THE *new* EXPLOSION OF TERRORISM

THE *new* EXPLOSION OF TERRORISM

BEAU GROSSCUP

NEW HORIZON PRESS
Far Hills, New Jersey

Library of Congress Cataloging-in-Publication Data

Grosscup, Beau, 1944–
    The explosion of terrorism.

1. Terrorism. I. Title.
HV6431.G764 1991   303.6'25   87-7731
ISBN 0-88282-101-6 (Hardcover)
ISBN 0-88282-074-5 (Tradepaper)

To Fannie, Zillah, Giah and Julia
In memory of Morris and Sarah

Contents

Acknowledgement

When one goes about challenging the conventional wisdom of the times, as I attempt to do in the pages of this book, rare is it that one actually has the opportunity to precisely gage the validity of one's critical endeavor. In the last months of writing I was fortunate to have two such opportunities. The first came about as a result of the revelations concerning the Reagan Administration's selling of arms to Iran. The second was of my own making and demonstrates the extent to which we in the West, including the author of this book, have fallen victim to a politicized vision of terrorism. For example, in writing on terrorism in the Middle East I discovered to my horror that I had named the computer file ARABTERR. Obviously, even after seven years of analyzing the political biases of our vision of terrorism, I, too, remain influenced by the popular Western notion that the Arab world is the single source of Middle East terrorism. From this "mistake" the strength of certain political biases and the degree to which they unknowingly guide our thinking became even more evident to me as did the need to challenge them.

I wish to extend my gratitude to all those who in various ways made important contributions either to the book or to the intellectual development of a most grateful author. First and foremost, I am indebted to Zillah Eisenstein who, through her initial questioning and later through her analytic clarity, forced me to develop and defend the conceptual framework. For this and ever-so-much more, I thank you. I thank Fannie Eisenstein, Isaac Kramnick, and Ros Petchesky for their reading of early drafts. From West Germany, I am indebted to Brigitte Hartmann, Gordon Jones, and Wolf-Dieter Narr for their assistance and friendship during my trips to Europe. I am also indebted to Sharon Seymour, Donna Freedline, and Dorothy Owens at Ithaca College for their grammatical and typing skills and to Mary Grosscup, for her patient editing and her lifelong support. I also thank my friends in Santa Barbara for their interest and constant inquiries during the final year of writing. My special appreciation to Jacqueline Berkaw, whose encouragement and support during a very difficult time can never be adequately repaid.

I am indebted to several organizations who provided the opportunity for me to share my ideas in a public forum including the Columbia University Seminar on Human Rights, the Peace Studies Seminar at Cornell University, the Political Science Department at the University of California, Santa Barbara, and the Political Economy Panels at the National Association of Political Science conferences in 1980 and 1981.

My deep appreciation goes to Dr. Joan Dunphy, President of New Horizon Press and her editorial staff, particularly Margaret Russell, for the assistance and encouragement in bringing the book to fruition.

Finally, to all my students who have tested and challenged me as a teacher and have been a vital part of my intellectual growth and the development of this critical assessment of the conventional wisdom on terrorism, I trust your contribution is evident in the following pages.

Introduction

When Iraqi President Saddam Hussein ordered his troops into Kuwait to settle a longtime border dispute—and an even longer enmity between the two countries—in early August, 1990, little did he know that his desire to bludgeon his way to the top rank in the power constellation of Middle East politics would collide head-on with an emerging American-sponsored new world order. Neither did he nor anyone else realize that in occupying and ransacking Kuwait he would crystalize in dramatic fashion the multiple dimensions, political complexities and moral contradictions inherent in the contemporary explosion of terrorism. As the Persian Gulf crisis has unfolded, the comfortable and uncomplicated vision of terrorism that has guided us for nearly two decades has been shattered. After over a decade of holding each other responsible for the global plague of terrorism, the leaderships of the United States and the Soviet Union have now joined forces to fight what they have unilaterally determined as the new terrorist poison boiling up from the caldron of Third World politics. With the end of the Cold War in Europe, and the start of the Persian Gulf crisis, the claims of Western leaders about a Soviet-sponsored international terrorist network have given way to alarms about a new Iraqi international terrorist conspiracy headquartered in Baghdad under the maniacal control of Saddam Hussein. President George Bush, who, as vice president, was a central player in the Reagan Administration's condemnation of "terrorist" states, openly urged the same "terrorist" leaders to join the rest of the international community in his anti-Iraq alliance. In what may be the most important development for future confrontations with terrorism, after two decades of funding and coordinating Western national and multinational forces, institutions and policy to battle the explosion of terrorism, the Persian Gulf crisis may bring shocking new evidence to bear on the reality of terrorism today and the pragmatic measures it requires. In open defiance of national and multinational anti-terrorist policy, former Western political leaders and laypersons alike travelled to Baghdad to negotiate with the "Hitler-like" Saddam Hussein for the release of nationals and family loved ones.

Finally, along with the dangers inherent in the Persian Gulf crisis, the disclosure in November 1990 of an anti-Soviet guerrilla network operating throughout Western Europe has further awakened the American public to the contradictions in past terrorism policy. After years of being told that only the sinister agents of the political left and Islamic fundamentalism stooped to the level of terrorism, evidence has come to light that the Central Intelligence Agency, in conjunction with West European intelligence services and member governments of the North Atlantic Treaty Organization, have been directing well-armed, anti-communist agents since the 1950s. These agents, who were prepared to conduct guerrilla operations in the event of a Soviet takeover of Western Europe or overthrow any democratic government who went too far to the left, have been linked to numerous instances of savage rightwing terrorism throughout Europe. The "realities" of terrorism in the early 1990s are clearly very different from what we thought we knew in the 1970s and 1980s.

The goal of this book is to end our confusion as to the realities of terrorism and, thereby, lessen the vulnerability of the democratic electorate to partisan anti-terrorist politics. To do so, we shall challenge the conventional understanding of terrorism as it has developed over the past two "fright" decades. We shall then offer a new framework that should serve us well as we confront the terrorism of the future.

In our journey through the past, we shall address several important questions. First, we will explore what do we know and what don't we know about terrorism? The purpose here is to alert us to how little even the "experts" know about this phenomenon and that much of what they do "know" is political biased. Consequently, laypersons have much to contribute to our understanding of terrorism and the right, if not obligation, to challenge political and "scientific" expert opinion. Secondly, we will address how and why terrorism became the headline issue for much of the 1970s and 1980s and is again resurging in the '90s. We discuss—in chapters on United States' domestic and foreign politics—how some proponents of past crisis ideology utilized public fears about terrorism and manipulated those fears into political support for their agenda, while some Russian leaders similarly manipulated their constituencies fears about terrorism into political support for their leftist agenda.

In the second part of the book, we turn to the realities of terrorism and ask: Who is responsible for the explosion of terrorism? What is the scope and nature of this contemporary phenomenon? How can we best confront terrorism without losing our cherished liberal democratic rights? In answering these questions, we offer the Middle View: a theoretical framework that de-politicizes the terrorism issue and centers our understanding in more distressing, yet less mythical, political terrain. Through chapters on West Germany and Great Britain, we document the need for the Middle View by discussing rising terrorism during the last two decades in these industrialized democracies and how reactions to this threat has, at times, undermined treasured democratic values. The in-depth section, which details the ominous spread of terrorism in the Middle East, verifies the usefulness of the Middle View as a guide for the future.

We end the book exploring the political realities of the post-Iran-Contra scandal era, the new Soviet-American coalition against terrorism, the aftermath of the crisis in the Gulf and assessing the degree to which the Middle View—though it met with considerable resistance five years ago—has begun to guide our thinking and assessment of terrorism.

Ultimately, through examination of both the past and present, we hope to understand the current explosion of terrorism as underscored by the volatile Persian Gulf crisis. Armed with this fresh understanding, we should be better prepared for the inevitable new explosion of terrorism sure to result from the clash between the great power architects of a new world order and those lesser powers, groups and individuals whose interests and aspirations will be denied by the imposition of that order.

THE EXPLOSION OF TERRORISM:
what
we know
and don't know

On April 14, 1986, a confident and resolute Ronald Reagan announced on national television that American air and naval forces had launched a series of air strikes on Libya in retaliation for Libyan leader Muammar Kaddafi's "reign of terror" against American personnel and property, saying:

". . . this mission, violent though it was, can bring closer a safer and more secure world for decent men and women."[1]

During the first optimistic days after the air strike resolute American citizens, weary of being paralyzed by terrorism, believed that a solution had finally been found, but in the weeks following, a vengeful explosion of terror struck back at America and its friends in three continents and quickly dashed any hope that Ronald Reagan had found a simple and direct answer to the problem of terrorism.

Terrorists in Lebanon executed one American and two British hostages, Peter Kilburn, Leigh Douglas, and Philip Padfield, with bullets to their heads. The murders raised fears that the delicate negotiations to gain the release of other hostages held by Arab terrorists were now doomed and that other British and American kidnap victims faced a similar fate. As western Europeans scrambled to leave the Middle East, additional hostages were taken; some, like British television cameraman John McCarthy, were abducted on their way to the airport. Gunmen in Khartoum shot and critically wounded an American Embassy technician. This attack, along with other anti-American demonstrations,forced an evacuation of all American personnel from Sudan. In Tunis, two young Tunisians fire-bombed compounds housing United States Marine guards and embassy personnel. Three people were injured when a bomb went off in front of the American Embassy in San Jose, Costa Rica. Throughout the world, United States embassies and consulates were besieged with an average of a dozen bomb threats a day and violent anti-American protests, causing some to close and all to dramatically tighten security. Several flights from the Middle East and western Europe were either cancelled or delayed by bomb threats. International trade shows were cancelled for fear of terrorist revenge. A potential air disaster was averted in London only when alert El Al officials discovered a package of explosives in the baggage of a passenger about to board a flight to Tel Aviv carrying 340 passengers.

For a short time thereafter, there appeared to be a world-wide lull in terrorism, but in the late summer and early fall of 1986 acts of terror around the world turbulently erupted.

Pan American's jumbo jet flight 073 was hijacked by Arabic-speaking gunmen who held it on the ground for sixteen hours, shot scores of passengers and set off grenades in the cockpit. The tail of the storm of violence lashed out. Of the 384 people aboard, at least sixteen were killed and more than one hundred were wounded, at least fifty of these seriously.

The very next day, two men entered the Neve Shalom Synagogue in Istanbul, Turkey, during sabbath prayers, fired submachine guns, detonated grenades, and killed at least twenty-one of the thirty worshippers.

During this same week, other parts of the world felt the effects of the terrorist outbreak. Dozens of bombings rocked Chile. Three people died and more than twenty were injured after two days of protests against the military government.

In Lima, Peru, bomb explosions killed two watchmen and badly damaged a gambling casino.

In Paris, hundreds of shoppers were lunching in a self-service cafeteria of a suburban shopping mall when a bomb exploded, devastating an eight-hundred-square-foot area, wounding forty-one people. The blast came only four days after another bomb had ripped through a crowded post office at the Paris City Hall, killing one person and wounding eighteen others. Prime Minister Jacques Chiroc declared war "on this leprosy of modern times."

On September 12, in Baghdad, Iraq, a long-range Iranian missile struck a residential area downtown, killing twenty-one civilians and injuring eighty-one. According to Iraqi officials, the missile was a Soviet-made Scud that had been fired from Iranian territory one hundred or more miles away.

Contrary to President Reagan's expressed hopes after the Libyan invasion, the military approach only seems to have compounded the difficulties, contradictions, controversies, and dangers of this age of terrorism. Multiple acts of random violence as well as acts of savage revenge have confirmed this point in dramatic fashion.

Also, there have been serious effects in international diplomacy due to the climate of terrorism and the strikes on Libya. The Soviets, calling the Libyan attack a "criminal action" and "state terrorism," cancelled top-level talks between United States Secretary of State George P. Shultz and Soviet Foreign Minister Eduard A. Shevardnadze on future superpower summits. The achievements of the November 1985 Geneva Summit were clearly undermined. The Soviets warned that further military action would force them to draw "more far-reaching decisions." The diplomatic fall-out also affected relations between the United States and its western European allies. Long-standing disagreements within the NATO alliance over American anti-terrorist policy festered into open sores as only Britain and Canada defended the military action. The other allies, including the Italians, who that day had warned American envoy Vernon Walters against military action, and the French, who refused to allow their airspace to be used in the bombing runs, harshly criticized the decision as a "Rambo response" that would cause further terrorism in western Europe. While opinion polls in the United States showed seventy-seven percent approval rating of President Reagan's decision, many polls in Europe indicated deep anger and disagreement with the air strikes, especially as damage assessment in Tripoli revealed substantial civilian deaths and injuries. Among the dead was Kaddafi's fifteen-month-old adopted daughter; two of his young sons suffered injuries. Former President Jimmy Carter, after hearing about Kaddafi's family loss, stated that the present administration was morally wrong to fight terror with terror. Secretary of State Shultz, angered by the charge, defended the air strikes by claiming that civilians who place themselves close to military installations are sure to become an "unfortunate by-product" in the war on terrorism.

Today, many people in both the East and West openly wonder what is next.

The depth of protest, the level of diplomatic fallout, and the escalated terrorist attacks since the Libyan bombing demonstrate that terrorism is not conducive to easy or quick-fix solutions like shooting missiles at Muammar Kaddafi. Events of the recent past, particularly during the explosive summer of 1986, have forced many people to conclude that terrorism is a complex phenomenon requiring careful study and measured response.

The ricocheting back and forth of proposed solutions on the part of those who are respected as experts in dealing with terrorism, the American public, and new revelations of underground dealings by officials of the Reagan Administration concerning the sale of arms to Iran has prompted attitudes reminiscent of the ones expressed at the height of the Beirut hostage crisis in June 1985, initiated by the hijacking of a TWA airliner over the skies of the Middle East, when a baffled President Reagan, admitting he was unable to act decisively against the current episode of terrorism, said:

"I've pounded a few walls myself. . . . I'm as frustrated as anyone."[2]

This startling admission caught most Americans and many others around the world by surprise. Its bitter, frustrated tone differed dramatically from the confident and militant anti-terrorist speeches we Americans had heard from presidential candidate Reagan during the 1980 Iranian hostage crisis. But it also took us by surprise as it was the first public confession by President Reagan, who has always assured us that he knew how to deal with terrorists, that he, too, was now caught in the complexities, contradictions, and follies that mark the contemporary age of terrorism. Indeed, the events surrounding the hijacking of TWA flight 847 and later Pan Am flight 073 have forced the world to witness once again the multiple facets of contemporary terrorism: the frustrations, the contradictions, the combinations of tragedy and farce, love and anger, stress and relief. For Americans especially, just five years after the trauma of the Iranian hostage crisis, the hijacking first of flight 847 and then of flight 073 were nightmares revisited. How did these new nightmares begin?

The first two months of summer 1985 brought a veritable explosion of terrorism that raged across the globe from Sri Lanka to Peru to Denmark. Most of our attention was focused on the hijacking of TWA flight 847, the explosion of an Air India flight off the coast of Ireland, and airport bombings in Japan and West Germany. In June both the print and broadcast media focused on spectacular and contradictory events of the Beirut hostage crisis that began with the savage murder of an American sailor and ended with the farce of the murderers' final press conference. These two events by themselves said a great deal about the dual facets of seriousness and facetiousness that mark contemporary terrorism. In between, we were exposed to more subtle contradictions, including President Reagan's awakening to the complexities of battling terrorism, a saga played out on network television newscasts by juxtaposing 1980 film clips of Reagan as a presidential candidate ready to invade Iran to free American hostages with President Reagan admitting that nothing could be done to gain the immediate release of the Beirut hostages. In other scenes, we saw television reporters ducking sniper bullets as they brought the crisis live into our living rooms while commentators and government officials debated the roles of the media in terrorism. Not surprisingly, the excitement of the immediate events brought concern over the long-term threat of terrorism and how to respond to it without sacrificing national and personal values.

Lost in the excitement, controversy, and debate over the events was an important message that kept flashing between the lines of the newspapers and across the television screen. Simply put, it said: contrary to what we think or have been told by our political leaders and scientific experts, what we know about terrorism is very little and highly contentious, and what we don't know is substantial and as yet elusive.

In the end, the Beirut crisis was by itself sufficient to get this point across. But in June and July there was a series of other incidents that, while not as spectacular, provided additional support for this cold fact.

In early June 1985 the trial of three Bulgarians accused of

helping convicted would-be assassin Ali Agca shoot Pope John
Paul II began in Rome. Some of the intrigue surrounding the trial
concerned not the innocence or guilt of the accused but the attempt
to document "the Bulgarian connection" to the shooting and with
it to confirm the theory that the Soviets were the sinister force
behind it (and terrorism in general), a theory espoused by terrorism expert Claire Sterling, some members of the American
media, and various people in the Reagan Administration. On the
first morning of the trial, Ali Agca shouted to the courtroom, "I am
Jesus Christ. . . . I announce the end of the world."[3] In the days
following, he made a spectacle of himself and of the trial with wild
contradictions in his story, all the while holding to his messianic
identity. Agca's testimony was the heart of the prosecution's case.
As it fell apart so did many of the supports for the theory
concerning a Soviet connection. In the end, the trial that was to
link the shooting of the Pope directly to the Soviet Union, adding
fresh evidence to President Reagan's charge that the Russians were
solely responsible for international terrorism, only served to cloud
the issue of culpability in the assassination attempt. It also spread
an aura of confusion and doubt over the issue of international
terrorism just when Ms. Sterling and others had predicted things
were about to clear up.

Our assumptions about who is involved in international
terrorism became even more muddled during June 1985 with the
discovery by the FBI of a Sikh terrorist plan to assassinate Indian
Prime Minister Rajiv Gandhi during his visit to the United States
and the subsequent explosion of an Air India jetliner that killed 329
people off the coast of Ireland. In both cases the FBI said that the
Sikhs suspected of involvement were graduates of a private school
for mercenaries located near Birmingham, Alabama. This revelation, in combination with an earlier discovery in the fall of 1984
that the CIA was training Nicaraguan rebels in terrorist tactics and
had published a training manual in terrorism, and earlier reports of
terrorist training camps in Miami, Florida, and San Bernardino
County, California, served to color our image of Soviet culpability
in and American abstention from terrorism.

It was also during the summer of 1985 that we came face to
face with the fact that, even after the most up-to-date security
systems are installed at obvious terrorist targets such as major
diplomatic institutions and airports, they are easily compromised.

Before that summer, for example, from 1981 through the summer of 1984, there had been a series of bombings at United States diplomatic and military installations in the Middle East, Latin America, and western Europe that caused great concern about the safety and vulnerability of United States diplomats and military personnel to terrorism. On October 19, 1984, in the wake of the bombing of the United States Embassy annex in East Beirut, President Reagan had signed the Embassy Security Bill passed by Congress authorizing $366 million over two years ($110 million to be spent immediately) to enhance security at United States diplomatic posts abroad. In Washington, D.C., the White House, State Department, and Pentagon were also fortified, at considerable cost, with the latest in anti-terrorist technology, including anti-tank ditches equipped with electronically-operated metal plate covers, and metal arms at all garage ramps and entrances capable of stopping most automobiles.

However, barely eight months after the elaborate security system had been installed, a lone man bent on matricide penetrated it. The security breakdown occurred June 21, 1985, and was recorded in a secondary headline on the front page of *The Los Angeles Times*. The headline, which read "Two Slain Near Shultz's Office," was followed by the account of a man, carrying a .22-caliber rifle, who had foiled the security system at the State Department and made his way close to Secretary of State George P. Shultz's office where he killed his own mother, who was a State Department employee, and then himself. The report went on:

> **At the State Department, cement barricades intended to block car bombs, as well as metal detectors similar to those used to spot weapons at airports, have been installed to protect against a terrorist attack. Officials said they were uncertain how the man was able to enter the building with the collapsible rifle and reach the seventh floor to carry out the shootings, within 100 feet of Shultz's suite of offices.[4]**

In a similar vein, airport security became a high priority for the Reagan Administration in the aftermath of the TWA hijacking in June 1985. In late June and early July the United States sought to isolate the Beirut airport by banning any Lebanese planes from landing at United States airports and attempted to organize an international agreement denying landing rights to nations permitting flights from Beirut to land at their airports. These measures failed to gain any support from the international community. Indeed, they were roundly criticized by most parties, including American allies in western Europe, as an overreaction to the Beirut hijacking. Yet, the United States was able to convince Lebanon to beef up its security system at the Beirut airport by installing earthen barriers to prevent unauthorized vehicles from driving onto the runways and by putting Lebanese police, supervised by Syrian security experts, in charge of airport security in place of the unreliable militia forces. Also in late June Secretary of Transportation Elizabeth Dole announced new measures to counter the recent upsurge in air terrorism, including the elimination of curbside baggage check-in for international flights, expansion of the federal sky marshall program, and intensified passenger searches. During the same period the Reagan Administration charged that the security system at the Athens International Airport in Greece, where the hijackers of Flight 847 had embarked, was inadequate. The administration issued a travel advisory against the Athens facility, warning tourists and commercial interests that Athens was an unsafe destination. By the time the advisory was lifted on July 22, 1985, after an inspection of the airport by a team from the Federal Aviation Administration, the Greek tourist industry had suffered over forty thousand cancellations and a major drop in advance bookings for the next two tourist seasons, with estimated losses to hotels and cruise ship lines running into the hundreds of millions of dollars. In November, four months after the Athens International Airport was declared "one of the best guarded airports in the world" by the International Air Transport Association, an Egyptian airliner enroute from Athens to Cairo, with the sky marshalls on board, was hijacked and flown to Malta where the shooting of hostages coupled with a rescue assault by Egyptian and United States commandos resulted in the deaths of over sixty people.

Anti-terrorist measures are taken with the best of intentions and with the idea that they are necessary and effective in deterring terrorists. But as in these cases, the validity of these contentions is undermined if not negated completely by events. The fact that a lone armed man was able to penetrate without too much effort a major United States institution that was recently overhauled with the latest in security technology and place himself dangerously close to a high-ranking official raises serious questions about what we know concerning anti-terrorist security. At the very least this breach of security should have reminded us that anti-terrorist security is not as yet an exact science but an endeavor that continues to demand serious thought and new approaches if our efforts are to succeed at all. Yet, it is difficult to conclude that any serious thought was given to the implications of this potentially dangerous event when, only three days after it occurred, the Reagan Administration announced without hesitation further plans to "improve security" at United States embassies around the world at an estimated cost of $3.5 billion.

The final event of this period revealing what we know and don't know about terrorism exposes the impact of terrorism on the nature of society, in particular, liberal democratic society. In the aftermath of the Beirut hostage crisis a major debate raged in the United States and Great Britain over the roles of the media in reporting terrorism. In Britain, Prime Minister Margaret Thatcher, speaking before the annual meeting of the American Bar Association, argued forcefully for some level of "voluntary" press censorship as one means of starving future terrorists of what she alleged was "the oxygen of publicity on which they depend."[5] Thatcher's statements were quickly echoed by members of the Reagan Administration, in particular Attorney General Edwin Meese, who said that newspapers, magazines, and broadcasters might be asked to agree to "some principles reduced in writing" including delays in reporting terrorist incidents and the withholding of hostage interviews.

Executives of American and British news organizations responded with concern and criticism to the Thatcher-Meese censorship proposals, arguing, at least in the American case, that the Constitution provided the appropriate guidelines or code of conduct for media policies. While the merits of each side warrant discussion, the point is that the heated exchange over the proposals for news censorship served to remind us that, as controversial as the terrorist event itself is, measures to counter terrorism are even more contentious. They are politically subjective, largely untested, and involve a wider range of issues, values, and changes than those with which most people, in particular persons in positions of political power, are prepared to deal.

The lesson taught by these and other events during June and July 1985 is that though terrorism is nothing new to us, we are virtual novices when it comes to dealing with it. If we are to successfully understand and cope with contemporary terrorism we need to first carefully evaluate what we know and don't know about it. We must then sort through the political implications of our approach to terrorism by asking the central question: how does what we know about terrorism affect our present and future, particularly in relation to those political principles, values, and traditions of liberal democracy we hold dear?

WHAT WE DON'T KNOW ABOUT TERRORISM: A PROBLEM OF DEFINITION

The central question to which we have no agreed-upon answer is: What is terrorism? Not one of the numerous definitions offered so far, including those by such authoritative sources as Webster's Dictionary, the United Nations, or the Federal Bureau of Investigation, has fostered any kind of consensus on the central components of scope, motivation, or objectives. While we have many conceptions of terrorism to choose from, its precise meaning remains elusive.

We also face considerable disagreement on how to arrive at a definition. One popular method is to define terrorism in very broad terms so as to include a multiple of sources, motives, and objectives. This is the approach taken by both Webster's International Dictionary and the United Nations. Webster's says terrorism is 1: The systematic use of terror as a means of coercion; 2: An atmosphere of threat or violence.[6] The United Nations' definition of terrorism, stated in Item 92, reads:

> **Measures to Prevent International Terrorism which Endangers or Takes Innocent Human Lives or Jeopardizes Fundamental Freedoms and Study of Underlying Causes of Those Forms of Terrorism and Acts of Violence Which Lie in Misery, Frustration, Grievance and Despair, and Which Cause Some People to Sacrifice Human lives, including Their Own, in an Attempt to Effect Radical Changes.**[7]

These two definitions are too broad, as they include a wide range of activities, actors, and motivations and they fail to make some important distinctions. For example, the United Nations definition presupposes we know how to distinguish between innocent and non-innocent lives; it assumes there is universal agreement on which freedoms are fundamental and those that are not; it assigns acts of terrorism to the realm of those deeds done to effect radical change, which, depending on what one means by "radical," could be a very broad or very narrow category. It says nothing about whether terrorism is a political or criminal act or both: whether one has to endanger or actually take a human life or merely threaten to do so. It leaves wide open the meaning of "endanger" so that we don't know whether a corporation that endangers the health of its workers with unsafe working conditions or a company that dumps toxic waste, thereby polluting the public water supply, is a terrorist in the same sense as an individual or group who blows up an airliner and its passengers.

A second approach, and, judging by recent books, also a popular one, is to mention the difficulty or impossibility of defining terrorism and then proceed to discuss the subject as though, in some general sense, everyone knows what it is. This is the approach taken by Robert Kupperman and Darrell Trent in their often-cited book *Terrorism: Threat, Reality, Response.* There are also a number of works, important among them Claire Sterling's *The Terror Network* and Christopher Dobson and Ronald Payne's *The Weapons of Terror,* that skirt the issue of definition altogether, yet offer information on the problem of terrorism.

The basic problem we encounter when defining terrorism is that it is a politically loaded concept, meaning that it is a subject entangled in contending political priorities, perspectives, and interests. The familiar statement that "one person's terrorist is another's freedom fighter" reflects this predicament. What appears to be only a problem of semantics is in essence a conflict of different ideologies, meaning that whether or not we see an event as terrorism depends on our political views. For example, President Reagan used the term "freedom fighters" to describe the United States backed "Contra" rebels trying to overthrow the Nicaraguan government. Others, including Sandinistas, refer to the rebels as terrorists, arguing that the Contra violence against civilian noncombatants constitutes terrorism. In another example, applying the term "terrorist" to anti-colonial nationalist forces who use violence to further their cause depends, in part, on our view of colonialism or other methods of pursuing decolonialization. In

South Africa, where violence is used by both sides, use of the label "terrorist" for either the black nationalists or the white minority government depends on our assessment of apartheid as a just racial policy or as racism, as well as our views on law and order, civil disobedience, and a host of other concerns. Finally, to characterize the policies of "totalitarian states" as "terrorist" while rejecting the terrorist label for the use of coercive power by the liberal democratic states is based on a subjective measure of political legitimacy and rests on a politically democratic interpretation of events and interests. The point is, even if we assume the best of intentions, our definitions of terrorism have been expressions of political priorities.

The political nature of terrorism is compounded by the pejorative connotations attached to it. Most of us view terrorism as a phenomenon that every decent, rational person is or should be opposed to. Terrorism seems to be an inhuman, uncivilized, and irrational activity for which there is no viable justification. Terrorism represents the darker side of human nature and constitutes a fundamental threat to our notion of civilization. We think it a strategy of the weak, the politically illegitimate, or the criminally insane.

Because terrorism has these and other negative connotations, the concept can be manipulated for political purposes. The negative image of terrorism can help mobilize support for a political constituency claiming to be anti-terrorist. When an individual, group, or state is characterized as "terrorist" or even "terrorist sympathizer," its political legitimacy is undermined and public opinion set against it.

One instance of political leaders of different persuasions trying to convince their constituents that their political beliefs were sound and their opponents evil is well illustrated by President Reagan's four-year effort to convince us as to the evil of the Sandinista government in Nicaragua and his charge in July 1985 that five nations, including Cuba and Nicaragua, are "a confederation of terrorist states" engaged in "outright acts of war" against the United States.[8] On the opposing side, Cuban president Fidel Castro, a day later, called Ronald Reagan "the worst terrorist in the history of mankind,"[9] and accused him of terrorist acts in El Salvador, Nicaragua, and Grenada. What appears to be a case of childish name calling between bitter political foes is in fact support for the argument of Noam Chomsky and Edward Herman that, "Among the many symbols used to frighten and manipulate the populace of the democratic states, few have been more important than 'terror' and 'terrorism.' "[10]

Due to the ambiguous perceptions of it, defining terrorism is difficult, but there are a few points of agreement. First, it is generally accepted by those offering an opinion that terrorism is a type of surreptitious warfare separate and distinct from conventional war, which is defined as "a major armed conflict between nations or between organized parties within a state."[11] Second, most definitions include a reference to violence or the threat of violence. Indeed, the negative impressions associated with terrorism arise, in part, because it is viewed as an activity of violence. As a form of conflict, violence carries its own negative meanings. Since most of us find violence deplorable as a form of social conflict, it follows that terrorism, projected as violence at its worst, carries with it those same connotations. Finally, authorities on the subject generally agree that the purpose of terrorism is to spread fear either by violence or by the threat of violence. Terrorism, it is argued, is a strategy of intimidation affecting the state of mind to force change. In this view, terrorism is more a psychological than military strategy, which separates it further from the accepted notion of conventional war.

If we combine these three criteria, terrorism would be defined as: a type of surreptitious warfare in which indiscriminate violence or the threat of indiscriminate violence is used to induce fear for the purpose of changing the state of mind or policy of the nation or group whose members are intimidated. As is true of all other definitions of terrorism, there are obvious problems with this one (for example, fear does not necessarily equate with terror), and its broadness could limit its applicability. But it does have the advantage of consensus to support it and could be proposed as an important starting point.

In strict definitional terms, we don't know what terrorism is, but we do know, somehow, that it is a major problem in today's world. Thus the explosion of debates, literature, and inquiry on "terrorism," however defined or undefined. But what we don't know about terrorism goes beyond definitional confusion. It is also evident in cases where there is an operative definition of terrorism and yet the application of that definition to actual events is inconsistent. For example, the FBI, in its 1982 and 1983 annual reports on terrorist incidents in the United States, defines terrorism as "the unlawful use of force or violence against persons or property to intimidate or coerce a government, the civilian population, or any segment thereof, in furtherance of political or social goals." Based on this definition, the FBI, in its 1982 report, included as a terrorist act an incident involving a single anti-nuclear activist who, on the pretense that his truck was full of explosives, parked at the base of the Washington Monument and threatened to blow it up. In its 1984 annual report, the FBI counted eight terrorist incidents in the United States but did not include in its tally the bombings of numerous abortion clinics. When asked about this apparent contradiction, FBI Director William Webster said the FBI investigated only "true terrorism" and the clinic bombings did not fit the definition because they were not "acts of violence committed in furtherance of an attack on a government."[12] Plus, he said, they were not activities carried out by an as-yet definable group whereas the event at the Washington Monument was.

There are other cases of inconsistency in the application of definitional criteria. Often terrorism is said to be violence directed towards innocent civilians. This is the criterion for listing the Palestine Liberation Organization (PLO) and the Irish Republican Army (IRA) as major contemporary terrorist organizations. Yet according to the United States Government, the 1983 bombing of the United States Marine base in Beirut that killed 242 Marines is one of the major terrorist events of the decade. In the Soviet press the indiscriminate American bombing of civilians in Cambodia is viewed as terrorism but the Soviet bombing of civilian villages in Afghanistan is not. The assassination of Britain's Lord Mountbatten was described as a terrorist act in the Western press but the assassination of Orlando Letelier, Chilean exile and leader of the resistance to the regime of General Pinochet, was not. According to some views, the Philippine rebels were terrorists, the killers of Philippine opposition leader Benigno S. Aquino Jr. were not. To some, the El Salvadoran rebels are terrorists, yet the right-wing death squads only violate human rights. To those who are not his followers, Libya's Colonel Muammar el Kaddafi is deeded as employing terrorist "hit squads" against political foes. It is reported that the death squads and secret police (SAVAK) employed by the Shah of Iran were said to "stifle" political opposition. To those who believe in its ideals, Angolan rebels are freedom fighters; to those who do not Namibia's South West African People's Organization (SWAPO) is a terrorist organization. The violence of the Tamil rebels is called terrorism, that of the Sri Lankan army is sometimes not, and so on. Even in cases where we establish a definition, understanding that there is no universality to it, our political priorities intervene to prejudice our definitions. If it seems silly and transparent, it is. But, it is also deadly serious. Public opinions and public resources are often shaped by power brokers who use the contradiction and complexity of terrorism to their own political advantages.

Our confusion over terrorism is aggravated by the scholarship of terrorism "experts" that fails to distinguish between discussions concerned with defining terrorism, the general problem of terrorism, and the problem of contemporary terrorism. Studies concerned with defining terrorism have a different focus than those which analyze the problems that terrorism causes for a national or international entity. Analyzing the general problem of terrorism—regardless of its political, social, or historical setting—is distinct from analyzing the problem of terrorism in a particular setting or time frame. In many cases, works written ostensibly on the subject of terrorism, which should include all three discussions, either focus on only one or two or present all three as though they were one. Yet, to many of us, this scholarship passes as the latest authority on the general subject of terrorism.

Since the late 1970s there have been several well-publicized books promoted as covering the general concept of terrorism which have focused exclusively on contemporary terrorism. For example, it is not the definition of terrorism, nor the general problem of terrorism in the historical sense, that concerns Claire Sterling in *The Terror Network*. Instead, it is the problem of contemporary terrorism, which to Sterling stems from "left-wing or Red terrorists, who have dominated the world scene in the harrowing decade between 1970 and 1980."[13] When Kupperman and Trent state in *Terrorism: Threat, Reality, Response* that terrorism is difficult to define but then provide us with a list of terrorists, it is because the focus has shifted to their conception of who is responsible for contemporary terrorism. Edward Micholas, in *Transnational Terrorism*, makes a serious effort to define terrorism. He then selects transnational terrorism, which is only one of many categories of terrorism he identifies for quantitative analysis, thereby shifting his concern from the general subject of terrorism to the problem of terrorism in a contemporary setting.

These examples, which we assume are studies and statements relating to the general subject of terrorism and accompanied by some comprehension of what terrorism is, are limited to particular aspects of terrorism. Too often, those particular works which focus exclusively on the problem of contemporary terrorism, most often defining it as a strategy of the political Left and totalitarian societies, we treat as the authoritative texts on terrorism: its definition, source, purposes, and effects. In reality, our knowledge and understanding of terrorism are narrowed rather than expanded by their inquiries. Too often, it takes an explosion of terrorism, like the one during the summer of 1985, before we are forced to admit that we really don't know much about it.

WHAT WE KNOW ABOUT TERRORISM: THE CONVENTIONAL WISDOM

If we don't know how to define terrorism, and there is great confusion and contradiction in the manner in which definitions are applied, what do we actually know about terrorism? We in the Western world have developed a vivid image of what a terrorist looks like, due in large part to media coverage of "terrorist" events, both real and fictional. The picture that most often comes to mind is of an olive-skinned male youth with a scruffy beard and a black beret sitting close over dark, half-wild eyes. He wears an army field jacket, combat boots, and designer jeans and menacingly waves a sub-machine gun as he spouts Marxist slogans. Supporting this portrait are some basic assumptions as to whom the terrorists are (left-wing revolutionaries in the pay of Marxist-Leninist states) and from what sources terrorism springs (a culture of permissiveness in the West and the very nature of totalitarian Communism in the East).

If these were simply the images and contentions of lay persons we could easily dismiss them as the products of watching too much television or too many movies. But they are duplicated in the statements of many policy makers and in the bulk of scholarship from our terrorist "experts." In fact, this vision and these assumptions then form an established conventional wisdom that has come to be accepted in the West as gospel on what we know about terrorism. More importantly, this conventional wisdom, which we will label the "ideology of terrorism," often guides the anti-terrorist policy of many liberal democratic states, including the United States.

The basic assumptions of the "ideology of terrorism" are:

1. Terrorism is primarily a strategy of revolutionary groups or individuals and directed against the state.
2. Discussion of state terrorism should be focused on totalitarian, fascist, or Communist states and cannot include the liberal democratic states.
3. Terrorism is primarily a strategy of the political Left in theory and in practice.
4. Terrorism is indiscriminate violence.
5. Terrorism is ineffective as a strategy of social or political change.
6. Terrorism is a criminal, not political, activity.
7. Terrorism is theater.

These points are listed separately here for the sake of clarity. But, if we are to understand them fully, especially in terms of sorting through their political implications for our democratic political tradition, we must treat them as a body of ideas, intricately interwoven, that reflect the political priorities of the liberal democratic state and its new Cold War agenda. We should know, too, that points one through four form the basis of the "ideology of terrorism" as they address the crucial questions: Who are the terrorists and from what source do they spring? Tenets five, six, and seven do not address such major issues nor are they as widely accepted as the others. Yet, they are important components of this conventional wisdom, particularly as they relate to the anti-terrorist policy of the liberal democratic state and thus, along with the others, deserve our attention.

Many analysts see terrorism as revolutionary in nature and limit their inquiries to non-state groups or individuals. Michael Stohl makes this point by arguing that terrorism is the "exclusive province of insurgents, dissidents, or anti-governmental forces."[14] Primary focus is on those who challenge state power. As a result, the names most familiar to us as terrorists are the Irish Republican Army, the Palestine Liberation Organization, the Tupamaros of Uruguay, the Baader-Meinhof Group (Red Army Faction) of West Germany, and the Shiite "Holy War." Individuals such as the infamous "Carlos" (Illich Ramirez Sanchez), Yasser Arafat, and, more recently, Mohammad Abbas, the alleged mastermind behind the hijacking of the Italian cruise ship, *Achille Lauro*, in October 1985, are also well known to us as major contemporary terrorists. Some authors explicitly ask: Who are the terrorists? and then provide us with a list. For example, in their *Weapons of Terror*, Dobson and Payne list a "Who's Who of Terrorism," which includes only revolutionary groups, with details of their ideology, goals, and international connections, if any. The revolutionary nature of terrorism can also be found to premise other major works, including those of J. Bowyer Bell, Ted Robert Gurr, Kupperman and Trent, and Sterling.

The particular irony of focusing the inquiry into terrorism primarily on revolutionary violence is that the concept "terrorism" was first used to describe state-sponsored violence: namely the violence of the Jacobin and Thermidorian regimes in France. Moreover, from an historical point of view, there are many cases of state-sponsored violence that match the characterization of revolutionary violence that we now label "terrorism." Germany under Adolf Hitler is the most obvious twentieth-century example.

Under the "ideology of terrorism," the customary exception to the exclusion of the state as terrorist are those regimes designated at present as totalitarian or Communist. In the West the list includes the Soviet Union, Cuba, Libya, Kampuchea, North Korea, and Vietnam. In 1984 the United States State Department announced the discovery of a new kind of terrorism: that of states sponsoring terrorist groups outside of their national borders. In addition to those mentioned above, Iran, Nicaragua, and Bulgaria were cited as terrorist states. Excluded from the list were the "authoritarian" states, including Chile, Guatemala, Paraguay, and Pakistan, all of which have horrific human rights records and have institutionalized terror in their national security systems, and all liberal democratic states including the United States, Israel, Great Britain, and South Africa. In fact, scholars who defend this part of the "ideology of terrorism" argue that it is impossible for liberal democratic states to be terrorists since their uses of coercion rest on constitutional bases and are guided by popular consent and rules of law. Paul Wilkinson has argued this point by distinguishing between force, which is the legitimate and legally authorized coercive power of the state, and violence, defined as the unauthorized and illegal use of coercive power by either the state or a non-state actor.

According to Wilkinson, terrorism is a form of violence. The liberal democratic state, therefore, cannot be terrorist, since its use of coercion is legitimate and thus defined as force. When defined by this measure, American bombing of Cambodian villages, even though done secretly by the Nixon Administration, was not terrorism, since President Nixon was a popularly elected leader and his decision-making powers continually subject to popular approval. On the other hand, totalitarian or Communist states, lacking popular bases, are assumed to use terrorism as a means of gaining and keeping power, as in the case of Joseph Stalin's domestic purges during the 1930s in the Soviet Union and the current Soviet bombing of Afghanistan villages. Depending on one's political allegiance, it is this distinction that separates the actions of the Soviet Union from those of the United States. Even though both are global powers, to those of Western persuasion Soviet support for revolution is terrorism, whereas United States aid and assistance of certain countries is undertaken to promote peace, freedom, and democracy, i.e., government without terror.

For many, the distinguishing feature between terrorism and other forms of violence is the indiscriminate nature of terrorism. The terrorist is said to be randomly violent, with no specific target in mind, a person or group who uses violence with no distinction between the innocent and the guilty. Anthony Burton's assertion that "the terrorist aims to kill the innocent,"[15] and Wilkinson's claim that "a major characteristic of political terror is its indiscriminate nature"[16] represents this viewpoint. For most people, the special evilness of terrorism, the very basis of its moral corruptness, is its indifference towards the innocent and the guilty. Even in cases where terrorists do identify a specific target, the act of terrorizing the innocent to punish the guilty and the randomness of terrorist weapons (bombs, kidnapping, hijacking, and hostage-taking) set terrorism apart from other forms of violence.

In theory, the indiscriminate nature of terrorism is a useful way of distinguishing terrorism from other forms of violence. But

here again, we confront the contradiction between terrorism, defined as indiscriminate violence, and the labelling of violent acts as
terrorist when there is a designated political target. There is also a
general failure to characterize the violence against innocents by
"our side" as terrorism. Somehow the current United States-
backed bombing of the El Salvadoran population and the Israeli air
attacks on the city of Beirut escape the label of terrorism. Yet, the
assassinations of West German businessman Hans-Martin
Schleyer and Italian political leader Aldo Moro in the 1970s were
tagged as terrorism. Either terrorism is indiscriminate or it is not. If
we agree that it is indiscriminate, then the application of that
criterion must be without political prejudice if it is to have meaning. But if we agree that terrorism is indiscriminate, then the
terrible destructive capabilities of the nuclear weapon make all who
possess it terrorist. We may not be ready to think in these terms
but such is the reality and complexity of terrorism in the nuclear
age.

Adherents to the "ideology of terrorism" contend that terrorism is ineffective in bringing about desired changes and thus
useless and senseless as a political strategy. According to re-
nowned terrorist expert Walter Laqueur, "Terrorism creates tre-
mendous noise. It will continue to cause destruction and the loss of
human life. It will also attract more publicity, but politically it tends
to be ineffective."[17] History, however, sometimes reveals a quite
different story. At least three states born during the twentieth
century, Ireland, Israel, and Yugoslavia, owe their existence in part
to successful terrorist campaigns against occupying powers. Both
the PLO and the IRA have employed terrorism with relative
success in contemporary times. At best, the record is mixed as to
the effectiveness of terrorism.

The same kind of argument can be made about the notion
that terrorism is a criminal rather than political activity. The purpose of this assumption is to deny any political legitimacy to
terrorists, especially in cases where there is a stated political goal.
The terrorist is portrayed as the criminal element. For instance, in
its struggle with the IRA, the British government has refused to
recognize the political status of its IRA prisoners even when faced
with hunger strikes that resulted in several deaths and political
pressure to alter its stance. Likewise, West German authorities
were adamant in their refusal to grant political status to the Baader-

Meinhof Group even though the terrorists' political ideology and goals were well publicized. Neither government wants to grant the terrorist political status. Having defined terrorism as non-state violence, government officials do not want to legitimize it by raising its stature to the political realm. It was based on this reasoning that the United Nations General Assembly for the first time passed unanimously a comprehensive resolution condemning international terrorism as "criminal" on December 10, 1985.

The final assumption of the "ideology of terrorism" concerns the purpose behind terrorist acts. Terrorism, it is sometimes believed, is theater, and contemporary terrorism a product of the revolution in mass communication. It was on this premise that the British government in July 1985 successfully "requested" that the British Broadcasting Corporation (BBC) cancel a program featuring Martin McGuinness, a suspected leader of the Irish Republican Army, on the grounds that to show the program would constitute a publicity coup for the IRA. Likewise, most of the criticism leveled at the American media during the Beirut hostage crisis, in particular coverage of the terrorist-controlled interviews with the hostages and the closing news conference with the actual terrorists, was based on the idea that terrorism thrives on publicity, good or bad. From this point of view, public opinion is the target of terrorism and the global communications system the vehicle used to sway that opinion. The notion that widespread death and destruction are the principal goals of terrorists is said to be outweighed by the minimal number of deaths resulting from terrorism each year and the large number of terrorist incidents in which a primary demand is the opportunity to publicize a cause through the media. The terrorists' targeting of communication installations, the regularity with which hijackers seek news conferences and hostage interviews, and the charge that reporters "cooperate" with terrorists in exchange for a story have helped promote this view. As in the BBC case, we are told that a major cause of terrorism can be dealt with, or at least diminished, by eliminating media coverages.

There is substantial validity to the idea that some terrorism is theater. The problem is that it neither tells the whole story as to the purposes of terrorism nor does it acknowledge the beliefs and obsessions of many, such as the Kamikaze pilots in World War II, who use terrorism as a strategy of political change whether they seek media coverage or not. It connects directly to the notion that terrorism is largely ineffective since its success depends totally on whether it is sensational enough to attract media coverage. It also plays into the hands of those public officials who, for whatever reason, seek to swing public attention away from any serious consideration of the terrorists' cause or who seek to limit the roles of the media. In short, this popular tenet of the "ideology of terrorism," while containing some merit, has serious policy implications for a society that values an informed public and freedom of the press.

The seven points of the "ideology of terrorism" discussed above constitute a large part of what we in the West know about terrorism. Our brief analysis of it shows that there are obvious anti-Left, anti-Soviet, and anti-revolution political biases operating here, and conversely the exact opposite prejudices operate in the East. As political ideology, this may satisfy many of us. But as objective inquiry into a major problem of our time it is flawed, since it fails to give us a solid basis for coping with the whys and wherefores of terrorism. Moreover, masquerading as truth, it skews our images of terrorism and the terrorist in favor of narrow political interests, so that we ask only certain questions and make choices from limited policy options. The upshot is that the process of developing anti-terrorist policy to counter a phenomenon that threatens us all becomes a politically partisan exercise that favors the interests of some and works against others. As we shall see, the political implications of this circumstance are significant.

Apart from the "ideology of terrorism," the balance of what we know about terrorism consists of a contending and equally biased view offered by the theoreticians of the Soviet Union and other members of the socialist world. While the specific details escape most of us, we are familiar with its general strains. According to them, terrorism is the strategy of the "Imperialist Camp," headed by the United States. It is used in both systematic and random ways to counter the rising tide of nationalist and socialist revolution and to maintain the superpower status of the United States. According to them, terrorism is clear evidence of the moral corruption and evil of the capitalist system. According to the Soviet view, it was CIA-backed terrorists who invaded Cuba in 1961, who backed the Solidarity Union in Poland in the late 1970s and early 1980s, who assassinated Indian Prime Minister Indira Gandhi in 1984, and who are behind the rebellions in Afghanistan, Angola,

Nicaragua, Kampuchea, and so on. As is true of its counterpart, "the ideology of terrorism," the political biases of this view are obvious. Its implications for political policy and public opinion are the same for the socialist world as ours are for the capitalistic world.

As we shall see, both of these contending theories of terrorism, though representing opposing political postures, contain aspects of truth as well as untruth. What is important is that taken together they constitute all we know about terrorism. The sad truth is that there is little awareness of and few attempts to build a middle analysis of terrorism, one free of the ideological trappings contained in these two and one that treats terrorism as the universal scourge it has become. This is our ultimate aim. For now our attention turns back to the "ideology of terrorism" and a look at how and why it has come to dominate how we in the West think about terrorism.

NEOCONSERVATISM AND THE SPECTER OF TERRORISM

In assessing the importance of the "ideology of terrorism" in today's politicized climate and why it came to define what we know about terrorism, we need to go beyond the simple statement that today's terrorists equate to yesterday's Communists. We need to acknowledge that the seven tenets of the "ideology of terrorism" spring from a deeper and more sophisticated analysis of terrorism, its sources, causes, and effects than that provided by a Cold War conspiracy theory.

Much has changed since the 1950s, and, for better or for worse, our analysis of the forces that shape our world has been sharpened by developments such as the nuclear arms race, *détente*, the evolvement of the democratic welfare state, the various social movements (civil rights, environmental, feminism, the sexual revolution) and, not the least, the phenomenon of contemporary terrorism. The most penetrating analysis of these developments has been provided by those on the left and right ends of the political spectrum. Beginning in the early 1960s, Left-leaning liberals, what remained of the Old Left, soon to be known as the New Left, spearheaded an attack on Cold War liberalism with an incisive exposé of the failures in domestic civil rights policy, employment, and poverty programs and the dangers inherent in our strategic nuclear doctrine of massive retaliation and Third World counterinsurgency. In the United States, these critiques fostered the civil rights movement and the passage of the 1964 Civil Rights Act, the War on Poverty programs and initial support for an end to the arms race and the American-Soviet Cold War. Ultimately coalescing into anti-Vietnam War sentiment, these ideas and events allowed the New Left to hold the political high ground in the Western industrial world from the mid-1960s to the mid-1970s. The right-wing or conservative revival in the West began at the end of the Vietnam War and continues into the mid-1980s. This new conservative movement did not spring from a simple mood swing against Communism. Nor can it be explained adequately by some pendulum theory of history whereby old-time conservatism rode back into power under the combined forces of gravity and momentum. To its credit, the contemporary conservative movement was spurred by some fresh ideas and a more sophisticated analysis of the domestic and international environment when compared to the Cold War ideology of the 1950s. These new ideas and a sharpened analysis of the Right are the product of a deep-seated repugnance for New Left politics and programs of the 1960s and a realization that without fresh ideas and inquiry, conservatism as a political force was doomed. Tagged by its critics on the Left and the major media as "neoconservatism," this analysis has captured the imagination and allegiance of increasing numbers of people in the industrial capitalist societies, including major political leaders such as Margaret Thatcher and Ronald Reagan. Its analysis of what it calls "the crisis of democracy" and the answers it provides for dealing with that crisis are now the dominant political themes preached by the top policymakers of the industrial West. As we shall see, a central part of this analysis focuses on what are viewed as the disruptive and divisive forces in liberal society who advocate and practice violence and terrorism. It is the neoconservative analysis of the crisis of democracy that gives the "ideology of terrorism" its complexity and sophistication. Along with a new life for conservative political fortunes, neoconservatives have contributed their own analysis of contemporary terrorism. The neoconservative view of how and why the "ideology of terrorism" has come about and how it influences our political sympathies impacts heavily on today's view of terrorism.

NEOCONSERVATISM AND THE CRISIS OF DEMOCRACY

Neoconservatives really don't like the label "neoconservative," nor do they see themselves as members of the conservative political camp. Rather, they view themselves and their interpretation of the crisis facing contemporary liberal democratic society as liberal. In part, those like Senator Daniel Patrick Moynihan, who protest that the neoconservative label distorts the fundamental liberal grounding of their analyses and in particular their firm commitment to the liberal notion of freedom as equal opportunity, are correct. On the other hand, there is a conservative impulse to their analyses of the historical development of liberal society, the cornerstone of which is that in the 1960s, liberalism's celebration of the self was distorted. The result, they argue, has been a crisis for liberalism. Some argue that this crisis can only be resolved by reconstituting the present political climate to that of the Cold War years of the 1950s. This posture of looking back to yesteryear places this group of liberals in a political light more in tune with conservatives than it does with contemporary liberal and progressive political forces. Also, neoconservative proposals for managing the crisis of liberal democracy, which call for a political, cultural, and social environment geared to authority, tradition, and an elitist notion of democracy, are very much in line with the political and social order advocated by traditional conservatives. This does not mean that neoconservatism is the same as conservatism, although on both the question of what is wrong with contemporary liberal society and what to do about it, there is common ground. What it does mean is that neoconservatives are part of a coalition of conservative political forces that finds fault and danger in the democratic welfare state. Indeed, as early as March 1971, a full five years before the term "neoconservative" had gained any degree of public acceptance, the editors of the conservative *National Review*, led by its guiding force, William F. Buckley Jr., recognized the conservative message of those writing for *Commentary*, a major journal of neoconservative thought, and welcomed them into the conservative fold.

Most prominent neoconservatives such as Norman Podhoretz, Daniel Bell, Irving Kristol, Samuel P. Huntington, Daniel Patrick Moynihan, Edward Banfield, James Q. Wilson, Nathan Glazer, and Robert Nisbet, to name a few, began their intellectual careers as part of the American Liberal Left and have impeccable liberal and even socialist credentials. The catalyst for their eventual shift from the Left to their present position as leading members of the neoconservative fraternity was the political and social turbulence in Western industrial societies during the 1960s. Frightened by the advent of "protest politics," civil disobedience, and racial militarism that marked some civil rights and anti-Vietnam War movements and disgusted by the accompanying lifestyle of many 1960s liberal types who indulged in drugs, public nudity, flamboyant and unkempt clothes, long hair, casual sex, and pornography, neoconservatives came to espouse a perspective committed to political and cultural moderation with a priority for authority, order, and social stability as prerequisites for justice. Arguing that by the end of the 1960s the United States and other major industrial democracies were deep in crisis, neoconservatives offered a new analysis of what caused the crisis and how to manage it. It is this doctrine that began to attract powerful adherents with influence in major governmental and corporate circles by the mid-1970s. Some neoconservatives, like Moynihan, used neoconservative ideas to win high public office. Others, in particular Chase Manhattan Bank President David Rockefeller, began to organize public and private officials and public policy organizations such as the Trilateral Commission around neoconservative themes. Although Senator Henry Jackson was the neoconservative candidate in the 1976 Democratic primaries, the election of Jimmy Carter and his cast of trilateralists, among whom neoconservative Zbigniew Brzezinski proved dominant, was the first fruit of Rockefeller's efforts. From the mid-1970s on, neoconservatives began to dominate several major private think tanks like Rand Corporation, the Hudson Institute, the Heritage Foundation, the American Enterprise Institute, the Georgetown University Center for Strategic and International Studies, and the Institute for Contemporary Studies in San Francisco. In addition to *The Public Interest* and *Commentary*, their themes were featured on a regular basis in *Foreign Policy, American Scholar, Time, Newsweek, Business Week, The New Leader, Harper's Magazine, The Washington Monthly, The New York Times Sunday Magazine*, and other publications in which neoconservatives have established ties. Conservative publications like *Readers Digest, U.S. News and World Report, Fortune*, and *T.V. Guide* also carried neoconservative essays. By the 1980 American presidential election neoconservative themes dominated the debate between the Republican and Democratic parties and were carried into the White House by the election victory of Ronald Reagan.

According to neoconservatives, the Western liberal democracies are in trouble because of a general crisis of authority. The anti-war protest movements and the large welfare programs undermined the legitimacy of governing institutions and eroded the authority of traditional political and social leadership in government, the military, the family, the church, business and labor, the university, and other public and private associations. Neoconservative Samuel P. Huntington of Harvard University connects the crisis in authority to the idea that "people no longer felt the same obligations to obey those whom they had previously considered superior to them in age, rank, status, expertise, character, or talents."[1] The power and effectiveness of major political parties, the courts, and the presidency were reduced while a new importance was given to the "adversary" media, the "critical" intelligentsia, Congress, and the "independent voter" or nonvoter. Abuse of people and property by militant racial minorities and students, rising crime rates, the politics of confrontation and violence, sexual liberation, and the peace and women's liberation movements are all said to spring from the political and social chaos caused by this general crisis of authority.

To major neoconservative figure Daniel Bell the threat to liberal democracy is found in the cultural realm with the real crisis being a matter of values, morals, and manners. The rise of modernism or a modern culture has caused a disjunction between the socio-economic and cultural realms that has a disruptive effect on liberal society. Culminating in the counterculture of the 1960s, this adversary culture challenged, at every turn, the established order and convictions of traditional democratic life through its street and guerrilla theater, nudity, its celebration of the drug culture and sexual experimentation, and its emphasis on self-determination and personal freedom in art form, politics, and lifestyle. To Bell and other neoconservatives, social permissiveness was the order of the day, "a point in life-style that the liberal mentality—which would approve of such ideas in art and imagination—is not prepared to go."[2] Most troubling to Bell is the dilemma created by the reality that liberalism, the culture of choice and opportunity, finds it difficult to say why it rejects the permissive lifestyle. In the end, Bell writes: "In culture, as well as in politics, liberalism is now up against the wall."[3]

In judging the elements of crisis, most neoconservatives do

not blame the capitalist socio-economic system, nor do they see the Johnson and Nixon Administrations' Vietnam War policies or racial inequality in America as valid justifications for the turbulence and attacks on authority of the 1960s and 1970s. Neoconservatives feel that the "new class" in the bureaucracy of the federal government, the courts, prisons, and parole boards of the criminal justice system and the cultural institutions, including museums and galleries, publishing houses, major news and cultural magazines, the theater, and the film industry is the result of negative influences of counterculture. They feel that its influence is evident throughout the educational system, particularly at the university level where liberal and left-wing faculty and administrators preach their radical ideas under the guise of academic freedom. According to Michael Novak, these "Know-everythings" are entrenched in the industrial society, and their activities account for at least thirty-five percent of the gross national product. According to the neoconservatives, this "new class," from these lofty positions of power, has undermined the traditional democratic values of hard work, honesty, decency, competition, and religious faith with its commitment to hedonist culture, its celebration of individual liberty to the point of knowing no bounds, and its purposeful expansion of government and economic regulations.

It is the "new class" that many neoconservatives hold responsible for the crisis of governmental authority that resulted in the social chaos of the 1960s. It is the "new class" that has led government into an unfamiliar activist stance on economic and social problems and into new areas of public policy, including public welfare, environmental policy, and the War on Poverty, minority employment quotas, busing programs, and workplace health and safety, where it does not belong and where it can only fail. The problem is, says Samuel Huntington, government failed within a context of a "democratic surge" in which people, in particular the previously disenfranchised, came to participate in and expect more from the government. The result was the development in the 1960s of a "democratic distemper" in which the expansion of government activity was paralleled by a reduction in government authority.

Most neoconservatives blame the liberal establishment in the industrial West that engineered the experiments in social welfare such as the New Frontier and Great Society programs of the

Kennedy and Johnson Administrations for the democratic surge
that overwhelmed government institutions. They also view the
emergence of an "underclass," a large element of mostly urban
black and brown populations, who are desperately poor, unedu-
cated, and unemployable, as the source of many poverty, housing,
education, and employment problems. The demands and needs of
this "underclass" are additional strains on the governments of
industrial democracies already burdened with problems and, according to the neoconservatives, the problems of the underclass
should be solved by the private sector and not by government.

Finally, according to the neoconservative view, it is the demand for socio-economic equality by a host of special interest
groups that has unreasonably added to the responsibilities of
government. These special interests include the poor and their
demands for food stamps, welfare checks, public housing, free
medical service, public transportation, and care for the homeless
and racial minorities demanding jobs and job training, school
integration, voting rights, taxpayers' money for minority business,
cultural and education programs, and racial quotas in hiring and
firing policy. There are also women wanting equal pay with men,
equal access to the labor market, professional training programs,
sports and social institutions, public child care programs, rape
crisis and battered women centers, police protection, abortion, and
family planning programs. Health activists and environmentalists
concerned about chemical and nuclear contamination, air and
water pollution, safe living and working conditions are also part of
the special interest lobby. These are the problems the liberal forces
of the early 1960s, the government of the "new class" responded
to, promising aid to them all. Unable to deliver on its promises,
liberal governments by the end of the 1960s faced a growing
challenge to their legitimacy and authority. To counter the institutional and cultural political crises brought on, the neoconservatives
believe, by the forces and programs of the "new class," management strategy must center on reestablishing the authority of the
state. To do this, they believe, a battle must be waged against the
notion of egalitarian democracy that has distorted the original
meaning of democracy as laid down in the American Constitution
by the Founding Fathers, and the meaning of the Constitution as
neoconservatives perceive it. To neoconservatives like Martin
Diamond, democracy has nothing to do with the concerns of

"equality of the human condition" or political participation as espoused in the 1960s but rather describes the situation in which all citizens have equal rights. Popular or democratic consent is necessary only to establish government, not to operate it. Translated, this means that once we have elected our officials, they should be left alone to govern.[4]

With this as their guiding principle, neoconservatives hope to restore the context in which demands upon government can be minimized. The provision and distribution of social goods, be they jobs, housing, health, or school lunches, are once again placed in the hands of the market system or private sector so that if and when there is failure, it is these arbitrators of the market that are to blame, not government. Neoconservatives argue that if government operates within its proper political context, the state's authority can be restored, allowing it to perform well with confidence its duties in the limited but legitimate domain of crisis management and national security.

To help restore the authority of the state, neoconservatives ask the public to lower its voice and expectation. In giving less governmental assistance to the poor, racial minorities, women, the working class, environmentalists, homosexuals, and others of the disenfranchised population, neoconservatives hope to rid the system of its "democratic excess," thereby countering the suicidal tendencies they see as inherent in liberal democracy by lessening demands on government. They also hope to convince the "responsible" elements of society, or the "silent majority," as Richard Nixon tagged it, of the legitimacy of neoconservative belief that there are connections between modernism and nihilism, radical critiques of the United States and anti-Americanism, poverty programs and cheating, feminism or homosexual rights and the destruction of the family, leftist politics and terrorism.[5]

The neoconservatives' goal is the authorization of a new elite establishment, one grounded in their conception of democracy and in traditional culture and freed from the crazed world of "fringe politics." Under their restructured state, they feel they can shape a "pre-crisis" management system ready and able to ward off any danger, be it the Third World debt crisis or Libyan terrorist "hit squads." Once empowered and secure in its authority, the reinforced state can focus effectively on other dangers threatening the industrial democracies, such as international Communism (in particular the Soviet Union and Eurocommunism), Third World revolutionary movements, a troubled international economic system, and parochial nationalism.

To neoconservatives, the purpose of government is effective management, which requires a special kind of political context and special leaders. The state must stand above the political chaos, insulated from the special interest groups and mass movements. Operating within its limited domain, government must serve as the voice of authority and rationality in societies increasingly faced with difficult choices over scarce raw materials and energy sources, inflation and unemployment, work and leisure, the environment and economic growth. Many neoconservatives believe government leadership must be provided by those embued with the wisdom that can only come from status, wealth, professional management experience, and some traditional values. These "blue ribbon" managers are found in the boardrooms of such companies as General Motors, Bank America, and Bechtel or in the prestigious law firms in Washington, D.C. and New York City. In effect, what neoconservatives feel is the best hope for the survival of the Western industrial society is a form of "authoritarian democracy," where a strong state apparatus, guided by a professional elite, enforces political and economic cohesion and discipline within an overall ideological context of individual freedom.

These neoconservative prescriptions for crisis management are by now familiar to Americans, Canadians, and western Europeans as the popular conservative themes that helped conservative politicians and parties win recent elections in the United States, Britain, West Germany, Canada, Belgium, the Netherlands, Norway, Sweden, and Denmark and aided in sustaining conservative political fortunes in France, Italy, and Japan during the 1970s and 1980s. Their most important expression is in the Reagan Administration's social, political, and economic agenda. The neoconservative attack on the "new class" and its expansion of the duties of the state is embodied in the Reagan campaign against "big government" and the efforts to dismantle the social programs of the "liberal establishment" by cutting the federal budget and shifting programs and responsibilities to the state and local government level.

Returning the state to its proper and limited domain by allowing the market to provide and distribute social goods and services is expressed in the Reagan campaign slogan "Getting Government Off Our Backs." Since 1980, this slogan has been at the core of the Reagan Administration's domestic efforts to privatize the National Park Service; to sell off the government railway system to private interests; its emphasis on volunteerism; its plans to dismantle the public housing program, the Interstate Commerce Commission, and the federal farm support bureaucracy; and its deregulation of the banking, trucking, natural gas, airline, and telephone industries. In a renewed effort at privatization, President Reagan has proposed the sale of several electric power authorities and the Elk Hills, California and Teapot Dome, Wyoming petroleum reserves in his 1986 budget.

Extending this theme to foreign policy, the Reagan Administration has placed heavy emphasis on the "magic of the market" as the vehicle for coping with the international economic recession and the general economic malaise in the West. It is the message President Reagan has given at every annual economic summit meeting of the industrial nations, and it is one of the main guiding principles behind his Caribbean Basin Initiative.

President Reagan's claim during the 1984 presidential campaign that Walter Mondale's candidacy and the Democratic Party were held captive by "special interest groups," labor unions and women's organizations in particular, and dominated by the "single issue politics" of the peace and nuclear freeze movements as well as the National Women's Organization, was aimed at distinguishing the responsible "silent majority" from the "marginal population" and its raucous brand of dissident politics. The Reagan Administration's anti-ERA stance, its insistence upon proof of intent to discriminate under the 1965 Voting Rights Act, to enforce the relaxation and postponement of environmental and mandatory safety devices such as air bags and seat belts in the automobile industry, its dismantling of the Occupational Safety and Health Administration (OSHA) and Legal Services Corporation, its emphasis on the "truly needy" that has resulted in cuts in food stamps, medical care for the poor, public welfare, consumer information services, and a host of other programs used primarily by the disenfranchised, is viewed by those of neoconservative persuasion as attacks on "excess." Rejecting the ideas of the "new class" and what neoconservatives see as its hedonist culture is behind the renewed emphasis on traditional values and process in law, education, art, religion, sexual practice, and family lifestyle. According to President Reagan, the Great Society programs of the Johnson Administration often were responsible for increased levels of poverty, "family breakups, welfare dependency, and a large increase in births out of wedlock."[6] They also financed "jobs for an army of federal bureaucrats and consultants and put a huge burden on the productive sector of the American society."[7] For President Reagan, the choice is between "greater freedom or big government."[8] If we only "strengthen the family, we'll help reduce poverty and the whole range of other social problems."[9] In March 1984 President Reagan told an audience of religious fundamentalists that the 1970s was a time when America lost its "religious and moral bearings" and pornography "was available in virtually every drugstore in the land."[10] During this decade, the "social mores of our country were being undermined" and "liberal attitudes viewed promiscuity as acceptable, even stylish."[11] Attorney General Edwin Meese's attacks on the activist judiciary shortly after assuming his post in 1985 as head of the Justice Department only echoed earlier campaigns by Reagan Administration officials against the "insanity plea," the Miranda decision, the Supreme Court decisions against the death penalty and in favor of a woman's right to an abortion. It was Reagan's first attorney general, William French Smith, who initially sounded the alarm about activism in the courts by accusing some liberal judges of "subjective policymaking," of taking over the administrative duties of prisons and public housing projects and of entering areas of the law only implied by the Constitution such as the right to marry, to procreate, and to sexual privacy. Since coming to office, Reagan Administration officials have blamed certain liberal judges and their control over the criminal justice system for enhancing the rights of the criminal element at the expense of the moral law-abiding citizen.

The Reagan Admnistration has relied heavily on policy commissions staffed with neoconservative leaders to study and develop public policy on a host of concerns ranging from poverty in America to the crisis in Central America. Important among these is the Central American Policy Commission headed by Henry Kissinger and citizens such as Boston University President John Silber, AFL-CIO President Lane Kirkland, former Supreme Court Justice Potter Stewart and Wilson Sidney Johnson, President of the National Federation of Independent Business. Other commissions assigned policy-making duties by President Reagan include the President's Foreign Policy Advisory Board, headed by Anne Armstrong with corporate president H. Ross Perot and corporate lawyer Leon Jaworski as initial leading members; the Presidential Task Force on Private Sector Initiative, led by C. William Verity, chairman of Armco, Inc., and given the task of promoting volunteerism; the National Productivity Advisory Council, chaired by William Simon, to seek ways of increasing capital formation and worker's productivity; the Commission on Strategic Forces, guided by Brent Scowcroft and assigned the job of justifying the administration's MX missile deployment plan; and the Task Force on Food Assistance, a citizens' panel on hunger in America chaired by J. Clayborn La Force, Jr. and organized to refute the claims of liberals that Reagan Administration programs were responsible for increased numbers of hungry children in America. The administration has also waged an intense campaign to "depoliticize" existing government commissions, in particular the Civil Rights Commission, the National Endowment for the Humanities, and the National Labor Relations Board, by replacing political appointees with the new commission members. These efforts and others are premised on the neoconservative prescription for reinforcing the legitimacy and authority of the state by assigning neoconservatives to policy-making positions. Operating above the political fray and guided by professional management principles, these citizens, serving only bi-partisan interests from these committees, can best apply their expertise and experience of wealth and status.

It is the Trilateral Commission, largely the product of David Rockefeller and Zbigniew Brzezinski, which epitomizes the kind of elite policy-making body that neoconservatives view as the best hope for turning the industrial West away from the brink of disaster and guiding it back to democracy. Described by Rockefeller as "a group of concerned citizens interested in fostering greater understanding and cooperation among international allies,"[12] the Trilateral Commission is the stepchild of earlier elite planning organizations like the Council on Foreign Relations and the Bilderberg Group that set the political and economic agenda of the Western world in the Cold War decades. In 1975, the Trilateral Commission issued a report, "The Crisis of Democracy: Report on the Governability of Democracies to the Trilateral Commission" which, though initially controversial even among its elite members, established neoconservatism as the guiding intellectual force behind the conservative revival in the trilateral nations of Japan, western Europe, and North America. Authored by neoconservatives Samuel P. Huntington of the United States, Michael Crozier of France, and Joji Watanuki of Japan, its neoconservative themes are worthy of our brief explanation.

The report begins by connecting the success of liberal democratic societies in the first two and a half decades of the post-World War II era to the positive political leadership of the United States, spectacular economic growth, the lessening of class conflict, and the assimilation of large portions of the population into middle class values, attitudes, and consumption patterns. It argues that in foreign policy there was general success in meeting the domestic and foreign challenge of Communism by collective and individual resistance.[13]

In the 1970s, the authors of the report claim, this recipe for success is threatened as trilateral governments suffer from overload brought on by excessive demands, rising expectations, and the adoption of the new lifestyles and new sociopolitical values. Parochialism has invaded foreign policy, commonality of purpose has withered away, the political party system is in the process of decomposition, and state authority has been undermined. According to this view, evidence of crisis appeared in the United States during the 1960s, has occured in western Europe in the 1970s, and shows signs of affecting Japan in the near future. Now, say the authors, all trilateral societies suffer or show signs of suffering from a crisis brought on by the "excess of democracy" in which the claims for participation and equality have overwhelmed the need for order and stability.

The authors feel that the solution to the crisis in the trilateral region is to be found in moderation and restraint of the forces of egalitarianism and fringe politics. It is now necessary to reassess democracy as a guiding principle of government as "in many situations the claims of expertise, seniority, experience, and special talents may override the claims of democracy as a way of constituting authority."[14] Indeed, to the neoconservative authors of the report, "The heart of the problem lies in the inherent contradictions involved in the phrase 'governability of democracy.' "[15] The balance between governability and democracy is tilted against government. To reestablish balance, and thus restore governability, political parties need to reassert their legitimacy; the power of the critical media must be curtailed; formal education must be related to economic and political goals; discipline should be re-established in the workplace; new incentives must be given to industry; and the "leadership vacuum" must be filled by experts with professional skills and experience. Overall, governability must be stressed over democracy if the crisis is to be resolved and further excesses prevented.

NEOCONSERVATISM AND THE IDEOLOGY OF TERRORISM

"I would say that the terrorist needs democratic permissive-ness as a fish needs water."[16]

This comment by Professor Walter Laqueur, an internation-ally respected expert on terrorism and a senior associate at the think tank at the Georgetown University Center for Strategic and International Studies, reflects succintly the connections between the rise of neoconservatism as a mainstream of ideology and the way we in the West have come to think about contemporary terrorism. On one level, these connections involve commonality of purpose as both neoconservatism and the "ideology of terrorism" attempt to pinpoint for us the root causes of each particular crisis, identify for us those we should hold as responsible for the crisis, and offer us an anti-crisis strategy. Secondly, and more signifi-cantly, neoconservatism and the "ideology of terrorism" intercon-nect analytically. For instance, both view the political milieu of the "open" liberal democratic society as dangerously vulnerable to the practice of "political excess and extremism" of which, both agree, terrorism is the ultimate manifestation. Neoconservatives and some prominent terrorist experts alike tell us that the authority of traditional institutions, values, and modes of life have been under-mined by societal misfits, left-wing dissidents, and members of the hedonist "counterculture" who have usurped the power of the traditional leaders in setting the priorities and goals of liberal society. In their advocacy of "excess," they have expanded the boundaries of legitimate political discourse and action to the point where society operates under the extremist principle that "any-thing goes," including violence and terrorism. Both argue for crisis management policy that restores the traditional order in the cultural and social realm, reconstitutes the authority of the state, and reinstalls elite leadership. Both stress governability over democracy as the preferred political order in which liberal society can be saved from its suicidal tendencies and made less vulnerable to terrorism.

In short, both the proponents of neoconservatism and the architects of the "ideology of terrorism" sponsor the political culture and climate of "authoritarian democracy" as the best solution to crisis.

In the writing of some prominent Western terrorism experts we are told that contemporary terrorism is the product of the rise of the New Left in the 1960s, its critique of Cold War liberalism, its celebration of violence, and its practice of revolutionary politics. These experts single out contemporary leftist theorists, in particular, Herbert Marcuse and his theory of repressive tolerance, French writer and activist Jean Paul Sartre and the African nationalist and Marxist, Franz Fanon, as responsible for influencing the modern terrorist groups of Africa, western Europe, and North and South America through their celebration of violence and their development of philosophical rationalizations for terrorism. For example, Paul Wilkinson argues that Sartre was the most important radical thinker on violence and terror because he "dares to seek to give philosophical respectability to the notion that terror, far from being a cancer of the body politic, is indeed its very lifeblood."[17] Ernst Evans, in *Calling a Truce to Terrorism*, says that Franz Fanon, through his book *Wretched of the Earth*, is responsible for justifying terrorism by proposing that violence is a "cleansing agent" for the individual and by arguing that violence is a constructive factor for oppressed peoples. Dobson and Payne, in *The Terrorists*, discuss at length the "philosophers of terror." They say Fanon is largely responsible for Western Left-leaning intellectuals, American civil rights activists, and some students supporting violence and actually turning to terrorism. They argue that "his books instilled that sense of guilt, that feeling that the Third World of the ex-colonies had right on its side, which has provided so much support for international terrorism."[18]

Collectively these authors accuse a wide spectrum of leftist theorists, some of them Marxists, others neo-Marxists, Maoists, or Third World nationalists, of having fostered a "culture of permissiveness" through which various theories of violence become popular and are adopted by young students and intellectuals. The writings of Latin Americans Carlos Marighella ("Minimanual of the Urban Guerrilla") and Regis Debray ("Revolution in a Revolution") are often cited as evidence for this claim. Others, like Marcuse and the Strasbourg "situationalist" school of scholars, are blamed for undermining the authority and legitimacy of liberal democratic institutions with their "elaborate arguments explaining why democratic free elections, party systems, and representations are a gigantic fraud, a conspiracy to dupe the masses."[19]

These experts on terrorism tell us that these and other heavy-handed attacks on liberalism became part of the basic curriculum at some universities throughout the Western world and were celebrated by Western literary figures and the media, only to end up forming the core of certain terrorist strategies. From these seeds of dissent, they point out, also sprang numerous cults and the worship of "cult figures" like Leon Trotsky, Che Guevara, Mao Zedong, and Emma Goldman. The large congregation attached to these cult heroes and heroines and their ideas are said to have reveled in the adversary culture and are active in left-wing dissent and violence. A few joined the Italian Red Brigade, Japanese Red Army, the West German Baader-Meinhof Group, the June 2nd Movement, the Red Army Faction, and the American Weather Underground, and became terrorists. But the majority became active in "democratic" politics where, as members of various student, minority, anti-war, environmental, and women's groups, they provided sympathy, support, and comfort for others in the terrorist ranks. Their patrons, if not their parents, are members of the bourgeoisie and the liberal-thinking "new class" that came to dominate the major institutions of society in the 1960s and whose members, according to Dobson and Payne, often sheltered terrorists, supported them financially, and gave them sympathetic exposure through their control over political and cultural journals, newspapers, plays, movies, and news reporting on radio and television.

For both neoconservatives and certain experts on terrorism, the decade of the 1960s was an era in which nobody, including state authorities, examined or questioned where the celebration of revolutionary ideals was taking liberal society. According to this view, it was clear that the climate of "democratic excess" was provoking a crisis of governability in the industrial democracies.

The rise of terrorism in western Europe, Japan, and North America is viewed as the ultimate and most extreme manifestation of this crisis.

For both the neoconservative and the terrorist expert, liberal middle- and upper-class youth, in acting out their political fantasies, provided a breeding ground for terrorism and a network of terrorist sympathizers that include some judges, lawyers, government bureaucrats, journalists, university officials, social workers, psychologists, and politicians.

As proof that terrorism has some of its origins in the antics of "democratic excess," several historians of contemporary terrorism single out 1968 as the benchmark for the contemporary terrorist movement. For example, British terrorist expert Tony Geraghty argues that the West German Baader-Meinhof Group, the Irish Republic Army of Northern Ireland, and the British Angry Brigade, terrorist groups active in the 1970s, were greatly influenced by, if not direct products of, the revolutionary student and workers' movements that challenged the government of French President Charles DeGaulle in May 1968. Claire Sterling, in *The Terror Network*, also pinpoints 1968 as the year of birth for what she says is an international terrorist network, backed by the Soviet Union and actively involving members of the European and Latin American upper class such as Italian publisher Giangiacomo Feltrinelli, one of Europe's richest men.

The neoconservative thesis about the dangers of the "culture of permissiveness" and mass movement politics is also the basis for explaining why terrorism grew in the industrial democracies during the 1960s and 1970s. The statement by Walter Laqueur connecting terrorism and the permissive society is echoed by other terrorism experts such as Olig Zinam, who writes: "The revolution of rising expectations and entitlements, anomie, and the spread of a philosophy of pseudohumanitarianism with its downgrading of personal responsibility and growing permissiveness on the part of law-creating, -interpreting, and -enforcing agencies, have contributed to the preference for violence and greatly expanded the opportunity for it."[20] To Zinam, Laqueur, Sterling, Dobson, Payne, and other proponents of the "ideology of terrorism," today's most dangerous terrorists are the spoiled, bored children of the middle and upper classes, full of egotistical self-confidence and naive idealism, who have "come under the influence of those political thinkers who preach that violence is essential to make the world a better place for the masses."[21] Or they are common criminals and social misfits who take advantage of the "politics of excess" and the "adversary culture" to wrap their individual criminal pursuits and personal pathology in the garb of democratic mass movement politics and an ideology based on the social respectability of violence.

These neoconservative themes are expressed specifically in discussion of why women, in particular middle- and upper-class women, were involved in the infamous terrorist groups of the 1970s. Dobson and Payne address this question by looking at how and why women became an instrumental part of the West German terrorist movement. One theory they suggest is that German women are terrorists out of a need to free themselves through violence from the chains of male domination. According to some who hold this view, terrorism is part of the bourgeois feminist movement, as women from good homes with good educations see themselves as superior to men and need to display that superiority in violence, a realm of action traditionally reserved for men. Another theory suggests that women are sexually dependent on their male counterparts and that sexual freedom and political violence are intimately connected. Sexual liberation and feminism are sometimes seen as springing from the political and cultural milieu of the 1960s, where permissiveness and sexual freedom were encouraged. It is a case, say Dobson and Payne, where "many who take to the gun and the bomb start out by living in communes where partners are easily swapped and where experimental sex is part of everyday life. Many of the most active terrorists are active marijuana smokers and some have taken heavier drugs. Excitement, sensual pleasure, and comfortable living outside normal routines, while enjoying widespread approval for the high-minded ideology they preach, are all incitements for young people to enjoy themselves."[22]

In her treatment of German terrorist leader Ulrike Meinhof in *Hitler's Children*, Jillian Becker supports many of these themes by describing Meinhof's commitment to terrorism as coming from her own sense of private despair rather than from serious political concerns.

In essence, neoconservatives and some terrorist experts have influenced contemporary views of terrorism, seeing terrorism as a product of a widespread social malaise instigated by dangerous political forces and ideas. They believe that the problem of terrorism is much larger than simply hunting down and arresting those few actually involved in terrorism. Rather, the fight against terrorism in the liberal society must focus from the start on those who have cultivated the breeding ground for terrorism: the members of the liberal "new class" and the leftist community who advocate excess and permissiveness in all realms, who seek to rationalize their violence as a positive social phenomenon, who promote economic equality over equal opportunity, socialism over capitalism, modernism over tradition, feminism over patriarchy, and choice in sexual preference. If we are to free ourselves and our society from the ravages of terrorism, the excesses of democracy as practiced in the 1970s must be delegitimized, the institutions and programs of the counterculture dismantled, the youth subculture tamed, and the "subversive" political Left exposed and eliminated.

In addition to having its origins in the political climate of democratic permissiveness, the current "epidemic of terrorism" springs largely from the disorder and instability brought on by the Communist forces in the Third World, according to neoconservatives and advocates of this "ideology of terrorism," and since, they maintain, in Africa and Asia the process of breaking free from the European colonial grip has also brought new political parties and Communist groups into the forefront and brought together once-isolated ethnic, racial, and tribal groups and splintered the old and often corrupt stable political coalitions of the old colonial order. Out of this new general breakdown in the established order arose the politics of protest, violence, and terror, sometimes advocated by Third World nationalism, which is often anti-capitalist and anti-imperialist.

According to Daniel Bell and Samuel Huntington, the continuation of terrorism after the yoke of colonialism is thrown off and independence established is connected to the industrial or modernization process that Third World societies experience. Huntington says that modernization changes the relationships between communal groups, that the move of the rural population to the city breaks down the isolation of various ethnic and tribal groups and creates feelings of relative deprivation that are eventually manifested in violence and terrorism.[23] Bell argues that the advancements in global communication, travel, the development of international and transnational organizations like the multinational corporation, and the industrialization process have radically changed the world since World War II. With these major demographic transformations, differences are exposed and begin to affect a broad audience. As contrasting values, priorities, needs, and desires confront each other the consensus of the old order breaks apart, producing instability in all realms. From this instability, says Bell, come the forces of revolution or counterrevolution.[24] Some of the most notorious Third World "terrorist" groups of the past and present, namely the Mau Mau of Kenya, the Viet Minh in Vietnam, the Tupamaro of Uruguay, the Algerian FLN, the Patriotic Front of ZANU and ZAPU in Rhodesia, SWAPO of Namibia, the African National Congress (ANC) in South Africa, and now the Philippine New People's Army, are said to be products of the decolonization or modernization experience.

Finally, the coalition of neoconservatives and terrorist experts believes that the Soviet Union and its client states who train, fund, and direct the modern terrorist groups are a major source of the contemporary explosion of terrorism. In particular, members of the Reagan Administration have said that the Soviet "evil empire" is behind terrorist attacks in the Middle East, the United States, the Philippines, southern Africa, St. Peter's Square in Rome, and Belfast, Northern Ireland. Neoconservative Charles Horner, writing in the June 1980 issue of *Commentary*, affirms the charge by some members of the Reagan Administration that the Soviet Union, Cuba, and Libya sponsor an international terrorist network, and argues that evidence to prove Soviet complicity in international terrorism is abundant but ignored by Western media and intelligence institutions. Taking the neoconservative "new class" thesis one step further, Horner says that Soviet terrorism is hushed up by the Soviet agents and sympathetic Western liberals as part of the overall Soviet propaganda campaign of "disinformation" to which Western policy makers are either naively or purposely vulnerable.

This thesis about Soviet disinformation raised by Horner and others and popularized in fictional form by conservative journalists Arnaud de Borchgrave and Robert Moss in their novel, *Spike*, has been said by Reagan Administration officials to underscore the charge by neoconservatives James Q. Wilson and Norman Podhoretz that terrorism has become a major part of the Soviet

Union's campaign to disrupt the capitalist system and export Communist ideology. This particular charge, cited by both neoconservatives and right-wing anti-Communists from the American old and new Right, like Samuel T. Francis of the Heritage Foundation, writing in *The Soviet Strategy of Terror*, is the principle reason why many critics of the Reagan-inspired New Cold War characterize the emphasis on international terrorism as old-fashioned anti-Communism—or simply new wine in old bottles.

The contributions of neoconservatism to an understanding of their views of the "ideology of terrorism" and vice versa give us greater comprehension of the West's stand on terrorism and how we have come to think about it.

THE NEOCONSERVATIVE PROFILE OF A TERRORIST

In our discussion in Chapter One of what we know about terrorism, we suggested that many of us actually have a sharp, concrete image of what a terrorist looks like and what political and cultural milieu he/she is likely to come from. Briefly restated, the media image is of a bearded, olive-skinned male youth wearing army fatigues and designer jeans and armed with Marxist slogans and a machine gun. As part of understanding how we came to know what we know about terrorism, we need to address the question: Why is it that the stereotyped image is accepted by many of us, including television and fiction writers, movie makers, news analysts, airport security officials, and even intelligence analysts, as the portrait of a contemporary terrorist? The answer lies, as we have detailed, in the predominance of neoconservative ideas among certain prominent Western terrorist experts and the general public. This ideology has narrowed our vision of who terrorists really are and from what sources they spring. The most concrete evidence of this can be found in the efforts to build what terrorist expert Juliet Lodge calls a "typical sociological profile."[25] To date, the most prominent and often cited study of terroristic character is "Profile of a Terrorist" by Charles A. Russell and Bowman H. Miller.[26]

Russell and Miller begin their portrait of a terrorist by acknowledging the explosion of terrorism over the 1965–1975 period and indicate that they hope to contribute to the study of terrorism

through an examination of individuals involved in urban terrorism. Their task, as they see it, is "to determine if there truly are
common characteristics and similarities in the social origin, political philosophy, education, age, and family background of those
individuals engaged in terrorist activities within Latin America,
Europe, Asia, and the Middle East."[27] To construct their portrait,
Russell and Miller compile and analyze data on more than 350
individual terrorist cadres from Turkey, Ireland, West Germany,
Italy, Spain, Palestine, Japan, Argentina, Brazil, Iran, and Uruguay
who were active between 1966 and 1976.

Although they announce their goal to be the construction of a
typical portrait of a terrorist, Russell and Miller have narrowed
their analysis considerably by selecting data drawn from the terrorism of a ten-year span, not terrorism per se. More importantly,
their study is also politically selective as the authors, "in order to
insure an accurate portrait,"[28] collect data on members of eighteen
revolutionary groups specializing in urban terrorism. Those selected appear to be, in the main, Marxist, Trotskyite, anarchist, or
urban revolutionary (nonstate) organizations. By collecting data on
a narrow constituency consisting of individuals operating from
some form of left-wing revolutionary ideology and engaged in
urban terrorism between 1966 and 1976, Russell and Miller seem to
invoke the same political criteria as neoconservatives to determine
who constitute the dangerous terrorists of today.

Russell and Miller analyze these individuals on the basis of
age, sex, marital status, rural versus urban origin, social and
economic background, education or occupation, method and place
of recruitment, and political philosophy. Based on these criteria,
the authors draw a profile of the typical terrorist as being a single
male, aged twenty-two to twenty-four, having some level of university experience, in many cases a college degree. The majority
are from affluent, urban, socially prestigious middle-class families,
who were exposed to an anarchist or Marxist world view and
recruited into terrorism while at the university.

By all accounts, including Colin Smith's *Carlos: Portrait of a
Terrorist*, Illich Ramirez Sanchez, code name "Carlos," matches
perfectly the profile developed by Russell and Miller. He is young
and comes from an affluent, politically active family. His father is a
lawyer, a self-proclaimed Marxist, and active in leftist politics in
South America. Carlos's early political education includes partici-

pation, as a child, in rock-throwing demonstrations on behalf of the Communist Party and the rural guerrillas of Venezuela. While attending school in Moscow, Carlos was allegedly recruited by the Soviet KGB and trained in terrorism.

Smith claims that Carlos displays all the characteristics of a frivolous youth with a special fascination for guns, sex, and money. Claire Sterling agrees, characterizing Carlos as an "amiable, party-going, skirt-chasing, guitar-playing Latin."[29] At the same time, he is a "senior member of the international terrorist circuit"[30] and involved in many successful terrorist operations. But according to those accounts, he is a careless fugitive, especially in covering his tracks, with an overwhelming weakness for women, which, according to Smith, has made him vulnerable to arrest more than once. He appears to escape capture only through his connections to the international terrorist network and his professional ties to the Soviet Union.

Carlos is presented to us as more interested in his own personal image and power than in political or social change. As the leader of the 1975 terrorist raid on the Organization of Petroleum Exporting Countries (OPEC) ministers' conference in Vienna, Austria, Carlos is said to have spent long hours talking with Sheik Zaki Yamani of Saudi Arabia. At the end of these discussions, Yamani says he was unimpressed by Carlos's political convictions yet very conscious of Carlos's high self-esteem, particularly as a sexual actor. We get further confirmation of the portrait of this internationally famous and feared terrorist as frivolous and self-important and consumed by the "cult of the revolutionary" from Dobson and Payne, who describe Carlos at the OPEC conference as having "dressed dramatically for the occasion in a long trenchcoat, with a beret tilted threateningly forward. In this portrait it is said he affected a thin beard, the badge of an anarchist, which also conveniently hides a double chin."[31] Their assessment of his background parallels Smith's and leads them to conclude that "with such an upbringing it was inevitable that he would make his career terrorism."[32]

In addition to Carlos, other terrorists who have gained notoriety, for instance, Andreas Baader and Ulrike Meinhof of the West German terrorist group that bears their names, Petra Krause, called the "terrorist of the century" by Swiss police, members of the Red Army, Red Brigade, leaders of the Tupamaro, the Irish

Republican Army, the PLO and so on, possess similar qualities to those in the portrait drawn by Russell and Miller. The media attention of the activities of those terrorists tends to reinforce a specific image of whom terrorists are and what motivations, politics, and general background we should attach to them. Information and public awareness about terrorists who do not fit this portrait, such as gray-suited government officials and uniformed military officers engaged in state terrorism, the leaders of right-wing terrorist groups in Northern Ireland, West Germany, Italy, Turkey, South Africa, the Philippines, and the members of the Latin American death squads, is scanty.

We cannot quarrel with the conclusions drawn by Russell and Miller as, based on criteria chosen for study, what they discover about the individuals in the eighteen groups is no doubt true. What we do need to question is their claim that they have compiled an accurate universal portrait of a terrorist, since they have drawn data from a very select part of the terrorist world. However, security officials at New York's Kennedy or Miami's International Airports trying to foil airline hijackings see a very different type of terrorist.

Russell and Miller's research appears to support the neoconservatives' claim that the source of the current "epidemic of terrorism" is to be found in the rise of the adversary culture, the "politics of democratic excess" and the power and influence of the "new class." For example, their conclusion that "the philosophical underpinnings of most modern terrorist groups may be found in a loose synthesis of the views developed by Mao, Trotsky, Marcuse, Fanon, and particularly those of Marighella,"[33] corresponds to the neoconservative claim that anti-liberal ideologies of the New Left are solely responsible for encouraging violence and terrorism in contemporary liberal society. In their analysis of the social background, education, occupation, and method of recruitment of the eighteen urban terrorist groups, Russell and Miller's data uncover evidence of the neoconservative "new class." For example, they said that the parents of the terrorists are:

Professional people (doctors, lawyers, engineers, and so forth), government employees, diplomats, clergymen, military officers, or sometimes even police officials. Although these parents were part of the existing social and economic

systems, many of them had been frustrated in their efforts to use them as vehicles for upward social and economic mobility. Liberal in political outlook, they also frequently advocated significant social and political change.[34]

Russell and Miller also contend that the university serves as the major recruitment center for terrorist groups. Their research finds many university environments dominated by administrators and professors with strong Marxist biases. In fact, conclude Russell and Miller, when the liberal views of the parents were "coupled with radical socio-economic doctrines so popular in most university circles during the 1960s, this combination of forces often added to the general student distrust of 'democratic institutions' as effective media for implementing social change—may have moved some young people towards terrorism."[35] Further, they find that many of the leaders of terrorist groups tend to be older and well trained in the humanities, giving them a similar kind of power over younger people.

Connecting the rise of terrorism with participatory politics and the "new class," Russell and Miller go beyond their announced intention to provide us with a profile of a typical terrorist. In fact, they try to substantiate the central proposition that the contemporary explosion of terrorism is a result of a political, social, and cultural climate where questions about equality, voting rights, patriarchy, public housing, workplace health and safety, nuclear weapons, peace, the roots of poverty, civil rights, child day care, and social justice are taken seriously. They also confirm that many enemies of the traditional democratic order and those sympathetic to the terrorist cause are entrenched in the major institutions of society with considerable power over state policy. Their profile and the analysis behind it has found its way into public consciousness. In a dramatically visual fashion it connects neoconservative crisis ideology with the specter of contemporary terrorism that we have come to fear.

ANTI-TERRORIST MOBILIZATION

If terrorism is defined as indiscriminate violence against innocent people, then it is viewed by most of us in the most negative of terms. Therefore, political forces of all kinds can use public fear and connect concern about terrorism policies to their enemies. It is a powerful political weapon to mobilize support for their political agenda. Major political leaders from both East and West have sensed the political gains to be made by playing to our fear of terrorism. For instance, during President Reagan's first presidential campaign he effectively portrayed the Carter Administration as weak and indecisive in its efforts to gain the release of the American hostages and convinced the American public that in a symbolic sense their president was being held hostage in the White House rose garden by Iranian terrorists. Reagan charged that Carter was caving in to the terrorist demands in order to secure the release of the hostages and left the impression that under Reagan's leadership American pride and power would not be held hostage by terrorists. In his enthusiastic welcoming home of the fifty-two American hostages, newly-inaugurated President Reagan showed he understood the pent-up public frustrations and demands for revenge. He promised an American policy of "swift and effective retribution" against any terrorists who up till now have been "confident that they can go to sleep, waking up in the morning and the United States wouldn't have taken any action."[1]

According to the Reagan Administration, much of the explosion of terrorism is caused by a Soviet-directed international terrorist network, and the battle against domestic and foreign terrorism is his primary priority. To effectively fight this battle, Reagan theorists tell us, we must return to a Cold War policy of open hostility and vigilance against the Soviet Union and Communism and a rebuilding of American military and intelligence capabilities.

Judging by public reaction in the United States to the events of the summer and fall of 1985, it appeared that the American public felt vengefully outraged. This was most obvious in October when United States Navy jets violated Italian airspace and forced the landing of an Egyptian airline carrying four Palestinians suspected of involvement in the hijacking of the Italian cruise ship *Achille Lauro* and the murder of one American passenger. This single act of American retaliation provoked, in many citizens frustrated by mounting terrorism against America, a sense of patriotic euphoria and cries for additional acts of revenge. Some Americans wanted the four suspects kidnapped from Italian authorities flown to the United States to face American justice. In his survey of American opinion during this period, *The New York Times* reporter Samuel G. Freedman says this one anti-terrorist success "unleashed a taste for retribution that has been building for years."[2] Freedman noted that the reaction across the country from the subways of Manhattan to construction sites in Los Angeles was not one of celebration as evidenced by the flags, champagne, and yellow ribbons that accompanied the release of the Iranian hostages of 1981, but rather an angry mood calling for deliberate and open revenge. The call for swift and bloody justice for the hijackers and support for Reagan's decision to intercept the plane cut through all levels of the American public. For example, a Chicago nightclub owner expressed open support for "Reagan Rambo" while a San Francisco municipal worker and admitted pacifist saw the action as "positive." In Miami, a stockbroker advocated a return to the gunboat diplomacy of President Theodore Roosevelt. A California construction worker, apparently not satisfied with the capture of terrorist suspects, said "we should have shot the plane out of the sky."[3] Across the country, newspaper editorial opinion reflected the feelings of the dissatisfaction and the anger of the public mood with headlines hailing capture of the "bloody-handed thugs," "cowardly pirates," and "human rodents."

The Reagan Administration moved quickly in reaction to the public mood. In late October 1985 Secretary of State George P. Shultz renewed his public campaign for a policy of "swift and sure measures" against terrorism. He reiterated his official support for an anti-terrorist posture advocated in May 1985 by senior administration officials Fred Ikle and Robert Oakley in which American military force would be used against terrorists where the loss of civilian life was a definite possibility. Although Defense Department and senior intelligence officials were reported to be more cautious than Shultz on the use of American military power against unidentified terrorists, they were said to be in agreement with him concerning the need to galvanize the American public behind a tougher response to terrorism.

Shultz encountered little if any editorial or public criticism for his suggestion that the United States fight terrorism with terrorism or for his urging Americans to get used to the idea that innocent civilians might be routinely killed or injured in the pre-emptive and preventive use of military power against terrorism. According to many news sources, Secretary Shultz actually improved his standing with the public and within the power circles of the administration for his willingness to tell the unpopular truth about the difficult and dangerous options required to combat terrorism. The public reaction illustrates the extent of public fear about terrorism as well as public acceptance and support of a militant defense policy as the proper approach to fighting America's enemies.

At different times the Reagan Administration has been openly criticized by members of other political and some media establishments as counterproductive in the battle against terrorism. Though there was genuine relief and bi-partisan applause for the Reagan Administration's handling of the TWA hostage crisis at the Beirut airport in June 1985, the president's militant stand after the hostage release brought many expressions of concern. The chorus of critical voices included *The New York Times'* foreign affairs correspondent Flora Lewis, who at other times has advocated the use of military force to counter terrorism and Communism. In this instance, she took issue with Reagan's July speech in which he laid the blame for terrorism at the feet of a Soviet-backed "confederation of terrorist states" before the American Bar Association. Lewis called the speech a diatribe that "served to magnify and elevate terrorists into crusaders for a world cause, giants instead of gnats stinging solid nations peevishly and ineffectively."[4] She claimed that it must come as a pleasant surprise to America's enemies and of grave concern to its friends that it is so easy to drive the United States into a frenzy. Lewis was of the opinion that Reagan's position is the wrong way to fight terrorism, since it "risks stoking the furies of American impatience, and scaring away allies and friends whose help is critical." Moreover, she says it isn't likely to scare terrorists; "it enhances them."[5] Around the same time, journalist Peregrine Worsthorne of the British *Daily Telegraph* echoed Lewis's sentiments, saying that President Reagan started off on the wrong track in his battle with terrorism by pledging to be tougher on terrorists than his predecessor had been. Worsthorne warns that this stance will only play directly into the terrorists' hands, and that the more frenzy created about terrorism the greater will be the humiliation when efforts against terrorism fail. Like Lewis, Worsthorne counsels that effective counterterrorism must be more sober, less indignant, and begin with the acceptance of the inevitabilty of terrorism. In addition to these journalistic voices of dissent, former President Jimmy Carter publicly admonished President Reagan's loud denunciations of terrorism and suggested that "terrorism can be dealt with quietly and effectively rather than with threats addressed to a world audience."[6]

In counselling President Reagan to take a less aggressive stand in dealing with terrorism, these critics offered the point that public hysteria is counterproductve in battling terrorists to whom publicity is lifeblood. However, in the months that followed his speech, President Reagan and his senior officials ignored the advice of their critics and sought public support of more militant anti-terrorist policies.

The conservative establishment and those terrorist experts who share its views have warned that the incidence of international terrorism is on the rise (which it is), that the majority of terrorist acts occurred in western Europe (40.5 percent in 1984), followed by the Middle East (20.6 percent), and that Americans are the primary target of terrorists (30 to 35 percent during the 1980s). The task of collecting, tallying, and reporting these figures is performed by various diplomatic and intelligence agencies like the United States State Department (the Office for Combatting Terrorism), the Central Intelligence Agency, the Federal Bureau of Investigation, and private organizations such as the Jaffee Center for Strategic Studies in Tel Aviv, Israel. These reports are dominated by the assumptions of the "ideology of terrorism" as to whom the terrorists are, what constitutes a terrorist act, and what kind of terrorism produces the greatest threat to most people. For example, to the authors of the annual report from the Office for Combatting Terrorism, titled "Patterns of International Terrorism," the problem of terrorism is limited to only those incidents of terrorism involving different nations or states. This highly regarded and often-cited survey does not include incidents of national terrorism. One of the conclusions sometimes drawn from this report is that the citizens of Chile, Guatemala, the Philippines, Paraguay, and many other countries, brutalized by their own "national security state," do not face as great a threat from terrorism as do the citizens who live in West Germany or Italy and American citizens who travel and live abroad. The terrorist groups held responsible for the bulk of international terrorism are, because of extensive media coverage, well known to many of us and most are left-wing in origin. Right-wing terrorists are excluded, according to the survey's authors, because there are no international connections between them, and their terrorism is confined to the domestic or national context. The many Latin American exiles who find themselves pursued abroad by government intelligence agencies and mercenaries and who have over the years been victimized by assassinations, bombings, and other acts of terrorism, often go uncounted and unreported as victims of international terrorism. Utilizing these and other distinctions, some terrorism "experts" warn the citizens of the industrial democracies that terrorism from the Left is a rising threat requiring increased vigilance and that Americans in particular are under duress. But they do not warn of terrorism from the Right and its similar consequences.

Realistically, the United States in the recent past has not been plagued to the same extent, by either indigenous terrorist groups or by the "international terrorist network," as have other industrial democracies in the 1970s and 1980s. However, our president and other officials urge a high level of public awareness and concern. Presidential advisors on terrorism Robert Kupperman and Darrell Trent in their 1979 book, *Terrorism: Threat, Reality, Response*, were among the first to warn that the low level of terrorism in the United States was a matter of temporary good luck, that Americans needed to prepare for the worst as it won't be long before the United States becomes a major terrorist target. This warning continues unabated, even though official reports show lower numbers of terrorist incidents in the United States. In early 1986 Robert

Oakley, head of the State Department's Office for Combatting Terrorism, contended that domestic terrorism remained a "serious problem"—even though terrorists managed to carry out only 7 attacks inside the United States in 1985, compared with 112 in 1977.

Terrorism does remain a serious problem in the United States, but not only from the sources included in Oakley's estimate. Among those incidents not included in his 1985 survey were attacks on abortion clinics by right-wing pro-life organizations and the family planning community, the surge in threats and assaults on the American Arab community, for instance in Dearborn, Michigan, where family members of Lebanese Shiite leader Nabih Berri live, and bomb threats and attacks on Soviet airline offices and the Soviet United Nations mission by the Jewish Defense League and increasing attacks against Jewish synagogues and properties by anti-Semitic groups. Here again, we find the political biases of the "counters" guiding the "science" of tallying terrorist incidents. In this case, their survey hides the magnitude of the terrorist problem in the United States because a more objective count, with terrorism coming more from the Right as well as from the Left, is not admitted.

CRISIS MANAGEMENT AND COUNTERTERRORISM

Even as conservative political fortunes have risen in the industrial democracies, the neoconservative crisis management proposals which call for strengthening the authority of state security institutions and the re-imposition of order and social discipline remain controversial. The conservative alliance has taken a "hard-line" counterterrorist position favored by terrorism experts. Advocates of the "hard-line" school of counterterrorism argue that the battle against terrorism requires the expansion of domestic and foreign intelligence operations, extensive security agency organization and policy coordination, constant public vigilance against terrorists and terrorist sympathizers, and the sacrificing of some of the traditions and privileges of open society.

In specific terms, many terrorism experts in the United States suggest that the central purpose of the anti-terrorist policy must be the protection or enhancement of state authority. They contend the primary goal of the contemporary terrorist is to portray the government as weak and ultimately to provoke public doubts about its legitimacy. According to this view, any concession or sign of government vacillation only encourages the terrorist. Paul Wilkinson and others feel that the process of bargaining, particularly if it entails concessions to terrorist demands, damages the credibility and authority of government, with long-term consequences. Wilkinson, an admirer of the "hard-line" counterterrorism first practiced by Israel and now adopted by other governments, including the United States, contends that "A necessary corollary of the hard-line principle is that there should be no political negotiations or conferences with groups or movements engaged in, or aiding and supporting terrorism."[7] Wilkinson concludes that "Governments have nothing to lose but possibly much to gain from holding firm to the policy of no capitulation, no concession, and no deal, when confronted with terrorist blackmail."[8] Expert Juliet Lodge agrees in *Terrorism: A Challenge to the States* that government legitimacy should be the greatest concern in the state's response to terrorism by arguing that "recourse to security measures may help to reassure the public that the legitimate authorities are 'in command' of the situation."[9] Besides, she says, policymakers in liberal democracies are not really interested in long drawn-out discussions that blame the rise of terrorism on the ills of society and government represssion. Their immediate concern is to protect their societies and innocent people from the terrorist by employing the science of security technology and law-enforcement processes.

If we survey the multitude of proposals on counterterrorist policy produced by many panels, study groups, conferences, and think tanks, we find the majority to be in basic agreement with Wilkinson and Lodge on the essentials of effective anti-terrorist policy. For example, there is almost unanimous agreement that effective intelligence gathering is imperative. Lord Grey of Naunton, who was governor of Northern Ireland from 1968 to 1973, contends that the scope of intelligence gathering must be broad and deep as "both for prevention and for cure, a prime requisite is knowing who is doing wrong or about to, what wrong he is doing or about to do, where he is and who his friends are, what their methods are and how best to counter their wicked designs."[10] Advancements in the science of intelligence-gathering technology are hailed as essential to effective counterterrorism. Computers are singled out as especially useful in the centralization and analysis of information. Terrorist expert John Wolf is amazed by the capabilities of the CIA's sophisticated computer system known as "Octopus." With an enthusiasm untempered by the political implications of this magical technology, he tells us that "Octopus"

> . . . can match television pictures of known terrorists and their associates against profiles contained within the system. The television pictures are taken in various overseas airports, bus terminals, and other transportation centers. In microseconds, "Octopus" can analyze a picture along with the information already in its file on targets in the area and the equipment and skills required to attack them successfully. Within a few minutes after the analysis, a radio alarm can be transmitted into a counterterrorist team who can in turn apprehend the terrorist.[11]

There is a great support by major anti-terrorist experts for international uniform penal codes, stronger penalties, including the death penalty, for terrorists, swift and efficient court procedures, a uniform no-negotiation stance, police and special anti-terrorist squads and a centralized oversight policy group responsible for continued assessment of threat and response. These experts feel effective anti-terrorism is a matter of deterrence and favor the use of video technology like IBM's controversial "Big Blue" software packages with service level reporter (SLR) and remote access control facility (RACF) that is being used to monitor Italian workers' activities. To enhance the legal authority of the deterrence function, many urge the passage of anti-terrorist legislation even if it encroaches upon traditional liberal democratic rights to privacy, free speech, or political activity. The "hard-line" school contends that only by using science to harden terrorist targets and by legislating an increase in the capabilities of detection and punishment can terrorists and their community of sympathizers be successfully thwarted.

To bolster their case for the hard-line policy, many experts in anti-terrorist theory say that their proposals are a product of scientific investigation. In their discussions of the important breakthroughs in counterterrorism resulting from scientific advancements in security technology or organizational and management strategy, there is little if any mention of political implications. Effective counterterrorism is presented as a matter of employing the magic of science to stay ahead of today's explosion of terrorism. Fortification of the authority and scope of state security institutions is another strategy advanced. But no-one has yet been able to confirm that the rise or fall in the number of terrorist incidents correlates with the adoption of hard-line counterterrorist posture. Indeed, there are important voices within both the anti-terrorist and conservative communities, like the highly respected terrorism expert J. Bowyer Bell, and some editors of *The Wall Street Journal*, who feel that these measures to counteract terrorism do not have any degree of certain success, but many feel something, indeed almost anything, must be tried.

While the political preference for "authoritarian democracy" among many anti-terrorist experts is evident, most anti-terrorist experts are cognizant of the political dangers to liberal democracy provoked by their recommendation of the hard-line approach. Yet, only a few mention the necessity for safeguarding the democratic process and fewer still expend any effort to detail or develop those safeguards. The prevailing assumption among many anti-terrorist experts is that in the battle against terrorism individual rights must give way to state authority. This indeed may be true, but as yet few of these experts have researched the erosion of individual rights by anti-terrorist measures and technology, how much erosion is necessary, or which individual rights and which individuals' rights are to be tampered with. Both history and the current debate over neoconservative crisis proposals tell us no consensus exists on this issue.

The refusal of many anti-terrorist experts to examine closely the political impact of counterterrorism on liberal democratic rights is part of their political preference for state authority. Terrorism experts like John Wolf openly accuse Americans of being blind to the dangers of terrorism and to the need for deterrence because of their desire to maximize their individual freedoms. Others like Walter Laqueur assume that "societies do not voluntarily commit suicide, they will rather give up some of their freedoms, if facing a moral threat,"[12] without being challenged as politically partisan. But the arguments of Laqueur, Wolf, and some of their colleagues which contend that terrorism is a major threat to industrial democracies and that reluctance of the public to give up traditional freedoms is tantamount to suicide, are politically and ideologically consistent with some of the political themes of neoconservatism.

Finally, many anti-terrorist experts have noted the absence of terrorism, other than state terrorism, in authoritarian or totalitarian societies in comparison with liberal democracies. This point, while not a recommendation for totalitarianism, is often used to suggest that the "open society" can be a fertile political milieu for terrorism and thus can be critically flawed. It implies a relationship between the absence of terrorism and a political, cultural, and social context of governability. In his survey of terrorism, Walter Laqueur notes that "Terrorism today occurs either in Parliamentary democracies or in halfhearted, inefficient authoritarian regimes."[13] Laqueur's observation is supported by government and private studies which show western Europe and North and South America having the bulk of the "terrorist" incidents and the Soviet Union and Eastern Europe consistently on the lower end of the scale. These surveys from the anti-terrorist experts help confirm the basic assumption that terrorism is best combatted in a political culture of "authoritarian democracy."

TERRORISM AS INDISCRIMINATE

Many of the industrial democracies have geared their counterterrorist policy to the premises that terrorism is indiscriminate, that everyone is a target, and that state policy is and must be aimed at protecting everyone. In such a view, state power must be sufficiently reinforced to deal with a "public enemy" presumed to be everywhere and targeting everyone. In the public interest, individual rights must be curtailed to provide security against terrorists who make no distinction between the innocent and the guilty. In cases where terrorists do identify particular targets, the indiscriminate nature of the acts of terrorism—bombings, hijacking, and hostage-taking—is invoked to support the state's position.

Acting on the assumption that terrorism is indiscriminate, some liberal states have installed security apparatus aimed at protecting the innocent and identifying the guilty by surveillance over everyone. Increasing the inconvenience to everyone, and infringing further on individual rights of privacy, movement, and political association, public and private officials have approved a haphazard array of security measures, including identification cards and badges, video and audio surveillance, x-ray sensor machines, polygraph tests, and searches of persons and personal belongings.

Many world policymakers, especially those in the West, treat terrorism as exclusively criminal activity. This holds true for both individual governments and international and regional institutions like the United Nations, the European Community, and the Organization of American States. Such leaders feel that the political claims of various terrorist groups are untrue and officials have denied political status to members of terrorist and revolutionary groups imprisoned in western Europe and North America. For example, in the early 1970s the Nixon Administration, backed by United Nations Secretary General U Thant, who said that hijackings should be judged by their "criminal character not their political significance,"[14] proposed that in civil aviation, hijacking be defined as a criminal act of political violence against innocent people. The "European Convention on the Suppression of Terrorism," passed by the European Parliament in 1976, defined terrorism as a criminal act to facilitate the extradition of suspected terrorists. On December 9, 1985, in what was hailed as a landmark resolution by all parties, including the Soviet Union, the United Nations General Assembly condemned all acts of terrorism as "criminal," a move that is expected to coordinate extradition procedures between nations by enforcing the code that no political rationale can be used to deny extradition. In February 1986 the United States Senate voted unanimously to fill a gap in American law by backing a "Terrorist Prosecution Act" sponsored by Republican Senator Alan Spector that would make it a crime liable to prosecution in the United States of anyone who wounded, killed, or even attacked an American citizen anywhere in the world. The Spector Bill, which has the backing of Secretary of State George P. Shultz, encourages the use of "moderate force" by the United States to abduct and bring back for trial in American courts on criminal charges anyone who seeks to harm or does harm to Americans travelling or living abroad. The United States Senate is also re-examining a number of extradition treaties it has with various nations that exempt from extradition those accused of "political" crimes.

However, by accepting the idea that only criminals are terrorists, many conservative policymakers seem unaware of the multiple sources and political nature of much terrorism. Further, the position on terrorism currently held by many political leaders and analysts permits anti-terrorism to be used as a tool of political intimidation and social control in much the same way that anti-Communism was used during the Cold War decades of the 1940s and 1950s. As Communism was said to be the force of subversion, now it is terrorism that is said to threaten liberal democratic society. As those who questioned Cold War assumptions were labelled Communist appeasers or "fellow travelers," opposition to conservative anti-terrorist measures, even when they erode cherished civil rights, is viewed as detrimental to the public interest, undermining the constitutional authority of the state, an obstacle to those responsible for security, and, ultimately, sympathetic to the terrorist cause.

In the war to combat indiscriminate terrorist-criminals, neoconservative policymakers have told us that individual rights may have to be sacrificed to the security needs of the state if we are to survive. Acting on this thesis, they have attempted, without considering divergent or more liberal views, to install technology and pass legislation that erode many aspects of our right to privacy, due process, and political association. The application of this technology and legislation threatens, in particular, the democratic rights, powers, and privileges of any political force that opposes the neoconservative program for ending terrorism.

ANTI-TERRORIST TECHNOLOGY AND INDIVIDUAL RIGHTS

The growth of the security industry for both state and private use has been staggering over the past twenty years. It was only two decades ago, in 1967, that the Federal Bureau of Investigation pioneered the use of computer-based files when it established the National Crime Information Center. Until then, all of the FBI files had been stored in a labyrinth of filing cabinets and had to be pulled individually by hand. A large part of this growth is due to efforts to strengthen security at airports, government and corporate installations, and, lately, at nuclear facilities. But counterterrorism is only part of a general trend to develop technology that can secure or protect public and private property and increase the capabilities of social control.

The impact of this technology and its centralization function on the traditional rights of individuals is a fiercely contested political issue in the industrial democracies. The Age of the Computer, while it brings with it increased efficiency in the gathering, storage, and dissemination of information, also reduces the means to individual privacy. The increased capability of public and private authorities to predict, prevent, or influence natural and human "disasters" by using advanced instruments of surveillance and detection runs counter to the idea of an "open society." The private sector's enthusiasm for the profit potential of new technology, be it video surveillance systems that survey the assembly line or polygraph and drug tests on employees and prospective employees, has generally outweighed the concern for its political impact. Public officials who have tried to strike a balance between technological advance and individual rights have usually approved technological innovation, particularly in the areas of crisis management and national security. The arguments concerning the increased vulnerability of modern, interdependent systems of transportation, communication, and energy have proven persuasive.

The rise of terrorism has helped ease the tension and contradictions posed by the growth in the private security industry to democratic control over the instruments of violence and coercion. In democratic societies it is traditionally the sovereign function of the state to monopolize the instruments of coercion and social control. The rapid development of the private security industry, especially the buying and selling of hardware and software and the training of employees to perform the police functions of investigation and surveillance, have challenged this sovereign purview. If, as is the case in the United States, half of all agents fulfilling police functions and carrying arms are privately employed, the power of the democratic state to control the spread and use of arms and to coordinate the various systems of crisis management and domestic security is greatly subverted.

This particular aspect of the crisis of modern democracy is less obvious when both the private security forces of the corporate sector and the state security agencies join in the battle against terrorism. Since terrorists do not discriminate between public and private installations, personnel, or property, there is ample reason for both public and private counterterrorist capabilities. To the extent we presume terrorism to be a permanent feature of contemporary democratic society, the co-existence of the two systems becomes tolerable, and, indeed, mutually supportive. In addition, since officials of both systems use similar if not the same kind of technology for their security functions, public confusion occurs about the use of force for national security versus private security purposes. This situation makes it possible for officials from both sectors to undermine the rights of those individuals in society who are denied possession or control of this technology of coercion. Indeed, the majority of individuals in society do not control the instruments of force, yet are virtually powerless against those in the private and public security who come armed with the instruments of force and an ideology that says the individual's right to know, right of privacy, freedom of speech, assembly, and due process of law must be curtailed if democracy is to survive terrorism and the political agencies behind it.

In some cases, the battle against terrorism has served to justify the adaption or application of technology devised for military security forces by public and private police and security agencies. The most thorough testing of technology against terrorism as an instrument of social control has been done by the British Army in Northern Ireland, although The Netherlands, Belgium, Italy, and West Germany have also tested it extensively. Because of the secrecy surrounding such technology and its national security application, our discussion of the latest advances and how and where they are applied is both sketchy and dated. But even with the veil of government and industrial secrecy, it is possible to get a sense of this technology, how it is being used, and some of the political implications for individual rights.

Much of the technology adopted in the name of counterterrorism has been in the area of prevention and consists of three basic components: detection, intrusion, and surveillance.

DETECTION TECHNOLOGY

Trained dogs. Trained dogs have proven to be effective for the detection of explosives and drugs. While they are mobile, they are also expensive to train, difficult to manage, and labor-intensive.

Electron capture vapor detectors. Electron capture vapor detectors are effective against explosives such as TNT, dynamite, RDX, and ANFO, which give off vapors. They are useful in cases where manufacturers impregnate explosives with vapor-emitting chemicals.

Tagging. Tagging is a method of identification used to detect explosives by "tagging" them with detectable chemical agents or with "coded" microspheres. Tagging can also be used for keeping track of and protecting military hardware and software. As a method of detection, tagging almost always necessitates mandatory regulation of manufacturing processes.

Trace detectors. Trace detectors are used for the detection of chemicals that by themselves or in combination with other chemicals become highly toxic agents and thus potential instruments of terror.

Metal detectors. Metal detectors are employed to detect small-arms traffic at airports and other transportation centers. They are widely used today and seem to have gained public acceptance with little fanfare, even though the amount of metal in "innocent baggage" does cause inconvenience and intrusion on the right of privacy of both people and property.

X-ray machines. X-ray machines are used to inspect carry-on baggage and, increasingly, to investigate larger volumes of material. Shadowgraph interpretation is not perfect and it requires inspectors to be constantly attentive. In addition, plastic explosives come in all shapes, forms, and sizes and are not always detectable by x-ray, as the March 1986 explosion aboard a TWA airliner enroute from Rome to Athens has proven. Shadowgraphing does remove some of the inconvenience of having to manually open and inspect personal property.

Personality and physical profile. Profiles are used primarily in skyjacking security to detect potential terrorists. Persons fitting the profile as interpreted by security personnel are subject to detainment, questioning, searches, and revocation of travel rights. Due to the subjectivity involved in both the construction of the profile and its application, the use of the profile is more of a political exercise than an applied science. There are reports of security personnel abusing their powers of search and seizure. Some travelers who were detained because they "fit the profile" have filed lawsuits. As use of the profile spreads there is the potential for even greater infringement.

INTRUSION TECHNOLOGY

Security architecture. Security architecture is the utilization of security devices in the planning and construction of architectural design such as moats, narrow bridges, single access buildings, and office isolation to impede access by either individuals or groups. Other security concerns of architectural design include fireproof and bombproof construction materials, emergency exits, internal security rooms, and automatic alarm and entry-exit security systems. Limitations on both freedom of movement and access are the major concern of this design.

Visual, audio, and physical barriers. Fences, walls, and soundproofing are the most common examples of this technology. The chain-link fence of galvanized steel with strands of barbed wire at the top is widely employed for perimeter security. If well lighted and maintained, these fences are effective against unwarranted intrusion. Walls act as both visual and physical barriers and, though common, are costly to maintain. In cases where "sensitive" installations are in need of protection, the public is barred.

Sensor devices. Sensor devices consist of a whole range of intrusion sensors, including door switches, conductive tape, photo-electric sensors of vibration, sound, and heat. This technology was developed for use in Vietnam to detect intrusion by North Vietnamese troops into South Vietnam, especially along the Ho Chi Minh Trail. Allegedly labor saving, these sensors do need constant maintenance and operational investigation. Their successful operation also necessitates development of an adequate security system to protect them from sabotage. The British have used sensors in their operations in Northern Ireland. According to its "Land Operation Manual," the British military has six different applications for remote sensor devices, including equipment that can sense people at up to 150 meters and vehicles as far away as 500 meters. These sensors can also detect animals, vibrations caused by marching troops, and moving trucks, and are sensitive to sound, heat, metal, and the smell of urine. Newer sensors can exclude unwanted noise, can combine different capabilities, and can electronically classify the information they receive.

SURVEILLANCE TECHNOLOGY

Television cameras. Closed-circuit television systems are widely utilized to expand the surveillance area. Camera technology now includes laser beam cameras and is standard equipment for most police forces. The placement of television cameras at strategic points or known "trouble spots" allows constant surveillance. Several cities, including New York, Cleveland, and London, have twenty-four-hour surveillance over many city blocks. British police survey major highways with cameras which are linked to police stations. In the post offices there is monitoring of the areas. A new phone-line television system (S.S.TV) installed in Great Britain sounds an alarm in the police station and produces a picture of what is occurring in the areas under camera surveillance. The Dutch installed an automated police report room in Rotterdam that includes the latest in video display units (VSU) and an assistance surveillance unit (ASE) complete with fixed and mobile telephones, concentrators, modems, and the technology to record incident number, geographical area, and priority code. It also produces an incident printout on a twenty-four or forty-eight-hour basis.

Night vision devices. Night vision devices have been developed for increased surveillance capability at night and have been tested extensively in Northern Ireland and Vietnam. An instrument called "Twiggy," which is an image intensifier capable of surveillance against persons in starlight up to 600 meters, has proven effective in giving security forces an advantage after dark. The Individual Weapon Site is more mobile than "Twiggy" and can be fitted to rifles. It, too, can be used in starlight, but with a range of 300 meters. Other night devices include infrared viewers, which can take pictures at night, and thermal viewers, which have long-range image capability that can be used in the daylight or at night and have the added advantage of distinguishing between warm and cold objects. One disadvantage of some night vision devices is that they are ineffective in artificial light. To overcome this disadvantage, British forces have been known to shoot out all the streetlights in the area under surveillance.

Helicopters. Since Vietnam, helicopters are widely used for police aerial surveillance and for transporting people and materials quickly to a crisis area. Equipped with the latest camera technology such as zoom lenses and image stabilizers and communications systems, helicopters have proven effective for dealing with traffic problems, crime watch, demonstration assessment, and riot control. In Kansas City, police employ helicopters for political demonstration surveillance, photo flights, and routine surveillance. In Cleveland, helicopters equipped with powerful searchlights are used to patrol the city's ghetto areas at night. Police and military personnel are also reported to be trained in using helicopters as mobile staging platforms for crisis management. Increasingly, helicopters operate as aerial patrol cars, with the added advantage of being free from ensnarling ground traffic that can inhibit and delay security force response.

While the use of surveillance technology may be effective against troublesome traffic patterns and in high crime areas, the increasing capability to monitor large and small areas during the day or night diminishes the privacy of average citizens. In its surveillance, the television camera does not discriminate between the innocent and the guilty. Moreover, the placement of surveillance equipment has: an assumption of who the enemy is or is likely to be; what political forces are likely to be violent or cause trouble for state authorities; who the criminal element is and where they live and operate. With the advancement of surveillance technology, especially its deployment and use as part of routine police work, the sense that "big brother" is watching becomes a reality for vast numbers of people. To many people, the response of police and state officials to questions or objections about the surveillance capability that "people with nothing to hide have nothing to fear" rings with danger to individual rights, especially since it is the state and the corporate sector that control this technology and oversee its use.

There are other counterterrorist preventive measures that have been proposed which raise even more complex issues. For example, there are proposals to limit the sale of certain weapons, chemicals, technology, and information about technology as a way of denying terrorists access to weapons. The American experience with no-sale legislation in the hand gun market and the politicalization of the issue by the powerful hand gun lobby in Congress gives us a hint of the controversy involved in these proposed laws. Such no-sale legislation, besides running counter to the democratic political tradition and increasing monopoly of the state over the instruments of coercion and technological information, is in many cases impractical. No-sale legislation of certain chemicals would involve the state in making constant exceptions to its no-sale rule, since the chemical industry is so complex and there are a large number of other industries that depend on having access to chemicals. Exceptions to the law not only increase the chances of these materials falling into the wrong hands, thereby defeating the purpose of the legislation, but also involve the state authorities in a continuous process of making judgments about who should or should not have access to this material. In the end, the rights of some individuals are going to be upheld while others are limited.

COUNTERTERRORIST INTELLIGENCE

Phone taps. Telephone taps are used for gathering intelligence and for surveillance purposes. There is an array of sophisticated electronically-operated phone "bugs" that operate by signal back to the central operation unit and indicate when a particular phone is being used. Every FBI office is equipped with a SUTECH system, which is a technical surveillance facility activated by use of a telephone or electronic signal. Names overheard on this system are filed in the Washington, D.C., central office in the ELSUR system.

Identification cards. Identification cards permit easy and rapid identification of persons, occupations, addresses, and associates. While some nations, including the United States, continue to debate the political implications of a national identification card, others, like West Germany and Britain, have an actual identification card or a system that serves the same function through vehicle registration, housing permits, and occupation cards. Social security numbers are an important source of personal identification in all industrial securities.

Electronic tagging of license plates. Electronic tagging of vehicle license plates is a surveillance system that enables security forces to keep track of the whereabouts of persons and to apprehend them if necessary.

Statistical analysis. Statistical analysis is a process for improving the intelligence function through the development of heuristic models that attempt to predict riots, political activism, and now terrorism. The study group at Rand Corporation, headed by anti-terrorist expert Brian Jenkins, has done the pioneer work in this area and has developed a project called Rule-directed Interactive Transaction Agent (R.I.T.A.) that provides researchers of international terrorism with a series of computer programs to aid in the analysis of terrorist activities.

Computers. Computers are used for the centralization, organization, storage, and dissemination of information. In the industrial societies, extensive use of computers by police and security agencies that can gather, organize, and store vast amounts of information and then make that information available, complete with cross references, numerical calculations, frequency data, and a whole range of other indices in a short time has revolutionized the intelligence and security industry. For example, with the aid of a high-speed microcomputer, flying spot scanner (in color display), table unit, and general purpose computer unit, it is possible to identify latent fingerprints and voice prints. ACCESS is a totally computerized police recording system that offers a centralized CRT display of microfilmed images that are automatically tracked and loaded with their most salient points abstracted by a FORTRAN computer program into RTE-IV operated data base for instant access.

The FBI has two IBM 3033 mainframe computers to maintain fifteen million records on missing persons, warrants, stolen property, securities, criminal history, and registered property. It is estimated that in the near future these files will include dossiers on ninety percent of all American residents with arrest records—or about forty percent of the labor force. More than sixty-four thousand federal, state, and local police agencies, government prosecutors, and judges have authority to access these files through the seventeen thousand terminals. According to a former employee at the top secret National Security Agency, the NSA has the largest computer complex in the world, estimated at around five and a half acres of computers, by which it secretly monitors telex messages, radio transmissions, and other communications, then channels and sorts this information for the president, the FBI, and the CIA. Included in this arsenal of electronic espionage is the IBM-designed "Stretch," a computer so large and powerful that it can only be used by the NSA and the Atomic Energy Commission.

The British have an information network called Police National Computer system that can link details of at least 3.8 million persons recorded to lists of "known associates." Britain also has the Thames Valley Police, a system with the capacity to store one hundred and fifty thousand personal records—or about ten percent of the Thames Valley population. This computer system can store two hundred and fifty thousand occurrences and over one hundred and twenty thousand crimes; almost every house and vehicle are entered and it is estimated that over half of the records involve people who have committed no crime. In this system, each person can be linked up to one hundred known associates, vehicles, crimes, and occurrences (non-criminal acts entered at the discretion of a police officer).

From the outset of the computer age, the issue of personal privacy has been paramount. The gathering, centralization, and storage of vast amounts of information and intelligence by public and private officials in the name of security have raised new questions about the danger to individual rights. It is the use, or abuse, of the computer's capabilities that is most threatening. Complaints have become common with respect to employment records and credit ratings and the issue of privacy. The lack of control over what is fed into the computer by law enforcement officials has raised fears about the political nature of the information. There are numerous reports of individuals' rights being abused by the monopoly control over information and access to information exercised by government officials. For example, after years of denial, the United States Justice Department now admits that it spent the mid-1970s building dossiers on dissidents. British police officials have been convicted of selling information from the computer file. In Britain a man was rejected from jury duty and accused of being an associate of a criminal because the computer file reported that a convicted criminal had parked his car in front of the man's house. In the Netherlands a woman was denied employment because information in the computer identified her as a member of the West German Baader-Meinhof terrorist group. The charge was proven to be false. British journalist Duncan Campbell, who has done extensive research on police use of computers in Britain, says that some police personnel select for their permanent record events that match their prejudices and predispositions and that their range includes a widely defined definition of "subversives" and "criminals." He says that when researchers have been allowed to see the police collections, "These predilections have been apparent; one divisional office had a card index marked 'cows, queens, and flashers.' Cards for men stopped on street checks included notes that individuals were 'grossly obese' or had 'effeminate appearance.' "[15] In a similar vein, Senator William Roth, Jr. of Delaware, in a complaint to the Office of Technical Assessment in August 1983, charged that the FBI National Crime Information Center computer system has been converted from an electronic bulletin board into a nationwide network for monitoring whereabouts of persons merely "of interest" to the government.

In reaction to the procedural abuse of individual rights, there have been legislative efforts to protect the rights of privacy and political freedom by restricting the use of computers. Some western European nations have passed privacy legislation, but its effectiveness has been undercut by the ease with which evidence of abuse can be hidden. In the aftermath of the Watergate scandal, the United States Congress passed the Privacy Act of 1974. Critics have charged that the law is not very effective in protecting the privacy of citizens from government abuse because it allows agencies to change information virtually without notification, it allows too many exceptions, and because there is no one person or agency assigned to its enforcement.

There also must be a willingness to police the system for abuse by those in control. So far, there has been greater concern for and funds spent on protecting computer secrets from the public than protecting the secrets of the public from the information collectors. In 1984 the British were planning to link the computer files of eight police forces with the Police National Computer in what was described as the first step towards a national network of police computers. But there were no plans for Parliament to develop a national policy on the use of police computers, a circumstance that dismayed even some senior British police officials. Carol Ackroyd, Karen Margolis, Jonathan Rosehead, and Tim Shallice charge in their book, *The Technology of Political Control*, that all the existing safeguards, such as code words, program checks, and security measures around computer installations are aimed at the small-time crook while "the big-time crooks (like the CIA and FBI in the USA) can enter, process, or look at almost any information they please."[16]

If the use of the computer by British police and other government agencies, including the Criminal Intelligence Squad, the Fraud Squad, the National Immigration Intelligence Unit, and the Central Drugs Intelligence Unit, is an indicator of how and for what purposes this technology is being used, then individual rights are in danger. According to the British government's Data Protection Committee report of 1980, the committee's attempt to gain access to details of the computer system used by British intelligence units M15 and the Special Branch was severely limited.

Yet the information the committee was able to obtain showed that the real culprit in the process of collecting and storing data was not the computer but, rather, the official policy of pre-emptive policing and surveillance in which a substantial proportion of the material computerized could only be described as "unchecked bunkum."

The Scotland Yard computer system was found by investigators from the Data Protection Committee to have twelve systems collecting information on people. Half of the twelve systems concerned criminals and contained seventeen thousand names. The other six systems held 1.3 million names and simply listed them as "persons." The Special Branch, described by British authorities as the best organization for counterterrorism because it already permeates every corner of the country and has a long history of close contact with the population, collects and computerizes large amounts of data, calculated to be as much as twenty thousand names a month. These data include indices of addresses and telephone numbers allegedly collected from telephone tappings and mail openings. The Special Branch also has a subject index where it holds details of political and other organizations it keeps under surveillance. The name file and subject file can be cross-referenced in twenty-seven "areas of interest." In his assessment of the impact of government intelligence procedures enhanced by the computer function, Duncan Campbell claims that, in addition to the instrusion on privacy, a lot of mistakes are made, so that inaccurate and unsubstantiated information is fed into the computer with little recourse open to the individual other than a plaintive pleading for civil liberties. Campbell asks, "What of the common rights of one hundred thousand or more people recorded in immediately accessible files as 'suspect' or 'of interest to the Special Branch' and treated accordingly?"[17]

Media technology. Media technology pertains to the use of film, advertising, television, and radio to enhance the intelligence-gathering capability by encouraging public awareness and participation in the security process. For example, the Anti-Terrorist Squad at Britain's Scotland Yard has produced a film entitled "A Time of Terror" for television broadcast in the initial stages of a terrorist campaign. The film attempts to rally the support of the British public by warning them that terrorism is indiscriminate and projecting a "we are all in this together" camaraderie with questions like, "Are you sure you are not living next door to terrorists?"

It also encourages public vigilance against bombs and asks the public to assist the police in their anti-terrorism efforts. It very bluntly warns that many more innocent people will be affected by counterterrorist security than will the terrorist. Finally, the film offers a terrorist profile that the public is to use to spot persons who might be terrorists. The profile says terrorists are likely to be young, keep to themselves, live near an underground subway system, include women acting as couriers, do not work regularly, visit pubs but do not drink excessively, and pay for goods with cash.

RESPONDING TO THE TERRORIST THREAT

The industrial democracies have become heavily involved in developing and coordinating an effective military and rescue response to terrorism. Several states maintain military forces trained in counterterrorism. The United States has a number of units trained in both pre-emptive and responsive action. The best known is the Army's Delta Force, which is backed up by two Army Ranger battalions. There are nineteen platoons of Navy Seals, Marine landing and reconnaissance teams, and Air Force Special Operations Forces. The Pentagon is reported to have at its disposal a supersecret anti-terrorist unit called CTJTF. The British, as a part of their "flexible response" posture on internal security matters, have developed special military units that are similar to those of the United States. The Special Air Services (SAS) is one of the most important and functions as a "dirty tricks" unit of the British Army. Critics charge the SAS has been involved in setting up assassinations and liaisons with "friendly" terrorist forces operating against a common enemy. The British conduct joint exercises in urban areas between their special military and police units to coordinate security activities. Special anti-terrorist exercises are conducted on board North Sea gas platforms on a routine basis and involve the Royal Air Force, Navy, Army, and police units.

Special Weapons and Tactics (SWAT) units have also been set up to counter the commando-like tactics of many terrorist groups. The most famous of these small, highly trained, and extremely mobile teams are the Israeli Saiyeret, which engineered the successful rescue at Entebbe, Uganda, in 1976, and the West German GSG-9, said to be the best prepared anti-terrorist group in the world. Created after the terrorist group Black September murdered eleven Israeli athletes at the Munich Olympics in 1972, the Grenzschutzgruppe-9 has been involved in numerous domestic and international counterterrorist actions, including a raid on a Lufthansa airliner at Mogadishu, Somalia, in 1977. Other SWAT teams of note are Britain's Special Branch, Police Special Patrol Group, Anti-Terrorist Squad, and Atomic Energy Authority Constabulary: France's National Gendarmerie Action Group, its Foreign Ministry's anti-terrorist brigade, Belgium's Brigade Diane, and Italy's Squadro Anti-Commando, DIGOS.

The need for this special counterterrorist capability may be obvious, but the aura of secrecy that surrounds these commando teams presents dangers to the democratic tradition. This aura helps stifle any open public debate about the usefulness, effectiveness, and appropriateness of their actions and, conversely, helps strengthen the arguments of those who want more secrecy and less public scrutiny of their policies.

Such secrecy enhances the potential for abuse of power by government officials at a time when there is evidence that such abuses are already a reality. For example, the activity of the Anti-Terrorist Squad (ATS) in Britain is deep in political controversy. According to its critics, who include the British civil rights community, the ATS has been used to gather information on left-wing political groups, to evict squatters from public housing projects, and to conduct raids on the homes of persons said to be anarchists. Critics maintain and trial records confirm that most of these actions were not in any way related to terrorism. In cases where ATS has been successful at apprehending terrorists, there are accusations of prisoner maltreatment, falsification of evidence, and of "confessions" extracted under duress. According to researchers of the *State Research Bulletin*, the short history of the ATS reveals four lessons:

1. The threat of terrorism has been falsely used as the justification for the large size of the Special Branch and other specialist units, when the real specialists in countering terrorism have been recently reduced by over seven hundred percent.

2. Use of ATS for general and unjustified intelligence gathering is growing under the "justification" of anti-terrorism activity, just as in West Germany.

3. The ATS has been relatively unsuccessful in persuading the courts to convict British citizens it has arrested on charges of terrorism.

4. The ATS has been involved in the use of agents provocateur.[18]

The governments in power today in industrial societies are also increasingly concerned with the security of nuclear facilities and fissionable materials. Traditionally, the SWAT teams have been assigned this special task and given far-reaching and often open-ended powers. In Britain the Atomic Energy Authority Constabulary, which guards nuclear installations and the movement of plutonium, was empowered by the Act of Parliament of 1976 to "carry arms at all times; to engage in what is termed 'hot pursuit' of thieves or attempted thefts of nuclear materials; the right to enter any premises at will; and the power to arrest on suspicion."[19] There is no elected body to which this unit is accountable. The Secretary of State has oversight responsibilities but may not intervene in the detail of its operations except in national security cases. Leo Abse of the House of Commons contends that the arms and new power of the AEA Constabulary conflict with every British tradition of civilian and political accountability. Commenting on the political dangers of this Act of Parliament, he argued that it "in effect created a private army which is not ultimately answerable, as are other police forces, to the elected body or to the Home Secretary."[20]

ANTI-TERRORIST LEGISLATION

Unilaterally and collectively, Western states and organizations like the United Nations, the European Community, and the Organization of American States have sought to counter the rise in non-state terrorism with specific laws aimed at enhancing the crisis management powers of the state. Embodied in these laws are the prerogatives of internal order, discipline, and national security over individual rights. Terrorism is treated as *the* crisis facing modern society that can only be countered by extending the legal powers of the state.

The only reference to terrorism during the first two decades of the United Nations was a draft code developed by the International Law Commission on offenses against the peace and security of mankind. In the late 1960s a rash of skyjackings prodded the development of conventions under the auspices of the International Civil Aviation Organization with the encouragement of several United Nations members, including the United States and the other industrial democracies. The major campaign by the United Nations against international terrorism began after the 1972 Munich Olympics. But, except for the unanimous vote in the General Assembly in late 1985 that declared terrorism a criminal activity, the United Nations has been unable to draft and pass a convention on terrorism, although numerous attempts have been made.

Though the United Nations has experienced great frustration in its attempt to pass anti-terrorist conventions, there are important lessons to be taken from it. As an international organization, the United Nations represents many diverse political positions, opinions, histories, and realities. As a result, there is no unanimity among its members on the definition of terrorism, its cause, or who the terrorists are. Also, the United Nations' experience differs with the efforts of individual states and regional organizations like the European Community in passing and implementing anti-terrorist legislation. That is, where there is political homogeneity or where there are dominant political interests to be served by anti-terrorist legislation, it has been possible to ignore questions of definition, cause, and source or, as is more often the case, to enforce certain assumptions on these issues as though they were self-evident and apolitical. In sum, the United Nations' effort exposes the political nature of terrorism and stands in marked contrast to the apolitical nature posited by many neoconservative leaders and terrorism experts.

The European Convention on the Suppression of Terrorism, passed by the member states of the Council of Europe in January 1977 is a good example of anti-terrorist legislation passed by a Western regional organization and represents an important step in coordinating European efforts to legalize anti-terrorist crisis management. The most important part of the agreement concerns the issue of extradition. The member states, with a few qualifications, agreed that terrorism is a criminal rather than political act and thereby subject to criminal prosecution. The act empowers governments to "extradite or try" all cases of terrorism. So far, efforts to implement the convention have been stalled by the qualifications to the extradition rule. These qualifications have been dictated by political realities and differences that exist within the European political community.

The European Suppression of Terrorism Act has spurred extensive cooperation among the various European security ministries and agencies. European security officials meet regularly to coordinate the exchange of information, to discuss anti-terrorist techniques, organize working groups in the technical fields of forensic science, computers, and police communication, the exchange of police personnel and collaboration on police training, and the cooperation in aviation security. But critics from many civil rights organizations in Europe charge that this cooperation goes far beyond the realm of counterterrorism to include the continuous exchange of information on those described as "subversives" and "potential terrorists." They present evidence that many individuals placed in these categories are students, often trade unionists, and left-wing political activists. These principles of European counter-terrorist strategy lead to the same claim as the neoconservative one: that the "enemy" is larger than the actual terrorists and extends to a political social milieu that fosters democratic excess and terrorism.

The Organization of American States (OAS) passed its anti-terrorist convention in early 1971.[21] In its effort to condemn acts of terrorism, the OAS found itself in a political quagmire similar to today's experience of the United Nations. But unlike the United Nations, the OAS was able to gain enough of a consensus (the actual vote was thirteen in favor and three opposed) to adopt a convention that its critics say contains the double flaw of being too narrow in scope and yet open to broad interpretation. Indeed, six members withdrew from the negotiations, objecting that the document was too narrow and did not deal with terrorism in any way.

The OAS document is heavily weighted to favor the authority of the state. For example, Articles 1 and 2 establish the purview of acts covered by the convention and the persons to be protected. In both areas, the scope is narrowed to cover only acts of "kidnapping, murder and other assaults against the life or physical integrity of those persons to whom the state has a duty to give special protection according to international law."[22] The limit on the acts covered and the exclusion of any mention of the word "terrorism" in Article 2 occurred because OAS members were unable to agree on a definition of terrorism and were afraid that a broad definition could be used as a tool of political repression by the state against opposition groups. The OAS also debated whom the state has the responsibility to protect and decided to follow the precedents of Western law and designate the protected class of people as foreign diplomats, consuls, and members of the family of a diplomatic agent. It is unclear how extensive a community of persons this definition covers. Depending on political conditions and the political interests of the protecting government, enforcement of Article 2 can either be all-encompassing or limited. In either case, it only covers state officials and their families and does not apply to the average citizen.

In its designation of persons to be deterred or punished, the OAS Convention is left open to various interpretations, thereby giving the state broad discretionary powers. The initial draft designated that persons taking part in the conception, preparation, or execution of the acts described in Article 1 were subject to state enforcement powers. But the actual convention makes no mention of this category. Thus, if it chooses, the state can employ its powers against those who commit any of the designated acts against the specific persons covered in Articles 1 and 2, or it can apply its powers against all members of a group or organization to which the "terrorists" belong. This ambiguity makes it possible for the state to violate the rights of a wide range of individuals if it chooses to interpret the convention in the broad sense. It was because of this particular ambiguity, which allows the state broad coercive powers, and because the convention defined terrorism as a criminal act with no recognition of political motivations that the Left-leaning governments of Chile, Bolivia, and Peru voted against it. Conversely, the other six member states who objected to the convention were all conservative governments and included Argentina and Brazil. These states argued that the convention did not give the state enough power to deal with terrorism. At the time, both Brazil and Argentina faced serious political challenges from opposition guerrilla forces, and the right-wing governments had sought to crush these forces under the sanction of an OAS convention on terrorism.

INTERNAL TERRORISM

Of central importance in the political shift toward neoconservatism has been a renewed emphasis on domestic national security. Traditional conservative beliefs in patriotism, political loyalty, and discipline in the home, workplace, and, most importantly, in state institutions connected to national security, have been espoused with renewed vigor as necessary to a revitalized America. The Reagan Administration has sponsored measures to strengthen and protect American institutions from Soviet influence, to root out subversive elements in political and cultural institutions, and to enhance the state's crisis management system so that it can deal effectively with the various threats posed against it. A major focus of this national security campaign involves preparations against the terrorist threat which some terrorist experts feel is sure to come to American soil.

NATIONAL SECURITY AND THE THREAT OF DOMESTIC TERRORISM

Immediately after their 1980 election victory, the Reagan campaign staff and transition team announced that a major priority of the new administration's domestic agenda would be the renovation of the national security system and that the problem of terrorism would be of central concern to the architects of that system. The specific proposals of this renovation and its linkage to the threat of terrorism were precisely and forcefully advanced in two sources: the "Mandate for Leadership," a thousand-page study authored by some members of the Reagan transition team under the direction of Edwin Meese, and "Terrorism: Threat, Reality, Response" by Robert Kupperman and Darrell Trent. In

"Mandate for Leadership," the authors make clear their deep concern with the erosion of internal security, law enforcement, and national security institutions during the decades of "democratic excess." The report states that "it is axiomatic that individual liberties are secondary to the requirements of national security and internal civil order"[1] and, backed by what they argue is a clear electoral mandate for their political agenda, the authors submitted a number of proposals on national security:

1. Appointment of persons to head the intelligence agencies and Justice Department who understand the nature of the threat and professional internal security work.

2. Presidential emphasis on the nature of the threat, on the rise of Soviet bloc intelligence activity, the nature of the terrorist threat, the reality of subversion, and the un-American nature of so-called dissidence.

3. Appointment of federal judges who understand both internal security laws and the nature of the threat from extremist and subversive groups.

4. Presidential veto of all legislation that would weaken existing internal security laws.

5. Exemption of the FBI and all other agencies connected with internal security from the Privacy Act and the Freedom of Information Act.

6. Restoration of a capacity to investigate the loyalty of federal employees and an updating of the Attorney General's List of Subversive Organizations.

7. Establishment of a standing congressional committee on internal security matters.

8. The establishment of central files on counterintelligence and internal security.

The report also proposes expanding and strengthening counterintelligence agencies by empowering counterintelligence officers with the right to investigate any American without restriction. It calls for the revision of present guidelines to permit surveillance of groups who might develop violent functions. Intelligence agencies would be free to use wire-tapping, mail covers, informants, and illegal entry. The report also identifies the enemies of American society as "foreign immigrants," "radical and New Left groups," such as the California-based Campaign for Economic Democracy and the Institute for Policy Studies in Washington, D.C., as well as anti-defense and anti-nuclear lobbies. Some clergymen, students, businessmen, entertainers, labor officials, journalists, and government officials also are targeted for government surveillance. It urges the president to use the power of the Executive Order to bypass Congress and lift the restrictions imposed on the intelligence community that have severely limited its ability to protect the nation against terrorism, subversion, and direct military threats to impose new restrictions on public access to information under the Freedom of Information Act. In sum, although the "Mandate for Leadership" may help target possible terrorists, it will also afford a broad-based attack on civil and political liberties and the forces of democratic liberalism.

The authors who penned "Mandate for Leadership" represent the ultra-Right point of view on issues of national security. But many of their proposals have been backed over time by several major figures within the conservative camp, including Richard Allen, President Reagan's first National Security Advisor, and Senator Paul Laxalt, President Reagan's closest political and personal ally in the Senate. In fact, the majority of these proposals was introduced to Congress in 1980 as part of a Republican Party intelligence charter.

The Kupperman-Trent study, "Terrorism: Threat, Reality, Response," asserts that terrorism, while difficult to define, is instigated primarily by non-state leftist forces. The authors argue that the Soviet Union and Soviet-backed states are the primary sources of state terrorism. They also argue that terrorism is indiscriminate violence and is criminal, as opposed to political activity, and that one of its primary motives is "theater" or publicity. However, they go on to say that terrorism in which publicity is the primary motive is on the decline and that terrorists are being forced to find new targets of disruption. Therefore, "one of government's most important jobs is to 'out-invent' terrorists, assessing yet unexploited possibilities and devising countermeasures."[2] As members of the "hard-line" school of counterterrorism, they argue that effective policy should be based on an overall posture of "toughness" accompanied by an increased intelligence capability, the hardening of potential targets, and a mentality and institutional structure of crisis management.

The balance of the study is given to detailing effective counterterrorist measures and the particular threat of terrorism to American society. They point out that as of 1979 the United States has been spared direct experience with the contemporary explosion of terrorism. But Kupperman and Trent warn that this welcome respite cannot last much longer, since America's enemies can be expected to "export" terrorism to the United States. They argue that "As European nations step up their fight against terrorism, often at the cost of civil liberties (as has already occurred in West Germany and Italy), America's open society will attract foreign terrorists, both as a land of exile and as a potential stage for new terrorist activities. Transnationals will, of course, strike anywhere they think their actions will be effective, and America, with its vast global interconnections and relatively high degree of personal freedom . . . may appear as a vulnerable target."[3] Based on their views, Kupperman and Trent urge the United States to develop and employ domestic anti-terrorist measures as a deterrent against this eventuality.

Having confidence in the recommendations of the "Mandate for Leadership," the Kupperman and Trent study, and other voices within the conservative coalition, the Reagan Administration has moved to enhance the capabilities of national security institutions. The administration was successful in gaining new legislation from Congress that impeded the Freedom of Information Act, including Senate Bill S.1752, which contains a number of provisions that impede public access to information. They include redefining such concepts as "government record" to exclude information created for a government official's "personal convenience"; redefining "trade secrets" to a broadened category, making it virtually impossible for public access to business files; a broadened use of a "national security" cover for denial of information; and withholding of any information connected to the law enforcement agencies. The bill also proposed that the attorney general can authorize withholding of entire categories of information if they are deemed to have any connection with terrorism, foreign counterintelligence, or organized crime. Senate Bill S.587 amends the Freedom of Information Act to limit access to records of law enforcement agencies. Senate Bill S.586 changes the Privacy Act of 1974 to allow government officials access to law enforcement records while limiting such access for those who are not subjects of government files. Senate Bill S.3091 prohibits the unauthorized disclosure of information identifying United States intelligence agents and allows federal agents to stifle investigations and reports they consider damaging to their agencies. In 1984 the administration successfully supported a bill which tightened CIA secrecy by authorizing denial of access to operational files, denial of discovery proceedings in Freedom of Information Act lawsuits against the CIA, denial of access by plaintiffs to affidavits submitted by CIA attorneys to the judge explaining why requests for files should be denied, and use of summary court proceedings rather than adversary hearings thereby ending the hearing process in which both sides can present their arguments. This legislation came on the heels of an order by CIA director William Casey, issued one month after he assumed his post, that ended all formal background briefings for reporters on agency operations.

The administration also introduced new guidelines to protect government secrets and government officials from prosecution in national security cases. An interagency task force drafted a proposal to make it easier for government officials to classify information in their files as secret and far more difficult for documents to be declassified. This proposal, signed by President Reagan, reversed a trend begun during the Eisenhower presidency of making it more difficult to keep federal documents confidential. The Justice Department changed the Freedom of Information Act guidelines on fees charged for information, making it possible for government agencies to restrict the flow of information by charging high fees in advance of receipt of the requested materials. In January 1983 President Reagan ordered White House aides to limit their contact with the press. Two months later, based on an interagency proposal to extend the use of lie detectors to include examinations of thousands of federal government officials with access to highly classified material, there were plans to get one hundred thousand government employees to submit to lifetime nondisclosure contracts requiring lie detector tests when ordered by the government. In reaction to congressional pressure and public outrage, the directive was put on hold for the 1984 election year. After the election President Reagan reissued the order, but was forced to abandon its random application after Secretary of State George Shultz publicly threatened to resign if he were forced to take a polygraph test. Testing is now to be done only in cases where espionage is suspected. Despite the uncertain status of this order, by 1984 more than one hundred twenty thousand employees had already signed a lifetime censorship agreement that was imposed in 1981, according to the General Accounting Office. Also, the administration has now required that unclassified government-supported academic research be given to government censors before it is published.

In addition, the Reagan Administration, invoking the little-used 1952 McCarran-Walter Immigration and Nationality Act, has banned many controversial foreign speakers from the United States. The list includes Nobel Prize-winning author Gabriel Garcia Marquez, human rights activists Hortensia Allende, the widow of Chilean President Salvador Allende, Italian playwright Dario Fo and his actress wife Franca Rame, world-renowned authors Farley Mowatt and Carlos Fuentes, retired NATO General Nino Pasti, an outspoken anti-nuclear advocate, and two hundred Japanese anti-nuclear protesters. Since 1981 the United States Information Agency has compiled a blacklist of people whom it deems unfit to represent the United States in an overseas speakers' program. On the list of some eighty to one hundred people are Walter Cronkite, Coretta Scott King, Ralph Nader, and James Baldwin.

The Justice Department successfully opposed appointing a permanent special prosecutor whose mandate was to conduct prompt and independent investigations into misconduct charges levied against senior government officials. In addition, the administration proposed making government officials virtually immune from personal liability in cases where they illegally wire-tapped citizen's telephones or violated individual rights in some other way. In these national security cases, the federal government becomes the defendant, jury trials are abolished, and the legal fees are assumed by the American taxpayer. In essence, the administration has abolished the concept of individual liability for illegal actions which in the past served as an important deterrent to the violation of constitutional rights of individual citizens.

The main thrust of the administration's initial effort was to free the CIA and the FBI from restrictions imposed on them by previous administrations. Under special attack were the Levi guidelines passed during the Carter Administration that limited the FBI's ability to infiltrate and surveil protest groups. The present administration officials considered it essential that these guidelines be lifted if the morale and functions of security institutions were to be revitalized. It was proposed to lift all restrictions on CIA covert operations and to establish a separate covert intelligence agency. At the end of his first year in office, President Reagan signed an executive order authorizing the CIA, for the first time, to engage in domestic intelligence activity. The order also lifted restraints on the surveillance of United States residents and corporate officials abroad when "significant" information is being pursued. Confronted with a storm of protest over the directive, President Reagan said he had issued the order to fulfill his campaign promise to revitalize America's intelligence system in the face of an "increasing challenge of espionage and terrorism."[4]

During the same period, CIA Chief Casey requested legislation that would permit the CIA and the FBI to conduct surprise searches of newspaper and broadcast newsrooms. He was turned down by Congress. By the end of 1982 the Reagan Administration sought and gained court approval for 904 wiretap warrants for surveillance on suspected foreign agents, a dramatic increase over the Carter years.

The administration has placed national security at the top of its priorities. Decisions ranging from increased production of nuclear warheads and revitalization of the nuclear power system to renewed production of chemical weapons and rejection of the United Nations Law of the Sea Treaty are among those undertaken to protect national security. In a similar vein, the administration announced its intention to increase arms sales throughout the world, arguing that these sales are vital and constructive in facing up to the reality of Soviet aggression and thus an important part of national security policy. Reagan's 1982 designation of May 1 as "Loyalty Day" is indicative in a symbolic sense of the new emphasis on national security and patriotism.

The administration has also deemed it necessary to access information it considers damaging to its interests and policies. President Reagan invoked the Trading with the Enemy Act against American citizens who subscribe to literature from Cuba as a way of preventing "subversive" material from entering the United States, and he eliminated travel privileges of Americans to Cuba. In 1984 the Justice Department attempted to stop publication of one judge's opinion that criticized the professional behavior of Justice Department lawyers. At the end of 1984 the CIA tried to use the Federal Communications Commission to punish the American

Broadcasting Corporation for a report that documented CIA involvement in illegal activity. In more recent moves, administration officials have attempted restrictions of the United States's distribution of award-winning Canadian films on nuclear war and acid rain, which have been termed "political propaganda." Also, certification as educational, scientific, or cultural has been refused to award-winning American films on toxic waste disposal and on the Vietnam My Lai massacre. Noncertification makes dissemination of the films abroad prohibitively expensive, since they are not exempt from foreign import duties. As part of its campaign against the Sandinistas, the administration has targeted certain American groups and individuals upon their return from Nicaragua. Employing a whole range of federal agencies, including the FBI, the Customs Service, the Internal Revenue Service, the Postal Service, the Secret Service, and the Defense Investigative Service, the administration has organized a campaign to investigate, intimidate, and censor those it claims are a part of a massive Nicaraguan spy ring. Numerous break-ins, robberies of membership lists, and non-delivery of members' mail have been reported throughout the country by groups critical of President Reagan's Central American policy, including the Michigan Interfaith Committee on Central America, and the Committee in Solidarity with the People of El Salvador (CISPIS). When CISPIS members, who raise money and medical supplies for Salvadoran war victims, came under investigation in 1984, agents said they were being questioned in connection with a series of terrorist bombings of federal installations in the United States. In fact, the real purpose of the investigation was exposed by a leaked Defense Department document charging that CISPIS is sympathetic to the Salvadoran rebel Farabundo Marti National Liberation Front and disseminates Soviet disinformation. Many people returning from Nicaragua report they have been subjected to tax audits by the Internal Revenue Service and federal agents have interviewed their landlords and employers. FBI officials admit that they try to interview returnees from Nicaragua for counterintelligence reasons and that lists of names and materials for investigation are provided by customs agents who search, photocopy, and censor materials of journalists and scholars returning from Central America.

On the other hand, information favorable to the administration's Central American policies emanates from the White House.

A special organization, the Outreach Working Group on Central America, has published a series of "White House Digests" that depict Nicaragua as a "terrorist" nation and runs a weekly forum of right-wing speakers on Central America. At the State Department, the Office of Public Diplomacy on Latin America and the Caribbean publishes anti-Sandinista pamphlets including those titled "Broken Promises: Sandinista Repression of Human Rights in Nicaragua," "Misconceptions About U.S. Policy Toward Nicaragua," and "The Contadora Process." The information dissemination office in the State Department also distributes reports from anti-Communist groups and organizations like the Cuban American National Foundation and the Gulf and Caribbean Foundation. According to National Security Council background reports, these right-wing public relations offices played a major role in the administration's effort to discredit the 1984 elections in Nicaragua. The State Department issued a "public diplomacy guidance" study for use by government officials and published a pamphlet called "The Source Book: Sandinista Elections in Nicaragua" for selected members of Congress and journalists. The administration also coordinated the activities of all non-governmental experts and foreign journalists sympathetic to its position by requesting that they prepare in advance reports and interviews for television and newspaper editorial pages.

Several important Supreme Court decisions, including those against former CIA agents Philip Agee and Frank Snepp, have reinforced the administration's position on national security. The Agee case upheld the government's right to restrict the travel of American citizens who are deemed a threat to national security because they publicly criticize the United States. The Snepp decision placed investigative journalism under new restraints as, in effect, the Supreme Court gave the executive branch the right to regulate the speech and writings of any government employee or ex-employee. In the 1985 CIA versus Sims case, the Supreme Court ruled that the CIA could refuse to divulge the names of the researchers who participated from 1953 to 1966 in its controversial MK/U1TR program, during which mind-altering drugs were secretly tested on human guinea pigs and resulted in at least one death. In his analysis of the decision, journalist David Wise claims that the court's language was so sweeping that the CIA could, if it wished, hold back any piece of unclassified information it wanted

British hostages executed by Libyans in reprisal for the American raid on Tripoli.

Kaddafi in the wake of the American bombing of Tripoli.

Arab terrorists seize Pan Am 747, Karashi.

Terrorists hijack TWA Flight 847, Beirut.

Bombing of U.S. Marine Base, Beirut.

to, including newspaper clippings with no connection to national security. The administration was also aided in its efforts to clamp down on political dissent by congressional legislation that allows "preventive detention" of federal court defendants and gives federal court judges great discretion in defining whether or not a defendant is a threat to a community. Some critics from the civil rights community opposed the law, because political bias can be used only to deny bail or impose a prohibitive amount of bail against those deemed "a danger to the community."

At times the administration has also invoked existing legislation to throw a veil of secrecy over what it views as classified government actions and to restrict government employee activism unfavorable to its interests. In February 1985 union presidents Kenneth Blaylock of the American Federation of Government Workers, Morris Biller of the American Postal Workers Union, and Vincent Sombrotto of the National Association of Letter Carriers were charged with violation of the Hatch Act, a 1939 law restricting political activity by civil servants. They were accused of writing partisan articles in their union publications. Some labor leaders charge that the enforcement of the Hatch Act in this case is politically motivated and is an unprecedented attempt to punish the union leaders for their criticism of Reagan policies that affect the Civil Service.

Information on Space Shuttle Missions has been restricted since 1984. The Defense Department claims there is little that can be concealed from the Russian electronic surveillance systems, and thus there are no military secrets at stake in the shuttle program.

An executive directive that took effect in the fall of 1985 greatly restricts federal agencies from gathering and distributing statistics on the economy, health, housing, and the environment. Critics say this directive is the most extreme step yet taken by the administration to restrict public access to information. In other action, the Justice Department has initiated criminal proceedings against authors Antoni Gronowicz and Samuel Loring Morison. Morison is being prosecuted under the Espionage Act because he gave *Jane's Weekly*, a British military publication, three United States satellite photographs of a Soviet aircraft carrier. Critics charge that the Reagan Administration is using the Morison case to establish a precedent that extreme criminal sanctions will be applied against those who reveal embarrassing disclosures to the media. If convicted, Morison could get forty years in prison. Numerous New Right organizations, of which the best known is Reed Irvine's Accuracy in Media (AIM) whose "AIM Report" has a circulation of around thirty thousand, have also attacked certain views of the liberal press. Among other things, AIM has campaigned against television programs critical of nuclear power, Agent Orange, Nestle's Infant Formula, Senator Joseph McCarthy, J. Edgar Hoover, and Anastasio Somoza. It has also protested against programs it viewed as favorable to the nuclear freeze movement, actress Jane Fonda, the film "The China Syndrome," and the Nicaraguan Revolution. Other active New Right organizations include the National Legal Center for the Public Interest, the National Strategy Information Center, the American Security Council, the Capital Legal Foundation, an organization that has been particularly active since 1980 in filing Fairness Doctrine complaints, including one against CBS for its documentary on General William Westmoreland. It has also asked the Federal Communications Commission to revoke the licenses of the three major networks because of their liberal programming biases. Leslie Gelb of *The New York Times* became *persona non grata* in the State Department for writing an article from material already in the public realm exposing the United States's contingency plans to place nuclear depth charges in eight allied countries without previous consultation. Secretary of State George Shultz accused Gelb of causing considerable damage to United States interests. In December 1985 government officials threatened to place the entire media under a Defense Department investigation if details of the January space shuttle were even "speculated" on. When *The Washington Post* then published a story based on information already in the public record, Defense Secretary Weinberger accused it of threatening the national security and aiding the enemy. In May 1986 CIA director William Casey, citing increased terrorism against Americans, began a new "get tough" confrontational policy against the news industry. He threatened to prosecute *The Washington Post* and NBC news under Section 798 of Title 18 of the United States Code, an obscure 1950 law that bars publication of classified communication intelligence. Casey told editors of *The Washington Post* that they, along with *The New York Times*, *The Washington Times*, *Time*, and *Newsweek*, had violated the espionage laws by reporting on "Ivy Bells," a secret intelligence-gathering operation by the National Security Agency (NSA). Critics of the administration's effort to muzzle the press, like James Bamford, author of *The Puzzle Palace*, which details the activities of the NSA, say Casey's application of Section 798 is an attempt to apply an official secrets act in which news reporters would have to check their stories with government officials as they are required to do in the Soviet Union.

The Reagan Administration's efforts to revitalize national security institutions and to impose a national security consciousness on the American public have been vehemently opposed by many civil rights organizations, who claim that the administration and its supporters in supporting these views are eroding legal rights to privacy and access to information. The administration has countered by stressing, as Casey is doing in the "Ivy Bells" case, the connection between national security and the threat of terrorism. Echoing the arguments of Kupperman and Trent, they argue that American society is increasingly vulnerable to terrorism from abroad. President Carter, with the creation of the Federal Emergency Management Agency (FEMA), the special coordinating Committee of the National Security Council (twin agencies for combatting terrorism within the State and Justice Departments), and FBI-run anti-terrorist training programs for local law enforcement agencies, had begun to develop an anti-terrorism crisis management system. These initiatives have been increased. Military and domestic police forces are being trained in anti-terrorist methods and technology. Anti-terrorist offices within the federal government have been expanded and upgraded with additional funds and personnel.

During his short term as Secretary of State, Alexander Haig ensured that his department was "on board" the administration's crusade against the Soviet-backed international terrorist conspiracy. Haig rejected at least two drafts of the 1981 State Department report on international terrorism because they did not contain evidence of direct Soviet support for terrorism, as he had charged in his public statements. State Department officials responsible for the report protested that the evidence of a Soviet terrorist conspiracy simply wasn't there. With new "researchers" in place on the third time around, Haig got the report he wanted. In March 1981 CIA Director Casey also asked his analysts to review their draft report conclusion that evidence of Soviet-supported terrorism was inconclusive. Casey sent the draft around to other agencies for "advice." Based on the assessment of the other agencies that the conclusions of the draft were "weasel-worded," Casey asked for further review of the evidence. Eventually, the report was re-worded.

Under the Reagan Administration, anti-terrorism has become the central concern of many federal bureaucracies. For instance, the FBI now employs five hundred of its nine thousand full-time agents to battle terrorism. But it is in security agencies like FEMA where preoccupation with potential terrorism is most evident. FEMA is headed by "General" Louis O. Giuffrida who served as Governor Reagan's terrorism advisor in California and founded the Specialized Training Institute, the commando school located in San Luis Obispo. Working together in California with Edwin Meese and Frank Salcedo, Giuffrida developed a comprehensive strategy to deal with political protests and protesters in which National Guard personnel and military resources are called up in instances of civil disturbance, and surveillance is conducted against political militants. Under Giuffrida, the six-year-old FEMA devotes major attention and funds to counterterrorism. Unfortunately, among the anti-terrorism measures taken Giuffrida and other FEMA officials have attacked peaceful protesters, labelling them potential terrorists, in particular anti-nuclear activists such as the non-violent Livermore Action Group. Operating out of the National Emergency Training Center in Emittsburg, Maryland, FEMA also conducts seminars and training sessions in counterter-rorist operations. For example, in 1984 FEMA sponsored a four-day conference called "Planning for and Dealing with the Conse-quences of Terrorism in the Local Community; An International Perspective," which drew sixty-six top officials from fourteen large American cities. Among the issues considered at the conference were the prospects of a coalition between terrorists and radical environmentalists against nuclear facilities. A few weeks after the conference, FEMA sponsored a five-day drill called "Exercise Mari-time," whose stated agenda was to ascertain the nation's vulnera-bility to maritime terrorism during peacetime and wartime. In several cases, participants in flood-control programs run by FEMA personnel report that they were given a test to see how they would react if a group of terrorists took over a bank and made demands on city officials.

As of 1986, the Senate has set up a Subcommittee on Security and Terrorism. The subcommittee is the creation of those who put together the Heritage Foundation's Intelligence Report, which calls for the restoration of legislative committees in the tradition of the notorious House Committee on Internal Security (HUAC) and the Senate Internal Security Committee (SISS) of the McCarthy years to investigate threats to internal security. Senior members of President Reagan's transition team and Administration like Edwin Meese, Edwin J. Feulner, William Casey, and J. William Middendorf and right-wing organizations like the American Security Council and the National Committee to Restore Internal Security, which counts among its members ex-staffers of HUAC and SISS, and people like J. A. Parker of the Lincoln Institute, were influential in the creation of the subcommittee. Until 1987, the committee was chaired by Jeremiah Denton, a right-wing Republican closely affiliated with the New Right Moral Majority. Other right-wing members were John East and Orrin Hatch, who have reputations as hard-liners on national security issues and advocate increased surveillance of "dissident" organizations. After five years in operation, the jurisdiction of the subcommittee remains unclear as terrorism, questions of internal security, intelligence, and subversions are often linked together and tend to be the zealously guarded province of the Senate Committee on Intelligence. On its initial session on April 24, 1981, several "friendly" witnesses, including Claire Sterling and Arnaud de Borchgrave, appeared before the subcommittee. Both told the subcommittee that the Soviet Union heads a conspiracy of international terrorists and is the major source of "disinformation" being fed to a gullible Western press. Other witnesses, notably former CIA director William Colby, were more cautious in connecting the Soviets to terrorism but agreed with the subcommittee's overall thesis that terrorism is an "insidious" threat that requires constant tracking and surveillance even on legal and non-violent groups and individuals. In its next series of hearings, on May 8, the subcommittee set as its top priority the elimination of restrictions on the FBI's power to infiltrate and surveil law-abiding protest groups. During these hearings, Joel Lisker, chief counsel to the subcommittee, revealed a "secret agenda" for investigating left-wing and progressive protest groups, including the leaders of the May 3, 1981 march on the Pentagon. In addition, the subcommittee members assigned themselves the task of investigating the "Cuban connection" to domestic terrorism by placing on its agenda hearings on the Puerto Rican nationalists groups and the Weather Underground. Ignoring the intelligence data gathered by the Carter Administration, who in March 1980 embarked on a major effort against domestic terrorists and singled out numerous anti-Castro Cuban refugee groups for special investigation, the subcommittee also studied links between Cuba and American liberal and left-wing organizations.

Despite the efforts of this subcommittee and other right-wing forums, their warning that American society was threatened by a left-wing terrorist conspiracy remained highly speculative and to many Americans simply unconvincing. There was no credible evidence of a sinister terrorist danger to American citizens to justify the kind of changes in the national security establishment and intelligence community the Reagan Administration and its conservative constituency were seeking in Congress. But in the fall of 1981 two events, the alleged Libyan assassination teams and the robbery of a Brinks armored truck in Nyack, New York, caused the American public to reevaluate the threat of domestic terrorism. The Libyan "hit team" plot seemed to prove that foreign enemies were prepared to strike anywhere in the world against Americans and that America's time of terrorism was now here. But it was the Brinks robbery that quickly gave rise to increased fear on the part of American citizens. For it was discovered that the four persons initially arrested in the Brinks case were members of the radical American political Left.

The attempted robbery on October 20, 1981 of a Brinks armored truck ended with a shootout that left three law enforcement officers dead. Three of the four people immediately arrested in the robbery were said to be members of the Weather Underground, a radical organization stemming from the student and anti-Vietnam War movements of the late 1960s and early 1970s. The three were identified as Kathy Boudin, Judith Clark, and Davis Gilbert. During the 1970s all three were wanted by the FBI in connection with a 1970 bombing of a townhouse in Greenwich Village, New York. Sam Brown, the fourth person arrested, was not officially linked with any current radical group, although police alleged he had been a member of the Black Panther Party. In the days following the robbery, police conducted raids on suspected "gang hideouts" in New York and New Jersey that reportedly led to the discovery of weapons, ammunition, floor plans of police stations, bomb manuals, and literature from the radical Left. Allegedly seeking links to the robbery, police arrested a number of people suspected of being connected to the Weather Underground and other radical groups, including the Black Liberation Army and the Black Panther Party. At the end of a high-speed chase through Queens, New York, police shot and killed Samuel Smith and arrested Nathaniel Burns. Officials alleged both men were connected to the Black radical movement and linked to the Brinks case by their car license, which police said matched one on a car parked outside a suspected "gang hideout" in New York City.

Many conservatives in Congress and in the media responded to the police arrests and hints of a broad-based leftist conspiracy with a call for further investigations of other leftist and liberal groups and their foreign connections and new security measures to counter the widespread conspiracy. *The Wall Street Journal*, in an October 23, 1981 editorial headlined "Terrorism at Home," called for an investigation of links between the Weather Underground, the Soviet KGB, and the Cuban intelligence agency, DGI. The editorial stated that the Cubans had aided the Weather Underground for years and that the Soviets were obviously involved since they controlled the operations of the DGI. In its initial report of the robbery, *The New York Post* labelled the Brinks killers a "Bonnie and Clyde Gang." Upon learning the identities of those involved, the *Post* tagged the group a "terror gang" and "gang of hate." ABC News "Nightline" ran an excerpt from the documentary film "The KGB Connection" featuring Larry Grathwohl, who had infiltrated the Weather Underground in 1969 on behalf of the FBI. Grathwohl claimed that he had used the Cuban Embassies in Mexico and Canada as message centers for the Weather Underground members on the lam. Other media coverage, even the more moderate, expressed the idea that the radical Left had reorganized and was prepared for violent action and terrorism. For example, *Newsweek* gave a qualified "yes" to its own question, "Is the radical Left back in business and ready for blood?"[5] Yet four pages later *Newsweek* admitted that the FBI really didn't know whether there was a full-blown conspiracy or a marriage of convenience between two aging, shrinking radical groups.

In the halls of Congress conservatives insisted that the Brinks robbery justified the easing of restrictions on the intelligence

community, particularly on FBI investigations of political dissidents. Senator John East of the Subcommittee on Security and
Terrorism campaigned hard for administration national security
proposals, arguing that "This incident reveals not only the continuing threat of terrorism to American citizens, but also our nation's
lack of sound preparedness to deal with or prevent these attacks."[6]
Right-wing Congressman John Ashbrook of Ohio echoed Senator
East's sentiments, contending that in the wake of the Brinks
robbery "Congress must take immediate action to halt the growth
of terrorism."[7] There was some surprise when Chairman Denton of
the Subcommittee on Security and Terrorism did not schedule any
hearing on the resurgence of the Weather Underground. Sources
close to the political infighting of the Senate committee system
suggested that Denton was immobilized by debates over investigative jurisdiction between various Senate committees. Some subcommittee members were anxious to investigate what they saw as
a terrorist conspiracy but were unable to do so for political reasons.
Subcommittee staff member Samuel Francis said the robbery
showed a "resurgence of terrorism" and that it was obvious the
Weather Underground had graduated from simple bombings to
complex robbery and an alliance of radical groups.

Federal investigative agencies, especially the FBI, reported a
link between the Brinks robbery and domestic terrorism. New York
FBI Assistant Director Kenneth Walton, who headed the joint
Federal-New York City Terrorist Task Force, announced plans for a
sweeping government investigation of radical political organizations, specifically an inquiry into possible connections between the
Weather Underground, the Black Liberation Army, the Puerto
Rican Armed Forces of National Liberation (FALN), a clandestine
nationalist group seeking independence for Puerto Rico, the Black
Panther Party, and what Walton said was a clandestine Communist group, the May 19th Movement. Walton was quoted as saying,
"We are looking at this as a major racketeering investigation and
will look at possible links between all these groups and possibly
some foreign organizations."[8] Walton emphasized that there
would be a broad investigation and insisted that all terrorist groups
shared the common purpose of the "creation of a socialist state"
and "an end to the United States government as we know it."[9]

A federal and local law enforcement round-up of alleged
conspirators confirmed Walton's warnings. In addition to those

already arrested, Weather Underground members Jeff Jones and Eleanor Raskin, who at the time were negotiating conditions for their surrender to federal authorities, were picked up by FBI agents even though some members of the FBI said there was no evidence linking either one to the Brinks robbery. Police, backed up by one hundred federal agents and an armored car, raided the home of Cynthia Priscilla Boston (Fulani Sunni-Ali) in Gallman, Mississippi, and arrested her in connection with the Brinks robbery. Boston was later released when she proved she was in New Orleans at the time of the robbery attempt. Police identified Boston as the Minister of Information of the Republic of New Africa (RNA), described by police officials and the media as "a terrorist organization." The RNA is a small, above-ground group which seeks to set up a separate Black nation in the South. Eve Rosahn was also arrested in connection with the Brinks case. She had allegedly allowed her car to be used in the robbery. At the time of her arrest, Rosahn had just been released from jail after being held on charges resulting from September protests against the South African Springboks rugby team. Police also broke into a house in Garden City, New York, hoping to arrest prison escapee and black activist Assata Shakur. She allegedly had been seen riding in a van belonging to the occupants of the Garden City house. When the fifty heavily-armed police officers forced their way into the house, they found a cleaning crew of four black men who had never heard of Shakur. Police proceeded to arrest two members of the crew, one for "resisting arrrest" and the other for "possession of gambling records." In December, other arrests were made, including that of Betty Jean Abrahamson. She was alleged to be connected to the robbery, since her picture was found in a "safe house" rented by Marilyn Buck, also a Brinks suspect. Abrahamson was identified by police as a member of the "militant" and "terrorist" Wells Springs Commune, a group the FBI claimed was involved in guerrilla training. Police said they hoped the arrest of Abrahamson would help strengthen their case that there were political and organizational links between the Brinks case, the Symbionese Liberation Army, the followers of Charles Manson, and a San Francisco radical group called Tribal Thumb.

FBI officials felt that the Brinks robbery justified further surveillance and investigations of labor and workers organizations, Black groups, and Socialist or Communist movements, on the basis that the Brinks case was the lead act in a resurgence of left-wing political violence. FBI officials applied the label of terrorist to these various organizations and individuals as a way of connecting them to the Brinks case. For example, police publicly described the May 19th Movement as a "clandestine terrorist organization" with links to the Brinks case. However, the group was an above-ground organization with a public telephone listing engaging in support work for liberation politics. In citing the RNA as a terrorist organization, police opened the way for a federal court judge in New York City to bar Chokwe Lumumba, the general counsel for the RNA, from representing Cynthia Boston (Sunni-Ali), who had been arrested for a second time, in federal court. Objections to Lumumba were dismissed only after press reports exposed the obvious violation of civil rights, and a legal deal was struck between Boston's lawyers and the United States District Attorney's office. The FBI also attempted to link the Socialist Worker's Party (SWP) with the Brinks robbery and terrorism by alleging that Judith Clark, arrested in the Brinks case, was a member of the SWP. The charge was challenged by Jack Barnes, SWP National Secretary, who issued denial of any connection and accused the FBI of using false information to pursue its campaign of political intimidation against organizations it had unilaterally decided were subversive.

In December 1981 a federal grand jury was called in New York City ostensibly to investigate the robbery and evidence of a conspiratorial merger between the Weather Underground, the Black Liberation Army, and the Puerto Rican FALN. According to federal officials, the grand jury would inquire into radical organizations. But three of the four witnesses called to testify refused and there were reports that the FBI had harassed and attempted to intimidate several people, including poet Sonia Sanchez, who was alleged to have some connection to the grand jury suspects.

Federal officials invoked the 1970 Racketeering Influences and Corrupt Organization Act in their probe of the Brinks robbery. Many legal experts and civil libertarians saw this development as ominous, since under this Act, which was originally aimed at Mafia activity, any organization can be considered a conspiracy if in a ten-year period it commits two acts of any of the thirty-two types of crime listed by the statute. All members of the organization are subject to long prison terms even though they are not actually involved in the acts themselves. The statute gives federal prosecutors and investigative agents almost unlimited latitude in calling people before the grand jury and in pursuing their racketeering probes. In the Brinks case, Federal-New York City Terrorist Task Force Director Walton argued that this approach was entirely proper since there was evidence of communication and association between groups under investigation and some foreign groups.

However, the Racketeering Act invoked in the Brinks case has foreboding implications for individual rights and future political activism. First, because the employment of such a draconian law could become almost routine, even when there is little evidence to support conspiracy charges. Most of the major media took a "wait and see" approach to the political significance of the robbery, as, for example, *Newsweek*'s story entitled "The Plot Thins," which ran after the discovery that persons arrested by the FBI were unconnected to the Brinks case and had been released. Terrorist Task Force Director Walton denied he had ever made any public statement about a terrorist conspiracy after the FBI stated there was no proof to support the claim. There were many doubters, among them President Reagan's terrorist expert Robert Kupperman, who said he didn't think a comeback by the Weather Underground was possible as it simply wasn't a viable group. Rockland County prosecutor Kenneth Gribetz also discounted the conspiracy theory, as saying the Brinks case was "a simple case of robbery and murder."[10]

Others were even more skeptical. Activist lawyer William Kunstler argued that the Brinks robbery was an extremely isolated case blown out of proportion by the administration and its conservative constituency. Congressman Don Edwards warned against overreaction, claiming that there were people "waiting to jump in a panic and chip away at our liberties."[11] *New York Times* columnist Tom Wicker accused his fellow journalists of coverage "that was sufficiently hysterical to give the impression that widespread underground terrorism suddenly had thrown off its cloak and become a major threat to the nation."[12]

These skeptics were supported by the contradiction between the sudden assertion of a conspiracy and previous assurances by the FBI and other law enforcement agencies that a left-wing terrorist conspiracy did not exist. For example, six months before the Brinks robbery, FBI director William Webster declared that "there was no evidence of Soviet-sponsored terrorism within the United States."[13] After the Brinks robbery, the FBI stated that a clear picture of a national conspiracy could not be drawn from the evidence they had collected. FBI agents said they had uncovered no political tract or manifesto issued by any of the groups allegedly involved and that the groups were small in number, lacking in public support, and highly resented by most liberal and leftist groups, in particular civil rights organizations. Some FBI officials said that their case rested, in part, on old theories about conspiracy which they had held since the 1960s but had not been able to prove.

The most important revelations exposing the political motivations behind the Brinks robbery come from the FBI's own statement that the Weather Underground had long ago ceased to be a viable target for investigation and that for a number of years the agency had gathered little information on the group. An investigative report in the October 28, 1979 issue of *The New York Times* had stated that the FBI was no longer concerned with the Weather Underground, that it was ignoring it in the hope that it would fade into a footnote of history. During the 1970s the FBI had dropped most of the arrest warrants against individuals suspected of being connected to the group, including Brinks robbery participant Kathy Boudin. In fact, the FBI had reported that domestic terrorism in general had greatly declined from an average of one hundred incidents per year through the 1970s to twenty incidents in 1980 and sixteen incidents in the first seven months of 1981. Federal agents stated that most of these terrorist-related incidents were the work of the Irish Republican Army, Croatian Nationalists, and anti-Castro Cubans.

The notoriety of the Weather Underground as a "terrorist gang" developed exclusively after the Brinks case. During the height of its violence, including the Chicago "Days of Rage" in October 1969, and the bombing of the Capital building in May 1973, the Weather Underground was never referred to as a "terrorist" organization. It was variously described as a radical antiwar group, protest group, or radical faction of Students for a Democratic Society. The FBI contended that liberals and leftists resented the Weather Underground and opposed its political action program. Civil rights organizations and left-wing political groups almost unanimously condemned the Brinks robbery as an act of political desperation by politically isolated individuals. Numerous articles and editorials in liberal and leftist journals, in detailing the origin and history of the Weather Underground during the 1960s and 1970s, confirmed the group's isolation from the mainstream of the political Left. This point was reinforced by the biographies and autobiographies of members of the Weather Underground, including Jane Alpert's self-analysis of her radical days in *Growing Up Underground* and Lucenda Frank's article for *The New York Times Magazine*, "The Seeds of Terror." Both accounts catalogue the disparate, often desperate, nature of their acts, their flight from political reality, and their ultimate sense of political and social isolation. Among the most vehement criticisms of the Weather Underground and the Brinks robbery attempt were those of civil rights groups, including the American Civil Liberties Union and the NAACP, who feared the negative impact the robbery would have on civil liberties.

However, whatever the real significance of the Brinks robbery, terrorism has already come to the United States. Since the late 1970s there has been increased violence by right-wing organizations, in particular the Ku Klux Klan, neo-Nazi groups, anti-semitic groups, and anti-Castro self-confessed terrorists. In 1980, while Iranian and Soviet-sponsored terrorism was occurring, six blacks were killed by snipers in Buffalo, New York; Vernon Jordan, president of the Urban League, was wounded by sniper fire; a nineteen-year-old black youth was found hung from a tree in Mobile, Alabama; two black joggers were shot to death in Salt Lake City; and in New York City two black men and one Hispanic male were knifed to death. Senseless shootings of blacks by police in New York, Indianapolis, Miami, and elsewhere led black leaders to charge in the early 1980s that there was a national racist conspiracy engineered by whites against the black population. This surge of violence coincided with the re-emergence of the Ku Klux Klan and neo-Nazi movements. Much of the violence was directed at anti-Klan rallies and demonstrations. In 1979 five anti-Klan demonstrators were killed in Greensboro, North Carolina, after the police released information to Klansmen about the demonstration's parade route, then were conveniently absent when the shooting took place. Nazis and Klan members fired into the homes of NAACP leaders in Sylacauga, Alabama, killed undocumented workers in Texas and Arizona, beat people with chains in Tupelo,

Mississippi, shot five women in Chattanooga, Tennessee, and a youth in Wrightsville, Georgia. They fired into homes in Toms River, New Jersey, and Detroit, Michigan, harassed Vietnamese shrimpers in Texas, and engaged in cross burnings and vandalism in almost every state of the nation. The Klan was also openly and successfully recruiting members to its racist cause in the American military. As the political climate has shifted to the Right, some American Jewish citizens have also claimed they are being targeted by right-wing vigilantes. The more militant members of the Jewish community, spearheaded by the Jewish Defense League, Jewish Defense Action, and the Jewish Defense Organization, groups the FBI admits it has trouble infiltrating, have responded with terrorist campaigns of their own.

Until 1985, federal officials paid little attention to these charges even though they were fully aware as early as 1980 of Klan and neo-Nazi paramilitary training camps in the South and Southwest and in the northern states such as Illinois and Connecticut in which, according to reporters for *Newsweek*, Klansmen armed with M-16 rifles and wearing military fatigues practice "search and destroy" missions. In Texas, federal agents also uncovered a right-wing "blueprint for revolution" called "The Turner Diaries" which advocates genocide against all Jews and non-whites and public hangings for all who support racial justice.

The 1985 convictions of neo-Nazis, including the notorious Gary Lee Yarbrough, of the assassination of Alan Berg, a Jew and liberal talk-show host in Denver, Colorado, seemed to indicate a new awareness of the threat from the Right of racist and anti-semitic violence. However, groups like the Aryan Nations, which has a mailing list of six thousand persons, the White American Bastion, the Sword and Covenant of the Lord, the Order, and other right-wing organizations formed by known criminals who espouse white racism and anti-semitism publicly organize their troops for further violence.

The Reagan Administration's more militant approach to domestic terrorism is further evidenced in its treatment of anti-Castro Cubans and anti-Sandinista Nicaraguan terrorists. In 1982, amid confirmed reports of Cuban and Nicaraguan terrorist training camps in Miami, Florida, San Bernadino County, California, and other more secretive camps in the United States, the Reagan Administration ignored or denied charges that the operation of these camps violated international law, in particular the Neutrality Act of 1794. Some influential Reagan officials interpreted the training of these guerrilla forces intent on overthrowing the Cuban and Nicaraguan governments on American soil as harmless exercises. Groups like the anti-Castro Omega 7, which in 1980 was targeted by the Carter Administration as the major source of domestic terrorism, are no longer prosecuted.

But with a twenty-five-year track record in terrorism, Omega 7, Alpha 66, and various other less infamous anti-Castro groups have been anything but model citizens. In fact, this network of Cuban refugees allegedly aid the CIA and have never been disarmed by American authorities. Theirs is allegedly an international terrorist organization. Now in their third decade of operation, they have unabashedly taken responsibility for numerous bombings and murders, including forty attacks on Cuban diplomats, twenty-eight bombings of Cuban embassies and missions, and fourteen bomb attacks on Cuban economic facilities between 1973 and 1979 that resulted in ninety-four deaths. These terrorist acts have occurred both within the United States and in the international arena. These groups admit that terrorism is a central part of their strategy to maintain their political hold on the Cuban-American community. During the 1970s, when attitudes within the Cuban exile community toward Castro showed signs of softening, these groups responded with a reign of terror, including the bombings of homes and offices, death threats, and assassination of any exile leader and his or her family who suggested anything other than a continued militant anti-Castro posture. It was this reign of terror in the Cuban exile community that concerned federal officials during the Carter Administration and led to Omega 7's being designated as the major terrorist group operating on American soil.

Exile leader Hector Fabian, who admits he spent eight years directing the New York operations of anti-Castro terrorism for convicted Cuban-exile terrorist Orlando Bosch and who was hauled in for questioning about these activities more than seventy times by FBI officials and grand jury investigations between 1973 and 1980, boasted in late 1981 that "December 5, 1980, was the last time the FBI bothered me."[14] Fabian has said that under the Nixon and Carter Administrations the paramilitary training camps were treated as criminal activity but "with the Reagan Administration, no-one bothered us in ten months."[15]

By the end of 1981 American officials were confirming that a change in policy toward the training of Cuban and Nicaraguan anti-Communist guerrillas had indeed occurred. In response to the charges by the Sandinistas that the United States was aiding efforts to overthrow the Nicaraguan government by allowing guerrillas to train in the United States and then infiltrate back to Nicaragua, Reagan officials vehemently denied that they were violating any neutrality laws. Thomas O. Enders, Assistant Secretary of State for Inter-American Affairs, stated the official administration position on the guerrillas when he said "as long as they don't hurt anybody and as long as they don't actually conspire in a specific way,"[16] the exiles were not breaking any law. At the time, Enders and other administration officials knew that at least one hundred Nicaraguan exiles trained in Miami had infiltrated back into Nicaragua where, under CIA direction, they would soon become Reagan's "freedom fighters." Likewise, Justice Department spokesperson John K. Russell, in explaining why the department had refused to investigate the guerrilla training camps said that "officially, we're not aware of any military maneuvers taking place in Florida."[17]

While scholars of international law and experts on criminal law debated the legality of its position, the administration did not alter its interpretation of the Neutrality Act of 1794 and other laws governing questions of national sovereignty and terrorism, including the Organization of American States Convention on Terrorism.

Between 1984 and 1986 there have been more than fifty bomb and arson attacks or attempts against abortion clinics and medical facilities in the United States. Many of the attacks occurred during 1984 with nine bombings in and around Washington, D.C. alone. Physicians and their families, along with medical support personnel, have been threatened, kidnapped, or shot at by anti-abortion fanatics. One doctor and his wife were held hostage for a week. Another physician's wife and child were forced to flee as their home was riddled with rifle bullets. In Wheaton, Maryland, a bomb explosion destroyed an abortion clinic and damaged the adjacent offices of a gastroenterologist, podiatrist, and two optometrists, all unconnected to the abortion business. Another blast at a Planned Parenthood clinic in Rockville, Maryland, uninvolved in abortions, destroyed the offices of an obstetrician-gynecologist and a small computer business and blew out windows in nearby houses. In addition to actual bombings, terrorists from the Religious Right have been connected to a large number of bomb threats and attempts at intimidation, including death threats and right-to-life advocates locking arms in front of abortion clinics to forcibly keep pregnant women from entering them. Three men, including the pastor of a Lutheran congregation, were arrested and charged with conspiracy in eight Washington, D.C.-area bombings that damaged federal and state office buildings, banks, churches, a beauty parlor, and the entrance to the office of the American Civil Liberties Union. In addition, agents of the Federal Bureau of Alcohol, Tobacco and Firearms, the agency in charge of the case, seized heavy revolvers, shotguns and rifles, hundreds of pounds of explosive materials, fuses, cylinder casings, and maps pinpointing abortion clinic sites. The arrest and conspiracy conviction of four right-wing religious fanatics in Pensacola, Florida, failed to halt the violence. According to Barbara Radford, the head of the National Abortion Federation, arsons were down during the early months of 1985, "but death threats against doctors are up and there has been a lot of vandalism, of gunshots being fired through windows."[18] Indeed, a major campaign of bombings and threats began anew in the last half of 1985. On October 19, while national attention was fixed on the hijacking of the cruise ship *Achille Lauro* in the Middle East, "right-to-life" terrorists firebombed the Coram Women's Center on Long Island, New York. On October 25, they burned the Hallmark Clinic in Charlotte, North Carolina. Two more clinics were bombed and gutted with fire on October 25 and 30 in Baton Rouge, Louisiana. On December 2 anti-abortion terrorists sent anti-personnel bombs through the mail to the Feminist Women's Center, a Planned Parenthood office, and two other clinics in Portland, Oregon, with the clear intent to kill those working in the clinics. On December 10 they bombed the Manhattan Women's Medical Offices in New York City. These acts of violence are openly supported by many participants at "right to life" conventions who wear little pins shaped like sticks of dynamite with the slogan "have a blast" and come at a time where leaders of the Religious Right like John Burt and Joe Scheidler tell congressional committees that their cause is higher than the law and that they intend to shut down the abortion business by spreading terror among the medical professionals involved in family planning with the unabashed intent to "cause them pain."

Whether one is pro-abortion or pro-life, such terrorism is

obviously in violation of the Constitution of the United States and the law. Yet when asked by reporters in the initial stages of the clinic bombings why the FBI had not taken over the investigation, Director William H. Webster said that the FBI only investigates "true terrorism" and that the bombing of abortion clinics could not be considered terrorism as they are not "acts of violence committed in furtherance of an attack on a government," and because "we have not yet established that all the bombings are caused by activities of a definable group."[19] Webster's statement is in direct contradiction to the FBI's definition of terrorism as stated in its annual report of terrorist incidents in the United States. The report defines terrorism as "the unlawful use of force or violence against persons or property to intimidate or coerce a government, the civilian population, or any segment thereof, in furtherance of political or social goals."[20]

Moreover, according to Webster, the series of clinic bombings in 1984 and 1985 were not to be included in the annual FBI count of domestic terrorist incidents. If they were included it would triple the FBI's count for 1984 from fifteen to fifty. Other senior FBI officials, when asked about this obvious contradiction in the process of counting terrorism, admitted that a literal reading of the definition would result in the inclusion of the clinic bombings as terrorism but that there is always some level of subjectivity involved in deciding what terrorism is. Rather than taking the definition in its literal sense, Assistant Director William M. Baker and John B. Hotis, an aide to Director Webster, said the FBI relies on its experience in dealing with this complex issue although it is always "a matter of judgment." Another FBI official claimed that there are criteria used to establish whether an incident should be counted as terrorism or not but admitted they couldn't be found in any formal document. When asked to list the criteria, the agent refused. If the FBI won't list the criteria designating terrorist acts, Attorney General William French Smith will. In his instructions to the Bureau in March 1983 concerning terrorism, Smith authorized the involvement of the FBI in cases where the facts indicate that two or more persons were planning criminal violence to further political or social goals.

There is a clear contradiction in the administration's approach as defined by Webster and the criteria as established by the FBI and the Justice Department. In every sense, the abortion clinic bombings fit the criteria. According to the Supreme Court, abortion is legal; thus, the bombings are attacks on lawful institutions. As of 1986, the right of women to seek safe abortions and the right of the medical profession to aid them are protected by law. The twelve arrests and several conspiracy convictions of persons in connection with the bombings confirm that more than two people are involved in terrorism against abortion facilities and personnel. In fact, a definable group, the Army of God, has been identified as behind many of the bombings. In their public testimony, some right-wing religious leaders boast that they speak for millions of like-minded people when they threaten violence against the abortion profession. Finally, violence and the threat of violence are being used against both these people and their property with the clear intent to coerce and intimidate. Whatever personal or moral commitments those believing in right-to-life espouse, and whether we agree or disagree with their interpretations, there is no doubt that in using terrorist and violent measures to enforce their beliefs, right-to-life members act in defiance of our laws and in accordance with others labelled criminals who utilize terrorism to bring about change.

AMERICAN FOREIGN POLICY AND TERRORISM

Shortly after taking office the Reagan Administration began to repeatedly warn that El Salvador, a tiny Central American nation, would be where the new administration would "draw the line" against Soviet-backed terrorism. Insisting on the global importance of the civil war in El Salvador, President Reagan and his Secretary of State Alexander Haig declared their intention to support the Salvadoran ruling junta under the leadership of José Napoleon Duarte through additional military and economic aid, including United States military advisors. Administration officials defended the new aid package as necessary to counter a growing crisis in America's backyard fomented by Cuban adventurism and Soviet-sponsored terrorism. Haig said classified documents in his possession proved that leftist rebels in El Salvador were part of an international terrorist network "who have been through (Soviet supported) schools in East Europe or the Soviet Union"[1] and whose atrocities accounted for a majority of the civilian casualties in the civil war. Haig argued that other documents purportedly seized from leftist forces showed that the Soviet Union and Cuba were supplying the terrorists with massive amounts of arms and closely directing a campaign to overthrow the Duarte government and impose a Communist regime on El Salvador. According to Haig, these documents detailed a "hit list" for the ultimate takeover of the four nations of Central America. The war in El Salvador was the second stage in a campaign that had started with the overthrow of Somoza in Nicaragua. Resurrecting the domino theory of the Vietnam era and applying it to Central America, Haig asserted that unless "we seize control today we will find (terrorism) within our own borders tomorrow."[2]

Beginning with its initial commitment of $50 million and promises to do whatever was necessary to cut off the flow of arms, including military actions against Nicaragua and Cuba, the Reagan Administration has stuck by its premise that it is battling Soviet-sponsored terrorism in El Salvador. Under Haig's direction, the State Department, bolstered by the publication in February 1981 of its first "white paper" on the Central American crisis, "Communist Interference in El Salvador," has argued that many civilians who oppose Duarte are either Communists or unwitting dupes of Communist propaganda. However, the State Department has not given the public any details on the actual social and political opposition. Professor James Petras, a Latin American scholar who scrutinized the administration's analysis of the Central American situation, claimed the State Department was purposely manipulating American public opinion through its "white paper." He charged that "this collective omission is necessary if one is bent upon labelling the opposition as Soviet-Cuban manipulated."[3]

Administration officials also made a new distinction between authoritarian and totalitarian governments in clarifying their continued support of the Duarte government, which has used repressive counter-insurgency policies, including indiscriminate bombing by the Salvadoran air force of civilian villages and right-wing terrorism. This distinction, taken from a 1981 *Commentary* article by Jeane Kirkpatrick, argues that the right-wing juntas of Latin America, while extremely repressive, are worthy of American support because they are open to reform and militantly anti-Communist. On the other hand, totalitarian regimes, because they are Communist, are absolutely impervious to reform. Haig invoked this distinction in a speech before the Trilateral Commission in April 1981, to rally support for the Reagan Administration's hard-line anti-Soviet stance. Other conservative scholars, like Professor Robert Wesson of the Hoover Institute, have leaned heavily on Kirkpatrick's distinction in their campaign for the Reagan cause in El Salvador. Wesson argued in an article for the *San Francisco Chronicle* that the Duarte government was the most democratic and libertarian that we could expect in El Salvador and that after some reforms ". . . will have proved that there is a civilized remedy for terrorism."[4]

Reagan policymakers argued that the situation in El Salvador fits the Kirkpatrick-Francis interpretation of counterterrorism. The United States backs the authoritarian Salvadoran government because it has shown its commitment to democratic reform by holding elections in 1982, has announced a land reform program, remains under civilian rule, and continues to be under direct siege from totalitarian Soviet-supported terrorists.

For five years members of the Reagan Administration have argued that American power and resolve were at stake in an East-West confrontation in El Salvador; that the Soviet Union, through its international terrorist network, dominates the Salvadoran opposition forces, and that the administration was under serious attack from a large and diverse constituency of critical opinion, much of which questioned the authenticity and truthfulness of the administration's evidence. Many of the administration's critics came from the mainstream of American, European, and Central American politics. The list of critics includes State Department staff members and congressional aides who voiced their immediate opposition through an anonymous "dissent channel" paper and a report called "Democracy in Latin America," several leading United States officials, former CIA agents Philip Agee and Ralph McGehee, and former United States Ambassadors to El Salvador Robert White and Murat Williams. Opposition also came from European leaders, among whom Swedish and Belgium officials were the most vocal. Journalists and academics with special expertise in Central American politics have also challenged the Reagan policy. Finally, even though he had been the chief beneficiary of the Reagan Administration's support, Salvadoran President Duarte has, at times, publicly objected to President Reagan's insistence that the Salvadoran opposition forces are nothing more than Soviet-backed terrorists.

In its initial presentation of evidence, the Reagan Administration used Pentagon and State Department studies to support its claim that Salvadoran opposition forces were terrorists responsible for a high level of indiscriminate civilian deaths. These reports concluded that a majority of the deaths were the handiwork of leftist terrorists. Some administration officials, including Secretary of State Haig, went so far as to say the four American nuns who were killed by security forces in December 1980 deserved their fate since evidence collected on the scene proved they were on a mission for the leftist terrorists.

Critics have challenged these reports and the conclusions drawn from them in two ways. First, many independent reports from El Salvador in 1980 and 1981 concluded that the level of killing is so great that it is impossible to verify who is killing whom, and question how the Reagan Administration can discern without reservation that it is the anti-government opposition who is responsible for terrorism.[5] Secondly, private sources, such as the Catholic Church and paramedics of the Green Cross, who attempted to sort out responsibility for the terror, say the evidence supports just the opposite of what Reagan officials claim. Scores of interviews with peasant refugees appear to show that terror by government forces and right-wing paramilitary groups is pervasive and the major source of fear among Salvadoran civilians.[6] Private documentation of government and right-wing terror by the Roman Catholic Church, including the Archbishop's Legal Aid Commission, estimated that in 1980 sixty-six percent of the assassinations were the work of government security agencies and fourteen percent were attributable to right-wing death squads. Human rights organizations and the Organization of American States (OAS) have also issued reports accusing the Salvadoran military of widespread violence against the population. According to reports in *The New York Times*, in its last year in office the Carter Administration tied continued American economic and military aid to the Salvadoran government to progress in curbing the killings.[7]

The organized terror and violence by known right-wing organizations and their death squads such as the Democratic Nationalist Organizations (ORDEN), White Hand, and the White Warriors Union are no secret to anyone, especially the Duarte government. But the Reagan Administration contends that organized terrorism comes only from opposition sources under the direct command of the Soviets and the Cubans through the Salvadoran Communist party. Yet, when journalists like T. D. Allman of *Harper's* have gone in search of the guerrillas they found "only terrorized, hapless people—abused, barefoot women with no food or medicine for their malnourished children; landless, jobless, illiterate men and boys fleeing for their lives from the 'security forces' of their own national government."[8]

When Allman did catch up with some guerrillas he found them to be ill-equipped, untrained peasants who had been pushed to rebellion by poverty, illness, and violence.

Allman's interpretation is confirmed by many non-administration sources familiar with the development of Salvadoran political and social movements. They argue that the opposition to the government is deep, longstanding, and embraces many elements of the social fabric, many of whom believe in nonviolence. For example, Professor James Petras, in his analysis of the major political opposition coalition, the Revolutionary Democratic Front (FDR) found that "Almost all union members, peasant associations, university and professional people are members or supporters of social and civic organizations that are sympathetic to the front . . . the guerrilla movement is part and parcel of a larger political and social movement that has been and is repressed."[9]

Voices opposed to the Reagan Administration's claims that terrorism is chiefly leftist in origin also come from within the Duarte government. In 1981, Vice-President Jaime Abdul Gutierrez, a career military officer known as a "realistic conservative" who declared war on the opposition after a two-day strike in June 1980, warned that paramilitary and right-wing terrorism was undermining the campaign to win the loyalty of the Salvadoran population. His documentation, which was intended to absolve the professional armed forces of responsibility for the terrorism, included the following claims: more than four hundred national guardsmen have been dishonorably discharged for acts ranging from murder to rape; most of the people assassinated have been leading moderates or non-Communist liberals, including several close to President Duarte; most accused of assassination are members of the National Guard, the treasury police; and the peasant refugees in the camps hold little grudge against the army but do fear paramilitary forces.

The second contention made by the Reagan Administration was the alleged connection between Salvadoran leftist "terrorists" and the Soviet Union and Cuba. Administration documentation for the connection was presented in a "white paper" entitled "Communist Support of the Salvadoran Insurgency" issued by the State Department on February 23, 1981. The "white paper" was circulated to journalists accompanied by translations, glossaries, photographs, and copies of the guerrilla documents. Citing captured rebel documents, the State Department study claimed that eight hundred tons of arms shipments were promised and two hundred tons were actually delivered to Salvadoran rebels from the Soviets and their surrogates in Cuba and Nicaragua. It also charged that the Soviet Union had direct control of Salvadoran opposition forces through its dominance over the Salvadoran Communist Party or indirectly through the influence of Fidel Castro.

The administration's "white paper" was immediately attacked by a variety of sources. Several critics familiar with the complexities and manipulative potential of intelligence documentation, including former CIA agents Philip Agee and Ralph McGehee, suggested that the documents were either doctored or complete CIA fabrications. The charge was echoed in a more cautious manner by former ambassador to El Salvador Murat Williams, who said "Forged documents are an old story in Central America . . . I would not trust the perpetrators of atrocities to become suddenly more honorable men when they present displays of 'captured war material.' "[10]

Other critics charged that even if the documents were authentic, they did not support the administration's claim about arms supplies. The "white paper" is full of contradictions concerning arms shipments, the tonnage of arms shipped, where it was shipped from (Cuba or Nicaragua), and the type of weapons actually sent. Wayne S. Smith, who headed the United States diplomatic mission to Cuba between 1979 and 1982, is quoted as saying that "U.S. evidence of arms shipments—especially during the period of Cuban peace overtures—has never been solid. While some arms have been sent from Cuba to El Salvador, the quantities are almost certainly far less than alleged. If the guerrillas had received all the arms reported by United States intelligence, the Salvadoran army would be outgunned twenty to one."[11] Other sources echoed Smith, saying it is well known that the rebels are ill-equipped, and that Cuba provides funds to purchase arms on the black market but does not provide arms directly. According to journalist John Dinges, United States intelligence sources said the "white paper's" estimates of arms tonnage delivered to rebels were "unrealistic" and that even if the guerrillas received the alleged two hundred tons of arms, they would go through them in a week, hardly enough arms to sustain the kind of threat projected by the Reagan Administration.[12]

When *The Wall Street Journal* raised the issue in June 1981, serious skepticism about the administration's "white paper" was raised by Congress and the media. In the article "Tarnished Report? Apparent Errors Cloud US 'White Paper' on Reds in El Salvador," reporter Jonathan Kwitny, who interviewed Jon D. Glassman, the chief author of the "white paper," for at least three hours, admitted that he was surprised to hear Glassman:

> describe parts of it as "misleading" and "overembellished." . . . Policy planner Glassman freely acknowledged that there were "mistakes and guessing" by the government's intelligence analysts who translated and explained the guerilla documents . . . Several of the most important documents, it is obvious, were attributed to guerrilla leaders who didn't write them . . . Statistics of armament shipments into El Salvador supposedly drawn directly from the documents were extrapolated, Mr. Glassman concedes.[13]

Kwitny's investigations challenged the alleged connections between the Salvadoran rebels and the Soviets, between Nicaraguans and PLO leader Yasser Arafat, and questioned the authenticity of many of the documents. Kwitny asserts that the "white paper" was used by the Reagan Administration as a "launching pad for its anti-Soviet foreign policy," and that despite its false factual basis, it had served the administration well in garnering support in western Europe and in the American press for its foreign policy. It had also raised fears about a Communist takeover in El Salvador; the National Security Council immediately sent $25 million in additional military aid and $40 million in "economic" assistance to Duarte. The aid to the military would only encourage a right-wing coup against his moderate government.

Other critics contended that even if the facts reported in the "white paper" concerning arms shipments to the rebels were true, the level of American support to the past and present juntas was already sufficient. Former Ambassador Murat Williams claimed that when he first arrived in El Salvador in 1961 the military presence was so great that he sent a complaint to Secretary of State Dean Rusk, but to no avail.[14] Williams says that since 1961, "in addition to maintaining a large air and group missions we trained Salvadoran officers both in the United States and in a police school in Panama. It has recently been estimated that 1,971 Salvadoran officers have had American training—a large figure for an armed force of less than 20,000."[15]

In addition to the "white papers," the administration has advanced other evidence to bolster its case. The most important pieces of this evidence were declassified aerial photographs of massive Soviet presence in Nicaragua, the construction of an airport that can handle fighter jets at Puerto Cabezas, Nicaragua, and the confession of Orlando Tardencilla, a Nicaraguan captured in El Salvador, that he was trained in Cuba and Ethiopia. But the actual aerial photographs showed no Soviet missiles, only features like a "Soviet-style obstacle course." Plans for extending the airport at Puerto Cabezas had been drawn up in 1976 and funded by the United States AID agency. Questioned by the media, Tardencilla said he had "confessed" under torture and that a United States Embassy official had warned him to cooperate or face certain death.

The evidence brought forth in the "white paper" failed to confirm a Soviet-controlled network in operation in El Salvador. In fact, the documents show that the Soviet Union had been hesitant to get involved in El Salvador and that Castro's role in unifying the Salvadoran Left was minimal. Critics like James Petras claim that the reduction of the Salvadoran opposition by the "white paper" to a small element of Marxist guerrillas dominating the "non-Marxists" is an oversimplification resulting from scanty evidence and selective analysis of opposition forces. The coalition of political forces fighting the Duarte government include Christian Democrats, Social Democrats, and Liberal Democrats, plus independent groups and pro-Moscow forces. To Petras, the unique thing about the Salvadoran opposition is the large degree of leadership and popular support from the Christian communities. More importantly, the opposition forces now include members of what the Carter Administration and the American media dubbed "major political forces of reform" who could be depended upon to push the regime towards reform and democratization. By 1981, forced into the opposition by right-wing repression and violence, these same groups are described by the authors of the "white paper" as three small non-Marxist-Leninist parties brought into the opposition for the sake of appearance. It is true that the Salvadoran Communist Party is pro-Moscow, but it has always been a marginal force in the anti-government coalition. Conversely, three of the four major leftist groups are openly critical of the Soviet Union. Contrary to the "white paper" and its claim that Fidel Castro had directed the unity efforts of the rebel organization, the unification of the opposition was well under way before 1979. It was spurred first by government repression that increasingly limited the options of opposition forces to guerrilla warfare and second, in a symbolic sense, by the 1979 triumph of the Sandinista revolution against the brutal Somoza regime in Nicaragua.

The Reagan Administration also relied heavily on documents covering the travels of Salvadoran Communist Party Chief Shafik Handel to substantiate the Salvadoran-Soviet-Cuban connection. But the documentation of Handel's travels fails to uphold the administration's interpretation. Handel did visit some Eastern European nations, Ethiopia, Vietnam, and the Soviet Union. But he came away from Moscow disappointed at his cool reception and fearful of the impact of the Soviet refusal on other possible donors. In contrast to the Reagan charge that aid to the Salvadoran Left was selective and secret, Salvadoran opposition pleas for aid from all countries and agencies, including the United States, were made in public and generally well responded to except by the United States.

Some major critics also attacked the Reagan Administration's contentions that the Duarte government was progressive and bent on sweeping economic and social reforms. Whatever its original makeup after the 1979 coup against the right-wing junta, the junta lost much of its progressive membership either by resignation and self-exile or assassination between 1979 and 1980, leaving Duarte to work along with the ultra-rightists and his former torturers who are responsible for his missing fingers. The so-called social and economic reforms announced by the government had ended in increased violence against the peasants and military occupation of their co-ops. For most of the population, political rights continued to be non-existent while their economic condition only worsened. Finally, critics challenged the "white paper" claim that the lack of public demonstration against the government was proof of popular support for the junta by pointing out that the major opposition had been forced underground, leaving a terrorized population for whom "the scores of dead protesters, including mutilated and decapitated corpses that appeared in the wake of every protest march, no doubt had a dampening effect on demonstrations."[16]

In the face of conflicting evidence, the Reagan Administration still maintains its view that Soviet-backed terrorists are attempting to overthrow the democratic government of El Salvador. Even the eye-witness accounts of government repression told by the million or so refugees who have found their way out of El Salvador, reducing the population by one-third, which include tales of assassination "hit lists" against high school students who demanded longer library hours and more books, have failed to affect the official administration view on terrorism in El Salvador. Reagan officials in their annual appeals to Congress for more aid allege human rights conditions are improving and point to the elections of 1982 as proof of the democratic process at work. Most of all, they continue to blame the Soviet-Cuban-Nicaraguan terrorist network for the continuation of the civil war in El Salvador and the rising tide of civilian casualties. Indeed, the only time the Reagan Administration has seriously questioned its position was in the summer of 1981 when it pursued the idea of a negotiated settlement. However, Secretary of State Haig soon relinquished this idea and introduced the concept of "straight terrorism"—attacks on power stations and the transportation network—to publicize the special evil of the rebel forces and to explain why the United States dropped the idea of negotiation. Meanwhile, in nearby Nicaragua the United-States-backed rebels whom the Reagan Administration has labeled "freedom fighters" were, with alleged CIA funding and training, deeply involved in the same kind of "straight terrorism" campaign.

During his first three years in office President Reagan was able to sustain a moderate, and, later in his term, a greater level of public support for his foreign policy and to convince Congress to go along with supporting his administration's allies in Central America. Although some opposition is increasing, public support for his policies is clearly established. Despite some major setbacks in coping with terrorists, such as the attack on the Marine barracks in Lebanon, the present administration's inability to free the six American hostages held by Arab terrorists, and the collapse of the "Bulgarian connection" in the shooting of Pope John Paul II, President Reagan has continued to judge the terrorist issue by a narrow but consistent moral viewpoint. He has held tightly to this political position even when his critics feel that in so doing he has ignored the many shadings and sources of international terrorism and focused public attention and American policy on Libyan leader Muammar el Kaddafi, the man many leaders, including President Reagan, call "the mad dog of the Middle East."

FIGHTING KADDAFI

In late March 1986 the largest American peacetime naval armada ever assembled sailed from the Mediterranean Sea and across the "line of death" that Libyan leader Muammar el Kaddafi asserted marked the beginning of Libyan sovereign waters. The naval force sailed into the Gulf of Sidra off the Libyan coast in the face of Kaddafi's threat to attack any invader. As predicted by American defense analysts, Kaddafi responded by dispatching missiles and naval craft to attack the American fleet. The superior American military technology easily turned the missiles away, destroying a missile site and three Libyan naval craft in the process. Two days later, Reagan Administration officials hailed the action as a show of America's commitment to international law and a blow against international terrorism.

Two weeks later, on the morning of April 15, 1986, thirty-three United States jets left from their bases in England and, from American aircraft carriers in the Mediterranean Sea, bombed targets in and around Tripoli and Benghazi, Libya. The mission was described by Reagan and his senior officials as an act of self defense against past and future terrorism.

It is President Reagan's view that Kaddafi acts as a Soviet agent and is heavily involved in terrorism against the West.

President Reagan's full-scale campaign against Kaddafi began after a major administration review of American policies toward Libya in the summer of 1981. Reagan officials admit that since the review they have pursued ways to get rid of Kaddafi and, failing that, to punish him by isolating him politically and economically.

Reagan's campaign to mobilize the Western world against Kaddafi, who has supported many terrorist groups and waged a global terrorist campaign against Libyan dissidents, and eliminate him if possible actually began when American jets, on orders from a United States official to test Libya's extension of its air space, shot down two Libyan military aircraft over the Gulf of Sidra in August 1981. Questions still surround the issue of provocation, but from the Reagan Administration's point of view, the event was overwhelming evidence that Kaddafi was an outrageous maniac who not only dared to make absurd claims for Libyan air space and sea boundaries, but actually attempted to back up those claims against the most powerful military force in the world. Administration officials have continued to publicly ask: Who would be so crazy to do these things, except an insane, tormented dictator whose grandiose schemes of personal and global power have aligned him with the Soviet empire and involved him in international adventurism, intrigue, and terror?

In December 1981, following American allegations that Kaddafi had sent a "hit team" to assassinate the president and other major American officials, President Reagan ordered economic and political sanctions against Libya. The sanctions were relatively harmless to both sides, involving only travel restrictions on Americans to Libya and asking the 1,500 American citizens living in Libya to return home. There was open resistance from American oil companies and European business interests. But Reagan Administration officials felt the sanctions were necessary, claiming that Kaddafi was erratic, hostile, and irrational and that he could not be dealt with through normal diplomatic channels. Threatening to order harsher measures if the sanctions failed to change Kaddafi's behavior, President Reagan warned friends and foes alike that the days of American passivity were over. From now on terrorist attacks on citizens of the United States, especially by a crazed leader of a fifth-rate power and partner of the Soviets in their escapades of terrorism, could result in active retaliation by the United States using all its resources, including military power, if necessary.

The administration felt from the outset that its view of Kaddafi would strike a sympathetic chord in the West. Most European leaders, who have had extensive experience with Kaddafi, find him unpredictable at best and a repressive dictator, unyielding in his approach to dissidents and willing to take action on behalf of his grandiose plans for the Arab world. Still, there is a fundamental disagreement between President Reagan and most European leaders on how to counter Kaddafi's actions. This disagreement became public after the bombing of Libyan cities in April 1986. Among American allies, only Britain, Canada, and Israel defended the act as appropriate or justified.

From the start, many western Europeans have raised serious

questions about America's political policy against Kaddafi. Some
charge that the Reagan view is an oversimplification of political
realities and its dangerous militancy is largely based on tainted and
unreliable intelligence. From their view, Kaddafi's antagonism
towards the United States stems from his commitment to the Arab
cause and his hostility to American support of Israel.

The issue of Kaddafi's mental health remains highly speculative even among experts who have observed the Libyan leader
over a long period. Some aspects of his personal and political
history and his cooperative relationship with some Westerners,
including American business interest, raise doubts about the alle-
gation that he is completely unreasonable and irreversibly antagonistic to Western interests. As a young officer in the Libyan army,
Kaddafi was linked with Western intelligence agencies, including
the CIA. He became especially close to an Arab agent of the CIA,
Charles Boursan, who allegedly worked on behalf of smaller
Western oil companies in the Middle East. Even as political relations between the United States and Libya have soured, officials of
American corporations operating in Libya, in particular major oil
companies, report that Kaddafi has always treated them with
respect and correct business courtesies.

Since 1983 trade relations between the United States and
Libya have virtually ended. But before the boycott, Libya imported
goods from the West. The United States was one of Kaddafi's
major trading partners, supplying among other items sophisticated technology and communications equipment. Indeed, during
the first year of the Reagan Administration, American exports to
Libya rose by twenty percent. Kaddafi's track record in these
trading and business ventures is excellent.

There are also questions to be raised about Kaddafi's close ties
to the Soviet Union. It is true that as of 1986 between five thousand
and six thousand Soviet-bloc military advisors and technicians
were stationed in Libya. Between two thousand and three thousand are Soviet advisors, while the remaining are contingents of
East Germans, Poles, Czechoslovaks, and others. The East Germans are in charge of supervising Libyan intelligence and military
communications, a key position that allows them to monitor and
possibly intervene in the dissent within the Libyan armed forces.
But Soviet support for Kaddafi is very tentative. Several senior
Western diplomats describe the Soviet-Kaddafi relationship as "no

marriage of love." For example, the Soviets have refused to sign a mutual defense treaty with Libya, something Kaddafi wants badly, on the basis that the Libyan leader is too unpredictable. Soviet advisors maintain a low profile in Libya, wearing their uniforms only around military bases. During the March 1986 hostilities between the American Navy and Libyan forces the Soviets refused to share with their Libyan allies any satellite data or intelligence gathered from their Mediterranean fleet. During the American attacks the three hundred Soviet advisors remained in their underground bunkers at the anti-aircraft missile site on the Gulf of Sidra and refused to help the Libyans erect new launching pads. As American hostility and military threats have increased, the Soviets have been reluctant to supply Libya with spare parts and technicians. The Libyans had to call in French and British technicians to repair the Soviet-made radar and the guidance mechanisms of the SAM-5 anti-aircraft missiles that were fired at American jets during the clashes over the Gulf of Sidra. Finally, in October 1985, the Soviets backed away from their commitment to build a $4.2 billion nuclear power plant in Libya.

For his part, Kaddafi allegedly sees Communism as abhorrent and godless. He has opposed Soviet involvement in the Middle East peace process, in particular their plan for an international peace conference. Though he buys $1 billion in Soviet arms per year, he has fallen $6 billion in arrears in his payments. He continues to annoy the Russians by selling Soviet-made arms to the Iranians at the same time the Soviets supply Iraq in the Iran-Iraq war. Kaddafi has also refused to permit a Soviet military base in Libya. Though the Soviets have long wanted a deep-water port at Tobruck, he will not allow the Soviet fleet to enter the port for any reason. Overall, Western intelligence sources report that in truth, the Soviet relationship with Kaddafi is no better than those he has with the Europeans and, until the Reagan Administration came to power, about the same as that with the United States.

Despite the high level of Western commercial involvement entailing thousands of people on many different and complex levels in Libya, the Reagan Administration insists that a normal rational relationship with Kaddafi is impossible. In May 1981 President Reagan ordered the closing of the Libyan Embassy in Washington and the expulsion of the remaining diplomatic staff in retaliation for what the administration charged were provocations and misconduct by Libyan diplomats, including support for international terrorism. Kaddafi asked for permission to reopen the embassy and offered to pay for the rebuilding of the American Embassy in Tripoli which had been sacked and burned in December 1979 by supporters of Iran. Reagan refused this and other offers over the next months. In September 1981, after the air battle over the Gulf of Sidra, Kaddafi again made a bid at reconciliation by sending his personal envoy, Ahmad Shahati, to Reagan. This diplomatic overture was rebuffed by Reagan Administration officials who insisted that Kaddafi was a Soviet client seeking to overthrow pro-Western governments in Africa and the Middle East.

It is obvious that Kaddafi's personal and political actions and motivations are complex, contradictory, and provocative. It is plausible, given his controversial rhetoric and actions, that the confrontational approach of the Reagan Administration is appropriate. But it is also obvious that were Kaddafi a dictator with anti-Soviet and pro-Israel sympathies, his actions might be judged very differently.

It is true that other Western leaders who have been threatened with Kaddafi's wrath and terror are openly weary and wary of him. Being wary is one thing; it is another to blame him for every assassination or attempted assassination, every provocation against pro-Western and Western governments, and every act of terror.

Many European officials who are more vulnerable to Kaddafi's threats and violence than are Americans contend that since the late 1970s Kaddafi has been moderating his actions. From their view, further moderation of his acts can be achieved with measures other than the United States using military force. They, along with former president Jimmy Carter, point to the effectiveness of their quiet diplomacy in 1978 when they covertly warned Kaddafi to stop harboring hijackers or be isolated diplomatically and commercially by the Western nations.

Open European resistance to President Reagan's methods of dealing with Kaddafi began at the end of 1981 when President Reagan charged that a Libyan assassination team was headed for the United States and asked the allies to invoke stiffer economic sanctions against Libya. The administration announced that Kaddafi had sent a "hit team" to kill Reagan and other senior administration officials. Acting on the advice of American intelligence, the administration ordered close watch at border crossings, international airports, and local Arab communities. The president even abandoned his presidential limousine to travel in unmarked cars.

Although Kaddafi denied that he had sent a "hit team" President Reagan stated "We have the evidence and he knows it."[17] But if he did have proof he was unwilling to make it public even to the European allies. Instead, he asked the American public and the allies to take his word that this new Libyan terrorist plot required drastic action and a heightened level of American-Libyan hostilities. He did permit some sympathetic members of Congress to be briefed by intelligence as to the evidence. Sketches of the members of the alleged hit team were also circulated by the FBI to some journalists. Yet definitive proof of the assassination plot has remained inconclusive. Amid growing media and public skepticism, White House officials were forced to admit, "We are extremely frustrated that we can't catch even a single terrorist . . . We have no smoking gun."[18]

Media coverage of the alleged hit squad initially supported the administration's story. But even the most pro-administration members of the media, seeking substantiation, pleaded for hard evidence. For example, *Time*, which among the major news journals gave the most positive reading to the Reagan allegations, headlined its major article on the story: " 'Searching for Hit Teams' there was no proof, but there was sufficient reason to believe."[19] Contradictory evidence separately provided by the FBI, CIA, and Secret Service raised more suspicions. After hearing the CIA report, Democratic Senators Henry Jackson, Daniel Moynihan, and Walter Huddleston all said they were convinced that the charges were true. But fellow Democrats Christopher Dodd, John Glenn, and Clairborne Pell were openly skeptical after their FBI briefing. In the end, these briefings, rather than clearing up doubts, only created further skepticism and confusion among American and European officials.

Further confusion surfaced when conservative members of Congress, in particular Senator Harrison Schmitt, called for immediate sanctions based on their reading of the evidence. Neoconservative Senator Daniel Moynihan threatened severe military reprisals to any attempted assassination. Other conservative congressional members said they supported military action against Libya after being told that an interagency team had added air attacks on Libyan oil fields to a bombing list that included B-52 strikes on "terrorist" training camps. But many congressional moderates and liberals, including Senators Glenn, Dodd, and Paul Tsongas, powerful members of the Senate Foreign Relations Committee, voiced doubts about the existence of the hit teams and reservations about the administration's planned military response. The picture was further clouded by Senator Howard Baker, a solid administration supporter, who claimed that while the plot was real the threat had quickly diminished. Baker was publicly rebuked the next day by an angry president who attacked Baker's assertion saying that Senate minority leader Baker "did not have any intelligence or information that would give rise to such a statement."[20]

Adding to the confusion and doubts were the disparate and contradictory accounts describing the identity of the assassins, how many members and teams there actually were, and exactly where they were located. Initial reports placed a single team already in the United States. The National Security Study given to the White House in early December listed twelve to fourteen members with a brief description of each. Other intelligence accounts said there were two teams of five and six persons each, one thought to be headed by the notorious "Carlos" and located in Mexico preparing to cross the border. At times, two of Kaddafi's most ardent enemies, Nabih Berri and Mohammed Shamseddin, leaders of the Lebanese-backed political party Amal, were included by intelligence sources in the hit teams. Administration officials later said their inclusion was a computer error. Finally, some officials of the FBI, who wished not to be identified, said that while there were plenty of tips, none of the information about the hit teams had been confirmed. According to one FBI official "It's been blown way out of proportion."[21]

Additional confusion came from the intelligence "leaks" from within the administration and Reagan's contradictory reaction to them. At times the president and his aides seemed pleased that the information was leaked, even though its release violated administration guidelines. On other occasions they were openly troubled by the leaks—especially those that prompted questions for which they had no answers. By mid-December the controversy surrounding the leaks had become so pervasive that President Reagan, calling them a "disservice to the nation," ordered the FBI to investigate their sources.

The reliability and number of the informants providing the information about the hit squads caused further confusion and skepticism. During September and October several intelligence informants in the Middle East had reported various Libyan plots against American embassies and diplomatic personnel. In contrast, the intelligence on the presidential assassination teams came from a single source: a terrorist defector who said he knew of ten persons who had been trained for the assassination. As the hit team plot unfolded questions were raised about the wisdom of relying on a single source, especially one whose reliability and motives are openly doubted by Arab and Israeli supporters of the administration. One Arab diplomat, upon hearing the informant had been paid a quarter of a million dollars for his information, stated flatly that "A dissident who is asking for money will say anything."[22] President Reagan denied that the administration was relying on a single paid source and insisted that the intelligence was from several sources in which he had full confidence. FBI officials, while agreeing with the president that the threat was real and that numerous sources had been used, admitted that most of the sources provided misleading information and that, while the agency had been deluged with tips, most of them had proven to be dead ends.

The confusion and contradictions produced only greater skepticism and criticism about the administration's approach. Some skeptics doubted that the Libyan hit teams ever existed or that Kaddafi was involved. Most critics accepted that a threat probably did exist but questioned the administration's response. Some suggested that President Reagan was using the reports of hit teams to show the world and the Soviets in particular that his Cold War rhetoric was not idle talk and to bolster his case that Kaddafi was a madman who could only be removed by either overt or covert American military action. Others charged that the president had actually damaged American interests by publicizing Kaddafi's rhetorical threats, thereby building up Kaddafi's importance and support among America's enemies. Harvard law professor Roger Fisher publicly questioned the Reagan policy saying: "We built up Castro in the same way. Why do this for Kaddafi? Why make this guy equal to a superpower?"[23] Former officials in the Carter Administration accused the new administration of blowing the story out of proportion. Their case was supported by former president Jimmy Carter who stated he had received similar threats during his term but had chosen to keep them secret. Intelligence sources backed up Carter's claim and said that Kaddafi has been making threats against the United States government and its officials for more than ten years.

Specific questions were also raised about the Reagan Administration's handling of the crisis. For example, why didn't the United States react immediately if officials really believed Kaddafi had sent his terrorists? Why did Kaddafi's denial of involvement go unanswered by the FBI, the CIA, and the Justice Department? Why was it left to the State Department, which doesn't normally handle these matters, to announce that there really was hard evidence about a plot? Why was the administration leaking extensive details about such a sensitive subject? Why, with government officials, including President Reagan, calling on the media to show restraint in its reporting of the alleged plot, did Reagan accuse Kaddafi on national television of lying and claiming that the United States had evidence of an assassination plot? And why did administration officials first decline comment on the initial reports, then take an active role in providing information on the hit teams, and finally, amid probing questions and growing skepticism, limit information by retreating under the cover of national security?

It was these unanswered questions that seemed to make the European allies uneasy. Secretary of State Haig did little to answer or appease the administrations's European critics. At a meeting of NATO foreign ministers in December 1981 he chastised the allies for their "double standard" of morality that permitted them to do "business as usual" with Kaddafi. Haig's comments were taken by many NATO members as another attempt to force the oil-dependent allies in western Europe to support the American confrontational posture and join the United States in imposing economic and political sanctions against Libya.

On this occasion NATO allies politely refused to support the administration. Their suspicions are sustained by some White House officials. One official who asked not to be identified told *The New York Times* that the possibility of imposing sanctions had been under consideration for several months and that the assassination plot had provided a new and dramatic basis for imposing them in December 1981. According to the official, "It wasn't artificial, just lucky timing."[23]

There is little doubt, even among critics of the administration's policies, that Kaddafi is openly hostile to American policy, particularly its support of Israel, and that his support of guerrilla warfare and terrorism is a major problem in current international politics. Nor, given Kaddafi's record of terrorism, do they easily dismiss the alleged assassination plot. The real question for critics, in particular many of the European allies, is whether Kaddafi's hostility warrants the kind of attention and response of overt military force and whether that response will be effective against terrorism. In the view of some European allies, President Reagan's military action only increases the dangers to them. Finding that their advice and counsel have been consistently ignored or criticized by Reagan officials as "soft on terrorism," and because the threat to their economic and political interests is dramatically different from those of the United States, many of our European allies have continued to resist America's growing pressure for military measures.

Reagan's decision to bomb Libya in April 1986 created further consternation among Europeans and brought their opposition to American policy into the open. Italian officials contended that the American military action did nothing but reinforce an unpopular and faltering Kaddafi regime and endanger the lives of 15,000 Italians, 5,500 British, 1,500 West Germans and 1,000 French citizens who live in Libya. Polls taken in Europe after the raids on Libya indicated that most Europeans think terrorism is only aggravated by American military action and such action could eventually lead to a confrontation with the Soviet Union. This view is also shared by self-professed hard-liners like Pierre Lellouche of the Paris-based French Institute of International Relations who called the April bombing of Libya "the Rambo response" and argued that it made Americans feel good but did nothing to stop Libyan-sponsored terrorism. Former West German Chancellor Helmut Schmidt said the bombing was a sign of "arrogance of power" that jeopardized the command structure of NATO.

Many Europeans feel that they have dealt with terrorism for more than fifteen years while the United States has been faced with the problem only recently and far from its own soil. From the European view, Kaddafi has the propensity to isolate himself from both enemies and allies, even within the Arab community. Continued hostility, whether expressed through hostile rhetoric or American threats and military action, especially the bombing of civilian targets in Libya by design or mistake, only heightens sympathy and support for Kaddafi as the leader of a small Arab nation being attacked by a superpower. These members of the European community say the David and Goliath syndrome plays extremely well in the Arab community, fueling fanaticism and breeding terrorists in the Palestinian refugee camps and capitals of radical Arab nations throughout the Middle East.

European critics of current American policies toward terrorism admit they have not yet developed an effective method to deal with the complexities of terrorism. But they do believe a saner and more effective course in moderating Kaddafi and his support for terrorism begins with diplomatic pressure such as restrictions on the activities and movements of Libyans in foreign countries. Some members of the European community, correctly assessing that President Reagan was going to attack Libya, and hoping to forestall an attack, proposed measures of this kind only hours before the American air strikes. One week later, agreement was reached to enforce these measures. Over the next few weeks all EEC member states restricted the activities of Libyans in their countries or expelled Libyan diplomats, students, and other Libyan citizens. According to European diplomats, continued Libyan support of terrorism will bring the expulsion of all diplomats from all countries and a complete transportation and communications boycott of Libya. European disagreement with Reagan's policy is not that he used military power but that he used it before all other measures had been explored and that when he did attack, he singled out Kaddafi for air strikes while ignoring overwhelming evidence that Iran and Syria are also heavily involved in state-sponsored terrorism. This quarrel took on even greater significance three weeks after the Libyan bombing, when both Israel and Britain, who supported President Reagan's use of military power against Libya, revealed they had substantial proof that Syrian-sponsored terrorists were behind a number of terrorist incidents, including the attempted bombing of the El Al airliner at Heathrow in London, the December 1985 massacres at the Vienna and Rome airports which claimed eighteen lives including five Americans, and the bombing of a discotheque in West Berlin. In June 1986 Italian officials also alleged Syrian involvement in these and other incidents.

However, the Reagan Administration says it has no plans to

use military force against Damascus even if the allegations are true and that, unlike its approach to Kaddafi, the United States would exhaust all diplomatic and legal channels before giving consideration to the military option against the Syrians. In contrast, when Italian Foreign Minister Giulio Andreotti suggested taking the Libyan claim over the Gulf of Sidra to the International Court at the Hague, Secretary of State Shultz turned him down, saying Kaddafi was a criminal and that no one could talk to criminals in court. The United States needs Syria for some of its diplomatic efforts in the Middle East, in particular help in gaining the release of American hostages held in Lebanon. Besides, Syria has a highly effective air defense system equipped with sophisticated Soviet-made missiles including the SA-8 and SA-9.

Many Europeans also see contradictions in the American criticism of their reluctance to participate in economic sanctions against Libya. They feel that the Reagan Administration, after calling for a total economic boycott of Libya in December 1985, permitted a dozen American companies, including five oil firms, to remain in Libya until June 30, 1986 and do business with Kaddafi in direct violation of its own economic boycott. In defense of the decision, administration officials point out that to force the companies out of Libya at this time would mean great monetary losses for them and would leave Kaddafi with a gift of several billion dollars worth of capital resources. These are worthy arguments.

The European nations have far greater economic interest at stake in Libya than does the United States. The Libyan air strikes, then, coming on the heels of the American violation of Soviet territorial waters off the Crimea by an American destroyer and guided missile cruiser on March 13, 1986 and the testing of Kaddafi's "line of death" threat in the Gulf of Sidra in late March, clearly worry many Europeans, who feel that in the short term these guarantee increased terrorism against western Europe. In the longer view, they fear that, with or without Kaddafi in power, the most likely result of the current American policy is even closer ties between Libya and the Soviet Union and a greater Soviet presence in the Middle East. From the European perspective, not only does a heightened Soviet presence diminish the chances for an overall peace settlement in the Middle East that potentially could lower the level of terrorism, but it increases the potential for a Soviet-American confrontation. Some of these fears appear well founded:

for instance, in the aftermath of the April bombing of Libya terrorism in western Europe and the Middle East against British and American civilian targets has increased. For their part, the Soviets have pledged further arms supplies to Kaddafi and for the first time asserted the right of passage under international law for their ships in the Mediterranean Sea.

It may be that in the long run the crediblity of the administration's perspective and policies, while not undermined, has been seriously damaged for the European Community by the increase of terrorism around the world since the Libyan air strike and increased aid to El Salvador.

Despite all doubts and criticism by foreign governments of President Reagan's policies in Libya and El Salvador over the past five years, Congress, in large part, has supported these policies. But in the aftermath of the Libyan raids serious questions have arisen as to the eventual result of American policy decisions.

IN CENTRAL AMERICA

One week after the bombing of Libya President Reagan told members of the Heritage Foundation that the Sandinista government of Nicaragua was seeking to "build a Libya on our doorstep" by providng "a refuge for all sorts of international terrorists."[24] According to President Reagan, members of the Red Brigade of Italy, the Baader-Meinhof Group of West Germany, the PLO, and terrorists groups from El Salvador, Uruguay, and Spain had been given shelter, training, and political direction by the Nicaraguan government. The scourges of international terrorism now threaten Central America, Reagan charged, and "it's the Contras, freedom fighters, who are stopping them."[25] Building on this theme, Reagan asserted "the march of freedom in Central America and the fight against terrorism are connected."[26] Earlier on the same day, the president, citing what he claimed was the Sandinistas' refusal to negotiate a Central American peace treaty, had extended the year-old trade embargo against Nicaragua and with it the state of "national emergency."

Because of this crisis, President Reagan hoped that the sympathetic public and congressional response to his decision to bomb terrorist Libya would help his effort to gain congressional backing for his $100-million military aid package to the United States-backed Contra rebels and their crusade to overthrow the Nicaraguan government.

It is the viewpoint of the Reagan Administration that the terrorist Sandinistas represent the ultimate moral evil in Central America and that they are bent on setting up a Soviet-Cuba-backed Communist dictatorship in America's backyard. However, even among some of the administration's staunch supporters there are serious doubts as to the paramilitary Contras being our best hope for defeating Communism and terrorism in Nicaragua. Despite the fact that Congress finally passed the $100-million military aid package in June 1986, authorizing for the first time since 1983 public funding of the Contras, the president has had a difficult time convincing both his opponents and his supporters that the Contras are "freedom fighters." The Contra's image as freedom fighters is contradicted by their links with the systematic terror and atrocities of the brutal American-backed Somoza regime and their continued terrorism against the Nicaraguan population. In supporting the terrorist-linked Contras, many people in North, Central, and South America feel that the United States supports terrorism in the Central American conflict. This belief has complicated President Reagan's policy options as he tries to overthrow the Sandinistas and it threatens to undermine the moral basis of present and future American foreign policy.

The roots of America's support of the Contras were planted in November 1981 when President Reagan authorized $19.95 million for covert operations against the Nicaraguan government. The plan, which had the strong backing of CIA Director William J. Casey, Secretary of State Alexander Haig, and Secretary of Defense Casper W. Weinberger, called for the CIA to train and finance a paramilitary force of 1,500 Latin Americans that would operate on the Nicaraguan-Honduran border. The administration initially denied the existence of a covert plan or that it was taking steps to topple the Sandinistas. But subsequent evidence, including testimony by CIA intelligence analyst David MacMichaels and a National Security Council document, confirmed that President Reagan had indeed approved the CIA plan to send the Contras into Nicaragua to destabilize the government. In addition, Nicaraguan rebels being trained in paramilitary camps in San Bernardino County, California, and outside Miami, Florida, admitted that their mission was to overthrow the Sandinista government.

According to the plan, the Contras were to conduct hit-and-run attacks on key economic targets such as power stations, bridges, and dams to disrupt the Nicaraguan economy. The plan went into action in the early months of 1982. By July a Defense Intelligence Agency weekly intelligence summary confirming that the Contras had mounted eighty-five attacks between March and June 1982 in Nicaragua on "military or military-related" targets circulated through the administration. The summary labelled the 15 September Legion, one of the largest Contra organizations, consisting of six hundred former members of Somoza's ruthless and universally hated National Guard, "a terrorist group." By August 1982 members of the CIA were telling congressional intelligence committees that the Contras in Honduran base camps numbered over 1,500 and were receiving $23.00 each a month in United States aid for their efforts.

Congressional opposition to these reports quickly mobilized. In December 1982 Congress attempted to put a halt to the CIA plan by attaching the Boland Amendment to an emergency spending bill, making illegal any covert aid for the purpose of overthrowing the government of Nicaragua. But over the next four months the administration did not heed Congress's objections. In April 1983 congressional delegations returning from fact-finding missions to Central America reported to Congress that the Reagan Administration was violating the Boland Amendment by continuing its covert activities against Nicaragua. At the same time, *The New York Times* printed the text of a National Security Council document on United States policy in Central America confirming that a year earlier President Reagan had approved a $22 million regional plan to prevent "Cuba-model" states in Central America that included covert activities against Nicaragua. According to the authors of the document, this plan had not been affected or altered by the Boland Amendment.

In the summer of 1983 the Reagan Administration went public with its plan and asked Congress for funds for the Contras to "harass" the Sandinistas into ending their military support for El Salvadoran rebels. Congress balked at this request, since the administration could not prove that weapons had been sent by Nicaragua to El Salvador after early 1981. Despite this initial setback, the Reagan Administration continued to press Congress for Contra aid. In March 1984 it requested $21 million in emergency

CIA funding for the Contras, arguing that the rebel efforts would end in failure without the aid. In a shrewd political maneuver, the Senate Appropriations Committee tied the aid package to a food bill for Africa, hoping to insure its passage. Again Congress said no. A year later Congress did approve $27 million in "non-lethal" aid under the stipulation it not be distributed by the CIA. President Reagan immediately set up a special office in the State Department to distribute this aid and has not allowed an audit of its operations by the General Accounting Office of Congress. In October 1985 *The Washington Post* reported that current and former administration officials admitted the president had approved a secret plan to channel funds raised from private American sources to the Contras in order to replace the CIA funds cut off by Congress. At the time, Nicaraguan officials were telling the World Court that 3,886 people in Nicaragua had been killed and 4,731 wounded in the four years of Contra attacks. Finally, after an intense three-month campaign during which the loyalty and patriotism of those opposing a renewed request for aid were severely questioned by congressional supporters of the paramilitary effort, President Reagan asked Congress for a military aid package of $100 million for the Contras. Before the Libyan bombings the aid package was rejected once by the House of Representatives, passed in the Senate, and was back in the House for another vote. In the aftermath of the air strikes, Reagan hoped that his Libyan success would end the American fear and caution concerning military intervention in the Third World—known as the Vietnam Syndrome—and bring support for his military plans in Central America. On June 25, 1986 Reagan's hopes were rewarded as Congress approved, by a slim margin, his $100 million Contra aid package.

But public opinion polls run two to one against the president's policy. The Reagan Administration's policy toward Nicaragua is an oversimplified if not misinformed version of the political realities in Central America. As a result, the president has met with major opposition to his Nicaraguan policy and has been severely criticized for pursuing policy options rooted in controversial sources, possible falsehoods, and misinformation. For example, many of the allegations made against the Sandinistas in President Reagan's March 16, 1986 television address on Nicaragua were challenged as wrong by a variety of sources. The United States Drug Enforcement Administration said it had no evidence that any top Nicaraguan officials were a part of the drug trade. Instead, drug enforcement officials alleged there were indications that members of the Contra forces were heavily involved in drug trafficking, a charge also made by some former Contra members in June 1986. Congress placed these charges under investigation. President Reagan's claim that Jewish people were persecuted by the Sandinistas was opposed by the investigation of Rabbi Balfour Brickner of New York, who said the few Jews who had lived in Nicaragua before the 1979 revolution were supporters of dictator Anastasio Somoza and had left the country of their own accord. He also asserted that the Managua Synagogue, which had been abandoned in 1978, was never firebombed and to this day remains intact, though at present there was no Jewish community to support it. The government of Brazil took issue with President Reagan's claim that the Sandinistas were supporting Brazilian radicals. Brazil said it had no internal security problems since the Sandinistas came to power in 1979 and that Elliot Abrams, the United States Under Secretary of State for Latin American Affairs, had recently sent a letter to Brazil confirming that the Reagan Administration was aware of this fact.

But it is President Reagan's view that the Contras are democratic liberators fighting the Soviet-Cuban-Sandinista terrorists that is most frequently objected to. It is the administration's view that the origins of the Contra movement can be traced to the Sandinistas' betrayal of the democratic revolution against Somoza. Contra leaders are said to be former members of the Sandinista democratic movement forced out by the small coterie of Marxist-Leninists who now control the ruling Sandinista junta. However, according to Christopher Dickey in his book, *With the Contras*, much of the National Guard leadership was rounded up at the Managua airport by a mysterious American thought to be a CIA agent and hustled out of Nicaragua to Miami, Florida. Within weeks, with plans, money, and weapons provided by the CIA, they set up the command center of the counter-revolution. The rank and file Somoza Guardsmen, led by the murderous terrorist known as Suicida, managed to make their way to El Salvador, where, beginning in 1980, they hired themselves out to right-wing organizations in Guatemala, El Salvador, and Honduras. Dickey says it was some of the former Somoza Guardsmen who assassinated Archbishop Oscar Arnulfo Romero in San Salvador in March 1980. With CIA funds and training by the Argentine military, expert in the techniques of torture and terrorism, these former guardsmen, numbering around 1,500 men, were organized into the Nicaraguan Democratic Front (FDN) led by Adolfo Calero Portocarrero, who has long-standing CIA connections and is opposed to the Sandinistas because he considers them Marxists who must be overthrown by military means.

Calero and his close associates and relatives continue to dominate the military command. The most important of these are Mario Calero, Adolfo Calero's brother, his brother-in-law Enrique Sanchez, Sanchez's brother Aristides Sanchez, and Colonel Enrique Bermudez. All of these leaders and those who hold other top posts in the military command are former National Guardsmen or persons closely connected to the Somoza regime. The Sanchez brothers were large landowners and committed to Somoza's dictatorship. Colonel Bermudez served as a military attaché in Washington under Somoza and had close ties to the CIA. It is with these political convictions and violent pasts in mind that critics now ask: where is the proof that these torturers and murderers suddenly became interested in democracy? What evidence is there they represent a democratic alternative to the Sandinistas? Isn't it more likely, given their past and present actions, that they seek only personal and political revenge against those who ended their privileges and power?

More importantly, their cruel atrocities against Nicaraguan civilians, the very people they say they seek to liberate, contradict whatever verbal commitments to freedom and justice the Contras now make. Since 1982 many journalists and human rights groups, including America's Watch, Witness for Peace, and the Center for Constitutional Rights, have published extensive documentation concerning Contra terrorism. Beginning in April 1984, Senators Edward Kennedy, Christopher Dodd, Clairborne Pell, and Paul Tsongas presented before Congress testimony of systematic and wholesale Contra atrocities committed against the civilian population in Nicaragua. Senator Dodd was the first to publicly detail the contradictions between the Reagan Administration's worldwide anti-terrorist campaign and its support for Contra terrorism. Speaking before Congress on April 4, 1984, he asked why it was that the administration was quick to condemn as terrorism Libya's bombing of a radio station in Sudan, the destruction of an oil depot in South Africa by the African National Congress, Iranian-planted mines in the Straits of Hormuz, and the PLO bombing of a civilian bus but remained silent about Contra attacks on the Nicaraguan radio station at the Managua airport, the destruction of oil facilities in Puerto Sandino, damage to Dutch and Russian ships by Contra-planted mines outside the Nicaraguan ports of Cortino and Puerto Sandino, and the ambush of a civilian bus near Jinotega in which ten civilians were killed. Dodd pointedly asked the administration, "Are we going to have an office for combatting terrorism in the State Department and an office for implementing terrorism at the CIA?"[27] On the same day, Senator Paul Tsongas promised any fellow Senators who doubted the stories about Contra terrorism that he would personally take them to the Nicaraguan town of Esta-Lee and show them the brutalized fathers and the motherless children. After he dared anyone in the Senate to take the floor and say there had been no Contra terrorism, Tsongas told his colleagues, "It is easy to vote on these things but you are killing people. We debate school prayer. We care. And then we kill. That is what this amendment is about—killing mothers, children, sons. That is your vote."[28] In his comments, Senator Edward Kennedy detailed a series of recent terrorist acts by the CIA-backed Contras, including a December 19, 1983 attack on a farm cooperative in which fourteen people were killed, among them two women; the sinking of two fishing boats killing two crew members and wounding seven others on February 24, 1984; the indiscriminate mortar shelling of three border towns from Honduras on March 1, 2, 3, and 4, 1984; damage to a Panamanian freighter and injuries to its crew from Contra mines in the Harbor of Cortino on March 7, 1984; the deaths of three peasants and a school official in the town of Esta-Lee and seven members of a farm cooperative on March 16 and the March 17, 1984 ambush in which eleven peasants died and seven were kidnapped.

In the renewed debate over Contra aid during October 1984, Senator Kennedy placed before the Senate testimony of various witnesses to Contra kidnappings, indiscriminate shootings of civilians, rape, torture, mutilation, the burning of houses, health clinics, schools, and hospitals. Kennedy entered into the *Congressional Record* a report by Harvard Law School professor Henry Steiner who had visited Nicaragua in June 1984. The report detailed the "systematic assassination of civilian leaders, torture of civilians and devastation of civilian institutions by the Contras."[29] Also entered into the public record on October 3, 1984 were descriptions of various accounts of Contra savagery committed in the towns and areas of Ocotal, Waslalal, and Jalapa and on the Miskito Indians in Zelaya Norte. Witnesses told of a cartoon manual, later discovered to be CIA-inspired, containing instructions to the Contras on how to sabotage crops and farm machinery, how to pour sand into automobile gas tanks, and burn books. As late as March 1986 Kennedy was still detailing Contra terrorism before the United States Senate.

Numerous independent sources, including Reed Brody in his book, *Contra Terror in Nicaragua*, have confirmed what these senators told their congressional colleagues. British journalists Jonna Rolio and Gavin MacFadyen, who conducted a series of interviews with victims and witnesses in Nicaragua during the summer of 1984, submitted one of the most indicting reports of Contra sadomasochistic savagery. Their interviews led the journalists to conclude that the Contras were waging a systematic campaign of terrorism and that the greatest level of atrocities was committed in areas where Sandinista programs of health, literacy, and agrarian reform were being implemented successfully. Rolio and MacFadyen travelled to the town of Waslala just after the Contras had attacked it. Survivors told them many horror stories: a man was found thoroughly beaten and stabbed, a cross carved in his back and his eyes pulled out; thirty-seven women and children were dead; the Contras attacked the hospital first and then burned the school. Outside the town, seven more tortured bodies were found. The Contras had cut the fingers off of one of the militia members, skinned him and spread his skin across a rock and laid his identity card on top of it. In their retreat, the "freedom fighters" passed through the village of San Miguel and tortured five more peasants, gouged their eyes out, and then beheaded them. In El Achote, the rebels burned twenty-five houses, leaving thirty families homeless and penniless. A witness said a young man was cut to pieces in front of his wife before she was shot. Before she died she saw her eleven-month-old baby beheaded. Church sources in the region reported that six hundred people were kidnapped during 1982 from Waslala and two hundred more in the last raid in 1984. Peasants who escaped their nightmarish capture said the Contras used them for pack animals to carry their heavy equipment through the mountains. Many others were raped or left to die from disease or exhaustion once they were of no further use to the Contras.

In other towns and villages, Rolio and MacFadyen report, the scene was much the same as in Waslala. Many civilians were kidnapped, tortured, and later found dead, their bodies mutilated. The Contras save their most sadistic torture techniques for members of the local militia and deserters from their own ranks. Witnesses told of one wounded militia member who was found by the Contras. They answered his pleas for mercy by cutting off his testicles and stuffing them in his mouth to stifle his screams and groans. Captured Contras say they witnessed many cruel sessions of torture and beheadings of young boys who tried to desert from the rebels.

In areas where Sandinista reform programs have met with some success, the Contras target coffee harvesters, members of literacy brigades, government workers, teachers, nurses, and doctors for special attention. Between 1981 and 1983 the Nicaraguan Ministry of Health lost eighteen doctors and nurses, including two Europeans. One was the French physician Pierres Grosjean, who was killed during a random spraying of a village by Contra gunfire. A German doctor and two Nicaraguan nurses were ambushed on a road outside Wiwili and executed with shots in the head. On three separate occasions the Contras have kidnapped groups of West Germans who have volunteered their services to earthquake-ravaged Nicaragua. The most recent kidnapping took place on May 17, 1986, when members of the FDN took twelve West Germans who were in Nicaragua working on housing projects in the farming cooperative of Jacinto Baca. They released them only after West German officials threatened to intervene. The hostages claimed their Contras captors told them their seizure had been planned by the Contras well in advance with the approval of the rebel leaders. Three of the West Germans told of mistreatment at the hands of their Contra captors, including being shot at, threatened with death, and long and exhausting forced marches through the mountains during their twenty-five-day ordeal.[30]

During 1982 the Ministry of Education lost 153 teachers, popular educators, and literacy brigade members to Contra terrorism. One of those killed was an eighth-grade student who worked as a zonal technician for the teaching volunteers. Two days after being kidnapped by the Contras, her body was found in the area of Rio Blanco. She had been raped and then had her throat cut and her breasts sliced off. The Contras kidnapped a young boy, a popular teacher's aide named Giorgino Andrade, and sadistically murdered him. His hands were sliced off, his tongue and eyes cut out, and his body left hanging from a tree. In Matagalpa, the Contras killed fifty-five education workers between 1982 and 1984; more than sixty percent of them were tortured before they died. On March 5, 1985 America's Watch, an American human rights organization, issued a report documenting that between 1984 and early 1985 the Contras had raped, murdered, tortured, kidnapped and mutilated many unarmed civilians, including women and children. The report also accused the Sandinistas of human rights abuses against the Miskito Indians. But America's Watch said the Nicaraguan government repression of the Miskitos had been "in sharp decline" since 1982.

The charges against the Contras have been so pervasive that Reagan Administration officials have been unable to ignore them completely. They have attempted to counter the evidence of Contra terrorism by arguing that these incidents are random or isolated, are a normal part of any war, and are most often acts of revenge for Sandinista terror. President Reagan dismisses the reports of Contra atrocities as part of a Sandinista disinformation program in which Sandinista sympathizers dress up as Contras and murder and mutilitate civilians.

But the testimony of present and former Contra leaders undercuts many of the Reagan Administration denials of Contra terrorism. For example, in September 1985 Edgar Chamorro, who was a leader of the FDN until the fall of 1984, told the World Court in an affidavit that the Contras forcibly enlisted new recruits by publicly killing Sandinista officials and their suspected sympathizers in front of the gathered village population. Chamorro and other rebel leaders alleged that not only was the practice routine and widespread but that it was done with the knowledge and approval of the CIA. FDN spokesperson Bosco Matomoros, in responding to Chamorro's charge, admitted that rebel abuses against civilians had indeed occurred but said that since 1984 a code of conduct has been in place to punish those participating in atrocities.

The terrorism of the Contras shatters the Reagan Administration's portrait of them as democratic "freedom fighters."

Moreover, the discovery of the controversial CIA training

manual, *Psychological Operations in Guerrilla Warfare*, has further
eroded public opinion about American support of terrorist tactics
in El Salvador. This manual, for which Reagan eventually repri-
manded several middle-level CIA employees, was put together by
CIA operative John Kirkpatrick and his associates in the agency.
The contents of the manual were based on old Vietnam archives on
guerrilla tactics and from a 1968 instruction manual used in training by the psychological operations department of the United
States Army Special Warfare School at Ft. Bragg, North Carolina.
According to Contra leader Edgar Chamorro, the manual was put
together as part of an effort to control Contra atrocities in order to
change the terrorist image that was increasingly damaging to the
rebel cause in important circles of world opinion. But rather than
discouraging terrorist tactics, the manual instructed the Contras in
the art of systematic terrorism. In a section called "Selective Use of
Violence," the manual counsels, "It is possible to neutralize carefully selected and planned targets such as court judges, mesta
judges, police and State Security officials, CDS chiefs, etc."[31] At the
center of the controversy surrounding the manual is the precise
meaning of "neutralize." President Reagan says the term simply
means to go in and physically remove people from their offices.
But its appearance in the section called "Selective Use of Violence"
contradicts the president's interpretation. In its original form, the
manual also instructed the Contras to hire professional criminals
for demonstrations in order to stir up trouble during which some
people would be killed. Chamorro says he objected to this idea and
instructed that the pages containing this proposal be torn out of
the manual. It is still unclear as to whether or not his order was
obeyed.

        After Congress cut off funds to the Contras in 1984 the CIA
and the National Security Council (NSC) continued to be actively
involved in directing the private efforts of the Contras. In August
1985 the Reagan Administration admitted that NSC officials had
given advice on military actions and continued to have "tactical
influence" over the rebel command. Marine Corps Lt. Col. Oliver
L. North, a member of the NSC and an aide to then-National
Security Advisor Robert C. McFarlane, had coordinated Contra
activities. He had been in touch with both the Contras and the CIA
and had given briefings on the Contra campaign to President
Reagan. *The Washington Post* claimed it was North who had been

responsible for drafting the controversial terror manual that was sent to the Contras. By November 1986 North was forced to resign from the NSC for his part in diverting funds to Contra bank accounts in Switzerland. The money was raised from the sale of United States arms to Iran in the disastrous attempt by the Reagan Administration to secretly gain the release of American hostages held in Lebanon.

The CIA has tried from the start to influence the various rebel factions to end their internal squabbling and unify under one command. In November 1984 a significant step was taken in this direction with the unification of the three groups headed by Arturo Jose Cruz, Adolfo Calero, and Alfonso Robelo Callejas. In addition, a support system was set up between the unified command and various private right-wing groups in the United States who stepped in and kept funds flowing to the Contras during the congressional ban on aid. Most of the money is channelled through a paramilitary organization in Alabama called Civilian Military Assistance, which sends teams to Central America to train the rebels. During that time, retired General John Singlaub, at present head of the World Anti-Communist League and the United States Council for World Freedom and formerly involved in the Phoenix Program in Vietnam, took charge of the Contra military training in place of the CIA operatives. Contra leaders say they are receiving money and weapons from conservative and New Right organizations. These support activities are under the private sponsorship of several retired government bureaucrats, such as General Daniel Graham, who from their influential positions on many corporate boards of directors initiate and coordinate fund-raising efforts.

The CIA currently remains heavily involved in the Contra effort and has channeled millions of dollars to the rebels in direct violation of the guidelines issued by Congress. In interviews conducted in early 1986 by journalist Martha Holmes, several rebel leaders alleged that the CIA continues to direct Contra activities from a command center in San Jose, Costa Rica, in addition to conducting polygraph tests on Contra members. CIA officials claim they ordered the tests to help establish a new command structure in the Contra organization and to eliminate Sandinista infiltrators from rebel ranks. But Contra leaders argue that the tests are being used to weed out rebel leaders who are not compliant with CIA wishes or are loyal to independent Contra leaders—in particular,

Eden Pastora. According to Roger Monge Zelaya, an administrator in the Costa Rican-based Nicaraguan Armed Resistance Force (FARN), "The polygraph was not designed to detect enemies of the counter-revolution but enemies of the CIA . . . directing us."[32] It is alleged that anyone who refuses to take the test will be drummed out of the Contra ranks. As a result, many of FARN's top leaders have quit or been kicked out and many of its fighting troops have deserted because of the testing program.

By early May 1986 six of eight of Pastora's lieutenants renounced his leadership and joined forces with the CIA-affiliated FDN. On May 16 Pastora and his few remaining loyalists announced they were abandoning their fight against the Sandinistas and crossed into Costa Rica seeking political asylum. Pastora accuses the CIA of forcing him and his followers out of the counterrevolution. He said the agency cut off aid to his organization because he refused to join forces with the former members of Somoza's National Guard who run the FDN. It also appears that polygraph tests played a large part in Pastora's demise. Some Contra members say fighters under his command were regularly asked about their feelings toward his leadership. According to these sources, anyone indicating loyalty to Pastora was declared unfit for continued service in the Contra movement. As a result, what in 1985 was an estimated force of five hundred under Pastora's leadership and was expected to grow to five thousand, by 1986 was reduced to no more than two dozen fighting men.

Then an agreement was reached between the still-warring rebel factions within the UNO (United Nicaraguan Opposition) to give civilian leaders Arturo Jose Cruz and Alfonso Robelo Callejas more power. The agreement, which came early in June 1986, after two weeks of arduous and often hostile negotiations at a CIA-organized conference in Miami, Florida, gave Cruz and Callejas leadership positions and thus quieted congressional criticism that the rebels are led by former followers of Somoza. But the new alliance is very tenuous. As recently as August 1985 Cruz and Callejas were treated with contempt by Calero and Bermudez when they visited the rebel camps in Honduras.

In April 1986 a *New York Times*/CBS poll still showed that the American public is against aid to the Contras by a sixty-two percent to twenty-five percent margin. However, in mid-1985 the Reagan Administration had been successful in getting Congress to repeal the ban against giving aid to foreign police forces by arguing that a new United States-sponsored counterterrorist training program was urgently needed to battle the rising tide of Soviet-sponsored terrorism.

In September 1985 the State Department asked Congress for $22 million to train the police and security forces, including the notorious Treasury Police, in El Salvador. Some of the funds are designated for operations against legal Salvadoran labor unions, peasant groups, and student organizations that are involved in legitimate anti-government activity. In testimony provided by Ricardo Castro, a Salvadoran army officer, West Point graduate, CIA employee, and self-confessed leader of death squad operations in El Salvador, we have an idea of what these opposition groups are in for. According to Castro, death squad killings are a routine part of the Salvadoran military strategy. As a translator for the Salvadoran defense ministry, Castro says that in 1980 he began working for a succession of American advisors at the general staff headquarters, where he witnessed numerous training sessions of Salvadoran military personnel by American instructors on the techniques of torture. In its response to these and other similar allegations, the CIA contends it does not teach torture as an interrogation technique and that its agents are only "in the vicinity" when interrogation sessions take place. But this part of Castro's testimony has been corroborated by other Salvadoran military personnel, including Gustava Lara, a former officer of the Treasury Police. Castro further admits that he led death squad missions in the villages of La Lucha, El Polvillo, El Salto, and La Montana, during which fourteen civilians were killed. He says the selection by death squad commanders of the civilians to be killed is based on spurious criteria ranging from personal vendettas to unconfirmed rumors or off-handed accusations that someone is a subversive.

According to such reports, Salvadoran military and police personnel treat any activity out of the ordinary as "subversive." For example, in Course 0-47, a study of a counterinsurgency operations offered at the United States Army School of the Americas until the school was closed in October 1984, students were taught how to identify the presence of Communist guerrillas and support for their subversive cause. Evidence of subversion includes the disappearance or movement of youths and the failure of families to speak about them; the refusal of peasants to pay rents, taxes, or agricultural loan payments; local population hostility to government forces manifested in the refusal of children to fraternize with the internal security forces; short absences from work by government employees; poor information from the network of police informants or police; and growing hostility against government agencies of public order. According to reports about Course 0-47, outright subversive activity includes consciousness-raising activities by the Catholic Church, demonstrations, strikes, or any action that might gain the support of the people.

Castro testified that once there are several suspects in a certain area, the death squads, armed with a list of suspects and dressed in either civilian clothes or disguised as leftist or rightist guerrillas, slip into the area and murder the suspects and their families. In most cases the victims were hacked to death with machetes in front of their homes.

While Castro singles out the National Treasury Police as the main security force involved in the death squad terrorism, he says army forces also purposely murder civilians during their military exercises. Castro testified that he commanded the third company of the Zacatecoluca Brigade during a sweep by the Atlacati Battalion in November 1981. At the end of the operation, "there were twenty-four women and children captured and they were assassinated right in front of me—just one by one in cold blood."[33] In another case, Castro says he was asked to act as a translator in the interrogation of civilians during an army operation against two towns with three hundred people each. The officer who requested his assistance told Castro the people were all to be killed after being questioned. Castro was assigned other duties and did not participate in the operation but says he heard later from his mother, who he contends has strong pro-government sympathies, that six hundred civilians were indeed killed in Morazan during the military sweep.

Not only is it alleged that terrorism is used by the death squads, but in October 1983 the Salvadoran Air Force, with alleged aid from local American supervisors and American pilots and aircraft, began random aerial bombardment of rural areas of El Salvador. The aerial terrorism was and is designed to counter recent military successes by the rebel Farabundo Marti National Liberation Front by frightening the civilian population into fleeing from their home areas, thus depriving the guerrillas of their support network. All who remain in the bombed-out area are assumed to be terrorists and further blitzed from the air and by Salvadoran Army land assaults. The basic techniques of the air war are demolition and fragmentation and involve the dropping of five hundred- and seven-hundred-pound iron bombs that are fitted with devices that convert them into antipersonnel weapons: incendiary bombing with Israeli napalm, and United States-supplied white phosphorous and indiscriminate machine gunning with American-made A-37 fighter bombers and AC-47, Huey and Hughes helicopters.

A principal proponent and participant in the air war is Salvadoran Colonel Sigifredo Ochoa, who has been reported by American journalists as conducting depopulation sweeps through large areas of El Salvador since 1981. His troops first gained international notoriety when they crossed into Honduras and dragged "suspects" out of the refugee camps and back into El Salvador. Ochoa has dubbed the designation of free fire zones in El Salvador the "Israeli solution" to the rebel insurgency. On the assumption that only terrorists remain in these designated areas, Ochoa's command will not allow entry of any relief organizations or medical supplies after the bombings.

Since 1983 the air terror has been responsible for most of the 500,000 internal refugees and the 750,000 refugees who have fled El Salvador. At present, more than one-fifth of the Salvadoran population are refugees, a higher percentage than at the height of the war in South Vietnam. Although the American press has largely ignored the air terrorism and the Reagan Administration's connection to it, independent investigations by the Committee in Solidarity with the People of El Salvador and America's Watch, along with reports in *The Christian Science Monitor*, *The Dallas Morning News*, and the Pacific News Service confirm the reports.

The major American media have been very slow to report on the aerial bombing and have only covered it sporadically since 1985. In that reporting, there has been no mention of, let alone criticism against, the aerial terrorism. The media's silence and selective omissions are ominous signs. There is no excuse for the journalistic silence as the horrors of the aerial terrorism over El Salvador are easily documented by those reporters who have investigated it.

To this day, the bombing continues in El Salvador and will until it is recognized for what it is—a policy of indiscriminate violence against a civilian population, better described as mass terrorism in a ghastly form—and a determined public hue and cry are raised against it.

THE MIDDLE VIEW: confronting the reality of terrorism

In our examination of the explosion of terrorism and its political implications, the smaller purpose has been to illustrate the socio-economic and political nature of terrorism and the political climates which seem to foster it; the larger purpose has been to provoke the conclusion that we need to construct a new and different framework with which to approach the contemporary explosion of terrorism. We need a new conception of the reality of terrorism, one that attempts to depoliticize the issues involved and allows us in the West to battle terrorism with a minimum of sacrifice to our democratic process and tradition. Currently, we are focusing all our attention exclusively on the terrorism of the other side, which leaves us with a partial and thus distorted notion of the reality of the terrorist plague. There is another position from which to view terrorism, one we will label the "Middle View" of terrorism. It is hoped that it will provide a new framework and a better understanding about the wider implications of the explosion of terrorism.

The building of the Middle View begins with a hard look at the reality of terrorism in present circumstances, and this requires at least a tentative settlement of what terrorism is. We already know that there is no agreement on a definition and may never be. This leaves us with three options. First, we can scrap the concept of terrorism altogether, judging it to be hopelessly political in nature. Or we can stop looking for a universal definition and continue to operate on a series of definitions, asking only that they be consistently adhered to. Or we could continue to seek universality but confine our definition to the least objectionable yet obvious criteria. The usefulness of the Middle View does not necessarily depend on settling the definitional issue, but it would no doubt be enhanced by it. With this in mind let us choose the third option and adopt the criterion of terrorism as a type of surreptitious warfare in which indiscriminate violence or the threat of indiscriminate violence is used to induce fear for the purpose of changing the state of mind or policy of the nation or group whose members are intimidated.

Armed with this or almost any other serious attempt at a definition, one of our major conclusions is that all legitimate governments, whatever their ideological stances, beginning with the United States and the Soviet Union as the two major global powers in the current international system, must accept the responsibility for terrorism's resurgence. Both the United States and the Soviet Union have, at times, forced the global population to accept their premise that the world is a safer place with nuclear weapons than without. They have also tried, albeit unsuccessfully, to push the idea that the world is safer with nuclear arsenals under their monopolistic controls rather than proliferated throughout the community of nations. They have made it clear that the only efforts to limit the kind and number of nuclear weapons under their control will come when it is in their mutual interests and that these agreements, as the arrangements made under the Strategic Arms Limitations Treaty (SALT I and II) prove, have nothing to do with nuclear disarmament. More importantly, in rejecting a policy of nuclear disarmament they have adopted a strategy of terrorism called "deterrence" to manage the potential for nuclear war. The thesis of deterrence is premised on the assumption that nuclear aggression can be controlled by creating a "balance of terror" in which each side's population, and in reality the world's population and life on earth as we know it, is held hostage to the prospect of total annihilation from weapons capable of the worst kind of indiscriminate horrific violence. This "second strike" nuclear strategy is defended as preferable to disarmament because the presence of nuclear weapons is verifiable whereas their absence is not. And it is defended on the basis that it has worked so far. While the "ideology of terrorism" tells us that terrorism is an ineffective and self-defeating strategy, the initial point of the Middle View is that the superpowers, in their grand scheme of global nuclear policy, have bet the fate of the world that terrorism does indeed work.

The Middle View argues secondly that the Soviet Union and the United States have both used or supported terrorist tactics during the past fifteen years.

In its revolutionary aspirations to build an international socialist system, the Soviet Union trains, finances, and provides weapons to many nations and groups, some of which, for both the enhancement of direct Soviet revolutionary global interests and their own more limited goals, are engaged in terrorism. The Middle View suggests that, similar to the Soviet Union, the United States, as part of its global counterrevolutionary posture, has supported organizations and movements which use and advocate terrorist tactics and that at times the United States funds, trains, and equips with weapons and ideas surrogate governments, guerrillas, and terrorists. This is a most difficult and troubling conclusion for those of us in the West who believe there is a significant difference between the motives and operations of Soviet foreign policy and those of the United States. But the purpose of the Middle View is to end the mythology surrounding the issue of terrorism. The reality is that both superpowers and minor powers utilize terrorism for their own particular purposes. When we come to terms with this reality, no matter how uncomfortable, we will have taken a major step toward stripping the issue of terrorism of some of its political and manipulative capabilities.

Many critics at different times have made the claim that both the United States and the Soviet Union are sometimes active participants in international terrorism. Yet it remains a minority point of view mainly because the ideologues in both the United States and the Soviet Union have successfully mobilized their constituents against believing it. In addition, those presenting the case exposing manipulative terrorism have been unable to develop a framework that can successfully counter those who seek to negate this reality by embroiling the discussion in endless definitional disputes and distinctions between terrorism and guerrilla warfare, control and influence, force and violence, and totalitarianism and authoritarianism. Although some of these distinctions are central to our understanding of terrorism, no matter whether they are resolved or not, they cannot negate the reality that superpowers as well as minor powers utilize terrorism. The Middle View discussion of terrorism seeks to avoid these disputes by accepting the basic structure offered by conservative analysts like

Samuel Francis and Claire Sterling in their documentation of the Soviet terrorist network. These authors have argued that they (the Soviets) support an international terrorist network, a terrorist infrastructure, and an ideology of terrorism through their client-state arrangements. In more specific terms, the Middle View utilizes the criteria suggested by Dr. Ray S. Cline, a senior associate and terrorism expert at the neoconservative Georgetown Center for Strategic and International Studies, who, in discussing Soviet involvement with terrorism, says "What they do is supply the infrastructure of terror: the money, the guns, the training, the background information, the communications, the propaganda that will inspire individual terrorist groups."[1] The Middle View adopts this framework for an examination of both Soviet Union and United States involvement. It seeks to illuminate the terrorism complicity of each superpower.

Before we can use the framework, we need to define the concepts of *surrogate* and *infrastructure*.

In his book, *The Soviet Strategy of Terror*, Samuel Francis uses the terms satellite and surrogate. He says a satellite is "a government, country, or organization that, while ostensibly independent, is in truth firmly controlled by the Soviet government" and a surrogate is "a government, country, or organization that, while perhaps independent of Soviet control, acts as a substitute for the Soviets in certain ways."[2] Francis defines the infrastructure of terror to mean "surrogate support facilities in the form of training, weapons, and propaganda."[3]

For the Soviet Union and the United States, there are several advantages in these kinds of relationships. The supporting of surrogates allows the superpowers to separate themselves from disreputable policies and acts that are carried out by smaller nations. For instance, Francis argues that "Operations that conflict with the publicly stated goals or values of the Soviet Union, the Communist Party, or Soviet foreign commitments or which, if the Soviet role were known, would embarrass the Soviet leadership, are assigned to surrogates that appear not to be closely tied to the USSR."[4] The Soviet Union and the United States have publicly stated their opposition to terrorism. However, in backing states or groups that use terroristic tactics, both countries can further their ideological goals while not being accused of directly utilizing terrorism as a part of their foreign policy. Secondly, by supporting surrogates, the superpowers can avoid committing their own resources in operations far from their national base. Finally, the aiding of surrogates who may be viewed by other members of the international community in a more favorable light than the superpower garners less criticism and more support for the surrogate's activity and is clearly in the superpower's interest. For instance, both Czechoslovakia and Cuba enjoy greater support from more leftists in western Europe and the United States than does the Soviet Union. By supporting these states, the Soviets can keep a low profile and limit outside charges about their aggression. In much the same way, South Korean and Australian participation in the Vietnam War and British cooperation in the American air strikes on Libya bolstered the basically unilateral role played by the United States in these events.

SOVIET TERROR NETWORK

As a basically regional superpower with alleged global aspirations, the Soviet Union employs a number of client states and surrogates in its hegemonic system. It supplies both arms and military training personnel to states around the world. In the tables below, we see the value of Soviet arms transfers to some of its major supporters and the number of Soviet military personnel beyond its borders.[5]

Soviet Military Aid (1977–83)

Afghanistan	$1.8 billion
Algeria	$3.2 billion
Angola	$1.5 billion
Cuba	$3.1 billion
Ethiopia	$1.8 billion
Iraq	$7.2 billion
Libya	$5.8 billion
Mongolia	$625 million
Mozambique	$520 million
North Korea	$210 million
South Yemen	$1.5 billion
Syria	$9.2 billion
Vietnam	$5.2 billion
Warsaw Pact	$6.17 billion

Soviet Military Personnel In The Third World (1984)

Latin American (Cuba included)	7,900
Middle East and North Africa	9,000
Sub-Saharan Africa	4,000
Asia	3,500
Afghanistan	117,000

Soviet-bloc Combat Troops Outside Home Areas (1985)

USSR	in Afghanistan	115,000 since 1979
Cuba	in Angola	20,000 since 1975
	in Ethiopia	7,000 since 1977
Vietnam	in Cambodia	180,000 since 1978[6]

In Latin America, the Cubans serve as a major Soviet surrogate. Reliable sources indicate that through its control over the Cuban intelligence service, the Direction General of Intelligence (DGI), the Soviets have trained members of the Irish Republican Army (IRA), the Canadian Quebec Liberation Front (FLQ), and some members of the American Weather Underground. DGI agents are alleged to have been in contact with "Carlos" in Paris and with Italian terrorist Giangiacomo Feltrinelli. Some Al Fatah members of the Palestine Liberation Organization were trained at the military college in Havana. The Cubans were also active in supporting the Sandinistas in Nicaragua against the Somoza regime and reportedly trained some members of the Sandinistas in Cuba. CIA intelligence says Castro was involved with the Guatemalan rebel groups MR-13 and Armed Revolutionary Force (FAR) in the 1960s and then the Guerrilla Army of the Poor (EGP) in the 1970s. In 1979 Cuban officials attempted to organize a united front between the EGP, FAR, and pro-Soviet Communist Party of Guatemala (PGT). Rebel organizations in El Salvador, Bolivia, and Uruguay also received Cuban support and training. Cuban military personnel are stationed in areas of the Third World helping to train and support Soviet clients. As of 1984, there were an estimated 3,500 Cubans in Latin America, 37,000 in Sub-Saharan African, and 500 in the Middle East and North Africa. In other parts of Latin America, the Soviets have trained members of the *Movimento de Accion Revolucionaria* (MAR) in Mexico and the Revolutionary Armed forces of Colombia (FARC).

Soviet military parade, Nicaragua.

Americans train native troops, Nicaragua.

Death squad victims, El Salvador.

Salvadoran army utilizes American-supplied helicopters.

Soviet air base at Ghanzi, Afghanistan.

Destruction caused by Soviet invasion and Afghan resistance.

Major Soviet surrogates and clients in the Middle East and North Africa are Libya, Syria, and the PLO. They share Soviet hostility toward Zionism and Western imperialism and have been useful to Soviet interests. Libya is a major recipient of Soviet aid and in return has provided training facilities, sanctuaries, and weapons for guerrilla groups and terrorists. There are at least thirty-four known training facilities in Libya. They are specialized both in terms of personnel—with camps set aside for North Africans, as against Africans, as against Palestinians—and in terms of military training techniques with some teaching desert guerrilla tactics, others organized to teach demolition techniques, and still others for underwater warfare. Instructors from the Soviet Union, Cuba, East Germany, and several other Eastern European nations are reported to have trained recruits from Egypt, Sudan, Iraq, Algeria, Oman, Iran, Morocco, Italy, Yemen, Japan, Latin America, and the PLO. Colonel Muammar Kaddafi has been supportive of many guerrilla and terrorist organizations, including the IRA, a group of Palestinian organizations known as "Terrorist International" operating in western Europe, and Polisario, a group seeking to take control of the western Sahara from Mauritania and Morocco. He is accused of organizing ANYOLP, a terrorist group who hijacked a Luftansa airliner in 1973 and demanded the release of the three members of the Black September group who were involved in the attack on the 1972 Munich Olympics. He is also connected to "Carlos" and the group of terrorists who raided the OPEC ministers' meeting in Vienna in 1975. It is alleged that he has tried to assassinate or overthrow the governments of Egypt, the Sudan, Morocco, and Tunisia—all governments who are hostile to the Soviets. Kaddafi's terrorist activities rely heavily on the People's Bureaus, which, while serving as Libyan diplomatic missions in foreign countries, sometimes function as centers for purchasing arms, coordinating terrorist operations, and dispatching six-person hit teams to assassinate Libyan dissidents. In their efforts to control Libyan-sponsored terrorism, many western European nations began expelling Libyans connected to the People's Bureaus from their territories in 1986.

The ties between the Soviet Union and the PLO are multifaceted and well documented. The Soviets have been connected to the PLO since 1969, when several PLO terrorist operations against Israel fostered Soviet interest in the organization as a potential ally in the Middle East. In 1974 stronger ties between the Soviets and PLO leader Yasser Arafat were established after the Soviet Union allowed the PLO to set up a formal diplomatic office in Moscow that August and the Rabat Arab Summit Conference proclaimed the PLO as the sole representative of the Palestinian people in October. Since then the PLO has been granted embassy status. Soviet representatives and PLO leaders have met on a regular basis to coordinate policy and military actions. According to reliable sources, hundreds of meetings have been held between Soviet, Eastern European, and PLO leaders. On several occasions Arafat has met with the highest level Soviet Politburo members, including Soviet leaders Leonid Brezhnev and Yuri Andropov. During a six-week period in 1982, Arafat met seven times with the Soviet envoy to Beirut, Aleksandr A. Soldatov. Soviet leaders have consistently expressed their support of PLO aims and activities in the Middle East. In return, the PLO has declared common policy objectives with the Soviet Union on a worldwide basis. According to Arafat, the PLO and the Soviet Union are "in the same position against imperialism, Zionism, racial colonialism, and fascism."[6] In addition to these common political aims the Soviets and PLO have established extensive scientific and cultural ties, including the exchange of Soviet and Palestinian jurists and close cooperation between Soviet and Palestinian journalists. More importantly, they have a close intelligence and military operational relationship. In their discussion of the PLO-Soviet relationship in *Terrorism: The Soviet Connection*, American terrorist experts Ray S. Cline and Yonah Alexander offer several instances of KGB recruitment of PLO members and the sharing of intelligence between the KGB and PLO on potential terrorist targets in Israel. In one instance a Greek newspaper photographer was employed to send photographs of Israeli sites to KGB agents in East Berlin who in turn handed them over to PLO representatives. Reputable reports indicate that the Soviets have also provided training and arms to the PLO with more than one thousand members trained in the USSR since 1974 and thousands more trained in major camps in Hungary (Lake Balaton), Czechoslovakia (Karlovy Vary and Ostrava), Bulgaria (Varna) and East Germany (Pankow and Finsterwalde). The Soviet camp at Simferopol is said to be a primary training center of PLO cadres in sabotage and terrorism techniques with a special course in river crossing. PLO representatives reveal that the Soviet Union and other socialist countries have allowed PLO members access to their military academies through scholarship programs. It is reported that at the academies PLO cadres have received training in scientific and technical fields, political instruction in Socialism, Communism, and the Russian Revolution, tactical military exercises, topography, the use of light arms and hand grenades, expertise in explosive materials, air defense, and communications. PLO military officers from battalion commander on down through the ranks are reported to be graduates of Soviet and Eastern European military academies. Documents captured by Israeli forces in Lebanon in 1982 indicate that the Soviets have trained PLO members since 1973 and were aiming to build the PLO terrorist militia into a large regular army. To accomplish this mission the Soviets and their allies have supplied the PLO with enormous amounts of arms and tens of thousands of tons of ammunition, including T-34, T-54, T-55, and T-62 tanks, BM-21 and Katyusha rocket launchers, 60mm, 81mm, 120mm, and 160mm mortars, ZSU-4 radar guided anti-aircraft cannons, SAM-7 shoulder-launched missiles, SAM-9 anti-aircraft missiles, and thousands of antitank weapons.

The PLO has allegedly trained more than ten thousand revolutionaries from all over the world in camps in Lebanon, Syria, Algeria, Libya, Iraq, and South Yemen, including members of the terrorist Baader-Meinhof Group, the Italian Red Brigade, and the Basque ETA. Between 1980 and 1981 the PLO trained more than 2,250 foreign guerrillas from twenty-eight nations with the help of East German and Cuban advisors. The PLO has also supported Iranian leader Ayatollah Khomeini. In general, according to Cline and Alexander, the PLO plays a major role in enhancing Soviet interests as it serves as a "transmission belt for the export of KGB terrorists techniques to other regions and hence constitutes an essential element in Soviet regional and global strategy."[7] Even though the PLO is split into many factions, some of which are at war with each other and some of which, like the Democratic Front for the Liberation of Palestine, are stricter adherents to Moscow's policy than others, there is continued Soviet support for the PLO as an umbrella organization pursuing an independent Palestinian state. This support is obvious even as the Soviet Union, beginning in August 1986, seeks to upgrade its diplomatic ties with Israel for the first time since 1967.

During the 1970s the Soviets armed and trained the Syrian army. Syria suffered substantial losses in military hardware during Israel's invasion of Lebanon in 1982, but was rearmed by the Soviets once again. Damascus serves as the headquarters for several terrorist groups, including Al Saiqa, Muslim Brotherhood, and Abu Nidal, and its refugee camps are fertile recruiting grounds for Arab terrorists. In his discussion of Soviet connections to its clients in North Africa and the Middle East, Samuel Francis asserts that "The terrorism that has been conducted or sponsored by Libya and the Palestinians would not have been possible without Soviet support in the form of training and the provision of weapons. If the Soviets do not openly approve or oversee this terrorism, certainly they have done little to prevent or restrain it."[8]

Reportedly, the Soviet Union is also active in South African revolutionary movements principally through the presence of Cuban troops and East German advisors and in conjunction with Marxist governments in Angola and Mozambique. Both of these client states set up training bases for the Patriotic Front of Zimbabwe during the war against the white minority government of Rhodesia. Soviet, Cuban, and East German advisors trained members of ZAPU, and the South-West African People's Organization (SWAPO), in Namibia. East Germans trained Zimbabwe African National Union (ZANU) guerrillas in Mozambique and also the police forces of Mozambique and Ethiopia in North Africa. Cuban troops and advisors with the assistance of East Germany back up the government of Angola. Because of their support for the revolution against the white minority government of Rhodesia, the Soviets have some influence in Zimbabwe under the leadership of Robert Mugabe and in the South African guerrilla movement headed by the African National Congress (ANC). According to Soviet defector Dr. Igor S. Glagolev, the Soviets control the South African Communist Party, the ANC, and the South African Indian Congress. Former ANC member Batholomew Hlapane testified before the United States Senate Subcommittee on Security and Terrorism that the South African Communist Party was instrumental in the formation of the ANC's terrorist wing *Umkonto We Sizwe*, "The Spear of the Nation."

In western Europe the Soviets are connected to various left-wing individuals and organizations such as the IRA, Baader-Meinhof, the Turkish Revolutionaries, and Turkish People's Liberation Front, members of the Italian Red Brigade, including Renato Curcio, Alberto Franceschini, Giangiacomo Feltrinelli, Fabrizio Pelli and Augusto Viel, "Carlos," and Henry Curiel, the founder of the Egyptian Communist Party who supported the efforts of other western European terrorists until he was murdered in 1978 by a right-wing terrorist group called Organization Delta. The Eastern European Soviet client states of Hungary, East Germany, Bulgaria, and especially Czechoslovakia support these terrorist groups by supplying them with weapons and training. Czechoslovakian defector Jan Sejna testified that Italian terrorist leaders Alberto Franceschini and Giangiacomo Feltrinelli were trained in Czechoslovakia.

North Korea, a Soviet supporter state, has trained terrorists since 1967. Cline and Alexander claim its trainees have been traced to Latin America (Bolivia, Brazil, Colombia, Mexico), the Middle East, and Asia (Sri Lanka, Malaya, and Indonesia). North Korea was very active in the 1970s, having trained twenty-five hundred guerrillas and terrorists by 1975, arranged safe conduct for Palestinians and Japanese terrorists out of Singapore, coordinated in conjunction with East Germany terrorist activities in western Europe and provided sanctuary for the Japanese Red Army after they hijacked a Japan Air Lines aircraft in 1970.

Soviet Defense Infrastructure

Soviet revolutionary foreign policy goals and interests are organized and sponsored by an infrastructure that reaches to many of the major strategic places in the world. The so-called "nerve center" for this infrastructure is located in Moscow in the International Department of the Central Committee of the Communist Party of the Soviet Union, Soviet Military Intelligence (GRU), and the Soviet Security Agency (KGB). To aid in the Communist Party's revolutionary activities, the Soviets in 1967 founded the Lenin Institute in Moscow where members of Western and Third World Communist leaders have been trained in ideology, psychological warfare, armed and unarmed combat, and guerrilla warfare. Moscow's Patrice Lumumba Friendship University, established by Nikita Khrushchev in 1958, serves as a training center for non-Communist Third World "freedom fighters." According to Cline and Alexander, other training centers around the Soviet Union in

Baku, Odessa, Simferopol, Tashkent, and in and around Moscow provide more specialized training in guerrilla warfare and terrorism. The curriculum includes political films on subjects such as the Russian Revolution, Russian efforts in World War I and II; Soviet agriculture and industry; the lives and theories of Marx, Engels, Lenin, and Stalin, and Soviet ties to the Third World. Courses are also taught on the "Struggle against Imperialism," "Zionist Ties to Imperialism," "Expansionist Israel," "The Reactionary Nature of North Yemen and Saudi Arabia," "Egypt's Betrayal (at Camp David)," "Soviet Efforts on Behalf of Palestine Liberation," and Russian language courses. In addition to these political studies, the students are instructed for six months for three hours a day in subjects relating to incendiary charges and detonators, the art of mining munitions dumps, bridges, vehicles and personnel, exploding metals, chemical and biological warfare, commando field and escape tactics, urban guerrilla warfare, marksmanship and camouflage, and the use of Soviet weapons, including the Soviet RPG-7 rocket and shoulder-carried Strela missiles. Courses in these and other subjects are offered inside Russia and in Eastern Europe. According to Claire Sterling, thirty-five courses were offered in the Soviet Union, eight in East Germany, four in Bulgaria, four in Czechoslovakia, and three in Poland during 1977.

According to reliable sources, Cuba also trains Third World guerrillas, particularly from Latin America. A training center on an eighteen-hundred-acre estate near Guanabo offers a three-month course in urban guerrilla warfare and uses United States Special Forces manuals in the training. Other centers, like the one at Pinar del Rio, emphasize rural guerrilla operations, fabrication, use of false passports and documentation, and secret communications.

Libya has about twenty camps training more than eight thousand foreign recruits under the direction of Palestinian, Pakistani, Cuban, and former CIA and American Special Forces instructors. The better-known camps are located at Tarhuima, Zuwarah, Zawia, Baida, Sinawan, Tobruk, and Sebha. The largest center, which is capable of training five thousand people in a six-month infantry course, is located about forty-five miles from Benghazi.

East Germany also runs camps for the Soviets both in the German Democratic Republic and in South Yemen, Angola, Mozambique, and Benin with similar curricula in guerrilla warfare, surveillance methodology, the use of modern weaponry and how to set up and operate a terrorist network. In addition to these training camps, there is evidence that the Soviet Communist Party has set up some terrorist organizations far afield from its major areas of operation, such as the *Solidarité* and *Aide et Amite* network in Paris, France, headed by Henri Curiel until his death in 1978.

The provision of arms is also an important part of the Soviet terrorist infrastructure. Soviet- and Eastern-European-manufactured weapons can only be purchased directly through the Soviet Union and Eastern European countries, the People's Republic of China, or on the international black market. They can be obtained indirectly through Syria, Libya, South Yemen, Cuba, Angola, Mozambique, and Iraq. Probably the most common Soviet weapon used by revolutionary forces around the world is the Kalashnikov AK-47 assault rifle. Employed as standard issue by the National Liberation Front in South Vietnam and the North Vietnamese army in the 1960s and by many other Third World armies in the 1970s, the AK-47 is now in the hands of the IRA, Palestinians, Cubans, Sandinistas, and African nationalist groups like ZANU and Polisario. A newer version of the assault rifle is the Kalashnikov AKM. Among Soviet-backed terrorist groups, the Czech-made VX-58 assault rifle and the Skorpion VZ-61 machine pistol are also popular. The VZ-61 has been traced to a number of terrorist operations, including the Red Brigade's murder of Italian politicians Aldo Moro and chief prosecutor of Genoa Francesco Coco, assassination teams in Johannesburg, South Africa, the IRA, and "Carlos." Other weapons taken from terrorists or identified in terrorist operations are the Czech Vzor 7.65mm automatic pistol, the Soviet Makarov pistol, the Soviet Tokarev TT-33 pistol, the Czech Nagant pistol, the Soviet-made SAM-7 Strela surface-to-air missile and the Soviet RPG-7 rocket launcher. In addition to arming its supporters with the latest in Soviet weaponry, the Soviet Union and East Germany have supplied the PLO with MB-41 machine guns and ammunition, 57mm anti-aircraft cannons and ammunition, the Shilka NK; 37mm, 57mm, 100mm, and 122mm cannons and ammunition as well as automatic and improved automatic rifles. PLO warehouses are well stocked with spare parts for T-34 tanks, 122mm shrapnel shells and mortar shells, and other kinds of ammunition.

A third part of the Soviet terrorist infrastructure is the ideology network. Samuel Francis identifies three forms of Soviet ideology support for terrorists. First, there is overt endorsement of guerrilla insurgencies (national liberation movements) via the Soviet-controlled media such as *Pravda, New Times, World Marxist Review,* and Soviet-controlled broadcasting facilities. Second, there is covert Soviet-organized endorsement of terrorism through front groups like the World Peace Council (WPC) and the Afro-Asian Peoples' Solidarity Organization (AAPSO). Finally, Soviet ideology appears in the form of disinformation defined as the "dissemination of false or provocative information" organized through a special office in the KGB which attempts to blame terrorist acts on Western agencies and agents. For example, in the case of the kidnapping and murder of Italian politician Aldo Moro, Soviet and French Communist Party newspapers hinted at CIA and NATO involvement.

The ideological foundation of Soviet foreign policy is the revolutionary ideology of Marxism-Leninism. We will not attempt here an in-depth study of the theoretical formulations of Marxism and Leninism and the various contributions made by other Communist theorists. What is of central importance in our discussion of terrorism is that Marxism-Leninism maintains that class conflict is deemed inherent and a normal aspect of the history of humankind and that conflict is expected to be often expressed in violent form. Marx, Friedrich Engels, and Lenin are more circumspect about terrorism and have written that the tactics of terrorism, when practiced outside the organized political movement by anarchist or nihilists, are destructive to the Communist revolutionary cause. While political struggle is a major aspect of Marxist-Leninist revolutionary theory, armed struggle is seen as a natural concomitant of the proletarian class war against imperialism. Lenin argued it was up to the vanguard, now embodied in the Communist Party of the Soviet Union, to create the objective revolutionary conditions and give aid to the international revolutionary forces.

Marxism-Leninism remains the basis of Soviet strategy, although it has been greatly impacted by the coming of the nuclear age and the development of the Soviet revolutionary strategy of peaceful co-existence. Also, other leaders, including Mao Zedong and Lin Piao, Leon Trotsky and the Fourth International, Che Guevara, Franz Fanon, Herbert Marcuse, Regis Debray, and Carlos Marighella, have contributed to modern revolutionary theory. All of these theorists argue for an active role of revolutionary forces, using the means at their disposal to organize armed insurrection and political warfare against the yoke of imperialism in its colonial and neo-colonial forms.

Soviet support for revolutionary nations, groups, and organizations, some of whom are involved in terrorism, does not mean that the Soviets control all aspects of their operations. In most cases, it means that through their far-flung global systems the Soviets offer aid, weapons, and training to these groups without knowing precisely how and by whom it will be used. As Claire Sterling and other analysts who have researched the Soviet international terrorist system have argued, the Soviets put the gun on the table knowing that some of those who pick it up and use it are terrorists. In using the guns against the West, the groups of individuals, be they pro-Soviet or not, aid and abet the Soviets in their strategy of disruption and of creating havoc and chaos to destabilize and undermine the Western capitalist system. In short, as Samuel Francis concludes, "there is not sufficient evidence to prove that the Soviets directly or formally control, let alone coordinate or direct, many terrorist groups or activities, but there is massive evidence to show that Soviet support for terrorism is virtually essential for the scale and intensity of terrorist operations, for necessary logistical assistance to terrorist operations, for instigating a gradual public acceptance of terrorism as a 'legitimate' means of struggle."[9]

Soviet Terror in Afghanistan

Soviet military forces have occupied Afghanistan since December 1979. The Afghanistan "secret war" has been a large and costly venture for the Soviet Union, with estimates of Soviet army dead ranging from fifteen thousand to more than sixty thousand, forty-five thousand to ninety thousand wounded, and an annual cost to the Soviets of $12 billion by 1985. Soviet troop strength is presently estimated at around two hundred thousand, with six hundred fifty thousand Soviet soldiers having served in Afghanistan as of 1986. While the goals behind the Soviet invasion are subject to debate, there is little argument that the Soviet occupation has been marked by extreme brutality on both sides, particularly with regard to gross violations of the Geneva Convention on Prisoners of War. For example, American news sources reported that in late 1985 Afghan rebels were drugging and torturing between fifty and two hundred Soviet prisoners and forcing them to live in "indescribable horror" in cages. But, while constituting serious violations of human rights, these rebel atrocities pale in relation to the numerous incidences of Soviet terrorism.

In its occupation of Afghanistan and its attempt to "Sovietize" the country, the Soviet Union has used terroristic policies and cultural genocide and destroyed Afghanistan's social, religious, and cultural legacy while attempting to instill loyalty to Communist ideals. The Soviet campaign to depopulate the rural areas of Afghanistan to halt guerrilla resistance has removed fifty-three percent of the rural residents from their villages. Constant Soviet bombing and terrorism have forced the emigration of five million Afghans to Pakistan and Iran; the death of one million civilians; destruction or damage to fifteen thousand villages and hamlets; the slaughter of ten million livestock and incalculable damage to the nation's transportation and economic system.

Soviet leaders have attempted to tightly control the flow of information concerning their involvement in Afghanistan, in particular their military tactics, from both the world and the Soviet public. To this end they require army personnel to sign a secrecy agreement concerning their activities while in Afghanistan. Despite the Soviet news blackout, many reporters and diplomats have returned from Afghanistan full of horror tales of Soviet terror and massive atrocities, including the use of chemical warfare. The United Nations Commission on Human Rights in Geneva has attempted to closely monitor Soviet activities. In February 1986 the Commission heard the latest in a long series of reports detailing Soviet violations of human rights. The report from Felix Ermacora, an Austrian lawyer, accused Soviet and Afghan troops of pursuing a campaign of "systematic brutality" using sophisticated weapons, including bombs that explode twenty-four hours after impact, canisters of "liquid fire," a tar-like substance dropped from aircraft and new designs for booby-trapped toys. This report, charging that Soviet terror killed more than thirty-five thousand troops in 1985, updated many of the atrocities documented by a detailed interim report submitted by the United Nations Secretary-General to the General Assembly on November 5, 1985. Based on numerous depositions and interviews given to the Special Rapporteur of the Commission on Human Rights from individuals and organiza-

tions witnessing Soviet activity against the Afghan civilian population, this report, called *Situation of Human Rights in Afghanistan*,
stands as the most important documented account of Soviet terror
in Afghanistan to date and worthy of our close examination.

The report begins by detailing acts of brutality, including the
murder of women, children, and elderly people on a systematic
basis, committed by Soviet armed forces in their searches of
villages in several regions of Afghanistan during 1985. According
to witnesses, there is a regular pattern to Soviet troop behavior
following the bombardment of Afghan villages. In the words of the
Special Rapporteur:

> **Tanks surround the villages during the evening; in the
> morning, troops enter the villages—each village at the same
> time—houses are searched, money is demanded, women
> and children in particular are questioned, usually concern-
> ing the whereabouts of the menfolk, and during the interro-
> gation people are sometimes killed. After the withdrawal of
> troops, they return once again shortly thereafter and begin
> the same search procedure. In this context, Special Rappor-
> teur obtained information on an incident which took place
> on 2 February 1985 in the village of Sandaly in Nangarhar
> province, where soldiers, after overrunning the village, exe-
> cuted 20 people, including women, on the village square.**[10]

The report claims that from March 11 to 18, 1985, an estimated one thousand civilians were killed by the Soviet troops in
reprisal operations against twelve villages in Laghman province
during which "livestock was decimated, houses plundered and set
on fire, women raped and some of them summarily executed, and
several children locked up in a house were burned to death."[11] The
report claims these terrorist atrocities occurred in the villages of
Charbagh, Qarghay, Mindrawer, Kats Dehmezanj, Haider Khan,
Chalabajh, and Tchadihi. Between seven hundred and twelve
hundred civilians were massacred during a large-scale operation in
late March 1985, after which the Governor of Kundus province
decided to flee. Witnesses claim that during 1985 the Soviets
stepped up their systematic bombardment of Afghan villages using
FROG 7 ground-to-ground missiles which "wreaked destruction
on a larger scale than in the past."[12] The Special Rapporteur also

interviewed several victims of Soviet chemical warfare, some suffering with wounds from highly explosive devices called "nopalm."

Over the first nine months of 1985, the report says, 32,755 civilians were killed, 1,834 houses destroyed, 74 villages wrecked, and 3,308 animals killed. Refugees arriving in Pakistan claim that aerial bombardments have destroyed irrigation systems, crop fields, and livestock on massive levels.

In a section dealing with anti-personnel mines and booby-trap toys, witnesses claim that these weapons are now used regularly against the civilian population in areas where a large Soviet military operation is under way. Booby-trap toys, which are dropped by helicopter in rebel-held areas, are made to resemble pens, harmonicas, radios, matchboxes, and birds. Children, who find the toys along the road or who step on them and have their hands or feet blown off, are the main victims. One bomb is shaped and colored like a bird and consists of two wings, one flexible and the other rigid. It goes off when the flexible wing is touched. The records of an Afghan surgical hospital in Peshawa give vivid detail of the horrors of Soviet bombing and booby-trap toys visited on Afghan children. Among those listed as wounded were Mohamad Ighal, age 10, suffering from leg wounds; Amanullah, 14, wounded in both legs after stepping on a bomb; Abdul Rahmen, 12, bullet wounds in the right leg; Gamela, 11, wounds in both legs from Soviet machine-gun fire during a search of homes; Khatema, 11, who lost her parents and was seriously wounded during the bulldozer demolition of her home; Nyamatullah, 12, wounded in the head and arms when a bomb was thrown into her parents' house; and Mohamad Nuur, 10, who was blown up by a bomb and lost his leg below the knee.

The Commission's report also details the Soviet army's treatment of its prisoners, claiming that "prisoners belonging to the Afghan opposition movements taken by the army are executed on the spot; those who are suspected of belonging to opposition movements are tortured while being interrogated and are held without trial."[13] The report also details brutal treatment of prisoners by the rebel forces and concludes that in Afghanistan "as regards the treatment of prisoners the existence of the Geneva Convention is simply unheard of."[14]

The report states clearly the impact and purposes behind

Soviet terrorism in contested areas, concluding that "in these areas are devastated villages, partly or completely destroyed, which foreign and governmental forces are trying to devastate systematically to cut off supplies for the members of the opposition movements."[15]

Finally, in several vivid statements the report tells of the devastation of the economy and family, religious, and cultural life in Afghanistan as a result of the war and Soviet terrorism against the civilian population:

> 108. Generally speaking, the state of war endured by the Afghan population, by affecting all aspects of life, has only exacerbated the economic situation which had already begun to show signs of weakness in the 1970s.
>
> 109. The situation of children in Afghanistan has been particularly affected; whether they live in Kabul or in the main cities or whether they cross the border as refugees, the majority of the children who do not leave the country and who are not in the cities are helpless against the effects of high-altitude bombing and shelling, starvation and disease, the disruption of families and the destruction of family life and the collapse of the traditional structure.
>
> 110. There is apparently no health care for the majority of the population. As a consequence, the infant mortality has reached 300 to 400 per 1,000.
>
> 112. The Special Rapporteur also wishes to emphasize two new factors which illustrate the range of the actions taken in the country; on the one hand, a policy described as one of humiliation and religious intolerance, and, on the other hand, bombings of civilians during funerals.
>
> 113. Indeed, according to a number of witnesses, mosques have been desecrated, religious books destroyed and in some cases even used as toilet paper, while members of the Islamic faith have been obliged to eat pork and to drink alcohol. One witness from Qula, a village in the province of Kandahar, has described his feelings, based on an experience in February, 1985, as follows: "by destroying religious books and acting in that way, they hoped that Moslems would no longer fight in the name of Allah".

114. A number of witnesses stated that funeral processions accompanying the bodies of victims had also been bombed.

115. Another problem, caused directly by the vicissitudes of war, concerns the numerous orphans and abandoned children and the situation of women. In the traditional society, only children were always looked after by a family member and orphans did not exist as a known category. The fact that the traditional system has been destroyed, often as a result of the loss of the father of the family, has created, particularly among the refugees, a whole series of psychosomatic disturbances.[16]

Other sources report that, due to efforts to "Sovietize" the country, only eight million of Afghanistan's 1978 population of fourteen million were still in the country by the end of 1985. Representative of these reports is one by conservatives Jean-Francois Revel, a former columnist and editor of *L'Express* in France, and Rosanne Klass, director of the Afghanistan Information Center of Freedom House in New York City, charging the Soviets with a deliberate policy of attacking civilian targets, including wedding parties, farmers in their fields, villagers in the bazaars, and medical facilities. According to Revel and Klass, the Soviets "pursue, rocket, and strafe slow, plodding caravans of refugees—women and children, mostly—fleeing to sanctuary in Pakistan and Iran."[17] In April 1985, in one district alone "eight hundred people were slaughtered—from pregnant women and newborns to the aged—shot, burned alive, hanged, bayoneted, tortured, or beaten to death, killed with grenades, decapitated, mutilated."[18] Revel and Klass relate a story told by a French doctor of Soviet brutalization of an Afghan village after the defection of some Afghan troops in which "they tied them up and piled them like wood. Then they poured gasoline over them and burned them alive. They were old and young, men, women and children. Forty people were killed."[19]

Other accounts tell of twenty-seven thousand people being executed by the Soviets in Poli Charki concentration camp betwen April 27, 1978 and January 5, 1980, and of villagers being killed in a Soviet attack in June 1980 after which Soviet troops put the men's heads on the women's bodies and vice versa. In a report filed from Chamar Pass in October, 1984, journalist Edward Girardet, on special assignment for *US News and World Report*, tells of Soviet fighter jets swooping down from the skies and attacking a band of five hundred civilians, leaving forty dead and scores wounded. Girardet, who visited Afghanistan in 1981, says the country was very different in 1984 where "entire valleys of farms and villages have been turned into crumbling ghost settlements" by the Soviet policy of turning any region that continues to resist them into a wasteland.[20]

Girardet confirms what United Nations personnel and relief workers from around the world report as the purpose behind Soviet terrorism. According to Girardet, "The Kremlin's targeting of civilians clearly relies on the obvious inability of the rebels to provide the necessary support for survival. . . . With the country-side bereft of sympathetic civilians, the Soviets feel that the rebels cannot long hold out. They are heavily dependent on fellow Afghans for food, shelter, and, most important, local intelligence about enemy troop movements."[21]

As of late 1986 the problem for the Soviets is that their political strategy is only working slowly with regard to Afghan rebel forces. Complete Soviet occupation is possible but only by committing additional resources and increasing the scope of military action. The result of such a strategy would further Soviet casualties and possible unrest and resistance within the Soviet Union as well as worldwide condemnation. However, from the standpoint of humanitarian concerns, the current strategy of Soviet terrorism is decimating in horrific fashion an entire nation, its people and culture. This is another case where terrorism proves to be a successful political policy when pursued by a modern superpower. Regardless of intent, in the Soviet's "secret war" on Afghanistan, we have a case illuminating both the extent to which a superpower will go to hold onto and protect its interests and the level of carnage created by superpowers using terrorist tactics. In doing so, it helps substantiate the Middle View's major charge that the contemporary empire-building superpowers are active participants in and a dangerous force behind the contemporary explosion of terrorism.

UNITED STATES DEFENSE NETWORK

As the world's greatest power, the United States maintains a global empire that includes approximately three hundred forty

military bases in twenty-two foreign territories from Antigua and
Barbuda to Turkey. It has an extended system of support relationships with governments that receive aid and training from the
United States in exchange for protection of United States security
and economic interests and are instrumental in its counterrevolutionary strategy on a local and regional basis. The tables below
show states in a support relationship with the United States and to
whom the United States has given military aid as well as number of
nationals trained in the United States' military training program.[22]

US Military Aid

Europe

Greece	$2.7 billion (1946–75)
Portugal	$361.9 million (1946–75)
Spain	$920.2 million (1946–75)
Turkey	$4.5 billion (1946–75)

Latin America

Argentina	$263.6 million (1946–79)
Bolivia	$80.7 million (1946–79)
Brazil	$640 million (1946–79)
Chile	$217 million (1946–79)
Colombia	$240.9 million (1946–79)
Dominican Rep.	$43 million (1946–79)
El Salvador	$5 million (1946–79)
Guatemala	$41.5 million (1946–79)
Haiti	$5.9 million (1946–79)
Mexico	$100 thousand (1946–79)
Nicaragua	$32.4 million (1946–79)
Paraguay	$30.3 million (1946–79)
Peru	$239.7 million (1946–79)
Uruguay	$89.2 million (1946–79)
Venezuela	$152.3 million (1946–79)

Africa and Middle East

Tunisia	$62.4 million (1946–75)
Morocco	$138.7 million (1946–75)
Saudi Arabia	$295.9 million (1946–75)
Iran	$1.4 billion (1946–75)

Asia

Indonesia	$218.2 million (1946–75)
Philippines	$805.8 million (1946–75)
South Korea	$6.5 billion (1946–75)
South Vietnam	$16.5 billion (1946–75)

U.S. Military Trained Personnel

Europe

Greece	14,144
Portugal	2,997
Spain	9,878
Turkey	18,900

Latin America

Argentina	4,017 (1950–80)
Bolivia	4,896 (1950–80)
Brazil	8,659 (1950–80)
Chile	6,883 (1950–80)
Colombia	8,349 (1950–80)
Dominican Rep.	4,269 (1950–80)
El Salvador	2,097 (1950–80)
Guatemala	3,334 (1950–80)
Haiti	643 (1950–80)
Mexico	1,003 (1950–80)
Nicaragua	5,673 (1950–80)
Paraguay	2,018 (1950–80)
Peru	8,160 (1950–80)
Uruguay	2,806 (1950–80)
Venezuela	5,540 (1950–80)

Africa and Middle East

Tunisia	636
Morocco	2,209
Saudi Arabia	1,380
Iran	10,807

Asia

Indonesia	4,757
Philippines	15,245
South Korea	32,479
South Vietnam	35,788

The United States also has supporter relationships with Zaire
and South Africa in southern Africa and Israel in the Middle East.
President Mobutu Sese Seko of Zaire has been central to United
States interests since 1978 when White power in Rhodesia was
overthrown and the leftist forces won the power struggle created
by the Portuguese pullout in Angola. In addition to earlier support
of the Shah Mohammad Reza Pahlavi in Iran, Ngo Dinh Diem and
Nguyen Thieu in South Vietnam, and Ferdinand E. Marcos in the
Philippines, the CIA has funded $1.28 billion in military aid to
Zaire's leaders, particularly Mobutu and his army. Some of this
money has found its way into Swiss bank accounts. In one case,
Mobutu pocketed $1.4 million given to him by the CIA for distribu-
tion to Angolan counterrevolutionaries. In exchange for this aid
United States supporter countries are expected to protect American security interests and permit a United States military presence
if desired, including military bases, and create a favorable business
climate for American corporations by offering generous tax provisions, a quiescent labor force, profit repatriation, mineral claims,
and public spending for a transportation and communication
network that serves the private foreign section. However, many of
the United States supporters have closed their eyes to wholesale
misuse of United States funds.

Israel is a special case in United States supporter relations
because of its strategic importance in the Middle East. Between
1950 and 1984 United States military aid to Israel totalled $8.62
billion. In many ways the Israel-United States support partnership
is similar to the Soviet-Libyan relationship. Led by militant Zionist
leaders, particularly Menahem Begin and his Defense Minister
Ariel Sharon, Israel has often taken "independent" action to protect its own and Western interests in ways that raise contradictions
and difficulties for American policy-makers in much the same way
that Kaddafi's actions often do for Soviet leaders.

Yet there is a strong mutual interest or relationship between
the United States and Israel. Except from Arab sources and a few
rare Western scholars such as Alfred M. Lilienthal (*The Zionist
Connection*) and Noam Chomsky (*The Fateful Triangle*), we Americans know little about this relationship or American support for
Zionist terrorism.[23] It is Chomsky who takes us to the heart of this
special connection when, in discussing the charge levelled against
the few American critics of Israeli actions he writes:

It is surely hypocritical to condemn Israel for establishing settlements in the occupied territories while we pay for establishing and expanding them. Or to condemn Israel for attacking civilian targets with cluster and phosphorous bombs "to get the maximum kill per hit" when we provide them gratis or at bargain rates, knowing that they will be used for just this purpose. Or to criticize Israel's "indiscriminate" bombardment of heavily-settled civilian areas or its other military adventures, while we not only provide the means in abundance but welcome Israel's assistance in testing the latest weaponry under live battlefield conditions—to be sure against a vastly outmatched enemy, including completely undefended targets, always the safest way to carry out experiments of this sort. In general, it is pure hypocrisy to criticize the exercise of Israeli power while welcoming Israel's contributions towards realizing the U.S. aim of eliminating possible threats, largely indigenous, to American domination of the Middle East region.[24]

Israel's 1982 invasion of Lebanon and its bombing of civilians in Beirut are part of a long history of using terrorism to protect Israeli and American interests. For now, a clear example of Israeli terrorism and United States acquiesence to it was the recent Israeli air attack on the PLO "headquarters" in Tunis, Tunisia, in October 1985. The Reagan Administration initially condoned this terrorist act but then withdrew its public support after much of the world condemned the Israeli raid as an act of terrorism. In the future we should be prepared for continued American support of Israeli military policies, even when these include terrorist acts, since Israel's importance to American counterrevolutionary policy in the Middle East has increased dramatically now that the Shah of Iran is no longer available to support American interests and Turkey is not yet in a position to protect American power in the Persian Gulf.

The United States has also demonstrated extreme patience with South African terrorism and military aggression against its neighbors. The governing forces of South Africa invade its neighboring states and murder civilians. The most recent attack came in May 1986, when South African army troops struck at the capital cities of Botswana, Zimbabwe, and Zambia. South Africa also spends millions of dollars in American newspapers and on American politicians and academics propagandizing its cause. Neither its military aggression nor its propagandizing efforts have drawn meaningful criticism from or adverse relations with the United States supporter states. While he was in office, South Korean leader General Park Chung Hee engaged in extensive bribery of United States politicians for a number of years with no retaliatory action taken by the American government. Indeed, from 1950 to 1984 United States military aid to South Korea totalled $8.76 billion. Sudan's former President Jafar el Numeiry could round up thousands of people during the early 1980s in what Sudanese now describe as the "years of terror" or announce that he was training several hundred guerrillas for suicide missions in Libya to assassinate key members of Kaddafi's government without disapproval or accusations of terrorism from Reagan Administration officials. In July 1980 Argentina helped organize a right-wing coup in Bolivia to keep a democratically elected and reform-minded government from coming to power. The coup leaders, led by General Luis Garcia Meza Tejada, were major participants in international drug traffic and closely tied to organized crime in Bolivia. Argentina provided the coup leaders with a list of potential opponents of the new regime and sent advisors to instruct the Bolivian security forces in torture. The Carter Administration cut off aid to the Bolivian government for its gross violations of human rights following the coup but did nothing to Argentina for its intervention against democracy in Bolivia. From 1980 to 1984 United States military aid to Argentina's generals, several of whom have been convicted of gross human rights crimes including thousands of "disappearances," totalled $13.6 million. Ferdinand E. Marcos in the Philippines and Jean-Claude Duvalier in Haiti, both dictators recently deposed by their own people, were long supported by United States aid ($802 million in military aid for the Philippines alone between 1950 and 1984.)

In addition to military aid and military training of its supporter states' officer corps, the United States strengthens the satellite relationships through economic aid from both public and private American sources and the international financial institutions, in particular the International Monetary Fund and World Bank. When these organizations are unsuccessful, the United States has, at times, directly intervened with military force as it did in Guatemala in 1954 and in the Dominican Republic in 1965. There has been strong suspicion among many critics of the United States Latin American policy that the United States accepts or even condones counterrevolutionary subversion in its supporter states. For example, it has been alleged that in Latin America the United States supported and aided or participated in coups (Brazil, Chile, Dominican Republic, Ecuador), assassination or attempted assassination of leaders (Chile, Cuba, Dominican Republic), economic destabilization (Brazil, Chile, Cuba, Dominican Republic, Guatemala), buying political and military officials (Brazil, Chile,Cuba, Dominican Republic, Ecuador, El Salvador, Guatemala, Uruguay), disinformation (Brazil, Chile, Cuba, Equador, Uruguay), and subsidization of civil and social groups (Brazil, Chile, Ecuador, Uruguay) between 1950 and 1980. According to these sources, the purpose behind these different methods is to ensure that the right people are in power to carry out the proper programs that maintain and enhance United States public and private interests on a national and regional basis.

United States Defense Infrastructure

The American infrastructure of global defense takes several forms, but a major institution is the National Security States (NSS). Edward S. Herman, in his book, *The Real Terror Network*, calls the NSS "an instrument of class warfare, organized and designed to permit an elite, local or multinational to operate without any constraint from democratic processes."[25] The ideological basis of the NSS is the National Security Doctrine.

As a patron of the NSS, the United States has funded, armed, and trained the military of its supporter states in national security ideology and counterrevolutionary tactics. For example, United States training of the Latin American military began in earnest with the establishment in 1947 of the Inter-American Treaty of Reciprocal Assistance. It was given a large boost in 1951 with the Defense Department's Military Assistance Program (MAP) and became full-blown in 1961 with the development of United States global counterinsurgency policy. Since 1950 over five hundred thousand officers from eighty-five countries have been trained by the United States in its various institutes. The best known are the Inter-American Defense College at Fort McNair in Washington, D.C., the United States Army Institute for Military Assistance at

Fort Bragg, North Carolina, and the School of the Americas (known as the "School of Coups") located in Panama until 1984. Police officers from many parts of the world have attended the International Police Academy in Washington, D.C., where the curriculum includes lectures on basic electricity, introduction to bombs and explosives, and assassination weapons. A large part of the curricula in these military schools is centered on Communist and pro-American doctrine. Students are taught to recognize information that appears to run counter to United States interests. The range of subjects is very broad and includes courses on censorship, chemical and biological operations, briefings on the CIA, checkpoint systems, civil action and civic affairs, clandestine operations, counterguerrilla operations, defoliation, dissent in the United States, electronic intelligence, warfare and countermeasures, the use of informants, insurgency, intelligence, counterintelligence, subversion, countersubversion, espionage, counterespionage, interrogation of prisoners and suspects, nuclear weapons effect, intelligence photography, populace and resources control, psychological operations, raids and searches, riots, special warfare, surveillance, terror, undercover operations, handling of mass rallies and meetings, and cryptography. In a symposium called "Population Protection and Resources Management" given to Latin American police agents at Fort Bragg, the students are taught such techniques as search operations, checkpoints, curfew, national identity card system, and block control to monitor the movement of people and goods. Other subjects included the role of the mass media and pro-government propaganda.

Under the controversial Public Safety Programs, which were discontinued in 1975 under Congressional orders but restarted under the Reagan Administration, the United States has also sponsored national training centers and institutes in its supporter states. For example, in Brazil, the United States participated in the construction, equipment, and development of curricula, faculty, and staff at Brazil's National Police Academy, National Institute of Criminology and Identification, and National Telecommunications Center. Police agents and military officers from Chile, Paraguay, Bolivia, and Uruguay have been trained at these institutions. It is through these institutions that the National Security Doctrine of the NSS is spread. In *The Real Terror Network* Edward Herman argues that there is a causal relationship between the rise of police and military training and aid provided by the United States in the 1950s and 1960s and the epidemic of physical torture, estimated to have claimed hundreds of thousands of victims, on a systematic basis in United States supporter states and other allies within its sphere of influence over the same period.

Respected sources indicate that part of the NSS infrastructure is the so-called "death squad" composed of "off-duty" regular military, police, and intelligence personnel. Research by Amnesty International in Argentina shows that the death squad has been incorporated into the organizational structure of Argentina's security apparatus with a small operational force set up within each section of the armed forces for the eradication of "subversion." Terror, kidnappings, torture, and murder by death squads said to be "out of control" allows the NSS to deny responsibility for these terrorist acts. But it is reported by reputable sources that death squad members report their activities to military and political officials and that their members are current and former military and police personnel. Contrary to the mythology surrounding their alleged independent activities, the operation of squads in the National Security States are carried out under the orders of state authorities. Their role is to eliminate "subversives" and to intimidate the rest of the population into quiescent submission and obedience to national security needs.

During the United States military and intelligence involvement in Southeast Asia, the exact number of civilian deaths inflicted by indiscriminate use of both ground and aerial firepower is unknown but conservatively estimated at 400,000 dead, 900,000 wounded, and 6.4 million refugees. According to United States military officials, including Army Chief of Staff General Howard K. Johnson, the United States used indiscriminate violence and killing of civilians as a basic part of its war-making strategy. Johnson admitted that "We have not enough information. We act with ruthlessness, like a steamroller, bombing extensive areas and not selected targets based on detailed intelligence."[26] In addition to the well-documented My Lai massacre and the Vietnamese Tet Offensive are the United States Army's Operation Speedy Express and the CIA's Phoenix Program. Conducted during the first six months of 1969, Operation Speedy Express consisted of air strikes, using napalm, anti-personnel bombs, and high explosives against the guerrillas and civilian population in the Mekong Delta province of

Kien Hoa. At the end of the operation estimates of enemy dead were placed at 10,899 but only 748 weapons were captured. Later, it was discovered that unarmed "enemy" farmers were gunned down as they worked the rice fields and civilian villages were leveled. There is little doubt that the Phoenix Program, allegedly organized by the CIA, had used counterterror measures. The South Vietnam government estimated that this counterterrorist program aimed at the National Liberation Front's political infrastructure resulted in the death of 40,994 suspected enemy civilians from 1968 through 1971. Michael J. Uhl, a former military intelligence officer, gave his opinion on the priorities of those carrying out the orders of the CIA agents and the Phoenix Program director and later head of the CIA William Colby. Uhl testified that a Phoenix MI team "measured its success . . . not only by its 'body count' and 'kill ratio' but the number of CDs, (civilian detainees) it had captured. . . . All CDs because of this command pressure . . . were listed as VCI. To my knowledge not one of these people ever freely admitted being a cadre member. And again, contrary to Colby's statement, most of our CDs were women and children."[27] Perhaps the most telling evidence is American overt and covert bombing of civilian populations over North and South Vietnam, Laos, and Cambodia ordered by Presidents Lyndon Johnson and Richard Nixon. In Southeast Asia there are widespread reports of America's alleged use of terrorist tactics. Allegedly, Thailand, a major American supporter state in Asia, served as a landlocked aircraft carrier for United States air strikes, a "rest and recreation" stop for war-weary American troops, and a source of hired mercenaries. There are many indications that in 1965 the Johnson Administration hired South Korean troops for its Vietnam war effort. The systematic terrorist acts of these "rented soldiers" became public knowledge in 1972 when it was discovered that these "fierce" troops had committed My Lai-type massacres, with the bulk of those slaughtered being women and children and that the truth about those attacks was known by many American authorities.[28]

Apart from the Vietnam War, the United States allegedly backed several terrorist surrogate operations during the 1970s. One of the most important was the Cuban refugee network which was said to be armed and trained by the CIA in preparation for the Bay of Pigs invasion in 1961. These terrorists operate under various names, including Alpha 66, Omega 7, Brigade 2506, the Cuban Nationalist Movement (CNM), and the Commandos of United Revolutionary Organization (CORU). We have already discussed some of the activities of these groups against some members of the Cuban exile community in the United States and against Cuban diplomats and diplomatic installations around the world. Many reports allege that such efforts were made in conjunction with the CIA and aided at times by the mafia in the United States. Reputable sources report that these groups have conducted a "secret" war against Cuba for the past twenty-five years and have attempted to assassinate Cuban leader Fidel Castro at least eight times.

Operation Condor is another organization operating within the United States's sphere of influence. Organized in 1976 by Chilean dictator Augusto Pinochet, a United States supporter, and his secret police chief Manuel Contreras, Operation Condor is the culmination of a long-sought United States objective to coordinate the activities of the internal security forces in Latin America. It has operated effectively as a collective monitoring and assassination network of dissident refugees from Latin America National Security States. Member states in this operation include Argentina, Bolivia, Brazil, Chile, Paraguay, and Uruguay. According to reliable sources in the FBI, the scope of operations includes kidnapping, torture, and murder by members of Operation Condor. Allegedly these operations extend beyond the member states and "involves the formation of special teams from member countries to travel anywhere in the world to non-member countries to carry out sanctions, (including) assassinations, against terrorists or supporters of a terrorist organization from Operation Condor member countries."[29] It is reported that kidnapping-murder victims number in the hundreds and possibly thousands. Sources indicate that at least two hundred Uruguayan political refugees who had settled in Argentina have been kidnapped and murdered by Uruguay's security forces. Under the cooperative agreements of Operation Condor the Uruguayan forces were allowed to enter Argentina and, with the aid of Argentinian security forces, track down, kidnap, and murder the dissidents. In the fall of 1976, the terrorism of Operation Condor and the Chilean intelligence service DINA reached into downtown Washington, D.C., with a car bombing that killed former Chilean Ambassador to the United States Orlando Letelier and American citizen Roni Moffitt. Recently DINA has been mentioned in connection with the 1986 assassination of Swedish Prime Minister Olaf Palme. Although no firm connection has yet been established, convicted DINA assassin Michael Townley says Palme was targeted for murder by DINA in Madrid, Spain, in 1976.

In the 1970s the Reagan Administration has increased its support of anti-Communists who are also terrorists in several parts of the world. We have discussed the Contras in Nicaragua and the air war over El Salvador. As of September 1985, Moslem rebels fighting the Soviet army and Soviet-backed government forces in Afghanistan had received $250 million in covert CIA funds. In 1986 Congress passed military aid packages to guerrilla forces in Afghanistan ($300 million) and Angola ($15 million). As of 1985 American "secret" aid to Cambodia rebels was estimated to be around $5 million. The administration has considered supplying the rebels in both Afghanistan and Angola with advanced anti-aircraft missiles such as the hand-held Stringer or Redeye, the British-made Blowpipe, and heavy anti-aircraft cannons. As part of its new global anti-terrorism offensive, the United States is once again training national police forces around the world in anti-terrorist techniques.

In these and other efforts to support its NSS network, the United States has provided billions of dollars which have been used for arms of all kinds. American military aid to El Salvador typifies the standard equipment for the NSS armed forces. The Belgian-made G-3 rifle and the United States Army's M-16 rifle are the mainstay weapons. The interior security forces are armed with the United States M-1 Garand rifle while the National Police have the .38 Smith and Wesson United States-made revolver, M-1 carbines and M-1 rifles. Heavier weapons include recoilless rifles, .30- and .50-calibre and M-60 machine-guns, mortars, rocket and grenade launchers, fragmentation grenades, and millions of rounds of submachine cartridges. The Israeli Uzi submachine gun is most often used by NSS death squad members. The major aircraft for the counterinsurgency mission in El Salvador and other Latin American nations include United States-supplied C-47 transports, Bell Uh-1h helicopters, Cessna A-37B "Dragonfly" fighters and Cessna 0-2A "Skymaster" control spotters, Brazilian EMBRAER EMB-11 patrol aircraft, Israeli Arava STOL aircraft, and Fouga Magister trainers and French-supplied fighter bombers and trainers. These aircrafts dropped five hundred pound bombs on the civilian populations as well as on military targets in the counterinsurgency air war in El Salvador.

Like the Soviet Union "propaganda" and "information" network, the United States has its own network centered in the multiple programs run by the United States Information Service (USIS), the CIA, and State and Defense Departments. Major programs include Radio Free Europe, Voice of America (broadcasting into the Soviet Union and Eastern Europe), Project Truth, and the new Radio Marti, which is aimed at Cuba. The USIS is the principal agency coordinating educational, cultural, academic, and political programming about "The American way of life" for public and private officials and causes on a worldwide basis. The organizational chart of the USIS Bureau of Programs includes a Policy Guidance Staff, International Communications Policy Staff, Media Reaction Staff, three Foreign Press Centers, and two Media Services. The Voice of America produces and broadcasts news reports and analyses, editorials, and cultural programs over the radio in English and in forty-two other languages.

Disseminating information about America has always been an important part of American foreign policy, and this policy has been strengthened under the Reagan Administration. One example of an administration public-private effort is the National Endowment for Democracy, which has funded $375,000 to Leonard Sussman's Freedom House, a conservative human-rights organization. The funds are being used to set up what is called "a network of democratic opinion leaders . . . to end the isolation of democratic-minded intellectuals and journalists in the Third World."[30] Sussman's Exchange, as it is called, sends out "democratic" articles "representing no ideological bias" to outlets in each continent. So far, the authors of the distributed articles have been mainly neoconservatives such as Bernard Levin, Vladimire Bukovsky, Andre Gluckman, Jean-Francois Revel, Paul Johnson, Chapman Pincher, George Urban, Lord Beloff, and a smattering of more traditional conservatives and Eastern European dissidents. Their articles are printed in conservative publications like the *The Daily Telegraph* and *The Times*, both in London, *The Wall Street Journal*, and the *Daily Cleaner* from Jamaica. They have covered revolutionary activities in Afghanistan, Tibet, Angola, Poland, Grenada, Ethiopia, the Ukraine, and Cuba. The Exchange has distributed no information on the popular upheavals in Haiti nor on democratic activity in South Korea, Taiwan, Pakistan, Egypt, or Indonesia. Not one liberal or leftist writer is represented on the Exchange. Ideology is also playing an important role in building support for the anti-Communist rebels in Afghanistan, Angola, and Cambodia. In 1985 Congress approved $500,000 for a program to train the Afghan rebels in public relations and media techniques. Taking an active role in the counterrevolutionary campaign, President Reagan summoned rebel leaders from Afghanistan, Angola, and Nicaragua to Washington in the first half of 1986. In his campaign for further funding and popular support and their respective anti-Communist causes, Reagan introduced the rebel leaders to the American public and Congress, calling them "freedom fighters" in the struggle against international Communism and terrorism. Yet many allegations of "terroristic" conduct and violations of human rights on the part of these leaders have been made known.

The Middle View's first major point of departure from the currently held perspectives on terrorism is that the superpowers must accept their part of the responsibility for the current explosion of terrorism rather than laying blame solely on countries such as Iran, Libya, Syria, or imperialistic America or the evil Soviet Union, depending on whom is viewed as "the other side." Even in our skeleton account of the global military systems of each superpower it becomes clear that both the United States and the Soviet Union have at their commands a vast array of weapons, military and economic aid, and military expertise. The point is that, as superpowers with global interests and goals, both the Soviet Union and the United States cannot avoid nor have they avoided contact or involvement with terrorist elements in their supporter states. This occurs because the supporter states of each superpower are of central importance to the promotion and protection of superpower interests, be they revolutionary or counterrevolutionary. As abhorrent as we find it, such a connection to terrorism is seen as preferable and less threatening to the world and particularly to superpower interests than the other, more publicized, terrorism: nuclear holocaust. This does not mean we should breathe a sigh of relief and learn to ignore low-level terrorism as the lesser of two evils. But we should realize that there is on the part of both Soviet and American policymakers an acceptance of this kind of terrorism because it has proven to be an effective way to gain other goals and to counter threats to their power or interests in their respective spheres of influence.

The second assumption of the Middle View is that terrorism is a permanent feature of international politics. This revelation, which follows from the recognition that terrorism occupies a major place in superpower and minor power strategy, is disturbing because it runs counter to our best hopes and dreams. It also contradicts the underlying assumption of the American and the Soviet public views of terrorism through which both assert that if the terrorism or the sponsorship of terrorism by the other side could be brought to a halt or effectively countered the current explosion of terrorism would come to a quick end.

The Middle View's argument that terrorism is a permanent feature of our world stems first and foremost from the reality that terrorism is a part of the superpower struggle for global supremacy, particularly with the continued presence of nuclear weapons holding human existence in the balance. Thus, continued use of terrorism is guaranteed as long as it serves the interests of the two dominant powers. This prediction of the future rests on a realistic reading of the past. The history of the great empires, beginning with Rome and continuing through Charlemagne, Genghis Khan, Pax Britannia, and Hitler's Third Reich is one in which terrorism played an important role in both the consolidation and the protection of the imperial order. It is only realistic to assume that nations and groups who struggle for bounty, territory, supremacy and/or liberation against outward forces and each other will use terroristic means when it is in their interests do so. In addition, as long as terrorism remains a politicized and partisan issue, it will retain its effectiveness as a vehicle employed to mold and mobilize domestic and world opinion. While the level of rhetoric will rise and fall over time, we can expect to be hearing about our enemies' acts of terrorism for some time to come. In short, both terrorism and accusations about "the other side's" terrorism can be expected to be with us for the forseeable future.

Furthermore, terrorism will be a permanent feature in our lives because for many frustrated individuals and powerless groups terrorism either is or is thought to be an effective way to achieve their individual or collective goals. We know that some individuals are driven to terrorist acts by their personal pathologies. Unless we devise some way to detect and control all human pathologies, on this basis alone terrorism will be a permanent fixture. More importantly, the essence of the human condition has been and remains the pursuit of the "cause." History indicates that terrorism has been part of the search for freedom, for self- and national identity and various forms of self-determination, be it for religious, ethnic, national, racial, or sexual reasons. For example, a major part of contemporary Armenian terrorism has its roots in the early part of the twentieth century. Croatian nationals hijack airplanes as part of a longstanding struggle for national identity. Tamil terrorism in Sri Lanka and Sikh terrorism in India have ethnic and religious bases. Both political ideology and religion motivate the IRA. The recent explosion of Middle Eastern terrorism stems from a combination of factors, some historical, as in the case of the Palestinian-Zionist conflict, and some tied to the contemporary resurgence of the Moslem world and the Moslem revolution in Iran which has placed the reins of state power in the hands of religious zealots. In the United States religious and racially motivated terrorism is older than the Republic. Current anti-Castro, anti-Sandinista terrorisms are products of reactions to foreign revolutions in Cuba in 1959 and Nicaragua in 1979, whereas the growing anti-abortion terror stems from a 1979 Supreme Court decision. In short, causes and the fanaticism that often accompanies them cannot be expected to end soon or even subside.

The Middle View agrees with the many terrorism experts who argue that the contemporary explosion of terrorism can be tied in part to the opportunities and vulnerabilities stemming from the interdependence of the world's communicaiton and transportation networks and energy systems. In the context of interdependence, the disruptive proportions of the fanatical pursuit of causes are incalculable. As the world "shrinks" even further, those opportunities and vulnerabilities will only increase, giving more terrorists more reasons to hijack a plane, take hostages for publicity purposes, or tamper with the water supply of a metropolitan area as part of their "revolutionary" strategy or pathological act of revenge. We already know that the best security arrangements at airports or nuclear facilities can deter terrorism but cannot halt it completely. Tight restrictions on media coverage of "terrorist events" or news events in general can limit publicity but cannot eliminate it. The Middle View thus warns us that because of the basic human condition and the state of technological development being what they are and are likely to be we must expect terrorism by individuals and by groups and by states, be they superpowers or not, to be a permanent fixture in ours and our children's lives as it has been in our parents' and grandparents' times.

But the Middle View accepting these existing facts and hypothesis about the realities of terrorism structures a new framework that allows us to approach terrorism and counterterrorism from a less politicized and manipulative perspective than offered by either the American or the Soviet view. For instance, by recognizing that both superpowers as well as minor powers are involved in terrorism, that they all "put the gun on the table" for their own purposes, a totally different context of discussion and debate concerning terrorism is created. Indeed, our whole notion of the political nature of terrorism changes. Even if it allows us to take only the small step from debates over who is the terrorist to whom is the worst terrorist, our political context has changed, it is hoped, for the better. For example, adherence to the Middle View means that both superpowers and minor powers commit evil acts—if by evil we mean terrorist. If we, the public, accept this, superpower policymakers on both sides could no longer manipulate national or world opinion by simply placing the black hat of the terrorist on their enemy's head and dressing themselves up in the white garb of the anti-terrorist crusader. Thus, both powers would be forced to change their propaganda pitches for their respective systems, since terrorism would no longer be available for their manipulative purposes. Presumably this would lead to a more meaningful and less rhetorical dialogue. But even if government leaders are unwilling to acknowledge their overt roles in terrorism, a knowledgable public may force the issue and change either leaders or public policy.

The Middle View also helps us better comprehend many of the complex issues of the contemporary political world. For instance, it may help many of us understand why Americans and Soviets are singled out by Moslem terrorists in the Middle East. The murderous attack on the American Marines in Beirut in 1983 has more complex implications when we understand that their "peacemaking mission" was accomplished by the indiscriminate shelling of Lebanese villages from the decks of the American battleship *New Jersey*. The kidnapping and killing of Soviet diplomats in Lebanon take on a different light for Soviet citizens if connected to the Soviet war against Moslem rebels in Afghanistan. The Middle View will not lessen our outrage at the kidnapping of 104 American hostages from a TWA flight, but it will allow us to have a better understanding of the similar outrage of the families, friends, and national communities of the hundreds of Lebanese hostages held by Israel at the same time. It is just possible that with this different level of understanding and outlook that both kidnap victims and those affected by their hostage status will redirect their outrage at the culpability of all sides in the Middle East conflict rather than pointing an accusing finger at whomever appears to be the villain of the moment.

In the same way, if we accept the source of terrorism as being in the human condition rather than viewing it as a result of some temporary sinister godless force, our outrage at its occurrence and its perpetrators is not reduced. But our anger, instead of automatically turning toward vengeful thoughts and acts, has a better chance of being channelled toward trying to comprehend the frailties and deficiencies of the world we have built and trying to correct them. We are also less likely to be politically vulnerable to the pitches made by political leaders that we should support their military actions since they are aimed at bringing an end to terrorism and then eventually watching these actions fail and bring about increasing terrorism.

If the terrorism issue is to be depoliticized at all and its manipulative qualities decreased, we must approach the explosion of terrorism through a framework through which we can distinguish rhetoric from reality, thereby offering the possibility that such meaningless rhetoric will not be acted upon. This is an important step as it is well established that rhetoric that is ignored or fails to evoke the desired reaction is of no use to politicians and is usually discarded.

A major breakthrough in depoliticizing the terrorism issue would be to reach an agreement on a definition of terrorism and have it applied consistently regardless of the political persuasion of terrorists. A universal definition is unlikely at this time, given the current diversity of political opinion and the polarized international climate, but we must work toward this event. And if the prescriptions of the Middle View guide our vision of terrorism and from what source it springs, a more objective context is created which allows us to confront those who play politics with the terrorism issue. For instance, it would be more difficult to mobilize public opinion against specific political forces by accusing them of terrorism or terrorist sympathies if we understood that terrorism was not the exclusive province of any one constituency. If we accepted that acts of "terrorism" were substantively akin to acts under the direction of those pointing the accusing finger, our reaction would be more sober, more restrained, and more politically astute. We would be less vulnerable to the machinations of political crusaders who justify the terrorism of their own "freedom fighters" or who seek fundamental changes in the democratic political order by taking advantage of the current political biases expressed in the terrorism issue. For this to occur, we must expand our portrait of whom the terrorist is from our current vision as presented in popular film and on television or as developed by certain terrorist theorists. Our new vision must include men and women in gray suits and military uniforms of all political persuasions, and we must cope with the unfortunate reality that terrorism is here to stay. Only then can the dangerous political biases evident in the American and the Soviet views be challenged. This is exactly what the Middle View proposes to do.

In the following chapters, we shall explore why the Middle View is needed if we are to understand the complexity and permanency of the explosion of terrorism. We shall also examine how, during the 1970s, conservative governments in Great Britain and West Germany mobilized the democratic populace behind the politicized "ideology of terrorism" to install many aspects of their preferred political order of "authoritarian democracy" and in doing so eroded many cherished liberal democratic rights.

NORTHERN IRELAND, GREAT BRITAIN, AND TERRORISM

By the 1980s many of the industrial democracies, like West Germany, Britain, Italy, Sweden, and France, who experienced terrorism during the 1970s had passed anti-terrorist legislation. Even in states only marginally affected by terrorism, preliminary preparations for anti-terrorist legislation were made if not implemented. In every case, the deliberations, enactment, and application of this legislation have provoked a debate between civil rights organizations and state officials on the proper balance between state powers and individual rights. In most instances, terrorism is either undefined or its definition applied arbitrarily and is treated as a criminal offense. In every case the adoption of emergency laws or permanent legislation has increased the powers of state security agencies.

THE PREVENTION OF TERRORISM (TEMPORARY PROVISIONS) ACT OF 1974, 1976

First introduced as temporary legislation in 1974, the Prevention of Terrorism Act (PTA) was amended in 1976 and has been renewed on a yearly basis.[1] This legislation, coming in the wake of two bomb blasts in Birmingham that killed 21 people and injured 180 others, passed unanimously through both Houses of Parlia-

184

ment in only seventeen hours. The act, which extends executive and police powers to an unprecedented level, consists of three major parts. Part I deals with proscribed organizations and empowers the Home Secretary to ban any organization that appears to be involved in or encouraging terrorism in the United Kingdom and connected to Northern Irish affairs. Persons who belong to the proscribed organizations, or who solicit or invite financial or other support for the organizations, are subject to fine, imprisonment, or exclusion from Britain. Part II gives the Home Secretary the power to exclude persons from or prevent entry to the British mainland. If the Home Secretary believes the person is or has been concerned with the commission, preparation, or instigation of acts of terrorism—or may be entering Britain with the intention of doing so—that person may be denied entry to the country. Under section 7, the person has the right to appeal the decision to the Home Secretary.

Part III deals with the arrest and detention of those suspected of terrorism. It gives the police the power to arrest without warrant any person they suspect of being guilty of an offense under part I or part II and to detain a person up to forty-eight hours for interrogation. With permission from the Home Secretary, this detainment period can be extended for five days, and, if the arrest is made at a port of entry, for an additional five days. During this detainment, the person cannot have legal representation, does not have to be charged or brought before a court, and can be photographed and fingerprinted without consent, using "reasonable force." Police may stop and search any person without a warrant; the law allows the police to search every person found on the premises. Finally, the police have the power to arrest any person they suspect of withholding information about terrorism or information that might prevent an act of terrorism.

Critics have attacked the PTA on both general and specific grounds. As a general piece of legislation, members of the Irish community have compared it to the South African apartheid legislation whereby people can be removed from areas they have lived in for years to far-away places simply because they are a nuisance to government authorities. Other critics point out that the act was passed unaccompanied by a definition of terrorism and attack the ambiguity, evasiveness, and the broad discretionary powers to state officials. Many people agree with Roy Jenkins, who was Home Secretary when the act was passed in 1974 and who was the first to publicly call the law "draconian." During the first four months of the act, Jenkins's label seemed appropriate: of the three people charged under part I two were subsequently freed with charges dropped; forty-five Exclusion Orders were approved and only five to eleven appeals were successful; and while police detained 489 people at police stations, only 16 were accused of a criminal offense.

From the outset, civil liberties groups in Britain have raised fundamental questions about the PTA and its interpretation and application by the police. For example, the National Council for Civil Liberties objected to the 1979 renewal of the act on a number of counts:

1. The police already have sufficient powers to arrest people they suspect of a terrorist act.

2. Extended powers of arrest for questioning are likely to encourage the police to indulge in "fishing expeditions" (arrest and interrogation of unlikely suspects) in order to gather low-level intelligence.

3. Prolonged periods of detention of arrestees not suspected of any particular crime will have no meaning without a widespread disregard of the Judges Rules.

4. The attitude amongst the police, who have tended to treat all detainees as "terrorists," together with the stigma of arrest of suspects.

5. The power to photograph and fingerprint every person arrested under the act and retention of these by the police is a serious infringement of privacy for innocent people.

6. The existence of the act creates the impression that the police have general powers to detain persons for interrogation in cases that are not connected with terrorism. The police seem to have taken advantage of the misunderstandings by the public.

7. The NCCL believes that the power of detention for up to seven days violates the European Human Rights Convention and in particular Article 5.[2]

Several issues raised by the NCCL have substance to them. Some members of the Irish community in Britain have charged that the act is being used to intimidate political activity by Republican groups unconnected to the violence of the Irish Republican Army (IRA), and that people are being stopped, arrested, and detained not because they are terrorists but because they are Irish. For example, 801 of the 3,162 persons arrested under the act between 1974 and 1977 were taken off the ferries, the trains at Lime Street Station, and aircraft at Speke Airport by Merseyside police in Liverpool, a major port of entry from Ireland. Ulster Member of Parliament Gerry Fitt charged that most of the arrests were unnecessary and not one conviction had resulted from the cases with which he was familiar. Police repression and surveillance are also well documented against those in the Irish community who support Irish Republicanism, a legal political stance. It is claimed that in the attempt to discredit the Republican political movement, the police treat all those who favor an Irish Republic in Northern Ireland as terrorists. The vagueness surrounding which organizations are proscribed and on the meaning of "support" is said to be a deliberate effort to frighten the Irish community into self-censorship. Dawn raids by police in the Irish communities are common. One elderly Irish man who had lived in Birmingham for twenty-seven years and had never joined a political association of any kind found himself arrested in his home early one morning by twelve officers who had the power to take over his house if they desired. When police come looking for one person they often end up arresting everyone on the premises. Members of the Irish working class, like construction workers who live together in large lodging houses, often find themselves arrested en masse when police come looking for one suspect. These and other members of the Irish community have been brought before a court after a period of detention and convicted of "wasting police time," a charge allegedly made in lieu of any concrete accusation or if the accused did not have the information the police were seeking. As well, the power of exclusion is used against the Irish and other citizens considered to be involved in "deviant" politics or whose deportation is judged to be "conducive to the public good."

Figures released after the first two years of the PTA support the charges that the laws were being used against the Irish community rather than for capturing terrorists. During this period, 2,101 people were held by police for up to 7 days. Only 101 were accused of offences and only 10 were charged with crimes under the PTA. Ninety-one exclusion orders were issued and eighty-one served, with only five withdrawn on appeals. Fourteen supporters of the British Withdrawal from Northern Ireland Campaign were arrested and charged with conspiracy to contravene the 1934 Incitement to Disaffection Act for distributing a leaflet entitled "Some Information for Discontented Soldiers." The eleven-month trial ended in acquittal on thirty-one counts.

The NCCL charge that the act allows the police to engage in low-level intelligence work and political harassment is confirmed by a number of cases. The long investigation into the Angry Brigade bombings is one case in point. Several hundred "fishing expeditions" were conducted by police over several months in 1972 and again in 1973. In raids on the International Socialists, the International Marxists, and the libertarian Left, quantities of documents were taken away and recorded. In one raid, among the several hundred items carried off for examination were six chopsticks, a sheet of paper with the words "shish-kebab" written on it, a roll of toilet paper, and two clothespins. These raids provided no evidence of any link between the Angry Brigade bombings and the membership lists of the raided organizations but did afford the opportunity for the gathering of intelligence. In their investigation into the application of the PTA, the authors of *State Research* allege a shift of emphasis in police procedures from use of the major powers of the act to its peripheral powers. They charge that "In the earlier period people already resident in Great Britain were arrested by police more often in proportion to arrests or detention of people coming into the country . . . the emphasis has shifted to control at ports and airports. The statistics issued by the government show that very few indeed of those detained at the ports are subsequently charged or made the subject of exclusion orders. The act is now being used mainly at ports . . . as a means of harassment and attempted information gathering."[3]

The British Trade Union movement and leftist political groups have echoed the charge that the police use the PTA as an instrument of general political repression. During the 1970s thousands of people were stopped, arrested, and detained; hundreds were charged, yet only a handful have been convicted of terrorism. By 1977 the bombings had stopped, yet more people were excluded during 1977 than since the early days of the PTA. Of those people excluded from Britain, most went to Northern Ireland, where between 1974 and 1978 only one person was charged with a crime upon arrival. Finally, in their questioning of suspects, some police focus on knowledge of other persons, their trade unions, political activities, and their social and sex lives. The methodology of information gathering is varied and extensive. For example, the Special Branch notes and indexes names of all political activists appearing in the press, particularly if they are in the leftist papers like the *Morning Star, Socialist Worker,* or *Workers Press,* indexes all persons signing petitions to Parliament, solicits and checks letters sent to it from the public describing activities of their neighbors and often containing pictures of demonstrations, subscribers to left-wing journals, newspapers, and magazines through a post office box number and investigates trials of political activists to see who attends or aids the defense: often a room is rented opposite the court to photograph those going in and out. Special Branch officers also follow up on raids by the police to check and index address books, checkstubs, and letters, solicit information from employers and state officials including doctors, social security officers, and teachers, and prepare reports on all public meetings and demonstrations. In addition, the Special Branch taps telephones, opens mail, and employs informers—often using blackmail to force people to work for them—to gather intelligence. Critics claim that these police investigative procedures clearly demonstrate a wider political purpose than anti-terrorism acts.

Critics within the legal community argue that the Prevention of Terrorism Act allows room for broad interpretation by state authorities as to their powers of arrest, detention, and exclusion, and its vagueness means that its enforcement relies heavily on the personal integrity of the state officials in charge. One of these experts is Professor David Lowry, who warns that the wording of the PTA is so obscure and undefined that it constitutes a wholesale attack on individual rights and civil liberties.[4] Lowry claims that part I of the act, in particular sections 1 and 2 that give the Home Secretary the power to ban organizations and make it a criminal act to belong to or support them, severely limits the freedom of expression, assembly, and association. For example, under the PTA, the Home Secretary can ban any organization based solely on his or her opinion that "it appears" the organization is "concerned" with terrorism. Freedom of association is further limited by the addition of sub-section 1(I)(a) that was inserted into the act because membership is difficult to prove. It shifts the onus of proof

of membership in a terrorist or subversive organization onto the
accused, who must show that they have not actively participated
in the organization once it is proscribed. Lowry maintains that
"The offense of 'belonging' to a proscribed organization is broader
than a conspiracy offense as both active and nonactive participants
may be guilty without proof of conspiracy."[5] The act is especially
broad in section 2, which makes it a crime to wear, carry, or display
any article that may arouse "reasonable apprehension" that one is
in support of a banned organization.

In part II of the PTA, for the Home Secretary to exercise the
powers of exclusion he or she needs only be "satisfied" that the
suspect is or was "concerned in the commission, preparation, or
instigation of acts of terrorism." Legal experts say the inclusion of
the category "preparation" appears designed to circumvent com-
mon-law proximity rules with respect to attempted crimes. It
means that the Home Secretary may serve an exclusion order
against people planning a demonstration or other form of civil
disobedience if the Secretary is satisfied that there is the potential
for violence. Many legal critics say the powers of arrest and
detention stipulated in part III are so great and subject to so few
safeguards against the abuse of power by state officials that the
PTA, in conjunction with the Judges Rules, permits arrest on
suspicion and detention for seven days of continuous interrogation
with no right to counsel or silence. As of 1976, all police and Special
Branch requests for the detention of persons for an additional five
days were approved by the Home Secretary. Each of the two
thousand persons detained were fingerprinted, photographed,
and interrogated and the collected information indexed and stored
in centralized computer files. All requests to have police return
information on persons detained but not charged with a crime
have been to no avail, as the Home Secretary, with no legal power
to do so, has ruled that the information will be held for the
duration of the emergency legislation. All evidence collected under
these secret circumstances is admissible in court. According to
Professor Lowry, the heart of the argument that the PTA provisions curtail freedom of assembly, association, expression, movement, and personal security rests on the fact that "For seven days a
person can be held incommunicado, his rights suspended. This is
obviously a new form of pretrial detention with grave implications
for the rule of law."[6]

Defenders of the British anti-terrorist provisions have argued that the special powers given to state authorities are necessary to effectively counter any emergency situation. They also maintain that the provisions are temporary and thus only related to special conditions of the present danger of terrorism. The broad scope of activity permitted by the PTA, in particular the gathering of intelligence, is justified on the basis that terrorism is indiscriminate as well as difficult to define and pinpoint, so that any piece of legislation is important no matter how obscure it may seem. Some defenders, including Home Secretary Roy Jenkins, argue that virtually all of those arrested under the PTA provisions would or could have been arrested under normal police powers so that the act does not represent a new attack on civil liberties. In addition, they claim there are safeguards in the PTA against state abuse of power, in particular the right of the accused to appeal the exclusion decision.

Critics respond by charging that without the PTA the police would have to, according to the law, give a person bail if arrested or bring them before the court within twenty-four hours. In addition, the police would not have the power to hold people without bringing formal charges. Nor would any oral statements allegedly made by suspects to police be admissible as evidence at a trial. The status of the provisions as temporary responses to emergency conditions is undermined by their continuous annual renewal. Critics cite comparisons between the PTA and the British experience with other allegedly "temporary" emergency legislation like the Special Powers Act of 1922 in Northern Ireland. The permanency of this legislation spurs observers to ask what the true meaning of "temporary" is, especially when it is not clear that the PTA has been effective against terrorism. What is clear, critics charge, is that the PTA can be used as an instrument of intimidation against political activity in the Irish Peace Movement, the Trade Union Movement, and the anti-nuclear and peace movements, none of which have any proven connection to terrorism.

Many critics of the PTA agree that terrorism can be indiscriminate and the broadened scope of police activity may, at times, isolate and identify terrorists. But they also contend that this must all be judged against the reality that the process of low-level intelligence gathering is contrary to civil liberties and "involves hardship, deprivation of liberty and stigmatization of wholly innocent people whose relevance to police investigation is that they are of appropriate ethnic origin or inhabit a particular community."[7]

On the issue of safeguards against state abuse of power, critics claim that the appeal process does not provide adequate measures of redress or fairness and that it is symbolic at best and outright fraud at worst. For instance, appeals are heard not by an independent tribunal but by the Home Secretary who made the original decision to exclude. Even though the Home Secretary is required to seek the advice of one or more persons, these advisors are chosen by him or her, and he or she may dismiss the appeal out-of-hand if he or she considers it to be based on "frivolous grounds." The right to appeal is further limited as the Home Secretary does not have to inform persons living outside the country that they have been excluded, nor do persons making an appeal have the right to counsel or any right to see the evidence against them. In the hearing before the appeals advisor, neither the accused nor the advisor is permitted any information about the evidence against the accused. Finally, the accused are discouraged from appealing their cases both by police who advise against appeals and by the condition that bail is not permitted to those arrested after being served the exclusion orders. Thus, the accused can remain in jail without access to a lawyer and isolated from family and friends who are not informed by police about the arrest, awaiting their case to be judged in a process which, in the opinion of many, is a travesty of justice.

The controversy and debate surrounding the Prevention of Terrorism Act in Britain do not concern whether or not the PTA extends the purview of state power, as all parties agree that it clearly does. The debate is over whether or not such powers are appropriate in a liberal democratic society. British state authorities have responded to their critics through both word and deed that the system is indeed appropriate and necessary to protect democracy. Indeed, most of the powers authorized to the police under the PTA, including the vague and broad discretionary authority assigned to the Home Secretary, do not stem from any specific counterterrorist theory but from long-standing British principles of general crisis management. These principles have evolved since 1920 through the installment of emergency powers laws, including the Official Secrets Act, incitement laws, conspiracy laws, and the Emergency Powers Acts. In addition, they are the product of recent counter-crisis proposals offered by British security officials, specifically those of counter-insurgency expert Frank Kitson.[8]

The PTA can be best described as an important instrument of governability that expands state authority over individual rights rather than a temporary piece of anti-terrorist legislation. In Britain, both critics and admirers of Prime Minister Margaret Thatcher and her conservative agenda agree that this campaign for governability has been openly and aggressively pursued since her government came to power in 1979.

TERRORISM AND THE IRISH QUESTION IN NORTHERN IRELAND

On November 15, 1985 the Republic of Ireland and Great Britain announced an agreement giving the Irish government a formal consultative role in governing the six northern counties of Ireland, known collectively as Ulster. Like past efforts to resolve the longstanding conflict in Northern Ireland, the signing was given a high profile by the media and was accompanied by expressions of goodwill and hopes for peace from many political leaders around the world. A year later, all hopes for peace were dashed as television pictures of Protestant riots and police fighting protesters in Belfast revealed that the new accord had failed to end the conflict in Ulster.

Like previous attempts at a settlement, this latest political arrangement was entangled in political circumstances and provoked a myriad of passions and extreme reactions, including terrorism, that virtually guaranteed its failure. First, the Anglo-Irish accord set up an "intergovernmental conference" of British and Irish cabinet ministers charged with discussing legal, political, and security issues affecting Northern Ireland. For the first time, the Irish Republic was given a role in the affairs of Northern Ireland, which is absolutely unacceptable to Ulster's Loyalist community. Secondly, the agreement was negotiated and signed by representatives of Britain and the Irish Republic. But the warring Catholic Nationalist and Protestant Unionist communities in Ulster view either the British or Irish as foreigners with no legitimate right to force a settlement on Northern Ireland.

Thirdly, it was clear from the initial reaction to the accord that it would have difficulty building any kind of political consensus in

Ulster or, for that matter, in England or Ireland. While the settlement raised new hopes of peace and prosperity in some constituencies, it sparked renewed fury and sanctioned increased violence in others. For example, both Prime Minister Margaret Thatcher of Britain and Prime Minister Garret Fitzgerald of Ireland supported the settlement on the basis that it would break the murderous cycle of violence by protecting the political interests of both the Protestant Unionists and the Catholic Nationalists. To her Unionist constituency in Ulster and England, Thatcher said ending the violence was the "greatest prize of all" and promised that the accord did not threaten the continued union of Ulster with England. Fitzgerald told the Irish Catholic Nationalists to "raise their heads" now that their position is and is seen to be on an equal footing with that of the Unionists. To the Unionists he offered the prospect that the agreement was a way back to a "normal" life without violence or fear." Both Thatcher and Fitzgerald pledged not to change the status of Northern Ireland without the consent of the majority population of Northern Ireland.

Unlike the high hopes for peace exhibited by the signatory governments, the reaction from the Protestant Unionist and Irish Nationalist constituencies ranged from tentative support to absolute outrage and rejection. Most Unionists and some Irish Nationalists denounced the treaty even before it was signed. Top Unionist leaders, including Reverend Ian Paisley, the firebrand leader of the Democratic Unionist Party, and James Molyneaux, head of the Official Unionist Party, sent a letter to Thatcher denouncing her for treachery and for negotiating with the government of Ireland which they labelled "a foreign government which not only claims our territory but harbors the murderers of our people." Unionist Member of Parliament (MP) Peter Robinson, in a fit of sexist fury, called Thatcher an "unmitigated and habitual liar" and an "unprincipled hussy" for signing the agreement. Ian Gow, the British Treasury Minister of State, resigned as soon as the agreement was announced, charging it would only prolong the agony in Ulster. Unionist members of Parliament, who feared the agreement would lead to the withdrawal of British rule in Ulster and ultimately its unification with the Republic of Ireland, called for a Northern Ireland referendum on the accord and spoke of "treachery and deceit" by those "quislings" who had collaborated with the invading foreign power of Ireland.

In the days and weeks following the signing of the accord, the verbal rage of unionist leaders was coupled with a new wave of "Loyalist" terrorism. The Royal Ulster Constabulary (RUC), the local police force, bore the brunt of the Loyalists' wrath for attempting to maintain order during Unionist-instigated strikes and violence. Loyalist terrorists bombarded RUC members, their homes, and families with gas bombs. By April 9, 1986 there had been more than 138 terrorist attacks on off-duty RUC members and their families. Most of the assaults occurred in the predominantly Protestant Unionist strongholds of Ulster.

On the Nationalist side, John Hume, the Social Democratic and Labour Party MP (SDLP), was almost alone in his support for the agreement. Hume argued the accord eliminated the need to pursue the union of the northern and southern parts of Ireland through armed force. But Gerry Adams, leader of Sinn Fein, the political wing of the Provisional Irish Republic Army (PIRA), which seeks to unify Ireland by any means possible, denounced the accord as only reinforcing the division of Ireland. An IRA-planted landmine on November 15, which killed a police officer in South Armagh near the Irish border, accompanied Adams's angry denunciation of the agreement. In the Irish Republic, Charles Haughey, the leader of the opposition Fianna Fail party, echoed Adams, charging the new settlement was "a severe blow for Irish unity and Irish nationalism."

To those familiar with the historical efforts to settle the Irish question, the passionate reactions and renewed outbreak of violence and terrorism in Ulster following the signing of the accord are all too predictable. Indeed, the terrorism and political violence that have claimed more than twenty-five hundred lives since 1969 and caused a marked deterioration in the social and political order of Northern Ireland have only worsened over the past year. Seven months after the signing, opposition to the accord forced the British government to abandon its four-year effort to install a power-sharing arrangement in Ulster by dissolving the Northern Ireland Assembly at Stormont. The Assembly had never been a politically viable institution since its inception in 1982 because members of the Roman Catholic Social Democratic and Labour Party refused to take their seats and Protestant Unionists engaged in periodic boycotts. But the Assembly's fate was sealed by the signing of the Anglo-Irish accord. The Unionist majority suspended the normal business of the Assembly and used it strictly as a forum for criticizing the agreement. Reacting angrily to the Unionist politicalization of the Assembly, members of the Alliance Party, moderates attempting to forge a non-sectarian consensus, ended their participation by walking out.

On November 15, 1986, a year to the day after the signing of the accord, the largest protest rally ever held in Ulster (estimates range from one hundred thousand to two hundred thousand people, or fifteen to thirty percent of the population) erupted in widespread looting and violence between police and Protestant demonstrators. Two people died in the rioting and over seventy people were injured, including thirty-two police officers. At least three officers suffered burns when acid was thrown in their faces. Police arrested sixty-nine people but while doing so killed one youth. Rejecting the appeals of their leaders, Protestant paramilitary groups appeared in uniform at the Belfast rally and openly incited the rioting. With Protestant leaders James Molyneaux and Reverend Ian Paisley promising a comprehensive campaign of civil disobedience in the streets of Ulster and pledging to organize a private army to protect Protestant interests, peace prospects have actually taken a step backward during the Anglo-Irish accord's first year.

After nearly two centuries of failing to reach a political settlement, there is no consensus as to what is at the root of the Irish question. There is, however, no absence of theories. For example, some analysts say the struggle in Ulster is basically an economic one, a case study of class warfare in a capitalist colonial society. Others see it as a political struggle and blame nationalism and nationalist extremists for the carnage. Many see the conflict as grounded in religious prejudice and discrimination. Still others claim that whatever its origins, the Irish question is fueled today by a culture of violence involving nothing more than the continuous avenging of historical and contemporary martyrs. Finally, there are those, among them well known terrorism experts Claire Sterling, Robert Moss, Richard Clutterbuck, and Ray Cline, who argue that terrorism and violence in Ulster are the work of Soviet-backed IRA agents and Soviet support for national wars of liberation.

Attempts to explain the Irish question from a single factor approach fail to capture its complexity. From the Middle View, detailed in Chapter Seven, the situation is intractable precisely because there are a multitude of issues involved, some laden with the burdens of history, some strictly contemporary in origin, each definable on its own terms yet each impacted and thus complicated and at times contradicted by the others.

In the discussion which follows, we will lay out each issue separately with no attempt to rank or prioritize them. The point is to expand what we know about terrorism in Northern Ireland by illustrating the complexity and interaction of the issues involved.

The issue of nationalism is central to the conflict in Northern Ireland. In Ulster there are two nationalist traditions directly confronting each other which so far have defied all attempts at reconciliation. The first, known as Irish Nationalism, or Republicanism, is driven by the premise that Ireland is a single political entity and should be free from British control. The second tradition, called Protestant Nationalism, or "Settler Nationalism," is based on defending the Protestants' cherished position of equal citizenship in the United Kingdom and preventing any conspiracy to establish Home Rule in Ulster. Today this nationalist tradition goes by the name of Unionism.

Both nationalist traditions have roots deep in Irish and British history. They start with the sixteenth-century rule of British monarchs Henry VIII and his daughter Elizabeth I and Irish resistance to British colonialism. Irish hatred for the English was aroused specifically when the British monarchs mandated Protestantism as the religion for Catholic-dominated Ireland and when Protestant forces, led by William of Orange, defeated James II and his Catholic armies at the Battle of the Boyne River in 1690. From this time on a small Protestant business class dominated the political and economic affairs of Ireland. The migration of Scottish Presbyterians into Northern Ireland and the immigration policy of Oliver Cromwell, which removed the Irish from the productive land, intensified Irish hatred of the English. It also fostered a new population of Protestant immigrants whose sole loyalty was to the British Crown. Given land by the British rulers, these immigrants developed as intense an attachment to their holdings in Ulster as that held by the dispossessed Irish. From this time forward, especially as the British, in order to maintain their political and economic interests, continued to move large numbers of people into Northern Ireland, the two nationalist populations confronted each other. On one side was a Protestant landed population whose loyalty was to an industrial and prosperous Ulster, which they claimed to have developed, and to their British benefactors. On the other was the Irish Nationalist population seeking to reclaim its land and its right to national self-determination.

The modern concept of "Settler Nationalism" may best describe the Protestant Nationalist tradition. In his book *Conflict in Northern Ireland*, Professor Donald P. Doumitt claims the Protestants are convinced that contemporary Ulster is a direct result of their work and sacrifice and thus they have a special claim to the land. Doumitt suggests the Protestant loyalty to Ulster is similar to the fierce sentiment held by the French "colons" in Algeria and the Zionist settlers in Palestine. From this strong Protestant "settler" loyalty has come a siege mentality spawning an unwavering and passionate sense of duty to defend Ulster from any attempt, including those made by the British under the guise of Home Rule, to take it from them.

Another historical pattern exhibited by Ulster's Protestants is a propensity to use force to protect their place and power in Ulster and a systematic avoidance of concessions to the Catholic majority. The propensity for violence is especially apparent anytime the issue of Home Rule has been raised. Since the nineteenth century, Protestant leaders have viewed any Home Rule plan as a major step toward the unification of Ireland and the abandonment of the British commitment to Protestant Loyalists. From their view it is to be opposed by all means. In this struggle, particularly before World War II, extremism has been encouraged by Protestant Loyalists and has helped to foster an environment in which cold-blooded murder and social turmoil are acceptable ways of defending one's interests.

The Irish Republican movement developed concurrently with Protestant Nationalism. It was originally spearheaded by the Fenians, a secret nineteenth-century revolutionary organization, and then in the twentieth century by the Irish Republican Army (IRA). The central goal behind Irish Republican Nationalism is the establishment of an independent Irish state free from British control and the reunification of the whole island under the rule of a republican government. A major step was taken toward this goal at the end of the IRA's successful guerrilla war against British forces which took place between 1918 and 1920. The Anglo-Irish Treaty in 1920 founded the Irish Free State as a Dominion of the British Commonwealth. Under the treaty, Northern Ireland remained a separate British Dominion unless Northern Ireland's Parliament, which was dominated by the Protestant majority, decided otherwise. Rejecting the Anglo-Irish Treaty as a sellout of their political interest, Irish Republicans, led by Prime Minister Eamon De Valera, eventually eliminated all British authority over the Free State. After becoming an Associated State, republican in form, the Irish Republicans finally broke completely with British rule by declaring Ireland a republic on April 18, 1949. Yet, the island still was divided and thus a major goal of Irish nationalism remained unfulfilled and Irish nationalist passions alive and burning.

As long as the Free State remained within the Commonwealth the Ulster Unionists felt little fear of southern encroachment. But the southern Irish Republican break with British colonial rule and then Commonwealth status raised new apprehensions in the Protestant Unionist community over the future of Ulster's political status. Since the British-Irish split, the Unionists have kept their Nationalist and Loyalist cause ablaze by feeding these fears and by pressuring the British government to live up to its historical commitment to remain in Northern Ireland.

The founding of the Irish Republic obviously did not end the conflict between the two nationalist traditions. It simply shifted the struggle to Ulster where the Unionists, in complete control of the Ulster government from 1920 until 1972, ruled over the Catholic minority with a heavy and often violent hand. Beginning in 1968, Ulster's Catholic Nationalists, through a series of civil rights demonstrations, pushed the Ulster government for administrative and electoral changes. In 1969 reforms were announced by the British authorities in the form of the Downing Street Declaration. The IRA rejected the proposed changes as too little too late, contending that the only solution to the massive Catholic unemployment and institutionalized Protestant discrimination in Ulster was complete British withdrawal from Ulster and union with the Irish Republic. To force its view, the IRA began a campaign of violence and terror in Londonderry and Belfast intended to push the British out. Instead of leaving, the British reinforced the British army's presence in Ulster. Then in 1972 they dissolved the Northern Ireland Parliament and installed Direct Rule from London via the Foreign Secretary's office in Belfast.

At present, as reflected in the passionate statements following the latest Anglo-Irish agreement, the national cause remains alive and well on both sides with Republicans aiming their terrorism at the British security forces and Unionist paramilitary troops and civilians. The Loyalist terrorists continue to target anyone who attempts to enforce any agreement that would undermine the British presence in and the Crown's rule over Ulster. Their terrorism is aimed principally at the IRA and its sympathizers but has also victimized the larger Republican community, British troops, and, more recently, members of the RUC and "disloyal" constituents in the Loyalist community.

Added to its nationalist component is the issue of sectarian conflict. Indeed, in the judgment of many analysts, the Irish question is an out and out religious war. Clearly there is a religious component or dimension to the conflict, as Protestants are fighting Catholics in Ulster and religious symbols are used to rally people to both causes. In addition, Protestant resistance to north-south unity is provoked in large part by apprehensions over the power of the Catholic Church in the Republic of Ireland and from Rome. But Protestants and Catholics in Ireland are not fighting over theological issues, nor are the Protestant and Catholic Churches at war. It is thus improper to characterize the Irish question as a religious war. Yet, there clearly is a sectarian element involved.

In discussing the importance of the Catholic religion to the Irish population, Irish historian Lawrence McCaffrey writes "Catholicism was the symbol of an independent Irish identity. It was the only thing that commanded the loyalty of the Irish masses."[9] Irish Catholicism has always played an instrumental role in the Irish struggle for independence from the British. For example, the early British efforts to destroy the native religion and force the Irish Catholics into economic submission, embodied in the Penal Laws of 1795, sparked a militant Catholic national spirit. The Catholic Church's leading role in the independence movement and in the struggle for civil rights in colonial Ireland and now in Northern Ireland has kept this strong religious nationalism very much alive. The ultimate driving force behind this religious nationalism is encapsulated in the often-expressed sentiment: for one to be Irish one must be Catholic.

This link between Catholicism and Irish national identity came to be distinctly embodied in the public moral code of the Republic of Ireland. Though the Irish Church has recently advanced a more tolerant or pluralistic posture, for a long time the Catholic hierarchy held a monopoly over the issues of how Irish society should be run. In essence, the Church was, and for many people remains, the Irish State.

From the Protestant perspective, the power and influence of the Church over the Republic of Ireland rules out any scheme to unify Ulster with the Irish Republic. To Protestants, "Home Rule is Rome Rule," and unification would result in the assimilation of Northern Ireland's institutions, culture, and structures to fit the needs of the Irish Catholic Church. Ulster's Protestants are quick to point out that the present Constitution of Ireland recognizes Roman Catholic principles and that Catholic moral theology is reflected in the civil law on the issues of abortion, contraception, education, euthanisia, and divorce. They argue that while the Constitution sets forth democratic principles, such as in Article 40 which guarantees the right to form associations and free class, religious, and political assembly, the Catholic Church's influence on these matters has placed a legalistic moral code on the Constitution that could be used to deny individual rights to those expressing anti-Catholic views. Protestants are also troubled by the statute which outlaws divorce in the Irish Republic and which does not recognize marriages dissolved outside of the Irish state. Indeed, Protestant fears about minority rights in Ireland were further heightened when Irish voters upheld the law against divorce by a wide margin in a June 1986 referendum. Today Ireland remains one of only two nations in the world in which divorce is illegal.

Even though Vatican Council II liberalized canon law on Catholic marriages, Protestants point out correctly that application of Canon 1061 was left to the local Church hierarchy and that the Irish Church has been slow to implement Rome's liberal interpretations on marriage. Protestants accuse the Irish Catholic Church of "out-Poping the Pope" by its insistence that in mixed marriages non-Catholic partners must agree to raise the children as Roman Catholics. They accuse the Church of being extremely conservative to the point of intolerance on all matters. This intransigence, Protestants say, has so decimated the minorities in the Irish Republic that over time they cease to exist. To support their point, Protestants note that the one-time thirteen percent Protestant population in the Republic of Ireland now stands at under two percent. Ulster's Protestant Loyalists view the demise in Protestant numbers in the Irish Republic as what the future holds for them should north and south be unified. In short, regardless of changes that have curbed some of the power of the Church and evidence of an emerging pluralistic climate in the Irish Republic and Church hierarchy, Protestants continue to view the Irish Republic as a nation whose population is ninety-five percent Roman Catholic, and, most importantly, "a Catholic country determined to uphold the public moral order of the Catholic faith, whatever the wishes of its non-Catholic minority."[10]

Rightly or wrongly, Ulster's Protestants are a very insecure majority. Their fears over the Catholic Church and encroaching Catholic nationalism have provoked a Protestant-backed system of institutionalized violence and discrimination against Ulster's Catholic minority. Few Protestant leaders take the majority statute or the system of majority rule in Ulster for granted and are constantly on guard lest Protestants lose either or both to Catholic Nationalists or British traitors. For both Ulster's Protestants and the Unionists in their midst, political prejudice in the form of electoral district gerrymandering and economic discrimination in housing and employment instigated against the Catholic minority are legitimate and effective weapons for keeping the Catholics in their place or from becoming strong enough to challenge Protestant power. Protestant rage and terrorism is especially directed at Ulster's Catholic organizations, in particular the IRA, which is perceived as nothing more than a political-military vehicle of Catholic Nationalism. Still, Protestants must confront the reality that over the past two decades their systematic religious discrimination against Catholics in Ulster has only fueled Catholic Nationalism, bringing it to a boiling point. It has also given the IRA militants and Catholic fanatics in Ulster's Catholic-Irish Nationalist community contemporary justification for their terrorism against the Protestant majority and its British benefactors.

Many observers of the Irish question see economic factors and conditions playing a central role in the Ulster conflict. From this view, Catholic violence and terrorism in Ulster is a product of economic and social hardship resulting principally from institutionalized low-level discrimination in employment and housing. On the other hand, Protestant terrorism is provoked by the desire to maintain the system of economic privilege and power.

Capital in Ulster is dominated by members of the Protestant

community who hold a monopoly over commerce, industry, land-holdings, and government. As a result, the affluent class in Ulster's economy is predominantly Protestant. On the other hand, though there are more poor Protestants than Catholics, on a percentage basis the Catholic minority remains the working-class poor and subject to systematic discrimination at the hands of all Protestants, particularly in the areas of employment and housing.

Affluent Protestants are convinced that their privileged class position is tied to continued union with the British capitalist state and the maintenance of Protestant political control over Ulster. Thus, on an economic basis, Ulster's upper class remains adamantly opposed to British withdrawal and sponsors terrorist organizations to keep Loyalist forces in line on this issue. With British backing, the Protestant capitalist class in Ulster maintains its privileged class position through control of local electoral politics and a system of economic repression against Ulster's working class.

From the Protestant capitalist class perspective, the principal challenge to their power is the working-class-based Catholic Nationalist movement. This movement offers a double-edged threat by organizing both the Catholic and working-class communities against their control over Ulster's economic system. To protect their dominant class position, Protestant capitalists pursue a dual-purpose strategy. First, they seek to maintain the loyalty of the working-class Protestants through various mechanisms of economic bribery, including higher wages and systematic favoritism in employment, job security, and housing. Secondly, and most important in terms of understanding a source of Catholic terrorism, Ulster's Protestant capitalists attempt to control the economic potential and power of the Catholic minority through economic discrimination and political repression.

Utilizing the gerrymandering process to dominate the political system from Parliament to the local district councils, Protestant leaders have been able to refine the process of economic discrimination begun by the British. The systematic nature of this discrimination is clear. For example, Northern Ireland government voting tables from the 1960s show Catholics as an electoral minority even in districts where they constitute the popular majority. Numerous studies by government agencies, including the British-sponsored Cameron Commission and Fair Employment Agency for Northern

Ireland, show that Protestant political control on the district level has resulted in a clear pattern of discrimination against the Catholic minority in occupations, employment opportunities, housing and other social services, and educational opportunities. In his study, Irish sociologist Edmund A. Aunger shows that in areas of public employment, such as the university system, there is a clear employment imbalance based on religious affiliation. In the Ulster universities, few Catholics hold positions of authority. In the mid-1970s they constituted only seventeen percent of the faculty and fifteen percent of the school administration. Aunger sums up his findings of occupational imbalance saying: "While a clerk may be Catholic, it is more likely that the office manager will be Protestant; while a skilled craftsman may be a Catholic, it is more likely that the supervisor will be a Protestant; and while a nurse may be a Catholic, it is more likely that the doctor will be a Protestant."[11]

Housing is another major area of sectarian imbalance. The housing shortage has been a chronic problem in Ulster for most of the twentieth century, plaguing members of the working-class community be they Protestant or Catholic. But studies show a connection between poor housing and recent Catholic unrest. In 1969, the year of massive sectarian demonstrations and riots, twenty-two percent of the nation's houses were said to be unfit for habitation, meaning they lacked either baths, hot water, inside toilets, or all three. According to political analyst Geoffrey Bell, the Catholic areas of Belfast contain the largest number and worst housing units in Ulster.

Sectarian economic and political discrimination is not a one-way street in Ulster. Studies in areas where Catholics control the local district council also show clear patterns of discrimination in housing and employment against Protestants. What becomes evident is that the respective political bodies in Ulster are motivated to discriminate in kind against the religious minority in order to assure political support from their constituents. The result has been to further poison Ulster's social-economic environment with sectarian hostility and violence.

The Protestant capitalist class system of economic discrimination helped spawn the present era of social turmoil in Ulster. Catholics, bent on obtaining electoral rights and administrative reforms that would end their political/economic deprivation, began a series of civil rights demonstrations in Belfast during 1966.

Through the Downing Street Declaration in 1969, the British government attempted to address the elements of economic discrimination in Ulster with a series of institutional reforms in local government, the police forces, the electoral system, and public housing authority. But as we mentioned, the IRA viewed the British-backed reforms as insufficient to seriously affect the large Catholic unemployment in the Belfast ghettos. From 1969 to 1972 the IRA used terroristic acts to try to force the British out of Ulster and to bring down the Protestant political system which the IRA held responsible for the economic plight of the Catholic minority. Protestant leaders, seeking to save their system of economic privilege from British reforms and IRA terrorism, mobilized Loyalist organizations, particularly the Royal Ulster Constabulary (RUC) and the Ulster Special Constabulary known as the "B Specials," a contingent of the original Protestant-backed Ulster Special Constabulary (USC) and responded with terrorism of their own.

Most discussions of the economic dimensions of the Irish question focus on the economic discrimination of Catholics by Protestants. However, there are those, for example, former Catholic socialist MP Bernadette Devlin, who question whether there is a religious component to the economic factor. Devlin, arguing from strict class analysis, says the reason there are "ins" and "outs" in Ulster is that there aren't enough jobs nor will there be enough jobs in an economy based on profit (capitalism) rather than on the needs of the population. Devlin is joined in her argument by several Protestant analysts, notably Unionist writer S. E. Long. They argue that serious unemployment and chronic economic crisis in Ulster result from the system of competitive economics, British trade practices, the cost of Middle East oil, and the resulting drain on government spending. These factors force cutbacks in job training, housing, health, and welfare services that negatively affect both Catholic and Protestant members of Ulster's working class. Government is blamed for failing in its economic policies to act on behalf of all Ulster's citizens and instead giving primary concern to profit and profit-seeking interests. According to this class perspective, religion and nationalist traditions are used effectively as vehicles to divide the workers of Ulster and pit them against each other. In the end, the major division and thus source of conflict in Ulster is along class lines where the affluent minority of Northern Ireland's and Britain's capitalist class control the system of repression and are aligned against the combined Protestant-Catholic working-class majority of Ulster.

So far we have focussed on the interplay of political, religious, and economic factors connected to both historical and contemporary violence in Northern Ireland. But there is another factor which complicates the Irish question even further. Today Northern Ireland is a society brutalized by violence, murder, and terrorism. It has become a place where violence is the norm, where violence begets violence, and where martyrs are made and avenged daily on all sides and for all sorts of reasons. It is a climate where the normal and accepted reaction to discrimination, prejudice, social injustice, political defeat, loss of work or livelihood, death, or injury to one's family or associates is reacted to with violence and terror. Several social scientists have found that while most residents of Ulster condemn violence, they have come to accept it as part of their normal routine since the beginning of daily violence in the late 1960s.

The violence during this period has been horrific. As the British increased their military forces from 1969 on, IRA bombings took their toll on Protestant-owned businesses and security forces. Protestant paramilitary organizations such as the Ulster Defense Association (UDA) and the Ulster Volunteer Force (UVF) began random assassinations of Roman Catholics, reprisal acts known locally as "Paddy-bopping." By September 1972 the violence had claimed 343 Protestant and Catholic lives, including the direct assassination of forty Protestants and eighty-one Catholics. From January 1969 to March 1975 the violence totalled 4,456 explosions, 978 attacks on police stations, 83 tarrings and featherings, 857 murders, and 9,477 civilian injuries. In the judgment of several analysts, as of 1972 prejudice, discrimination, poverty, and hatred had weakened Ulster's social cohesion to the point where survival at any cost became the first priority. This only reinforced the concept that "the end justifies the means" and sustained acceptance of violence and violent retaliation.

From this period on the climate of violence and terror has been so pervasive in Ulster that it is proper to wonder if the conflict isn't sustained primarily by the legacy of violence and martyrdom. That is, even if redress of major grievances were possible and the fears of the warring constituencies somehow soothed, would or could the violence end? Or more to the point, as long as violence, particularly that of organized paramilitary organizations, is an accepted way of conducting the business of politics can any settlement be achieved in Northern Ireland? In a climate where extremists of both sides view any compromise as a betrayal of their ideological positions and who command powerful paramilitary forces ready and willing to use violence and terror to achieve their goals, is there any realistic hope for conducting Ulster's affairs without violence? As social scientists probe the pervasiveness of Ulster's cycle of violence and terror and report its disastrous psychological impact on the residents of Ulster and their children more and more people are answering "no" to these questions. Indeed, the emergence of consensus-building "peace first" groups in Ulster indicates growing support for the conclusion that the Irish question cannot be settled until the socio-psychological acceptance of violence and terrorism is destroyed. Yet, despite international recognition and support, including the Nobel Peace Prize for their leaders, the failure of the peace groups to forge an effective consensus indicates how deeply ingrained the acceptability of violence is and how intractable is this component of the Irish question.

As we might expect, the multiple dimensions involved in the Irish question have generated a variety of groups and associations, some well-known, some shadowy and elusive, most involved in terrorism, on all sides of the conflict. To further illustrate the complexity of the Northern Ireland problem, the pervasiveness of terrorism and the difficulty in finding a solution, we must briefly examine these major parties and their specific agendas.

The major Catholic Nationalist extremist organizations in Ulster are the Irish Republican Army (IRA) and the Irish National Liberation Army, both of which are committed to uniting Ulster and the Irish Republic by any means, including violence. The IRA was formed in 1919 out of the Irish Volunteers, whose cause was independence from British colonialsm. The IRA waged guerrilla warfare from 1918 to 1920 against the British forces in the Anglo-Irish War and was active all during the struggle for Irish independence. Since 1969 the IRA has been ideologically split between the "Officials" and "Provisionals." The Officials are agreeable to some participation in the current political process of Ulster and seek a united Ireland guided by Marxist economic theory. The Provisionals, or Provos, refuse to participate in the current government of

Ulster, claiming that it is illegal. Describing themselves as socialist in the tradition of western European socialism rather than Marxist, the Provos seek to expel the British from Ulster and unify the north and south by any means possible, including violence. Among their prominent assassination victims are Britons Lord Louis Mountbatten and Sir Norman Stronge. According to some sources, including Claire Sterling, both the IRA Officials and Provos have been funded, trained, or shipped arms by Libya and Czechoslovakia as well as connected to Palestinian, Italian, and Spanish terrorist organizations.

The Irish National Liberation Army (INLA) was created in 1975 and consists of breakaway members of the Official IRA who had refused to obey the cease-fire orders of the Official IRA and continued terrorist operations on their own. They have teamed up with the Irish Republican Socialist Party (IRSP) which serves as its political front. The goals of both the INLA and the IRSP are to end British rule in Northern Ireland by armed warfare and unite it with the Irish Republic.

Sinn Fein, a term meaning "We Ourselves" which implies a commitment to revive the Irish culture and language, is an Irish nationalist political organization established in 1905. By 1919 it was illegal. As a nationalist organization it supported independence from Britain and rejected Dominion status. Today Sinn Fein is legal in both the north and the south and acts as the political mouthpiece for the IRA Officials and Provos. In November 1986 Sinn Fein abandoned its sixty-five-year-old policy of abstention from the Irish Parliament. In doing so it formally recognized the Republic of Ireland as separate from the northern six counties, but did so in order to pursue unification via political as well as military means.

Finally, there is the Social Democratic Labour Party (SDLP) which speaks for the Catholic community in Ulster. It is seeking a reformist solution to the Ulster conflict by no longer stressing unification of North and South, but rather by greater political participation in the government of Northern Ireland.

Major organizations on the Protestant Unionist side start with the Unionist Party, which was formed in 1885 out of Protestant opposition to Home Rule. Associating Home Rule with Rome Rule, the Unionists fought for Ulster's continued union with Britain and a separate parliament for Northern Ireland. The Unionist party's constituency includes farmers, the wealthy business class, and the Protestant urban proletariat.

Protestant paramilitary organizations include the Ulster Volunteer Force (UVF), whose contemporary existence began in 1966 when it was resurrected to protect Protestant supremacy in Ulster and to defend the Constitution of Northern Ireland. It is currently illegal and viewed as the unionist counterpart to the IRA. In 1966 the loyalist UVF declared war on the IRA and began a terrorist campaign against the Catholic population.

The Orange Order is an armed semi-secret group founded in 1795 whose contemporary ideology is to defend the British Crown and Ulster on behalf of Protestantism against Catholic encroachment. It stages provocative annual marches in July to celebrate the Battle of the Boyne, a 1690 Protestant victory.

The Ulster Defense Association (UDA) is the largest Protestant paramilitary group, with a membership estimated at fifty thousand. Its primary loyalty is to Northern Ireland and it advocates the separation of Ulster as an independent state from Britain with a Protestant-Catholic power-sharing system of government. Following the British imposition of Direct Rule over Ulster in 1972, the UDA began attacking British troops. It has also been involved in shootouts with the loyalist UVF.

In 1973 two new Protestant terrorist groups, the Ulster Freedom Fighters and the Red Hand Commandos, surfaced. With a membership consisting mainly of dockyard criminals, these two groups have engaged in sectarian killings, extortion rackets, and property damage. They are said to be motivated by criminal pursuits and sectarian malice. Some sources argue that the UDA invented the Ulster Freedom Fighters (UFF) as a fictitious group to deflect blame from the UDA for sectarian murders and to mislead British authorities who were moving against the UDA for its terrorist acts.

The two other major constituencies in the explosion of terrorism in Ulster are the Royal Ulster Constabulary (RUC) and the British army. The RUC is a seven-thousand-man military force, ninety percent of whose members are Protestant. It was formed in 1922 to maintain security in Northern Ireland and given authority under the Special Powers Act of 1921–1922 to arrest and detain anyone suspected of being an enemy with no concern for constitutional rights. For most of its history the RUC has been an important arm of the Protestant movement and the British government and, since it took its orders from the Protestant-run government until 1972, a major target of IRA terrorism. Since then the RUC, with prodding from the British authorities, has slowly developed into a professional police force and by most accounts plays less of a leading role in Protestant partisan politics. In the aftermath of the 1985 Anglo-Irish accord, the RUC has become a target of Loyalist terrorist organizations because of its role in maintaining law and order against Protestant violence. The RUC has also had strained relations with the British army since British troops were mobilized in 1969.

The British army was ordered into Ulster in 1969 in the attempt to protect British economic and political power by control-ling sectarian paramilitary violence and terrorism. Since then the army has become a source of conflict and both a target and participant in the violence. Except in the Loyalist community, the British army is viewed by the majority of Ulster residents, particu-larly the Catholic Nationalists, as a symbol of old-style colonialism. For this reason, since 1969 it has been targeted by a Catholic population that it was ostensibly sent in to protect.

As the principal agent of the British government in Ulster and enforcer of the controversial British anti-terrorist policy, the army quickly turned its attention and guns on the Catholic community and their paramilitary organizations, in particular the IRA. In pursuing its duties in Ulster the British army has paid a high price in lives. Its professional reputation has been severely damaged by its involvement in terrorist activity. According to many sources, including the European Commission and former British army intelligence officers such as Fred Holroyd, the British army has been involved in terrorist activity which includes kidnapping plots, assassinations, forgery, political psychiatry, and postal death threats in Ulster.[12]

In conjunction with the presence of the British armed forces and its partisan terrorist activities, it is the colonial and anti-democratic aspects of British government policy in Northern Ire-land that have helped fuel nationalist hostility and violence in Ulster. Present British security policy in Northern Ireland is founded on the repressive security legislation enacted into law in 1922 as the Civil Authorities (Special Powers) Act (Northern Ire-land) 1922. This Act, which originally was to last one year, was enacted to deal with the outbreak of sectarian (Catholic) violence and was renewed every year until 1928, when it was given a life span of five years. In 1933 it was extended indefinitely until its repeal and replacement by the Northern Ireland (Temporary Provisions) Act in 1973.

The Special Powers Act provided for the death penalty for several explosive and firearms offenses and flogging and imprisonment for others. It prohibited inquests on people who had died while in police custody, empowered the Minister for Home Affairs to ban organizations, to intern suspects indefinitely without charge or trial, and made it an offense to refuse to answer questions asked by the police, special constables, or soldiers. It also gave the Minister of Home Affairs the right to delegate all his/her responsibilities, including the power to unilaterally make new regulations backed by the force of law, to any police officer.

In response to the Catholic civil rights movement in the late 1960s, the Criminal Justice (Temporary Provisions) Act was passed in 1970 providing for six months in prison for riotous acts. In 1971, faced with Catholic rent and rate strikes, the Unionist Stormont government passed the Bad Debt Act allowing the government to deduct arrears of rent and rates in addition to "collection charges" from the wages and social security payments of those on rent and rates strikes. Also in 1971, under the auspices of the British government, the Stormont government introduced a new internment policy. On August 9, 1971, British troops began an operation which over its first six months resulted in the arrest of 2,375 persons and the internment of 900 suspects without trial for an indefinite period. During their internment, detainees were routinely subjected to cruel and degrading treatment and released only after in-depth interviews. According to a European Commission report in 1976, some suspects were tortured by being forced to run barefoot across broken glass, beaten, or threatened with being tossed blindfolded from a helicopter. One common torture involved a sensory deprivation technique where suspects were hooded and forced to stand spread-eagled against a wall, placing extreme pressure on the fingertips, while being subjected to a loud whirring noise.

Following the imposition of Direct Rule in 1972, the British repealed the Special Powers Act in 1973 and passed the Northern Ireland (Emergency Provisions) Act. The new Act was passed to silence the international outcry against British abuse of civil rights in Ulster and the internment policy in particular. In many areas the new law actually extended the powers of British and local police authorities. For example, the 1973 Act, extended under the Emergency Provisions (Northern Ireland) Act of 1978, revoked jury trial for many pre-existing serious offenses including murder, manslaughter, causing explosions, and possession of firearms and extended the period of detention following arrest from forty-eight to seventy-two hours. Police were given the power to forcibly take fingerprints and palm prints and photograph those arrested. The new law also continued to allow internment of arrestees under the new label "detention." The powers of detainment reside exclusively with the British Secretary of State.

In addition, the burden of proof to show that a suspect's confession was not voluntary was put on the defendant's legal counsel: previously it had been the prosecution's responsibility. Any confession is admissible in court if the defense cannot provide prima facie evidence to prove it was obtained involuntarily by use of torture, inhuman treatment, or degradation. In 1984 Amnesty International was still requesting official British inquiry into the proceedings of Ulster's "Diplock courts," charging that the overwhelming number of cases in which convictions were based solely on confessions and where judgments are rendered by a single judge rather than by jury may not conform to international standards of fair trial. In another important change, local magistrates could no longer consider the question of bail on suspects charged with scheduled crimes, forcing defendants to appeal to the High Court Judge. The effect has been a dramatic increase in the number of persons held without bail and the length of their detainment.

In essence, the security legislation ostensibly passed to deal with sectarian terrorism and violence placed the police and British military in an almost insurmountable and unchallengeable position throughout the history of Northern Ireland. At the same time it denied much of the populace the rights normally associated with a free society: freedom from arbitrary arrest and detention, the right of the arrested to be brought before a court or released, and the right to remain silent. The result has been an armed Irish Nationalist movement violently fighting the contradiction between Unionist and British governments publicly committed to liberal democratic values and their enforcement of repressive anti-democratic measures in a quasi-colonial context.

Today Northern Ireland remains a polarized society with violence used by both sides as a method of protecting interests and pursuing goals. While deaths and injuries from sectarian violence continue to mount (the official death count from 1983 through the end of 1985 stands at 195), efforts by governmental bodies and various peace movements in and outside Northern Ireland—such as the Peace People Community—to narrow the political, social, and economic gap between the warring communities and to establish a middle ground that would end the violence continue to fail. The interplay between the nationalist, religious, economic, and sociological forces discussed here has simply forestalled all efforts to build a sustainable political consensus. Even the peace movement and its humanitarian cause has failed to cut through the partisan issues dominating Ulster. As the first anniversary of the Anglo-Irish accord passes, funds and sophisticated weapons for terrorism continue to flow into Northern Ireland from all over the world, increasing the potential of a holocaust with even greater loss of life and suffering.

The question remains: how and when will violence and terrorism end in Ulster? Many terrorist experts, including Claire Sterling and Ray Cline, answer by laying the blame for the continuation of the conflict on outsiders. Operating from the "ideology of terrorism," they suggest that there will be no settlement in Ulster as long as the Soviets and their network of international terrorists are allowed to train and equip IRA terrorists in hopes of fomenting social unrest and draining the resources of the British government. But the IRA is also funded and armed by many Western sources, including the Irish-American community, through organizations such as the Irish National Caucus and the Irish Northern Aid Committee. On the other side, proponents of the Soviet view argue that violence will continue in Ulster until the forces of national liberation and socialism have broken the power grip of the foreign imperialists and their local capitalist clients.

However, the explosion of terrorism in Northern Ireland is not the simple concoction of a Soviet terrorist conspiracy nor the exclusive product of British imperialism, though there are elements of both involved. Neither is it a case where responsibility for terrorism rests with a single constituency, as many Western journalistic sources suggest. Indeed, as we have seen, terrorism in Northern Ireland is openly practiced and publicly justified by all the major constituencies. Nor is the conflict confined to the timeframe of Claire Sterling's "fright decade" in the 1970s. Rather, what we see through the framework of the Middle View is that the conflict in Northern Ireland, though it has its international components, remains fundamentally Irish in nature, defined by its complex and disturbing historical record and by the contemporary interplay of numerous and often contradictory local and regional political, economic, religious, and sociological factors. It is the same conclusion, with some important differences, that we reach in our examination of terrorism in Sri Lanka and India. Indeed, given the opportunity to develop further the analytic context of the Middle View, it is a conclusion we will often reach in our study of the explosion of terrorism.

Firebombing on Belfast streets, Northern Ireland.

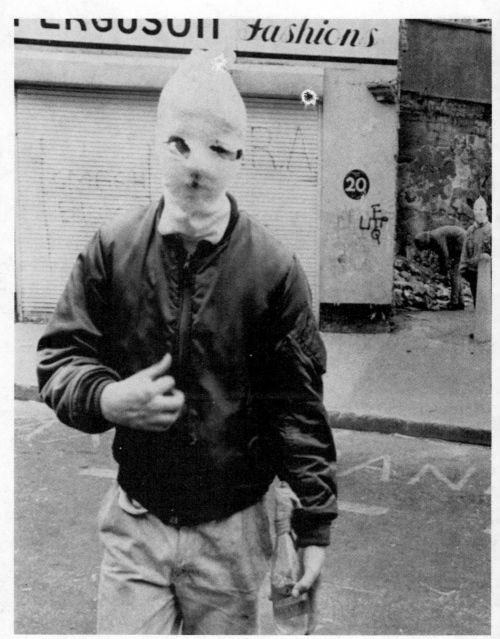

Terrorists roam the streets of Derry, Ireland.

Members of the Neo-Nazi Movement, West Germany.

The assassination of Karl Heinz Beckurts, Munich.

Sikh mutiny in Indian army, Delhi.

Bomb explodes in Paris department store, France.

WEST GERMANY BATTLES TERRORISM

The wave of terrorism in western Europe has caused grave concern throughout the Western world about the vulnerability and chances of survival of democratic institutions and processes. Nowhere was this concern greater than in the Federal Republic of Germany, more commonly known as West Germany. Many people inside and outside the Federal Republic feared that terrorism and the state's battle against it would force the return of authoritarian rule in Germany, thereby repeating the experience of the Weimar Republic in the 1920s when Adolf Hitler and his brown-shirted terrorist thugs overwhelmed a young and weak German democracy and engineered the rise of German fascism.

In fact, the fascism of the 1920s has not returned to German society. But in the 1970s West Germany battled with terrorism and many programs of liberal reform enacted in the 1960s were discarded, resulting in a political climate where the politics of law, order, and security have been given priority over individual rights. Chancellor Helmut Schmidt and the Right wing of the ruling Social Democratic Party (SPD), defined the problems facing West Germany in neoconservative terms and installed a crisis management system of "authoritarian democracy." These forces sometimes sponsor and use anti-terrorist legislation and policy as a political tool to mobilize West German society against progressive democratic groups to justify a political climate of intimidation.

The Federal Republic was created out of the ruins of World War II. The division of Germany into two separate states resulted from a breakdown in the victorious wartime alliance when France,

Britain, and the United States squared off against the Soviet Union. In 1949 the occupation zones of the Western powers were unified and the liberal democratic state of the Federal Republic, grounded in the conservative legal and constitutional basis of the Basic Law, was founded. Under the leadership of Chancellor Konrad Adenauer and the conservative Christian Democratic Union (CDU), the two major priorities of the West German state during the 1950s were economic recovery and anti-Communism. By the 1960s the German "economic miracle" had made the West German economy the strongest in Europe and on its way to becoming one of the most powerful in the world. Adenauer's strict adherence to the American-sponsored anti-Communist containment policy made West Germany an important member of the Western alliance. Because of its geographical position in Central Europe, it was assigned a strategic role in the containment strategy as the first line of defense against Soviet expansionism. Internally, anti-Communism was used to mobilize the German public against political parties of the Left (the Communist Party was outlawed in 1956) and against any hint of political radicalism. The passage of anti-Left legislation, including the Political Criminal Act of 1951, and the reinforcement of internal security forces like the Federal Border Guards and state emergency commandos, created a strong state apparatus whose mandate was to identify and repress Communists and their left-wing sympathizers.

The mid-1960s marked the beginning of the second period in the political-economic history of the Federal Republic. Adenauer's retirement in 1963 left West Germany without its guiding father figure and created a political void his successors Ludwig Erhard and Kurt Kiesinger could not fill. With the economic crisis of 1966–67, highlighted by the first government budget deficit since 1958, deep divisions, which had been subsumed by the drive against Communism and for economic affluence, surfaced in the West German population. The rise of the New Left, spawned by the radical student movement and militant trade unions, the activities of liberal reform-minded political forces, and the *Ost Politik* policy of SPD leader Willy Brandt, which directly challenged the containment policy, exposed the pluralistic nature of German society. By October 1969, against a backdrop of student riots and massive worker wildcat strikes, Willy Brandt and the SPD withdrew from the ruling alliance of the Grand Coalition. With promises of reform in domestic and foreign policy, a coalition of the SPD and the Free Democratic Party (FDP) was elected with Willy Brandt as chancellor.

Under Brandt, some political and social reforms were enacted. The demands for labor and university reform made by the trade union and student movements were instituted into the economic and educational process. A less strident anti-Communist tone was set in domestic and foreign policy by Brandt's implementation of *Ost Politik*, which included the signing of trade treaties with the Soviet Union, East Germany, and Poland. But anti-Communism remained the guiding principle behind state policy. Indeed, the proclaimed goal of the SPD reform program was to transform social conditions so that the basis for Communism was removed from German society. Even so, the tone was different, and Brandt's coalition was less inclined to view Communism as a disease that the state must constantly guard against lest it infest the healthy organs of German society.

The period of reform was short-lived; Brandt resigned the chancellorship in 1973, forced out by the discovery of a spy ring within his government. Actuallly, the end of the social reform movement had already begun with the economic crisis of 1973 and the rising discontent among German workers and students who were critical of the reform movement for not living up to its promises. Rising inflation and unemployment rates further shattered the glossy picture of the German economic miracle. The 1973 oil crisis exposed how vulnerable Germany's long-term economic growth was to foreign interests. While in office, Brandt attempted to downplay the crisis with forecasts of a rosy future and warnings that any retreat from the reform program would disrupt the social harmony in the Federal Republic. But with Brandt's resignation, the German state, under the leadership of neoconservative Helmut Schmidt and the conservative wing of the SPD, adopted a different strategy of governance. Pushed by its conservative critics in the Christian Democratic Union and the Christian Social Union alliance (CDU/SU) as well as by its own sense of crisis management, the new government ordered a period of economic and political consolidation and the evaluation of past achievements.

Upon taking power, the Schmidt government charged that the dimensions of the crisis were larger than originally conceived, and it began to define the crisis and its solution in neoconservative terms. Government officials argued that the legitimacy of the state was endangered by "a continual loss of authority affecting traditional institutions such as the state, the family, the schools, and the church."[1] They accused the liberalization movement of overextending the power of the state. Reforms proposed by the Brandt government were discarded and unemployment and welfare programs attacked. The mounting threats to internal security and social stability were blamed on the political and intellectual weaknesses of the reformers. In the bluntest of terms, Chancellor Schmidt and his Justice Minister Hans Jochen Vogel contended that the state had been undermined by too many concessions during the "bout with liberalization" and that these concessions had raised false hopes among the population and had broken down the consensus on the basic values of liberal democracy in the Federal Republic.

The crisis was also found in the cultural realm. Traditional values and cultural achievements were under siege in the major educational and cultural institutions. German political observers like Oscar Negt claim that it was the loss of cultural hegemony during the liberalization process that the conservatives were most worried about. The reform movements in the universities, cultural institutions, and media had pushed them aside, and a "New Class" and its liberal philosophy had taken charge. Helmut Schelsky and other conservative intellectuals argued that this "New Class" stood at the pinnacle of Germany's power structure where, as producers and mediators of meaning, they threatened the intellectual security of the state. As administrators of "psychosocial poison" in the state schools and as sympathizers who had control over important levels of government and society, the "New Class" was accused of trying to confuse the natural feelings and the natural discernment of citizens.

To counter this crisis of authority, culture, and democratic excess, the German government adopted a crisis strategy that used as a political vehicle the contemporary concern for both international and domestic terrorism. In West Germany, the Black September terrorist attack on the Munich Olympic Village had first aroused concern in the summer of 1972. The growing number of kidnappings, bombings, bank robberies, car thefts, and arson connected to the domestic terrorists of the Baader-Meinhof Group and June 2nd Movement intensified the concern. State officials, aided by the German media, used these incidents to fan the fires of public hysteria in order to prove that terrorism was the new threat to German democracy. It was no longer Communists but terrorists and their sympathizers who were the "internal enemy" and who must be driven from governmental and educational institutions. Chancellor Helmut Schmidt took a leading role in the campaign by charging that it was the terrorists of Baader-Meinhof more than the problems of inflation or unemployment that were unsettling German society. From Schmidt's point of view, the proper response to this crisis was to fortify and strengthen state security institutions, to pass anti-terrorist legislation, and to install a political climate in which public loyalty to the state was required.

The turn toward neoconservatism taken by the Social Democratic Party did not go unnoticed by conservatives inside and outside of West Germany. Many opposition leaders of the CDU/SU praised Schmidt, saying for a Social Democrat he was doing a good job. Schmidt was described as a "down the line right-winger" within the party ranks of the SPD and was known to complain about the "cumbersome requirements of parliamentary democracy." The editors of the conservative British journal *The Economist* applauded him several times for adopting a political course that was "blowing away the clouds of socialism."

In order to strengthen the authority of the state, the Schmidt government began a campaign to justify the legitimacy of the state's role in the battle against terrorism. Of particular use to this campaign was the assumption that society should be viewed and treated as an organism. Labelled as "militant" or "aggressive democracy," this view defines a political system "constantly vigilant against potentially corrosive influence, ever ready to flush those influences out of the political system."[2] The purpose of the state is to fight the disease and infection that are constant threats to the total organism. In this vision of "militant democracy," the police are viewed as the major institution of social hygiene and "the interests of society are joined with the interests of the state and a threat against one part of the system is seen as a threat against the whole." Since it is the state that identifies the threatening symptoms of societal disease, it is the state that must find a cure. Only a democracy that is militant or aggressive can protect society. And in a "militant democracy," the whole society must be united behind the efforts of the state to battle the "anti-democratic" infection. To be successful, it is argued, the state must have the power and the means to protect the "communal peace."

Communism was portrayed as the disease threatening West Germany in the 1950s and 1960s; in the early 1970s it was terrorism—undefined by West German officials—that infected German society. Though state violence increased during this period—between 1973 and 1976 the police killed fifty-seven people in shootings—it was the violence of the terrorists that constantly drew the attention of the media and government information agencies and led Attorney General Siegfried Buback to comment that "attentive readers of the newspapers will almost every day discover some activity which in some form or other can be traced back to anarchist terrorists."[3] The campaign to legitimize state authority and measures of repression made a careful distinction between those who supported the state and those defined as "public enemies." The "internal enemy" consisted of terrorists and their sympathizers who were disloyal to and out to destroy the German state. On the other side, according to Interior Minister Werner Maihofer, the friends of the state included "All of us who pay our taxes on time, stop at the red light, and are always on time in the office and factory."[4]

The conservative campaign to mobilize public opinion in favor of state authority raised other important issues. One brought up by government officials was the common problems faced by the Weimar Republic and the Federal Republic. They blamed left-wing terrorism as the most important factor in the destruction of German democracy. The issues of "infection" and "disease" were raised as they had been against Communism, in connection with the contemporary public enemy of German society. The Baader-Meinhof Group became known as the "gang" with a "hard core" leadership who even when captured and held in Stammhein Prison could still wreck chaos and havoc by reaching out to international allies and ordering more burnings, bombings, and killings. They were described as a "plague," as "freaks," or as a "cancerous sore." Schmidt claimed that the terrorist community had no rights under the law because the state couldn't apply laws made for humans to animals or the insane. On the other hand, state security forces, in particular special anti-terrorist squads like GSG 9, were given heroes' status and their accomplishments celebrated. According to political science professor Margit Mayer, this campaign was so successful that after the rescue mission by GSG 9 in Mogadischu, Somalia, in 1977, the German state "could present itself to the German citizens as victorious, clean, and solvent."[5]

The German state depicted terrorism as an indiscriminate and widespread threat by constantly focussing public attention on the "anarchist terrorists" of Baader-Meinhof, the June 2nd Movement, and the "anarchist political scene" in Frankfurt and Berlin. Every bank robbery, weapons theft, act of arson, or electric power failure was attributed to the terrorists. After fifty-three canisters of mustard gas were found missing from an army depot, officials reported that the German Parliament, hospitals, and health departments were going to be attacked by terrorists. The report turned out to be inaccurate, as did others, including the claim that terrorists had stabbed the bodyguard of CDU leader Helmut Kohl. As the campaign went on, new "anarchist terrorist" gangs were constantly being "discovered" by German security officials as proof that the threat still existed, even though the "hard core" of the Baader-Meinhof Group had been imprisoned or were dead by 1974. But in 1975 Justice Minister Vogel claimed, "The number of potential terrorists is greater than previously suspected."[6] Also in 1975, the government began to tell the public that the terrorist threat was part of an international conspiracy fostered by simple hate and fanaticism. Interior Minister Maihofer called it "international organized crime tourism" and claimed that the imprisoned Baader-Meinhof leaders had connections to other international terrorist groups including the Palestinian fanatics of the PLO and Black September.

By these means, state officials sought to appeal to the common sense and basic fears of the Germans by emphasizing the indiscriminate nature of terrorism. The political nature of these appeals and the dimensions of the crisis as portrayed by officials was best described by Hans-Magnus Engensberger in a 1979 speech to a New York audience. Explaining the nature and operation of what he said was a second system of state surveillance repression that was new to Germany in the post-World War II period, Engensberger said of those in power:

They place little store by the mobilization of enthusiastic masses such as Fascism needed; they merely urge us to be

sensible. The civilization on which our continued existence depends, they say, is extremely complicated and very vulnerable. Its success is bought at the price of risks that increase daily; crime, crisis of scarcity, sabotage, wildcat strikes, psychological disturbances, environmental pollution, radioactive poisoning, drug addiction, economic crisis, terrorism and so on and so forth.[7]

A major theme of the Federal Republic's anti-terrorist campaign was based on the neoconservative "excess of democracy" thesis. As early as 1972 the conservative forces within the state began an ideological and legislative campaign to isolate and intimidate those citizens failing to display "positive loyalty" to the state. Central to this effort, which intensified under Helmut Schmidt, was the identification of the "internal enemy." What began ostensibly as anti-terrorism quickly became an attack on liberal and leftist communities. The charges of "guilt by association" and "terrorist spawning grounds" were levelled at these political circles. Left-wing intellectuals who wrote or talked about class conflict or violence, or who tried to make distinctions between political activists and terrorists, were silenced by accusations that their theories only encouraged terrorism. Liberal lawyers, who tried to defend terrorists in special "74a courts" set up to try political cases before "suitably experienced judges" chosen by the government, were tagged as terrorist sympathizers, a label soon to have legal consequences. But the real enemies of the state and thus German society were identified as members of a "New Class" who "keep getting out of step," the "desk-bound activists" in the bureaucracies of the state, the "intellectual stone-throwers," the "criminals in the guise of left-wing reformers" whose "theories placed on virgin paper with clean fingers drove the Baaders to murderous conclusions." These "men behind the scenes" who appear to be supporters of the state are far more dangerous because they seek to bring down the state with the hidden weapons of the mind in schools, universities, churches, the press, and the cinema.[8] It is these "enemies" who combine terrorist activities with middle-class professional occupations, who disguise themselves as the "couple next door" and who also undermine the state with talk of class conflict, questions that challenge traditions, glorification of violence and revolution, and, ultimately, change attitudes. Increasingly, the state held the forces of "misguided liberalism" collectively responsible for terrorism, civil disobedience, wholesale attacks on the prevailing order, and grass roots reform movements. Together these various political forces were "melted inextricably into one context; its totality as the 'internal enemy' has become the object of a declaration of war."[9]

This political climate of intimidation took its toll on liberal and Left political, legal, and intellectual communities. Fearful of being labelled as terrorist sympathizers, scores of lawyers and judges backed away from defending or sitting on cases involving those accused of terrorism. Their enthusiasm for the courtroom was tempered by the experience of the defense attorneys for Baader-Meinhof, Eberhard Becker, Jorg Land, and Siegfried Haag, who were forced underground by legal actions instituted by the state against them, and attorneys Klaus Croissant, Hans-Christian Stroebele, and Kurt Groenewold, who were accused of complicity in criminal activities. Stepped-up police surveillance at political rallies, raids on bookstores, housing projects, and suspected terrorist hideouts, and censorship of any literature thought to be supportive of violence affected the political activity of the organized Left, including members of the SPD. Under pressure to prove their loyalty to the state in order to get or keep a position in civil service, thousands of citizens sought refuge by disassociating themselves from the political, cultural, and social reforms of the late 1960s.

The state also emphasized the middle- and upper-class background of the German terrorists and their memberships in the student movement and other liberal and left-wing causes during the 1960s to connect terrorism with the excesses of liberal reform and to characterize the source of terrorism as flowing naturally from the breakdown in state authority and cultural tradition. Terrorist leaders Andreas Baader, Ulrike Meinhof, Gudrun Ensslin, and Horst Mahler were routinely depicted as bored, spoiled youth, spouting left-wing rhetoric but with no real connection to or concern for the working class. The state persistently characterized these terrorists as criminals and their demands and actions as completely devoid of political meaning or purpose. Andreas Baader and Gudrun Ensslin were portrayed as modern-day versions of Bonnie and Clyde who were on a romantic spree of crime and terror. Baader's taste for women, fast cars, and plentiful amounts of alcohol and Deutschmarks were publicized to reinforce the notion that criminal motives were behind the many car thefts and bank robberies. The state also publicized the key role played by women in the Baader-Meinhof Group (twelve of the original twenty-two members and eight of the next twenty were women). The public was inundated with psychological theories blaming Meinhof's apparent Jekyll-Hyde transformation from a quiet, non-violent, and successful writer to a gun-toting bank robber and bomber on her fatherless childhood. Her "obvious" insanity was blamed on the insertion of a silver clamp in her brain to ease the pressure from a tumor. Baader's "craziness" was said to be a product of his being reared from the age of one by his mother, grandmother, and aunt after his father, an historian, was killed in the early days of World War II. Time and again, the scenario offered by members of the police to explain the rise of terrorism was "a direct causal line—broken family, the reading of Adorno and Marcuse, then the participation in demonstrations, and finally, terrorist."[10] The state sought to politically isolate the terrorists and their sympathizers from the average German citizen and linked the rise of terrorism with a larger political malaise fostered by the forces of excess.

The state repudiated the political proclamations of the terrorists and portrayed them as criminals. Even though they were tried in the political criminal court, the state treated their crimes as apolitical: a product not of economic or political failure in the Federal Republic but of the rise in various youth and criminal subcultures, of a breakdown in traditional German values, of the glorification of violence or of individual pathology.

The state sought to discredit those who challenged its interpretation of terrorism and the crisis facing West German society. The end result was a "witch hunt" atmosphere that by 1977 was so successful that both the liberal reform movement and the general public were sufficiently cowed. For example, when the distinguished International Russell Tribunal investigated the charge of political repression in the Federal Republic in 1977, state officials countered the unfavorable findings of the Tribunal by charging that anyone who supported the Tribunal's conclusion that civil rights were being violated by the government was disloyal to the state. In addition, all German citizens were asked to prove their loyalty to the state by being on constant alert for suspicious activity and persons. The public was recruited into the battle against an internal enemy said to be everywhere, who did not discriminate between the innocent and guilty and who represented criminality in its lowest and most threatening form. As individuals or in groups, citizens were told to report anything that attracted attention, to look closely at their surroundings—at cars and apartments with unusual occupants and especially at abandoned housing and industrial buildings. Failure to do so placed one under suspicion of harboring terrorist sympathies. Security officials were urged to "Activate the people, motivate them, bring them together . . . Hunt the criminals. Hunt them all the time."[11]

By the mid-1970s the growing conservative mood of the population encouraged by the state-sponsored anti-terrorist campaign was evident. Public opinion surveys found students to be more conservative, increasingly narcissistic, and more concerned with middle-class security and affluence than the previous generation. Conservative party fortunes were revived in local and *Lander* elections. Backed by a broad and increasingly conservative political coalition that cut across party lines and went deep into the membership of SPD, the government began to institutionalize a political climate of "governability" by sponsoring anti-terrorist legislation and by expanding the scope and functions of state security institutions. These actions, which had begun as early as 1972 with the Hamburg Decrees, gathered force in 1976 with the passage of a body of anti-terrorist laws. In this process, the rights of individuals to privacy, freedom of speech, and association gave way to the security needs of the state crisis management system. As we shall see in our examination of some of this legislation, the move towards "authoritarian democracy" created a political context where the realm of individual rights was redefined to coincide with the need for authority, order, and social stability.

THE LAW FOR THE PROTECTION OF COMMUNAL PEACE

The Law for the Protection of Communal Peace was first drafted in 1962 but not passed until January 1976. The most important part of the law is section 88a, which deals specifically with the question of violence. Its purpose is to punish the ". . . giving of support and approval to violence by means of words, publications, and films likely in the circumstances to disturb the public peace."[12] Penalties may be incurred by anyone who ". . . displays, suggests, presents, or otherwise makes accessible, produces, procures, supplies, stocks, offers, announces or recommends, seeks to introduce into the area covered by this law or to export from it . . . matter likely to disrupt the peace in order to use it or enable another to use it with the intention hostile to the state."[13] In his discussion of the legality of this law, lawyer and journalist Sebastian Cobler claims that it is unprecedented in Europe with two notable exceptions: the Press Law enacted in Greece by the repressive military junta in 1969 and Article 1b of the Spanish Emergency Law of August 1975, during the final days of dictator Francisco Franco. Under the law, a crime is committed if it is judged there is the "likelihood" of an utterance to disturb the public peace. The force of this law has been applied almost exclusively against socialist, Marxist, and other liberal-Left writers, artists, publishers, booksellers, and printers. It was on this basis that the state conducted searches and confiscations of the premises of the Munich *Trikont-Berlag* because of their publication of West German urban guerrilla Bommi Baumann's autobiography *Wie Alles Anfing*.

Numbered 129 StGB, the Law Against Organizations Which Threaten the State is based on the claim that dangers that threaten the civil order stem from people who are members of a collective or organization. It penalizes "anyone who forms an organization the purposes or activity of which are directed to the committing of criminal acts, or anyone who takes part in such association as a member, publicizes it or supports it."[14] The truly troubling aspect of this law is that it uses a broadened definition of what constitutes an organization. The law does not presuppose an "organization" with a structure guided by rules. Therefore, the external organization form is of no significance. The Federal High Court in West Germany has consistently ruled that the definition can be satisfied by a loose association of people with no vertical structure necessary, and that the only requirement is that there be a "sense of organization." The charge of belonging to, supporting, or publicizing a "criminal organization" justifies telephone tapping, surveillance, house searches, confiscation, interrogation, and imprisonment. Guilt by association and collective liability are also implied by the law. The additions of Section 129a and Section 112 of the criminal code now make it mandatory for a person suspected of belonging to a "criminal organization" to be imprisoned. It was this law that was invoked against Klaus Croissant, defense counsel for the Baader-Meinhof Group. He was imprisoned for organizing an interview in *Der Spiegel* for his clients and thereby supporting a criminal organization even though Baader-Meinhof had not yet been legally proven to be a "criminal organization." In another case, the Provincial Court in Karlsruhe convicted and sentenced a woman student and a doctor to six and nine months in prison for "conspiring to publicize a criminal organization." They were distributing leaflets describing the solitary confinement conditions of the jailed members of the Red Army Faction (RAF) and stating the RAF's political position. The court ruled their actions were intended to recruit others into the RAF cause. Critics of this law also charge that the state has extended the purview of this law to the point of stigmatizing as "gang behavior" any resistance or self-help campaigns which are collectively organized. Persons who work on these campaigns or show support for them are liable to arrest under this law. Police have arrested members of the Squatters' Movement, and the Federal High Court has upheld the arrests by ruling that those who took part in the housing occupation for the purpose of protesting high rents, housing conditions, and housing shortages had a common purpose and thus constituted a single organization that under 129 StGB was a criminal organization.

CONTACT BAN LAW

Passed in 1976, the Contact Ban Law has been labelled "the solitary confinement law" by its critics. The state passed this law under what is defined as a "supra-legal state of emergency." It gives the courts the power to prohibit prisoners accused of supporting or being a member of a "terrorist organization" from contact with the outside world. In reality, it enforces solitary confinement, since access to visitors, newspapers, radio, mail, or legal counsel is prohibited. Because of the enforced isolation it is extremely difficult and often impossible for those confined to prepare for and receive a fair trial. More importantly, it is a form of pre-trial punishment that critics charge is meant to destroy the identity of political offenders. A good example is the case of radical activist Peter-Paul Zahl, who in 1974 was arrested and convicted of resisting arrest. The prosecution appealed the ruling and the High Court ordered a new trial on the charges of resisting arrest and attempted murder. Between his 1974 trial and retrial in 1976 Zahl was held in prison. Upon his conviction his sentence was extended from four years to fifteen years. The judge ruled that even though there was no new evidence presented at the retrial, the longer term was justified because even after three years of confinement, prisoner Zahl had not changed his hostile attitude towards the Constitution, and therefore he needed to be further deterred, and the public needed to be protected from him.

UNIFORM POLICE CODE

The Uniform Police Code constitutes the body of laws which delineates the authority and coordinates the activities of the police. Most important of these is Section 43, paragraph 2. The so-called "Death Shot Provision" gives the police the right to "shoot to kill" troublemakers or use weapons against a group "if acts of violence are being committed or are about to be committed by it or from within it, and action against individuals seems unlikely to be successful."[15] Between 1967 and 1978 two hundred people were shot by police and critics of the "shoot to kill" provision say greater numbers of people will be killed since police no longer have to justify the use of firearms as self defense. The following examples help confirm the critics' fears. According to the Federal Criminal Investigation Office *(Bundeskriminalamt)*, the use of firearms in criminal offenses was on the decline between 1972 and 1977. Police, on the other hand, were shooting more often. Between 1973 and 1976 police shot and killed fifty-seven people. In 1976 and 1977 they fired 411 warning shots, 301 shots at men, killed 25 people, and wounded 165. Shots fired in self defense totalled 310 while shots fired by reason of police regulations numbered 2,826. Unintentional shots with effect came to sixty-two in 1977, up from eighteen in 1976. In 1979 a Berlin woman said by police to be a terrorist suspect was killed with a bullet in the back by a police officer. Police officials said she had attempted to escape capture by turning and running away. Witnesses claimed that she could have easily been apprehended without shooting her. Also in 1979 a man suspected of terrorism was shot several times and seriously wounded as he entered his Frankfurt apartment, his arms loaded down with sports clothes and equipment. Police, who were hiding in the apartment, said he had attempted to reach into his pockets for a gun. Later, police admitted that because the suspect's hands were occupied with the sports equipment it was impossible for him to reach for anything without dropping the baggage, which he did not do.

Paragraph 36 gives police the power to use military weapons, automatic weapons, pistols, machine guns, and hand grenades. It also empowers police to use heavily armored equipment for demonstrations, strikes, pickets, pursuits and arrests. Paragraph 10, "Checking of Identity"; paragraph 17, "Searches of Persons"; and paragraph 19, "Entry into and Searches of Dwellings" extend the concept of suspicion and facilitate police intervention into citizens' private lives and homes on the mere pretext that they are acting suspicious. Researchers for the *Newsletter on Civil Liberties and Police Development* claim that:

> Searching of persons and objects as well as entering private dwellings will be made possible in situations where the concept of danger is no longer related to persons as suspects (potential criminals), but to geographical locations (check points, endangered property, suspicious dwellings, etc.). When the police define certain locations as security risks on their own authority, all persons who are present in or in the vicinity of these locations are automatically suspected of crime.[16]

THE DECREE ON RADICALS

In January 1972 state and federal governments in West Germany announced a set of policy directions known as the Hamburg Decrees. This set of regulations is meant to enforce "positive loyalty" on civil service employees. Principle 1 states:

> According to the state Civil Service Acts for the federal and state governments, only those persons may be appointed as public officials who can at all times guarantee support for the free democratic basic order according to the Constitution, and public officials are obliged to actively defend this basic order both in office and out of office.[17]

Under this code, the Constitutional Protection Office investigates the loyalty of thousands of people. A determination that an applicant or employee has engaged in unconstitutional activities or even belonged to an unconstitutional organization justifies rejection or dismissal from the civil service. This set of decrees, which we will examine in greater detail later, was judged to be constitutional by the Constitutional Court in 1975.

The most obvious effect of the anti-terrorist legislation has been the broadening of the power and activities of the German security apparatus. For example, under a law passed in 1972, the Criminal Investigation Bureau was given the authority to operate under its own initiative and to use intelligence-gathering procedures against "movements hostile to the Constitution." New legal measures that impinge upon democratic rights of privacy were also institutionalized, including the control of mail and telephone communication between West Germany and socialist countries. Information gathered by agents of the Federal Intelligence Office (BND), an agency charged only with duties of foreign reconnaissance, by means of letter-openings and telephone-monitoring is classified in archives called "Information about persons concerning recruitment and gaining of intelligence information" and sent to the Federal Domestic Intelligence Office (*Verfassungsschutz*) as part of the hunt for "enemies of the constitution" within West Germany. Between 1974 and 1978 decrees were passed permitting/ requiring state governments to pass information to the Security Group Bonn, a secret police organization. *Lander* police forces and governments were authorized to gather and store information on citizens in computer systems that are linked to the national computer of the Federal Criminal Bureau where it is available to any state agency upon request. Police stepped up their surveillance of labor disputes and strikes in which they gathered information of strike "ringleaders" and passed it on to corporate management officials. Telephone taps are routinely provided by the post office upon request of the Secret Service. Persons who protest the telephone tappings, like nuclear physicist Klaus Traube, find their motives questioned by police and suspicions aroused. Photographic surveillance, the use of individual identification cards, and the use of informers have all become too commonplace in West Germany. The surveillance capabilities of the Berlin police have been enhanced by the creation of *Kontact Beamter* (KOB), a system of neighborhood police surveillance which utilizes "walking police" (one officer per three thousand residents) who record all activity in a particular area. Security officials defend the KOB as a method by which police can offer better security and faster response to residents of the neighborhood. Critics charge the KOB acts as an agency of political surveillance similar to Hitler's "neighborhood wardens," a system used to control local political activity, and maintain that police officers routinely gather the smallest detail, including information about the voting records of neighboring residents. Both police officials and their critics agree that with this increased authorized surveillance capability, police activity under the KOB has taken on a preventive character and purpose that leaves the scope of police power undefined and open to broad interpretation. Throughout the Federal Republic, Intervention Units (MEX) are also employed for quick response to activity designated as "criminal" or "possibly criminal." In all cases, questions about confidentiality and citizens' rights to privacy are countered by the prevailing attitude among state security officials that "someone who is sought by the police has no right to keep the details of his life private."[18]

A large and comprehensive system of military state security was also installed. Rationalized by the "threat of terrorism," the state police forces were enlarged in number to a total of 150,247 by 1978 and were armed and trained in crisis management procedures. In effect, the police were militarized by the Uniform Police Code. To aid them in their expanded duties, the Federal Border Guard has, since 1972, taken on a policing role in the interior of the Federal Republic. Both the equipment and training of the Border Guard reflect its new function as an internal security service and permanently available intervention force. In addition to its normal arsenal of military weapons, it now is armed with water cannon and batons. Under "PD 201," both the Border Guard and the police are given special training in the use of weapons in civil war. Anti-riot technology, such as "Chemical Mace," "pepper fog," and electrical and acoustic paralyzing devices, have been tested for effectiveness. Police operations like the 1974 "Winter Journey" against organizers of rent strikes and "other sorts of trouble" in Frankfurt, the eviction of housing project "squatters," and the large-scale manhunts for the kidnappers of CDU leader Peter Lorenz and corporate executive Hans-Martin Schleyer also provide opportunities for the testing of equipment and police coordination and the conditioning of the public to the expanded scope of police activities. In addition, there are new communication channels to facilitate the flow of information between federal and state security agencies. Due to their advance computer and information technology, police can stop any vehicle and within eight to ten seconds know the name, residence, occupation, and criminal record of any German citizen in that vehicle.

The meanings of "violence," "terrorism," and "anti-state intention" remain undefined in West Germany. The legal parameters of police power are vague and often established after the fact. Police-raid laws passed in 1978 ostensibly for combatting terrorism are now applied for so-called normal forms of crime fighting. Proof of innocence or guilt has shifted from being the responsibility of the state to that of the individual. For instance, a Berlin woman was awakened early one morning by the shouting of her name to find her bedroom full of green-uniformed police and a machine gun in her face. She was hauled into police headquarters for a week of questioning concerning her passport, even though she had reported it stolen from her purse at school immediately after she discovered it was missing. Police, assuming she gave the passport to someone connected to the terrorists, placed her under surveillance for a year because her missing passport had ended up in the hands of Baader-Meinhof member Gretta Tettermann on the Swiss border. State-sponsored investigations, surveillance, raids, and harassment against people of the liberal and leftist political persuasions while the state ignores or tolerates those of right-wing persuasion, such as "sports clubs" who practice full-scale war maneuvers in the forests of the Federal Republic, have led to the charge that the West German state is "blind in the right eye." Finally, numerous cases, including an individual's being sent to prison for calling the Federal Republic a "Coca-cola Stall," anti-terrorist provision 129 StGB being applied against the Frankfurt Women's Center for transporting women to Dutch abortion centers, and police monitoring of the anti-nuclear and the "Green" party, indicate that the targets of the state anti-terrorist campaign sometimes are not terrorists at all. In a very real sense, as Interior Minister Hans-Dietrich Genscher said, "the danger is the people."[19]

THE *BERUFSVERBOT* AND THE POLITICS OF INTIMIDATION

The enforcement of the Hamburg Decrees (*Berufsverbot*) permit bans on public service employment on political grounds. Starting in 1972, the state moved to curb the power and influence of the "New Class" in Germany that the conservative alliance between the CDU/SU and the Right wing of the ruling SPD held responsible for the social upheaval of the late 1960s and the loss of conservative hegemony over the educational and cultural institutions of West German society in the early 1970s. Through the Hamburg Decrees, the state sought to confront the "leftist spirit" at the universities before it spread into society at large by securing the loyalty of public servants, a category that includes professional educators. By invoking the State Civil Service Acts, which mandate extensive investigations of civil service applicants and employees, the government refused appointments to those who could not prove their "inner commitment" to the state. Claiming that "civil servants are to be duty-bound to the state, in fact 'this state,' "[20] government officials began a drive to "bring clarity back into German culture." According to Professor Margit Mayer, one purpose of the state campaign was to revise the total educational system through the purification of books and texts that deal with controversial themes and are thus likely to create conflicts and problems for students. The state put a terrorist interpretation on the crisis affecting the educational system. By 1977 this view dominated mainstream German politics, as evidenced by the recommendations of a CDU party convention in Lower Saxony. Party delegates unanimously backed a resolution contending that government suffered from overload, a condition instigated by an educational process in which, due to the "heightened intellectualization in the schools . . . young people are brought up to place demands on society and the state."[21]

Also by 1977, of the 1.5 million people investigated, 4,000 or so were rejected on the basis of being "disloyal to the state" or showing "hostility to the state." Only two dozen of those investigated were extreme right-wingers, even though there was a revival of neo-Nazi political views led by the National Democratic Party, whose expressed aim is the destruction of liberal democracy. Many of those charged and discharged with disloyalty were industrious and loyal civil servants whose level of political activism during their university days may have consisted of attending a protest rally against the Vietnam War or a demonstration in favor of the liberal reform program. These peaceful protestors were caught in the state's efforts at "unmasking the enemies of the state." When further justification for the *Berufsverbot* was needed, the state pushed the ideology of "aggressive or militant democracy." For example, in their response to French historian Alfred Grosser's warnings about the continuation of authoritarian and anti-liberal traditions in the Federal Republic, state officials asked:

> **Hadn't it been the intent of the fathers of the Constitution to construct an "aggressive democracy?" Hadn't it been the concern at the time to guard the Constitution against its enemies so that anti-democratic forces could not once again uproot the democratic Constitution by exploiting its own liberal spirit? Loyalty to the constitution must then be particularly binding for public employees.[22]**

According to German political scientist Wolf-Dieter Narr, the state's enforcement of *Berufsverbot* gives us a clear idea of the political climate known as the "free democratic basic order" (FDGO) in West Germany. He says, "The formula extracts only certain parts of the Constitution. For instance, it is much more explicit with respect to organizational principles than with respect to the specific fundamental rights of individuals. It relies generally on freedom and equality and emphasizes the 'right to personality,' but omits mention of the democratic and social state."[23] This one-sided interpretation of the Constitution is diagnosed by the state to be the essence, or "spirit," of the Constitution, and creates a kind of super-constitution in which the state's view supercedes the actual Constitution. Narr says the FDGO formula is used to reverse the responsibility of the government to its citizens to enforce a political climate where the responsibility of the citizen and the civil servant is to the government.

The civil service and the universities were the specific targets of the *Berufsverbot*, but the campaign of investigations, accusations, dismissal, and guilt by association resulted in a wide-ranging political climate of intimidation. External censorship and self-censorship in the political, cultural, intellectual, and economic activities of liberal and left-wing circles were important by-products of *Berufsverbot* and resulted from the abstract nature of the FDGO formula and its broad interpretation. Critics claim that a climate was created where no-one who opposed the state in any way knew exactly when, where, or how much they would be affected or whether there would be any reasons given for their being affected.

The government also waged a public campaign against those individuals and organizations like the Russell Tribunal who raised objections to the *Berufsverbot* and the politics of intimidation. According to a document obtained surreptitiously by the Russell Tribunal, the German Ministry of the Interior concocted a plan to discredit the findings of the Third Russell Tribunal's 1978 investigation into the human rights situation in the Federal Republic. The state instigated the plan under the premise that "the danger exists that such a happening (the Tribunal) has new protest potential, gathers together and intensifies what there is already, and in addition strengthens a new terrorist extremism as well as sympathy for the terrorists who are fighting the state."[24] The specific proposals of the plan give us a good idea about the scope of governmental activities against the Tribunal and its supporters. They include:

3.1 Steering the proceedings by infiltration and participation of democratic power groups with the aim of achieving acquittal . . .

3.2 To influence personalities and groups of the democratic spectrum not to participate in the Tribunal and not to support it . . .

3.3 Prohibitions
—in accordance with the law on meetings. The possibility of prohibiting the Tribunal, or its preparatory meetings, is to be tested by the existing agencies for public order . . .

3.4 Withdrawal of subsidies, etc.
If it be determined that groups which are subsidized by public funds support the Tribunal, this subsidy shall be withdrawn . . .

3.5   Forfeiture of the basic rights according to Art. 18GG.
      If it can be established that persons in preparing or
      conducting the Tribunal, misuse basic rights mentioned
      in Art. 18, e.g., freedom of expression of opinion (Art.
      5), freedom of the press (Art. 5, Abs. 1.), freedom of
      association (Art. 8), or freedom to combine (Art. 9) in
      the fight against the liberal and democratic basic order,
      the Federal Parliament, Federal government, or a *Land*
      Government can make application concerning the for-
      feiture of basic rights . . .

3.6   Explanations and Information to the Public.
      The public inside and outside Germany must be edu-
      cated through intensive explanation and information
      concerning
      —background and the real aims of the groups carrying
      out the Tribunal
      —the powers which really activate the Tribunal
      —a clear and as unanimous as possible condemnation
      . . .
      —the real circumstances concerning the states of affairs
      misrepresenting and distorted by the Tribunal . . .[25]

The Russell Tribunal found that state powers under *Berufsverbot*
had adversely affected human rights. A few of the specific findings
included: that people critical of the government are considered
"hostile to the Constitution"; that the intelligence service operated
on a broad scale and gathered information on every kind of legal
political activity; that suspects were assumed to be guilty rather
than innocent; that the concepts of loyalty, hostility to the Constitution, and the free democratic order are vague and applied
arbitrarily; and that even though people may be considered loyal,
they are, because of their associations, judged a risk and are not
hired by or are fired from civil service because they might become
disloyal.

The government and the major media reacted to the report
with deafening silence. When official comment was made, two
points were stressed to the German citizen: First, the Russell
Tribunal was an international organization and there was no need
for the German public to regard it at all. Second, attention was
brought to the word "tribunal," which was purposefully connected

World War II, whose unpopularity with Germans is well known. With these obvious plays to German nationalistic sympathies and by employing its armada of ideological, political, economic, and media weapons, the state was able to minimize the findings of the Russell Tribunal and to continue its hold over the conservative political climate.

COUNTERTERRORISM: AN EVALUATION

Throughout the 1970s the West German government defended the expansion of state power as necessary for the preservation of German democracy. Both defenders and critics, who agree that the expansion of state powers did occur and that it had eroded the purview of individual rights in West Germany, disagree on the political implications. Defenders say they are aware of the negative effects of German counterterrorism on individual rights but justify them as necessary to save democracy. Some critics have argued that the state policy against terrorism exposed the true fascist nature of German democracy, thereby fulfilling the prophesy of the Red Army Faction. However, a majority opinion, while critical of the politics of intimidation, rejects this view, saying there is an important difference between Nazi Fascism with its institutionalized terror and the "aggressive democracy" of the Federal Republic. According to this popular view, the climate of "governability" is temporary, a result of the state's "overreaction" to terrorism. It is said that once the threat of terrorism is over, Germany will return to normalcy.

The basic problem with the thesis of "temporary overreaction" is the assumption that terrorism alone was the target of state policy. From the very beginning, the Federal Republic utilized a formidable security apparatus and drafted repressive legislation which intimidated and repressed political opposition. For example, in 1951 both the twenty-thousand-strong Federal Border Guard and the Security Group Bonn were created. In 1956 the Communist Party was banned, the provisions of the 1969 Emergency Laws were drafted, and Germany was declared a military state. State officials also see a need for continued vigilance in the foreseeable future. In 1975 Chancellor Schmidt estimated the period of crisis would extend over the next twenty-five years and would require a centralized detective force comparable to those in Eastern Europe.

The state's own definition of the crisis includes the "misguided liberalism" of the Brandt government, the rise of the "New Class" in the civil service, and the vaguely defined "internal enemy"—all of which were viewed as basic threats to the preferred political order of "militant democracy." Finally, the following comment made in 1974 by a West German police official leaves ominous doubts about the purposes of anti-terrorism legislation and policy:

> Anyone who examines the background can see that the new laws are the product of developments stretching over several years, and that even the final versions were not produced in the last few weeks . . . if some politicians and the media still insist that there is a connection between the Baader-Meinhof gang and measures designed to improve the security situation this is false and dangerous. It implies that security laws are hasty reactions to current events which would justify later, when the situation is normal for their repeal and relaxation.[26]

It was the state's purposeful imposition of the rule, "thou shalt not be, nor show any sympathy for, the terrorist," that allowed it to define and sort out those loyal to and those against its conception of German democracy. According to the state, as long as the crisis of authority, culture, and democratic excess remained, as evidenced by the presence of an "internal enemy," there was a need for a permanently vigilant state and society.

However, mainstream media reporting and scholarship from many political realms also work against the "temporary overreaction" thesis. Media reports, articles, and books on Baader-Meinhof played up the middle- and upper-class background of its members in order to discredit them in the eyes of the establishment working-class and trade-union movements. In this literature, multiple connections were made between the rise of German Fascism and its terrorism and, following Jillian Becker, the Baader-Meinhof Group was tagged "Hitler's Children" in order to negate any favorable publicity that might affect domestic and foreign opinion. So successful was this campaign that as early as 1975 Melvin Lasky, a strong supporter of the state's anti-terrorist policy, confidently wrote that the urban guerrillas had isolated themselves from public opinion and had become an embarrassment to the political Left.

To most of the German Left, the terrorists were more than an embarrassment; they were a political liability. Left-wing critiques of the terrorists are probably the most scathing of all. Their single purpose was to disassociate Baader-Meinhof and its successors from the established political Left and the larger progressive community on both a personal and political level. They claimed that the terrorists lacked any legitimacy within the German Left since they held no position of power or influence and had only a small crazed following. They claimed that the terrorists' cause was politically as well as morally bankrupt due to its inability to create the socio-economic and political conditions of fascism in Germany that they claimed existed immediately beneath the democratic facade.

Through its various critiques of terrorism, the Left attempted to separate itself from the terrorists. But its claim that terrorism was an isolated, illegitimate phenomenon was argued against by the government's massive campaign to link terrorism with the Left. In doing so, the state tried to establish the point that the real danger to German society was those who aided and abetted terrorism from behind the scenes through their intellectual endeavors and their positions of influence in political, social, and cultural institutions. Government officials felt that they were not overreacting to an isolated phenomenon but reacting appropriately to what was a permanent and fundamental challenge to German democracy.

Other evidence weighs against the "temporary overreaction" thesis advanced by the government. Both in the German print media and in private interviews with persons close to police operations it has been alleged that German police directly aided the terrorists by supplying them with weapons, passports, and other paraphernalia required to operate in the depths of the political underground and engage in violence. However, these charges have not been conclusively proven. Some critics have contended that the state's battle was not with terrorism *per se* but only with terrorism of the Left. During the 1970s the state was accused of ignoring the real and potential danger of right-wing terrorism and violence. Large-scale military training exercises by known neo-Nazi organizations were dismissed by German authorities as meaningless sport and hunting outings. Indeed, many of these paramilitary organizations pass themselves off as *wehrsport-gruppe*, or sports groups. Probably the best known is *Wehrsport-*

gruppe Hoffman led by Karl-Heinz Hoffman, a man known to have Nazi sympathies. Active since the early 1970s and estimated to have four hundred heavily armed members, this organization is treated as harmless by Bavarian government officials despite accusations that its members have been involved in political and religious harassment.

In 1980, at the same time the number of terrorists wanted by the West German government was fifteen (all of them alleged leftists) and federal prosecutor Kurt Rebman was warning that the threat from terrorism was not yet over, government estimates of membership in neo-Nazi groups totalled seventeen thousand persons in sixty-nine identifiable organizations. Some of the neo-Nazi organizations had claimed responsibility for attacks and bombings of foreign and Jewish property and persons in the late 1970s. The state's passive response to these organizations and the *wehrsportsgruppe* is in marked contrast to the massive scale of police investigations, mass arrests, the enforcement of *Berufsverbot*, and the political intimidation that defined the state's confrontation with left-wing violence. State officials simply do not include right-wing extremists on its "internal enemies" list on the same scale as it does left-wing groups and individuals, since right-wing violence tends to support the state and its conception of "militant democracy."

The recent revival of leftist terrorism against NATO installations, coinciding as it has with increased levels of militancy and terrorism by the German Right against Jews and the southern European minority community in the Federal Republic, may conclusively reveal the true nature of the German government's counterterrorist policy. A continued passive state posture toward right-wing terrorism and the neo-Nazi paramilitary organizations while the state continues to crack down on the sponsors of "misguided liberalism" would further counter the thesis of "temporary overreaction." It would also confirm that the state used the rise of leftist terrorism to install and reinforce a political climate of "authoritarian democracy" and that under the direction of Helmut Kohl and the conservative CDU, the government remains committed to its perpetuation.

TERRORISM IN SRI LANKA AND INDIA

The suprapower rivalry is part of the current epidemic of terrorism but it is only one aspect. There are complex historical roots and a multitude of issues and forces behind other aspects of terrorism as evidenced in Sri Lanka, India and, as we have seen, in Northern Ireland. Our intent is to re-establish that, in both historic and modern times, terrorism is a complex phenomenon springing from diverse sources and for a multitude of reasons. It is this reality that has been obscured by the extreme politicalization of the explosion of terrorism in recent years.

COMMUNAL TERRORISM IN SRI LANKA

Sri Lanka, the teardrop-shaped island off the southeast coast of India, is a nation inflamed by communal terrorism that so far has defied all efforts at settlement. As of late 1986, the reality of open civil war between the Buddhist Sinhalese majority (seventy-four percent of the population) and Hindu Tamil minority (thirteen percent) threatens to undermine if not totally destroy what was once a solid democratic tradition.

The communal conflict on this paradise-like island, once known as Ceylon, has deep historical roots. The Sinhalese and Tamil communities co-existed in an uneasy relationship for over two thousand years. But since Sri Lanka gained its independence from Britain in 1948 the deep-seated antagonism between the two communities has grown steadily, inflamed by extremists in both communities and their horrific acts of terror. Beginning with the explosive communal riots in July 1983, which officially took 387 lives (unofficial sources say the death toll was in the thousands), Sri Lanka has been engulfed in a vicious circle of ethnic terrorism.

The major antagonists in the conflict are the Tamil guerrillas of the underground Tiger Movement and the Sri Lankan military and police forces. Increasingly, the two sides are fighting open pitched battles. But both continue to employ terrorism to brutalize the respective Sinhalese and Tamil civilian populations, with unarmed men, women, and children the major victims in what have become almost routine daily slaughters.

The reasons for the terrorism in Sri Lanka are varied and complicated. But a major driving force behind the explosion of the communal violence is that the militants in both the Sinhalese and Tamil communities pursue their terrorist acts with a deep-seated sense of righteousness; each is firmly convinced that justice and God are on their side. In this way, Sri Lanka's terrorism is not unique. Viewing right and wrong in terms of one's personal or country's moral beliefs is a situation that is, as we have seen, a major motivation of terrorism throughout the world.

As the dominant political force in post-colonial Sri Lanka, the Sinhalese majority has made several obvious attempts to institutionalize its political and economic power in Sri Lanka at the expense of the rival Tamil minority. The first of these government-sponsored decisions was the Citizenship Act, which in effect made most of the Indian Tamil plantation workers, who constitute about six percent of Sri Lanka's population, a stateless community. In 1956 the government of Prime Minister Solomon Bandaranaike, riding a wave of Sinhalese nationalism, passed the Sinhalese-only Act, installing Sinhala as the official language of Sri Lanka. The impact on the Tamil minority, who speak Tamil and practice Hindu, was disastrous. Under British rule the Tamils had invested more heavily in education than in land. As a result, they held a disproportionate number of high-paying jobs. The government's language decision effectively excluded the Tamils from the universities and most other positions of power. Then, in the early 1970s, the government installed a "standardization" system requiring that Tamil students possess higher marks than Sinhalese students for admission to the university. Finally, in what has proven to be the most controversial decision of all, the government, under the rubric of achieving racial balance, has sponsored a migration program of Sinhalese into the Tamil "homeland" of northern and eastern Sri Lanka where the Tamils are the majority population.

The political leadership of the Sinhalese majority has taken these steps with a righteous belief in the historical destiny of the Sinhalese community. From their reading of Sri Lankan history comes the claim that, as the original community to arrive from India, as the only people in the world speaking Sinhala, a language with deep Sanskrit origins, and as the "chosen race" of Lord Buddha, it is the right of the Sinhalese people to dominate the island. Indeed, it is the belief of many Sinhalese that unless they do dominate Sri Lanka they face racial extinction. Unlike the Tamil minority, who have fifty million fellow Dravidians across the narrow Palk Strait in southern India, the Sinhalese, if they are driven from Sri Lanka, have no brotherly community or "mother country" to turn to for support. There is a strong sentiment among Sinhalese that, though they are the majority population on Sri Lanka, they are a minority within the greater Tamil community that stretches across India's Tamil Nadu state. The Sinhalese view themselves as constantly under threat from this larger and antagonistic Tamil population.

In making their case, the Sinhalese point to a history of successful invasions by Tamil kings from southern India. Over the centuries these invasions have forced the Sinhalese community to move its capital progressively southwards from Anuradhapura to Polonnaruwa, to Kandy, and finally to the present location at Colombo on the southwestern coast.

Current militant Sinhalese politicians such as Cyril Mathew have invoked this history of Tamil invasion and forced Sinhalese migration to heighten chauvinistic and militant sentiments among the Sinhalese. Their claim is that if Tamil demands for a separate state are granted by the central government the majority Sinhalese population will be forced into a final retreat, this time to Dondra, the southernmost tip of the island. Eventually they would be compelled to jump into the Indian Ocean and to their extinction.

Sinhalese extremism and government anti-Tamil policy is also driven by strong feelings of resentment against the Tamil minority for its pampered condition under British colonial rule. It is true that the British did favor the hard-working Tamil community, rewarding them in many realms, particularly in education. This favoritism eventually enabled the Tamils to dominate the civil service and other professions during the colonial period and in the initial decade after British rule ended.

On the other side, the Tamils see themselves as Sri Lanka's

oppressed minority. Tamil leaders of every political persuasion accuse the government and majority Sinhalese population of treating Tamils as second-class citizens at best and at worst seeking to install a political system of racial domination if not complete Tamil racial extinction. For most Tamils, the government's downgrading of the Tamil language in 1956 gave immediate credibility to this claim. The government-sponsored settlement of Sinhalese in predominantly Tamil areas has only added fuel to the charge. Tamils see the settlement as the purposeful rearrangement of the ethnic makeup in areas where they are the majority. They see this as a colonial policy and compare it to Israel's controversial settlement of the occupied West Bank in the Middle East. To Tamils, the disastrous implications of the settlement policy to their political fortunes are clear in areas such as Trincomalee, where since 1948 the Sinhalese population has grown from a tiny minority to thirty percent of the population and parity with the Tamils.

Over the years the implications of government decisions on the Tamil community have led even moderate Tamils to conclude that racial superiority guides Sinhalese policy and must be resisted to the last Tamil. This conclusion has fueled Tamil militancy and extremist opposition to government authority. Over the past three years Tamil hostility and violence have been mainly directed at the government's settlement plan. The government has pushed ahead with its settlement scheme in the face of repeated Tamil hostility and acts of resistance. For example, the government implemented its migration plan in the Dollars and Kent farms in the Mulaitivu district despite public warnings from Tamil leaders. Under the guise of a "village expansion scheme," the army pushed Tamil owners off their land and replaced them with Sinhalese ex-convicts. In November 1984 Tamil guerrillas raided the farms and massacred at least seventy-two Sinhalese ex-convicts. But in January 1985 President Junius Jayewardene announced that no part of the island would be considered as the traditional homeland of any community and that he intended to go ahead with his program to settle thirty thousand Sinhalese from the south in the Vanni "dry zone" of Northern Province. Under this plan each Sinhalese family would be given a half-acre of land and money to build a home, and each settlement would be armed with twenty-five machine guns and two hundred rifles to protect itself against Tamil guerrillas.

In its resettlement scheme the government has used nationalized corporations and cultural "discoveries" to force Tamils off their land. Both tactics have further provoked Tamil hostility against the Sinhalese. In Mannar District, the government took four thousand acres of Tamil land and handed it over to the Cashew Corporation. Sinhalese laborers from the south were brought in to work the land. Cashew then declared it could not make a profit from the enterprise and divided the land up among the Sinhalese workers.

The government has also been found attempting to create a false cultural historical record in Tamil areas recently resettled by Sinhalese migrants in order to solidify Sinhalese claims to the land. The scheme involves setting up museums, such as the one in Vavuniya, which are stocked with Sinhalese cultural "discoveries" unearthed in the new settlements. Among the "discoveries" supposedly unearthed from Tamil villages all over the Vanni area were statues of Buddha and other remnants of Sinhalese and Buddhist civilizations. Confronted by archaeologists' doubts about the relics' authenticity, several senior Sri Lankan civil servants admitted that alleged "cultural discoveries" in Vanni were either bought or prepared and brought from Sinhalese areas. The purpose behind the deception was to establish that Vanni was a Sinhalese historical site rather than a Tamil traditional homeland.

Since the early 1970s the Tamils, provoked by the government's decisions discriminating against their language, culture, and citizenship and restricting their opportunities in education and the professions, have demanded the establishment of a separate Tamil state (to be called *Eelam*). The Tamil proposal calls for uniting the northern and eastern regions of the island where Sri Lankan Tamils have lived since antiquity. At the forefront of the Tamil separatist movement is the Tamil United Liberation Front (TULF). This organization consists of a number of major Tamil political organizations and was formed in 1972 under the name Tamil United Front.

In its early years, the TULF sought political power through the established political system. In 1977 the TULF took part in the parliamentary elections, seeking a mandate from the Tamil population for a separate independent state. The TULF won only 18 of 168 parliamentary seats, but the elections produced evidence of strong support for the separatist movement. For example, in areas where there was a Sri Lankan Tamil majority (who are different from the

Indian Tamils), TULF candidates won every constituency but one on a platform calling for a secular socialist state of Eelam and a party manifesto demanding that "Sinhalese imperialism shall quit our homeland."[1] Also during the early 1970s, an underground separatist organization composed mainly of Tamil youths surfaced in the Tamil community. Demanding a separate Tamil state, these self-professed "freedom fighters," known collectively as the Tiger Movement, embarked upon a terrorist campaign of assassinations, robberies, and bombings.

Since the end of the 1970s the Tiger Movement, though split into several separate and at times antagonistic factions, has managed to heighten militant sentiment within the Tamil community. Recently, the battlefield successes of Tiger guerrillas have been central to the extremists' political campaign. During 1985 the five main guerrilla groups of the Tiger Movement, possessing an armed strength of more than twenty-five hundred fighters, managed to forestall the government's brutal military campaign to stamp out the Tamil separatist movement by fighting the army to a draw. By early 1986 the Marxist-oriented Liberation Tigers of Tamil Eelam, the most violent and hard-line of Tamil organizations, emerged victorious from a series of fierce battles between rival Tamil factions to gain control of the militant opposition forces. Their political credibility bolstered by their battlefield success, they have directed the extremist Tamil elements in enlisting political support within the larger Tamil community for their armed campaign and the separatist state of Eelam. At present, as negotiations between the Tamil moderates and the government continue to falter or prove fruitless, many disillusioned members of the moderate political Tamil leadership of the TULF are moving to the extremist camp and supporting its terrorist campaign.

The first major incidents of communal violence between the Sinhalese and Tamils started in 1956 after the announcement of the official language decision. Retaliatory violence and terrorism began in earnest after the 1977 parliamentary election, with communal riots claiming at least three hundred lives. Several sources claim that the 1977 riots were provoked by Sinhalese hostility to Tamil separatist demands, the Tiger Movement's terrorist campaign, and alleged anti-Sinhalese campaign statements made by Tamil politicians.

The current tidal wave of rampant terrorism and violence,

which today threatens to end in outright civil war, began with nationwide communal riots in 1983. The rioting started in Colombo but the death and destruction from the wave of incendiarism, looting, and assault quickly spread across the entire island. Property damage was massive throughout the island, with much of the commercial section of Colombo, called "the Pettah," totally destroyed. The destruction and terror caused by the rioting also drove tens of thousands of people from their homes into grim refugee camps.

According to numerous sources, the 1983 riots stand as a turning point in the history of communal violence in Sri Lanka. For the first time the rioting involved a sophisticated level of organization and planning. Responsibility for the planning has been traced to a government ministry that sent out its employees armed with election lists to target Tamil property for destruction. The 1983 riots also underscored the vicious cycle of terrorist retaliation and counter-retaliation that has come to characterize Sri Lanka's ethnic conflict. For example, the Sinhalese claimed that their rioting began as retaliation for a Tamil Tiger ambush of a patrol of Sinhalese soldiers in which thirteen soldiers were killed. In turn, Tamil sources said their ambush was in retaliation for the kidnapping and rape of several young Tamil women by Sinhalese troops in the Jaffna district. Finally, the 1983 riots marked the beginning of an era in which the communal violence and terrorism between the Sinhalese and Tamils victimizes other ethnic communities. The official death lists from the 1983 riots include not just Sri Lankan Tamils, but also scores of Indian Tamils and Indian nationals, neither of whom had any ties or sympathies with the Northern Province or the separatist movement.

Since 1983 the level of terrorism by both sides has reached epidemic proportions. According to Western news sources, who have focused most of their attention on Tamil terrorism, the Tamil Tiger Movement has shifted its attacks from individuals and government installations to sending large groups of armed guerrillas into pitched battles with government military forces and large-scale assaults on major police installations. Sinhalese civilians, especially those who have migrated into the predominantly Tamil areas, continue to be victimized by Tamil terrorism. Among the recent reports of Tamil terrorism is one of Sinhalese children between the ages of nine months and fourteen years being forced to kneel beside an irrigation ditch in the town of Sipura and then shot in the backs of their heads.

Western media coverage of Sinhalese and official government terrorism is not as extensive as accounts of Tamil terrorism. Yet the government of India and Western human rights organizations such as Amnesty International have been among those charging the Sri Lankan government with terrorism and widespread human rights violations. These reports claim that government troops in the north are out of control and indiscriminately killing Tamil civilians. In its 1984 report on Sri Lanka, Amnesty International charged that government forces had randomly killed unarmed members of the Tamil community in acts of reprisal for the killing of thirteen soldiers by Tamil militants in July 1983.[2] According to the Amnesty report, the government finally admitted in November 1983 that its armed forces had gone "on the rampage" and killed fifty-one people. Six more Tamil civilians were reported killed by the army in four separate incidents in the late summer and early fall of 1983. Most Sri Lankan officials deny these charges. Yet independent reports coming from recent army offensives in the north, such as the one in April 1986 in which ninety civilians died, tend to verify the charges levelled against the government for its "official" terrorism. In its reporting of government terrorism, Amnesty International has also expressed concern that Tamils continue to be arrested under the provisions of the Prevention Against Terrorism Act (PTA), during which they are held without trial and in at least seventy-five out of one hundred and seventy cases were tortured by security officials. Torture reportedly includes hanging victims upside down from hooks, beating them with metal bars, applying chili powder to sensitive body parts, and driving needles under fingernails. Amnesty International investigators have charged that following the torture sessions a number of prisoners died while still in army custody. Amnesty International also recorded reports linking Welikada Prison officials to the deaths of fifty-three Tamil political prisoners who were detained or convicted under the Prevention of Terrorism Act in Welikada Prison. Official government reports claimed the prisoners died at the hands of Sinhalese inmates.

Since 1983 the communal conflict has claimed more than three thousand lives. Today there is no end in sight to the carnage. Indeed, in the summer of 1986 the fighting seemed to be entering a new and even more deadly phase. A powerful bomb destroyed an Air Lanka Lockheed Tristar airliner parked on the tarmac of Colombo's Katunayake International Airport, killing sixteen people. Four days later eleven people died and one hundred and fifteen were injured in the bombing of Colombo's Central Telegraph Office. A third bomb exploded in a processed food and soft drink factory in central Colombo, killing eight people and injuring fifty others. Sri Lankan officials blamed Tamil terrorists for the three bombings and used them to push a request to increase the military budget from $290 million to $420 million through the Sri Lankan Parliament. A further buildup of government military forces appears imminent. President Jayawardene warns that if current negotiations with the Tamil guerrillas produce no settlement, a larger military effort will be initiated to eliminate the curse of Tamil terrorism.

Guided by Jayawardene's claim that Tamil terrorists and their community of sympathizers are the major source of terrorism in Sri Lanka, the government and its security forces have cracked down hard in Tamil-populated areas by invoking the anti-terrorist provisions of the Prevention of Terrorism Act and the Emergency Regulations. The government's repressive "security" measures, ostensibly aimed at the terrorists, have caused a great deal of hardship on the entire Tamil population, particularly in Jaffna. Most of the peninsula is covered by a security zone and a dusk-to-dawn curfew. Residents are required to have a special permit to use their vehicles and bicycles. This has severely restricted the movement of people and goods. Exit permits are required of those wishing to leave the peninsula. The government has also declared a one-hundred-mile arc of coastal land covering the entire northern coastline as a prohibited zone. Anyone caught by security forces in the area is considered to be a terrorist guerrilla. This zone, along with a broader surveillance area covering coastal waters in the same region, is designed to end the logistical support coming to the Tamil guerrillas from Tamil Nadu in India.

The government's security measures have brought all Tamil commercial enterprise, particularly the all-important fishing industry, to a grinding halt. Five bridges have been blown up, leaving only one closely guarded road as access from the peninsula to the rest of the island. Many Tamil citizens claim the army destroyed the bridges. The government blames the Tamil guerrillas. Regardless of who destroyed the bridges, the limited island access clearly works to the advantage of the government's security strategy and its military forces. It has become an instrumental part of the government's effort to isolate the Tamil stronghold of Jaffna and cripple its economic base, forcing the Tamil people to abandon their struggle for an independent state. Contrary to the government's hopes, observers in Jaffna report that so far the repressive security regulations have only driven more and more people, including moderate political leaders of the TULF, into the ranks of the militants.

At present, there is no end in sight to the terrorism and counterterrorism that grips Sri Lanka as both sides continue their terrorism and reprisal killings. The government continues to operate under the Emergency Regulations, to enforce the PTA, and go forward with its migration plan. Meanwhile, relations between the Sinhalese majority and the Tamil minority continue to worsen and threaten to end up in an island-wide civil war.

Outside efforts, particularly those by Indian Prime Minister Rajiv Gandhi, to intervene as a neutral party and settle the conflict have so far failed. The Indian government has prodded the Tamil guerrillas to negotiate a settlement. For his part, Gandhi clearly favors the moderate, non-Marxist elements within the Tamil community. Still, for several reasons the Sri Lankan government and the Sinhalese community at large remain extremely suspicious of Indian claims of neutrality. The Indian army has provided training to all five liberation movements involved in the Indian-sponsored peace talks. Several Tamil leaders have taken refuge in Madras, where they reside in luxurious houses provided by the Indian government and essentially under Indian control. In addition, major support for the Tamil separatist movement comes from the Indian state of Tamil Nadu with little or no effort by the Indian government to discourage or end it. Taken together, these circumstances only reinforce the sentiment and fears within Sri Lanka's Sinhalese community that India acts as a protective "mother country" to a Sri Lankan Tamil community determined to push them into the Indian Ocean and ultimately racial extinction.

We have seen that the present battle of ethnic and communal terrorism raging between the Sinhalese and Tamil communities in Sri Lanka is connected to a long-standing historical conflict. It continues to be fueled at present by decisions, policies, fears, and antagonisms connected to a multitude of local racial, religious, and cultural differences. Yet, it is not completely divorced from the larger East-West global contest. For example, there are powerful Marxist elements within the Tamil guerrilla forces, a fact which largely explains why Tamil terrorism is reported in the Western media as the problem threatening Sri Lankan democracy. But the Soviet Union has no control over the Tamil Tiger Movement and little, if any, influence in the Tamil community. It is also true that the Sri Lankan government receives large doses of aid from the United States, Canada, Britain, West Germany, and Japan. Yet it finds itself at odds with these Western donor nations over its refusal to share the aid with the Tamil community in the north.

From the perspective of the Middle View, these international forces are not the principal reason for the terrorism in Sri Lanka. The Cold War political themes, which guide the "ideology of terrorism" and the Soviet View, do not help us expand what we know about Sri Lanka's place in the contemporary explosion of terrorism. Rather it is the complex constellation of local forces and issues, some of which we have discussed briefly, which deserve the bulk of our attention if we are to develop a sound analysis of Sri Lankan terrorism and of contemporary terrorism in general.

ETHNIC DIVERSITY AND TERRORISM IN INDIA

On June 5, 1984 Indian Prime Minister Indira Gandhi, in a military operation dubbed Operation Blue Star, ordered the Indian army to storm the Sikh Golden Temple in Amritsar in India's northwestern State of Punjab and seize it from the two thousand followers of Sikh militant preacher Jarnail Singh Bhindranwale. Until Gandhi's decision, the daily violence and terrorism between the Hindu majority and the Sikh minority in India had drawn little attention outside the Indian subcontinent. But since June 1984 terrorism in India has been front page news around the world. Indeed, in late October 1984 it became obvious that something was very wrong in India when Prime Minister Gandhi was assassinated by her Sikh bodyguards. Sikh extremists claimed Gandhi's murder was an act of revenge for the killing of Bhindranwale and at least one thousand of his followers and the desecration of the Golden Temple, the Sikh's holiest shrine, during Operation Blue Star. The horror of this single terrorist act was compounded a thousand times over as Hindus, in revenge-sparked riots, massacred over three thousand Sikhs throughout India.

Since Gandhi's assassination, Sikh and Hindu extremists have intensified their respective terrorist campaigns in India. Sikh terrorism has captured the most media attention, particularly since the Sikhs have made it clear they have few qualms about victimizing members of the international community if it serves their cause. In one well publicized case, Sikh terrorists set off a deadly explosion aboard an Air India Boeing 747 jet off the coast of Ireland in June 1985, killing 329 people. Yet, in modern India, the explosion of terrorism is not the exclusive province of the Sikh community but rather a multi-faceted phenomenon.

India is a multi-cultural society consisting of Kashmirs, Tamils, Bengalis, Muslims, and Sikhs. Over a period of several centuries each has developed a high degree of cultural and subnational awareness. During British colonial rule and the struggle for independence this consciousness was generally subsumed under the banner of Indian nationhood. In post-colonial India subnational sentiment has developed to the point where it often is at direct odds with and threatens to undermine Indian nationalism and the national political system.

Among the various cultural and religious groups of India, the development of Sikh subnational awareness is a recent phenomenon. Indeed, Sikhism is one of the world's youngest religions, founded in the fifteenth century by the guru Nanak. During its first two centuries Sikhism developed a reputation as a militant warrior sect steeped in a tradition of bravery and martyrdom. The Muslim Mogul rulers of India, through their genocidal persecution of Sikhism, which they considered as a heresy to be rooted out with vengeance, were largely responsible for the development of Sikh warrior lore. Later, both the British colonial authorities and the Indian government enlisted this fierce military tradition by incorporating large numbers of Sikhs in their respective colonial and post-colonial armies. The current leaders of the Sikh extremist movement have purposely embellished this warrior tradition and centuries-old martyrdom to recruit and train young Sikhs for their terrorist campaign against the Hindus.

It was also during the first two hundred years of their religious development that the Sikhs adopted their distinctive bearded and turbaned appearance, their long hair knotted under the turban. The purpose was to develop a Sikh identity and to distinguish Sikhs from other Indian communities. Today it is a major source of controversy within the Sikh community.

Under the forceful leadership of Maharaja Ranjit Singh, Sikh power reached its zenith in the nineteenth century. The Sikh empire ruled over northern India, Kashmir, and what is now Pakistan and stretched west to east from the borders of Afghanistan to Tibet. Despite its breadth and power, the Sikh kingdom was easily conquered by the British in 1849, only ten years after Ranjit Singh's death. Still, Sikh attachment to the idea of a separate Sikh kingdom was firmly established during this period. The traditional Sikh homeland was split into predominantly Hindu India and mainly Muslim Pakistan in 1947 and the Punjab partitioned again in 1966. Yet, the historical attachment to a separate Sikh state remains strong among Sikhs and a major reason for the current rise in Sikh militancy.

The philosophical foundations of Sikhism are a combination of Hinduism and Islam. But the majority of the first Sikhs came from Hinduism. Until recently most Sikhs have maintained close familial and kinship ties with the Hindu majority. In turn, until the rise and spread of the Hindu revivalist movement in Punjab during the late nineteenth century and early twentieth century, Hindus treated Sikhism as one of their own sects.

Even today most Hindus regard the Sikhs as one of their own. But the Hindu revivalist movement in Punjab forced the Sikhs to turn inward and fostered the development of Sikhism as a separate order. A Sikh reform movement further spurred Sikh subnational consciousness and managed to set up a centralized body to run Sikh temples and establish educational institutions to socialize Sikh children in the history, values, and behavioral norms of Sikhism. An exclusive Sikh-only political party called the *Akali Dal*, led by wealthy and educated Sikhs, was organized in the 1930s as the promoter and guardian of Sikh interests. Since its founding, the party has played a pivotal role in the political and religious mobilization of the Sikh community. In particular, the Akali Dal has consciously boosted Sikh subnationalist sentiment by demanding the creation of a Sikh homeland (*Khalistan*) in the state of Punjab and by insisting that the Punjabi language, which some linguists call a Hindu dialect, be installed as the national language of the Sikhs. Both demands were rejected, first by the British colonial administration and later by the Indian government.

The roots of contemporary Sikh militancy and, ultimately,

terrorism can be traced to the early years of Indian statehood. The Sikhs strongly supported the Indian nationalist movement against British colonialism. The subsequent division of the subcontinent into India and Pakistan once independence was won in 1947 brought great hardship to the Sikhs. The partition cut across the Sikh homeland of Punjab and forced millions of Sikhs, many of whom were very prosperous, out of the new Pakistan and into India where they arrived penniless and embittered. During the migration Sikhs and Muslims fought fierce and brutal battles against each other with both sides engaging in and subject to brutal killings. The march left a legacy of communal violence and murderous revenge that today smolders just below the surface in both communities.

Ironically, the system of Indian democracy has also been difficult for the Sikhs. Under British colonial rule Sikhs enjoyed special privileges, including separate elections which gave them more political power than their minority status warranted. Today the fifteen million Sikhs still comprise barely two percent of India's seven hundred and fifty million people, eighty-three percent of whom are Hindu. Under the Indian democratic system there are no separate elections. Forced to compete for power against larger ethnic communities in the "one man, one vote" system of Indian politics, Sikhs are now at a severe numerical disadvantage. In addition, their political leadership has proven to be inept or at least consistently outmaneuvered by the Hindu politicians in control of the central government. Provoked by these adverse political conditions, fervent Sikh nationalists exposed a raw nerve in the Sikh community shortly after independence with the charge that in the division of the Punjab the Muslims were given Pakistan and the Hindus got India, but the Sikhs got nothing. Their forceful agitation for a Sikh homeland or *Punjabi Suba*, which is a state for all those who speak Punjabi, was partially rewarded in 1966 when the Indian government divided Punjab into two states—Haryana and Punjab. At present, nine million Sikhs, or fifty-two percent of the population, reside in the new Punjab, with the remaining six million Sikhs scattered throughout the rest of India, with one million in New Delhi.

At first glance there appears to be little reason for Sikh extremism and the growth of terrorist organizations in the 1980s. After all, the Indian government conceded to the historical homeland demand in India where Sikhs now constitute a numerical majority. This majority position has proven politically advantageous, having helped the Akali Dal control the government of Punjab from 1977 to 1980. The Sikhs are also among the most prosperous Indians. Due to hardworking Sikh farmers, who produce sixty-five percent of India's food grain reserves, and the "Green Revolution" in Indian agriculture, the Punjab is now India's breadbasket. Sikhs have also fared well in the manufacturing and construction industries. Relative to their numbers, they hold a disproportionately high number of prominent positions on the national level in industry, the government, and the army. They are also greatly admired by other Indians for their hard work and enterprising spirit.

Despite their favorable position in Indian society, social turmoil began to dominate the Sikh community in the 1980s. Extremist sentiments and terrorist organizations found support among Sikhs and militants increasingly occupied positions of prominence and political power. Even before Indira Gandhi's fateful decision in June 1984 to activate Operation Blue Star and occupy the Golden Temple, violence between Sikh extremists and moderates and bloody clashes between Sikhs and Hindus were almost daily occurences.

Current Sikh militancy is driven by a profound identity crisis among Sikhs that is growing worse as modernization and prosperity come to the Sikh community. This identity crisis is summed up by the popular Sikh slogan "The Panth (religion) is in danger." Over the past decade many Sikhs began to openly express the fear that they and their religion would be engulfed and ultimately absorbed by Hinduism.

To Sikh extremists, the absorption of Sikhism by Hinduism and modernization is far advanced. Indeed, many of the more prosperous Sikhs have abandoned the outward symbols of Sikhism: the turbans, long flowing beards, and steel daggers, finding them inconvenient in dealing with Western culture and out of place in a cosmopolitan setting. Orthodox Sikhs, fearful that these trends will eventually lead to the extinction of their cultural and religious identity, have become fanatically attached to Sikh symbols and have forcefully promoted their preservation. In addition, though there are some dissenters on this issue, a large and extremely vocal sector of the Sikh community has argued that only political autonomy can safeguard Sikhism. While extremists demand a totally independent country, moderates have proposed that Sikhism can be protected and enhanced by a politically autonomous state within the Indian union.

The beliefs of the Sikh minority are also fueled by a combination of demographic, economic, and political factors. In Punjab, where the Sikhs have enjoyed a numerical majority since 1966, there are clear signs that the Sikh majority is now endangered. In 1971 Sikhs constituted 60.2 percent of the population. By the early 1980s the Sikh majority was down to fifty-two percent. Several factors have combined to reduce this majority. First, as a result of the successful "Green Revolution" in Punjab agriculture, hundreds of thousands of non-Sikh workers from Uttar Pradesh, Bihar, Rajasthan, and Orissa have migrated to and settled in Punjab. At the same time there has been a major outflow of Sikhs from Punjab to neighboring states in India and overseas. Census reports indicate that by the early 1970s at least one-fifth of the Sikh population in India lived outside Punjab, with more Sikhs leaving every day. Prosperous Sikh communities have sprung up in India outside the Punjab and in Canada, the United States, Britain, East Africa, West Germany, Thailand, Singapore, Hong Kong, and Malaysia. These wealthy immigrant Sikh communities serve as a powerful magnet attracting large numbers of Sikhs from the Punjab. For example, in 1970 sixty percent of the Indian immigrant population to England were Jat Sikhs. (Interestingly, those Jat Sikhs who stayed in the Punjab have become the major social support resource for the Punjab extremist movement in the 1980s and are actively urging members of their sect to return from overseas.) This outflow of Sikhs from the Punjab raises the very real possibility, and thus fear, among Punjab Sikhs that in the near future the Sikhs could again be a numerical minority in the one state where they have enjoyed majority status since 1966.

In addition to the reduction in its overall percentage, the Sikh numerical majority is severely undercut by political factionalism within the Sikh community. Major sections of the Sikh population, particularly the Scheduled Caste (Mazhbi), and members of the merchant castes such as the Khattris, Aroras, and Suds, have opposed the political and religious militancy of the Jat Sikhs. The lack of social homogeneity only fuels the fanaticism and paranoia of more militant Sikhs. In their view, Sikhism is threatened both by non-Sikh, particularly Hindu, populations and by those within the Sikh community who are unwilling to take the necessary steps to ensure its survival.

non-Sikh, particularly Hindu, populations and by those within the Sikh community who are unwilling to take the necessary steps to ensure its survival.

Also, while the Punjab is India's most developed agricultural area and the Sikhs the dominant and most prosperous population in its rural sector, it remains a backward industrial state. In the past, the Hindu-dominated central government, citing the Punjab's location as a border state and thus vulnerable to foreign invasion, has been reluctant to invest public funds in the industrial sector. Sparked by Hindu intransigence and control of the public purse strings, Sikh leaders have insisted that continued development and thus prosperity for Punjab's Sikhs requires a major commitment from the central government for the industrialization of the state, a larger percentage of the river waters flowing through Punjab, quick completion of the Thien Dam, and more electrical power for both industry and agriculture. The continued reluctance of the Indian central government to recognize the Punjab's industrial needs or move on them fuels the efforts of Sikh extremists to drum up sentiment depicting Sikhs as a persecuted minority. In this way, the Sikh demand for state autonomy is really a code term for increased control in the economic sector, particularly of the industrialization process, as the only way to guarantee Sikh prosperity and, ultimately, survival.

The minority mentality among Sikhs and the resulting fears and ethnic insecurity that flow from it have also been heightened by the inability of the Akali Dal to build a dominant political base in the Punjab despite the Sikh numerical advantage. The Akali Dal has never been able to maintain political control of the Punjab government or push the agenda of the Sikh population without cooperating with non-Sikhs. None of the three post-1966 Akali-led governments lasted a full term, as non-Sikhs and non-Akali Sikhs pursued their own political agendas. Now, with the rise of Sikh extremist sentiment, the moderate leaders of the still-prominent Akali Dal have been unable to dominate politically. Though moderate to the core, both their political instincts and events in India beyond their control are pushing the Akali Dal leaders to adopt a political strategy more in tune with the Sikh militant sentiment in order to solidify their present political position as well as secure their place in any future Sikh-dominated state.

Sikh extremism in Punjab was also spurred by the ultimately

disastrous political strategy of the Indira Gandhi-led Congress
Party in the early 1980s, which sought to split and weaken the
Akali Dal in the Punjab in order to regain power for itself. For their
vehicle they chose Jarnail Singh Bhindranwale, a charismatic Sikh
preacher. In the late 1970s Bhindranwale had successfully tapped
the hostile sentiments of poor Sikhs, especially farmers and young
people, who have not tasted the fruits of prosperity and feel that
their traditional Sikh lifestyle is under attack from the forces of
modernization. Emboldened by the backing of the Congress Party,
Bhindranwale played to this pent-up hostility by preaching a
fanatical Khomeini-style Sikh fundamentalism and demanding a
return to "pure" Sikhism and the founding of a separate Sikh
homeland. He quickly attracted large numbers of militant supporters, eventually organizing more than ninety thousand frenzied
youths into the All-India Sikh Students Federation. Urging his
supporters to use violence against their opponents, including
moderate Sikhs, Bhindranwale directed a campaign of intimidation
and terrorism that claimed the lives of more than four hundred
people, mostly Sikhs, in the first six months of 1984. By the time he
and his two thousand militant followers turned the Golden Temple
into an armed bunker in June 1984, Bhindranwale had become the
major spokesperson for the Sikh community even though he
represented the views of a minority of Sikhs. Contrary to the
political intentions and interests of the Congress Party, by mid-
1984 the Sikh community was more unified behind the radical
program of the extremists, in particular their demand for a separate Sikh state, than it had ever been behind the moderate agenda
of the Akali Dal.

The emergence of a paranoid minority mentality and the
erosion of Sikh orthodoxy by the modernization process helped
spur political extremism within the Sikh community. But there are
also specific political goals behind Sikh militancy. Bhindranwale's
preachings of violence and terrorism were designed to influence
the population flow into and from the Punjab. The trumpeting of
Sikh militant subnationalism, accompanied by violence, was intended to breed fear and insecurity among Punjab Hindus and
force them to leave. It was also directed at mobilizing Sikhs to
return to the Punjab "homeland." For its part, the Akali Dal,
whenever out of power, has historically resorted to civil disobedience, strikes, demonstrations, and protest marches to mobilize

those in power and to keep themselves in the public eye. In keeping with this political tradition, the Akali party, fourteen months after its defeat in the 1980 election, threatened to launch a mass campaign of agitation unless their demands were granted by the Indian government. These demands included greater state autonomy from the central government, recognition of the Sikhs as a nation (*Kaum*) rather than a religious community, and the redistribution of river waters between the states of the Punjab, Haryana, and Rajasthan. Though much more moderate than the Bhindranwale-led extremists, the Akali Dal leadership helped fuel the fires of Sikh extremism by its advocacy and threatened adoption of an extra-legal political strategy to regain political power.

The combination of demographic, economic, and political forces fomented support for Sikh extremist sentiments within the Sikh community. Emboldened by this support, the extremists initiated a terrorist campaign against the Hindu community two years before the raid on the Golden Temple. For example, in a terrorist procedure repeated many times since, a bus was hijacked by armed Sikhs and a number of Hindu passengers were dragged out and shot simply because they were Hindus. Still, Prime Minister Indira Gandhi's decision to attack the Sikh terrorists and occupy the Golden Temple stands as a watershed event in India's communal terrorism because it provoked massive sympathy and public support for the extremists' agenda among Sikhs. It also triggered her own assassination and has led to a dramatic increase in injury, suffering, and death from the reprisal terrorism of both communities since.

In the largest anti-terrorist operation ever undertaken, over four thousand crack Indian troops, including a newly formed commando unit, attacked the Golden Temple complex at Amritsar on June 5, 1984. The initial army strategy was to force the two thousand terrorists inside to surrender by raking them with heavy machine gun fire. Unable to dislodge the Sikh fanatics, the troops moved inside the complex. They were quickly forced back by withering and accurate fire from the Sikh militants, which caused heavy army casualties. Using howitzers, tanks, and heavy guns, the army began blasting away the Sikh fortifications, causing massive damage to two buildings within the Golden Temple complex. The Sikh's second most important shrine, the Akal Takht, was completely destroyed by the artillery barrage. The army then re-entered the complex and, after fierce hand-to-hand fighting, finally occupied the Golden Temple. Bhindranwale and Major General Shubheg Singh, the alleged mastermind behind the Sikh's two-year terrorist campaign, were found dead, their bodies riddled with bullets.

Sikhs are famous for their long-standing vendettas. With the desecration of their shrine in Amritsar, it was only a matter of time before they sought revenge. That act came five months later on October 31, when two of Gandhi's Sikh bodyguards assassinated the Prime Minister outside her New Delhi home. Hindus responded to Gandhi's assassination with riots and terrorism, including public burnings of innocent Sikhs. The violence was greatest in the north, especially in New Delhi, where the alienation between Sikhs and Hindus is the most intense. The reign of terror left more than three thousand Sikhs dead and the Sikh community cowering in terror.

Investigations conducted by citizens' groups in the aftermath of the riots allege that Hindu terrorism was purposefully aroused by several officials of the ruling Congress Party. For example, the investigative reports charge Congress Party leaders with making anonymous telephone calls and spreading false rumors about Sikhs poisoning the water supply of New Delhi, Sikhs killing passengers on a train from Punjab, and Sikhs killing Hindus in the cities. There are also accusations that some Congress Party politicians trucked in Hindu gangs from outlying villages to mobilize mobs and then, using voters' lists, set them to burning Sikh homes. Witnesses say that during the killing and looting, crowds of people and police officials looked on, afraid to intervene because the murderers had links to high officials in the Congress Party.

The Hindu riots following Gandhi's assassination widened the gulf of fear and distrust between Hindus and Sikhs and between moderates and extremists in both communities. But actions taken by new Prime Minister Rajiv Gandhi, the son of Indira, after he won the hastily-called election guaranteed that Sikh retaliatory terrorism would follow and eventually intensify. For example, Gandhi, after an initial refusal, reluctantly agreed to an official investigation of the Sikh massacres. But he also promoted several of the Congress Party leaders accused of being involved in the Hindu terrorism to new party posts. Then, in 1985, mobilizing political support under the banner of anti-terrorism, Gandhi initiated several repressive measures to clamp down hard on Sikh political activity in the Punjab. On February 2 the government extended its curbs on the entry of foreigners into the Punjab. In March Parliament passed Gandhi's request to extend direct central government rule in the Punjab for six months and added a provision to the National Security Act of 1980 (NSA) allowing preventive detention without trial for up to two years. The new legislation was hardly necessary, since, in addition to the NSA, India already had extensive preventive detention laws on the books, including the 1981 Essential Services Maintenance Act and the Public Security Act (PSA) covering Jammu and Kashmir. According to Amnesty International's 1984 report, the preventive detention provisions are routinely invoked by the Indian government to detain nonviolent political activists. For example, among those detained under this legislation in 1983 were student leaders in Assam, tribal leaders in Bihar, and trade union leaders in Bombay for trying to organize meetings; Sikh leaders in the Punjab for expressing their views in support of political autonomy; and political workers in Bihar for campaigning for minimum wages.[3] In May, Gandhi's government asked for and received parliamentary approval for a tough new anti-terrorist law that granted broad powers to government and police officials and immunity to authorities who abuse the new law. It also instituted the death penalty for terrorist acts that result in death and set up special closed courts to try suspected terrorists. The law prohibits songs, speeches, paintings, or pamphlets that in any way challenge India's sovereignty or territorial integrity. Later in the year, Gandhi pursued his anti-Sikh campaign outside of India. On his visit to Britain in October he called on the British government to take stronger police action against exiled Sikh extremists living in what he said were terrorist "breeding ground" communities in Britain. In support of Gandhi's anti-Sikh efforts, British Prime Minister Margaret Thatcher agreed to extend Britain's 1978 Suppression of Terrorism Law outside western Europe to India. This decision made it more difficult for Sikhs accused of terrorism to avoid extradition by claiming their acts were political.

Sikh militants responded to Gandhi's early initiatives with a stepped-up bombing campaign in New Delhi and other areas that claimed eighty lives. Among the victims in the Punjab were Raghunandan Lal Bhatia, secretary general of the Congress Party, and two other local political leaders, Krishan Lal Manchanda and Makhan Singh.

As the level of violence increased, Gandhi belatedly initiated conciliatory steps in an effort to raise political support for the Sikh moderate forces and their campaign to ease tensions in the Punjab. Negotiations between Sikh moderates of the Akali Dal and the government in the spring of 1985 ended in an accord in July 1985. In the accord the government agreed to several important Sikh demands, including the transfer of Hindu areas of the Punjab state to Haryana in order to increase the Sikh majority in the Punjab. The government also agreed to allow the city of Chandigarh to become the capital city of Punjab, ending its joint status as capital of Haryana and Punjab. Finally, Gandhi gave in to the demand for more lenient treatment of Sikhs arrested in riots during the previous three years.

Even though these were significant concessions, the accord failed to resolve the issue of religious and political autonomy for the Punjab. The government also refused to spell out specific steps for the promotion of the Punjabi language and it denied the Sikh demand that the special anti-terrorist courts set up under the new anti-terrorist legislation be abolished. More importantly, the accord failed to win the approval of or in any way mollify the Sikh extremists. They, along with several leading moderate leaders such as Prakash Singh Badal, former chief minister of Punjab, and Gurcharan Singh Tohra, president of a Sikh committee that manages Sikh shrines, rejected the accord as a "sellout" and betrayal of everything the Sikhs had fought for.

A month after the signing of the accord, Sikh militants made good on their pledge to continue their terrorist campaign by assassinating moderate Sikh leader Sant Harchand Singh Longonwal, who had struck the political deal with Gandhi. Since then, extremists on both sides have increased their violence and terrorism in Punjab. In January 1986 Sikh extremists occupied the Golden Temple again and for the first time called on all Sikhs to take up arms in a battle for independence. Encouraged by the Golden Temple takeover and the increased level of violence, the extremists issued a proclamation on April 29 founding the independent state of Khalstan. On April 30 five hundred central government commandos and paramilitary police, on orders from the Punjab state government and Prime Minister Gandhi, raided the Golden Temple. Meeting very little resistance, the army commandos seized the compound from the Sikhs. But Sikh violence again increased in the aftermath of the April raid. By the end of the first six months of 1986 communal violence in the Punjab had claimed an estimated 398 lives with 111 people dying in June alone. Over the first half of 1986 thousands of terrorized Hindus fled their homes in the Punjab to settle in neighboring Hindu states. Many of the agreements reached in the 1985 accord, such as the transfer of the city of Chandigarh to Punjab control, remained either unfulfilled or abandoned altogether. Meanwhile, Sikh terrorists continued to target key Hindu leaders. In August the Sikh extremists assassinated General Arun Vaidya, India's most decorated military officer, who had been high on the Sikhs' hit list since the army assault on the Golden Temple in 1984. Then in October, a lone Sikh attempted to assassinate Prime Minister Rajiv Gandhi during the Prime Minister's morning prayers.

In an ominous development for the Indian nation state, the communal terrorism between Sikh and Hindu communities has also provoked a revival of a militant Hinduism. Called the Hindutva, members of India's new religious Right claim to be the heirs to the oldest spiritual tradition in the world. Their proclaimed goal is an Indian Empire stretching from Afghanistan to Burma and a leading role for India in South Asia and eventually the entire Third World. Claiming to be tolerant of other religions, they insist that no-one, be they Sikh, Buddhist, or Muslim, will be allowed to take advantage of their "tolerance."

The revival of militant Hinduism has fed the separatist and fundamentalist sentiments within the Hindu community and among India's minority religions to the point where today it threatens to split India into multiple warring communities. Fierce fighting between Hindus and Muslims has already brought the imposition of a state of emergency in Khasmir. Since early 1985, riots between rival Hindu castes in the west Indian state of Gujaret have claimed hundreds of victims. Between July 9 and July 15, 1986 fighting between Muslims and Hindus claimed fifty lives. Seven Muslims, including a three-year-old girl, were burned alive by Hindu mobs.

Hindu militancy has further strengthened the political position of the Sikh fundamentalists. Emboldened by their newly-found support, they have used the 1984 attack on the Golden Temple to stir up further anti-Hindu sentiment among Sikhs, claiming Operation Bluestar was "the biggest blow against the Sikh nation." They have also fueled Sikh anger at the government in

New Delhi by referring to it as the "Delhi throne" comparable to another Mongol or British imperium and thus the hated enemy of all Sikhs.

The rising level of extremism and communal terrorism has complicated the already-complex political landscape in India. In particular, it has forced Sikh moderates into an extremely precarious position. Suffering from political isolation and victimized by Sikh and Hindu terrorists, Sikh moderates are being forced to reconsider whether they have a secure place in Hindu India. More and more they are limited to a choice between identifying as Sikhs and thereby forced to support the political agenda of the extremists and terrorists or opting to hold onto their moderate political position and face being ostracized as traitors by a majority of the Sikh community. Even if they choose to hold onto their moderate stance as the only hope for reconciliation between the two communities, they are confronted by a rising tide of Hindu militancy and anti-Sikh sentiment. Meanwhile their membership diminishes, a victim of political desertion and terrorist violence.

As of December, 450 people had died in ethnic violence during 1986. Four hundred of those killed were civilians. The death list includes twenty-four Hindus killed on November 30 in the worst Sikh terrorist operation of the year. For the second time in six months Sikh terrorists ambushed a public bus, this time in Khuda. Like the Muktsar assault in July, the terrorists separated the passengers by ordering all the Hindus off the bus. As the Hindu passengers descended, the terrorists opened fire on them with automatic weapons. In addition to the twenty-four who died, seven others were wounded. This latest attack is part of an escalation of violence which followed Gandhi's annual Independence Day speech in August in which he boasted that the government forces had the Sikh separatists on the run in Punjab. Contrary to Gandhi's statement, the Sikhs who are terrorists seem as formidable as ever and just as determined to have their way in India. In safeguarding their privileged position, Hindus are responding as they have traditionally done, with official and unofficial terrorism of their own.

The explosion of communal terrorism in India has now reached crisis proportions. The longer it continues the more serious the questions it raises about the continued survival of India as a modern pluralistic nation state. Indeed, it may be raising other, far more important, issues as well. For example, some observers of Indian terrorism believe that the stakes in the Sikh-Hindu conflict involve a fundamental challenge to the dominant post-World War II theory of nation-building based on cultural pluralism and the long-held assumption that ethnic, cultural, and religious loyalties disappear with time.

Our study of the explosion of terrorism in India reveals a complicated political situation involving a multitude of national and local factors, decisions, and policies. More important, we have seen that the rising tide of communal terrorism in India is also connected to the contemporary processes of modernization and the historical processes of building national and subnational movements. These processes are not unique to the Indian subcontinent but are also ongoing in a multitude of states in Africa, Asia, and Latin America. These processes have influenced the explosion of terrorism in many places, including Northern Ireland and the Middle East. Exploring the role of these countries in terrorism is particularly important, because it expands what we know about terrorism and also helps to uncover what we don't know by exposing us to the complexity and multi-dimensionality of terrorism. This can be an unsettling and confusing process because it forces us to question what we do know about terrorism by challenging the narrow political parameters set by the "ideology of terrorism" and the Soviet View.

MIDDLE EAST TERRORISM:
the past is the future

For many of us the contemporary explosion of terrorism is synonymous with events in the Middle East. The Middle East holds this dubious distinction even though the most recent data documents that the Middle East region is not where most international terrorism occurs. According to the annual report on international terrorism by the Tel Aviv-based Jaffee Center for Strategic Studies, that position is held by western Europe, where in 1985 forty-five percent of all international terrorist incidents took place.[1] Yet, as recent terrorist bombings in France and West Berlin indicate, a large proportion of terrorist activity in western Europe originates in or is connected to Middle East politics. Indeed, for 1985 17.2 percent of all recorded terrorist attacks are counted by the Israeli Institute as the work of Palestinians. Based on these numerical calculations alone we can safely conclude that terrorism is a major phenomenon and terrorists major components in the quagmire of Middle East politics.

To even the most casual observer of the Middle East it is obvious that the superpower contest plays a central if not quite defining role in the region's problems and prospects for peace and that the explosion of terrorism is part of a complicated and often contradictory situation. That being the case, our focus in this chapter will shift from substantiating the complexity of terrorism and address why the Middle View proposes that we view terrorism as a deplorable but permanent part of our future.

Terrorism has been and is likely to be a permanent fixture in our world because it is perceived as an effective policy for achieving both short- and long-term goals. This conclusion may seem strange to those who know that, like most aspects of Middle East politics, the story of Middle East terrorism, the reasons for it, and the players in it are extremely volatile. Knowing this, we might conclude that the current explosion of terrorism is only a temporary phase in the long history of Middle East conflict. Yet, that history tells us that beginning with the Assassins of the eleventh, twelfth, and thirteenth centuries, terrorism has developed as a permanent fixture in the Middle East political tradition. More importantly, since the end of World War II the major constant in the Middle East is the employment of terrorism as a policy option by all sides simply because it has proven to be an effective method of achieving discernible results. This tradition of permanency and effectiveness counters the conventional wisdom offered by many Western terrorist experts who, as noted in the discussion of the "ideology of terrorism" in Chapter Two, argue that terrorism is ineffective as a political strategy and thus likely to be a passing fancy employed by irrational zealots. Yet, led by both zealots and non-zealots, all the major participants involved in the conflicts of the Middle East, be they states—including the United States, Israel, Iran, and the Soviet Union—or sub-national organizations such as the Palestine Liberation Organization (PLO) or the Shiite Amal, have participated in or supported terrorism either directly or indirectly, because they have seen or experienced the effectiveness of terrorism; the benefits it can bring and the personal and political victories to be gained from it.

But there is another side to terrorism which is also evident in Middle East politics. For most of those who traffic in terrorism it has proven to be a two-sided accomplishment; triumph mixed with tragedy, success joined with failure. The examples in the Middle East are endless. Through its terrorist activities, the PLO triumphed by forcing the issue of Palestinian rights to the forefront of the international agenda and by building a strong political base for itself in the Palestinian community and among major Arab states. But the PLO's initial success has been tarnished if not completely negated by fierce intra-communal fighting and grisly acts of terror, political rejection by major Arab leaders and a politically disastrous reputation as little more than a ruthless terrorist organization within Western journalistic circles.

After being thrown out of Egypt in 1972, the Soviet Union

was able to remain a player in Middle East politics by arming the PLO and the radical Arab states of Syria and Libya and condoning the strategy of revolutionary violence against Israel. But today the Soviets find themselves held hostage and victimized by a terrorist monster they helped create. Since 1985 Russian diplomats have been kidnapped and murdered by Islamic terrorists, and political infighting within the PLO undermines current Soviet policy objectives in the Middle East. Because of its terrorism in Afghanistan and the terrorism of its Syrian and Libyan allies, the Soviet Union is the subject of worldwide condemnation. As a result, in the Middle East the Soviets have found themselves in the uncomfortable position of censoring news of the war in Afghanistan, attempting to hide the horrors of its terrorism from Soviet citizens and their Muslim allies, and downplaying their support for Arab terrorists while they focus their efforts on ending the political infighting in the PLO.

Israel also finds its employment of terrorism a mixed blessing of triumph and tragedy. The terrorism utilized by some major factions in the Zionist movement, led by the Stern Group, the Irgun Tsvai Leumi, and the Haganah, played a central role in the creation of the Zionist state of Israel in Palestine. Further utilization of terrorism by Israeli forces helped solidify and enlarge the Jewish state in the 1950s, 1960s, and 1970s. But its invasion of Lebanon in 1982, its aerial bombing of civilians in Beirut, Zionist extremist terrorism against Arab communities in occupied territories, and the terror of its "Iron Fist" policy in southern Lebanon have exposed Israel's heavy reliance on state terrorism in enhancing its interests. Today, as these major contradictions play havoc with Israel's long-cultivated reputation as a highly principled and moralistic state, the anti-terrorist rhetoric of Israeli leaders increasingly falls on deaf ears in the court of world opinion.

France has also experienced the double-edged sword of terrorism. For years French governments have successfully negotiated "peace" deals with various Arab terrorist groups, including an arrangement with the infamous Abu Nidal in early 1986. In this case, France agreed to release convicted Palestinian terrorists provided Abu Nidal would not carry out terrorist operations on French soil. In another earlier instance, in 1977 France arrested and then released Abu Daoud, who planned the Black September massacre of Israeli athletes at the Munich Olympics in 1972, to

mollify various Palestinian groups. France has also permitted
Libyan and Iranian terrorists to travel freely in France and operate
against their respective dissidents as long as they refrained from
terrorism against French citizens or in France proper. In general, it
has been official French policy that terrorism can be ignored so
long as it does not affect "innocent French." But a bloody week of
terrorist bombings in Paris in September 1986 in which eight
"innocent" French citizens were killed and one hundred fifty
wounded, shattered all French assumptions about their ability to
successfully negotiate from crisis to crisis by maneuvering between
terrorist groups. Indeed, the terrorists of the Lebanese Revolutionary Armed Faction, who carried out the bombings, insist they did
so because the French government had reneged on a promise
made during secret negotiations. The terrorists claim France had
agreed to release their leader Georges Ibrahim Abdallah, accused
of complicity in the deaths of American military attaché Lt. Colonel
Charles Ray and Israeli diplomat Yacov Barsimantov. Apparently
the French government, under pressure from the United States,
refused to release Abdallah for fear of antagonizing American
officials. They were confident they could out-maneuver the terrorists. But the September bombings proved the French officials'
confidence was misplaced and brought into question their ability to
thread their way through the maze of contemporary terrorism.
Today, according to *Liberation* editor Serge July, "France is the
special target of all kinds of murderous blackmail . . . due to the
fact that all our governments since the early 1970s have negotiated
from crisis to crisis with all terrorists and those who control them."[2]
The conservative government of Premier Jacques Chirac is also
under fire for taking actions which its critics say pose a serious
challenge to the French democratic tradition. The government did
arrest and attempt to expel a dozen Arab radicals after the initial
bombings, though there was no direct evidence linking them to the
terrorism. Several of these "undesirable immigrants," whom the
government attempted to expel without formal legal procedures,
had established residence in France for over ten years. Its new
repressive anti-terrorist measures, which include visas, border
controls, increased intelligence, and monetary rewards for information on terrorists, are also causing much concern among French
civil rights activists. In addition, French troops in the United
Nations Interim Forces in Lebanon and French diplomatic person-

nel in Beirut are under attack from pro-Iranian Shiite terrorists for the French government's participation in peace-keeping efforts in Lebanon and its support of Iraq in the war with Iran. In short, what was once a successful if extremely selfish and nationalistic method of dealing with terrorism has turned into a tragic nightmare for French authorities. Yet, the reluctance of the French government to support Britain's recent call for sanctions against Syria is a clear signal that the French continue to believe they can avoid the wrath of terrorism by making deals directly with the terrorists or their state patrons. The French refusal to participate in the British-sponsored sanctions against Syria stemmed from their desire to obtain Syrian aid on three key matters: an end to the terrorist bombings in Paris, the release of French hostages held in Lebanon, and the safety of French troops stationed with the United Nations in Lebanon.

Like France, the United States is also currently entangled in, if not trapped by, the contradictory politics of terrorism. As we have seen in earlier chapters, Ronald Reagan's triumph in the 1980 presidential election and his successful campaign to return the United States and the West to a Cold War posture was aided in large measure by the 1979 Iranian hostage crisis and his militant position on international terrorism, in particular the state-sponsored terrorism of the Soviet Union, Iran, and Libya. However, in November 1986 the American public discovered that the Reagan Administration had exchanged large amounts of arms for hostages with the terrorist state of Iran during the period Iran was sponsoring attacks on American citizens. So, just eight months after the April 1986 American bombing of Libya boosted President Reagan's reputation as the world's greatest anti-terrorist warrior to new heights, the political purposes behind the Reagan Administration's anti-terrorist position were publicly exposed. The secret deal with the Iranians and the lies told to American friends and foes has also severely damaged President Reagan's personal credibility. The long-term tragedy is that it has undermined the professional credibility of the American diplomatic corps at its highest level. This can only damage future American diplomatic efforts on a broad range of important issues, including nuclear arms reduction, which affect millions of people.

On the other hand, there are states, Iran, Syria and Libya among them, whose participation in or support of terrorism have so far gained them a place of importance and notoriety far beyond what normal instruments of diplomacy had brought in the past. The same is true of numerous, now notorious, Middle East terrorist groups such as *Abu Nidal*, the Christian Falange, *Fedayeen*, *Amal*, *Hezbollah*, *Jihad*, or the Palestine Liberation Front, who hold center stage in the power struggle of the Middle East. For decades the local and regional aspirations of these third-rate nations and the causes represented by the various terrorist organizations were subsumed under the dominance of bi-polar politics and the will of the superpowers. Now, by employing the instrument of terror, they have power and influence far beyond their actual capabilities or resources. As is often the case where there is little honor among thieves and where it is not difficult to be snared by the complexities of terrorism, their current triumphs may be short-lived. But as of late 1986, it is these states and groups, backed by the threat of terrorism, who are turning the screws on old and new enemies, righteously demanding concessions from extremely powerful foreign friends and foes, and defining issues and deals in their terms and to their advantage.

Since the General Assembly of the United Nations recommended the partition of the Palestine Mandate into two states, one Jewish and one Arab, Middle East terrorism has gone through four discernible stages. Both Arabs and Jews participated in terrorism. On December 2, 1947, Arab demonstrations in Aden marked the start of a three-day protest strike against the United Nations decision to partition Israel. The demonstration began peacefully but soon turned into an orgy of destruction as mobs broke into Jewish shops and set them afire. There was similar hit and run violence in Haifa, Jerusalem and attacks in Jaffa. British troops did not interfere; Jewish terrorists had killed and maimed so many of their number that their own opinions on attributing blame for violence were painfully unclear. The terrorist campaigns of certain militant Zionist groups, in particular the Irgun Tsvari Leumi led by former Israeli Prime Minister Menachem Begin and the Lehi or Stern Gang headed by present Israeli Prime Minister Yitzhak Shamir, had begun their anti-British campaign in 1944.

In essence, Israel is a state in which terrorism has long played a central role. Reputable accounts show that terrorism from certain Zionist groups began in earnest one month after the United Nations decision. Indeed, personal testimonies of prominent Zionist leaders at the time indicate they favored "a strategy of eliminating whoever stood in their way, including women and children, and proceeded to do so, murdering captured and wounded."[3] On December 18, 1947, Palmach, a Kibbutz-based force of the Zionist army led by Moshe Dayan, one of Israel's most revered and honored soldiers, terrorized the Arab village of Khissas, killing ten people, among them one woman and four children. In April 1948 the now-famous massacre of two hundred and fifty defenseless people in the Arab village of Deir Yassin by the Irgun-LEHI took place. The Haganah command condemned the operation, but Irgun commanders, led by Menachem Begin, praised the terrorists for their humanity and effectiveness. Researchers are still uncovering horror reports of Israeli acts of terrorism, including one told by a Zionist soldier who participated in the occupation of the Palestinian village of Dueima in 1948 and testifies that the Zionist army:

> . . . **killed between eighty and one hundred Arabs, women and children. To kill the children they fractured their heads with sticks. There was not one house without corpses. The men and women of the villages were pushed into houses without food or water. Then the saboteurs came to dynamite the houses. One commander ordered a soldier to bring two women into a house he was about to blow up . . . another soldier prided himself upon having raped an Arab woman before shooting her to death. Another woman with her newborn baby was made to clean the place for a couple of days, and then they shot her and the baby. Educated and well-mannered commanders who were considered "good guys" . . . became base murderers, and this was not in the storm of battle, but as a method of expulsion and extermination. The fewer the Arabs who remain, the better . . .[4]**

The first phase of Middle East terrorism by Israel began with its military policy from 1948 onward. This policy was geared to the creation of a Greater Israel by integrating "the bulk of the occupied territories within Israel in some fashion while finding a way to reduce the Arab population; to disperse the scattered refugees and crush any manifestation of Palestinian nationalism or Palestinian culture; to gain control over southern Lebanon."[5] In this policy, Israeli terrorism played a central role in provoking the Arab states into wars they did not want to fight and could not win. Zionist terrorism also produced the legend of the "cruelty of the Jews" which aided in the collapse of Arab forces in 1948 and caused millions of Arab civilians, victims of Israeli terror and psychological warfare, to flee from their homeland over the next three decades.

Until this dark side of Israeli policy was exposed in its invasion of Lebanon in 1982, accounts of Israel's military strategy and its terrorist content went largely unnoticed or were effectively squashed by a pro-Israel Western press. Documentation of this policy is provided by numerous sources. One of the most important is the personal diary of Moshe Sharett, the former Foreign Minister (1948–1956) and Prime Minister (1955–1956) of Israel.[6]

The major significance of Sharett's discussion of what he calls Israel's "sacred terrorism" is that it contradicts the widely-held belief that Israel only engages in retaliatory terrorism. Sharett, who was a central, if at times reluctant, participant in implementing Israel's "security policy," makes the following points in his diary. First, Israeli political and military leaders never seriously considered Israel's existence to be threatened by the Arabs and sought to push the Arab governments into a military confrontation with Israel. The Arab threat was an Israeli-invented myth to mobilize public opinion and political action in Israel and in the West and justify Israeli military acts of "reprisal." In turn, Arab leaders staked out a public posture of hostility and engaged in unwinnable military actions and terroristic acts. Secondly, Sharett claims that in order to transform Israel into the major power in the Middle East, Israel's leaders pushed the Arab states into wars that Israel was sure to win. Thirdly, to realize the goals of the Greater Israel policy, Sharett says several tactics were invoked to terrorize the Arab population and create tensions between the defenseless residents and the Arab governments who were unable to protect them. They include large- and small-scale military operations aimed at civilians across the armistice lines; covert terrorist operations deep inside the Arab world for espionage purposes and to create fear, instability, and tension among the Arabs; and Israeli-initiated military operations against Arab military units on the borders intended to demoralize the Arab military establishment and further destabilize the Arab regimes.[7]

Israel launched its security or "reprisal" policy in the early 1950s. In pursuing its goal of removing the Arab populations from their territory, Israel carried out regular terrorist operations deep within Arab territories. The best known of these include the Ariel Sharon-led Unit 101's attack on the village of Qibya in October 1953, in which sixty-six civilians were massacred, and Israeli attacks on civilian targets and Western installations in Cairo and Alexandria, Egypt in 1954. In December 1954 the Israeli air force committed the first major act of civilian air piracy by hijacking a Syrian civilian airliner. The purpose behind this little-known hijacking was to obtain hostages for exchange with Israeli soldiers being held by Syria. This hijacking and the purpose behind it served as a precedent for later PLO actions, such as the infamous operation at Ma'alot in 1974 in which Israeli hostages were kidnapped for exchange with captured PLO guerrillas.

In 1981 Prime Minister Menachem Begin made public a "partial list" of Israeli terrorist operations against Arab civilians by various Labor governments which included more than thirty incidents in which civilians were killed. While claiming the attacks were all retaliatory in nature, Begin admits that the Israeli Air Force bombed Arab civilians, canals, bridges, and transport on a regular basis. Begin's revelation is echoed by other Israeli leaders such as former Foreign Minister Abba Eban and Chief of Staff Mordechai Gur, who admit that terrorism is a central part of Israeli military policy. Eban even defends Israeli terrorism as logical, on the grounds that it can move innocent parties who have been victimized by terrorism to exert pressure on their political leaders to make peace. General Gur states that "For thirty years from the War of Independence until today, we have been fighting against a population that lives in villages and cities"[8] and admits that the Israeli army has never made a distinction between civilian and military targets. Sharett's diary documents that an essential element in resurgent Israeli militarism during the 1950s was a conscious campaign to justify terrorism and revenge as the new moral and sacred values of Israeli society.[9]

Acts of Israeli terrorism have induced the Arab population to flee from its homeland either by force or out of fear. For example, in the 1948 conflict over seven hundred thousand Palestinians fled or were expelled from Palestinian territories, most of them fleeing from Israeli terrorism or the legend of Jewish cruelty. In 1967 over four hundred thirty thousand Palestinians fled from the Golan Heights and the Gaza Strip after Israeli occupation. In 1970 Israeli bombing of the Jordan Valley drove a million and a half Arab civilians from their homes in the Suez Canal area. Finally, by October 1977, Israel's bombardment of southern Lebanon and the Israeli Army's "liberation" of West Beirut had created over three hundred thousand refugees, mostly Shiite Moslem, in Lebanon.

Debate continues over whether Israeli terrorism is retaliatory or provocative in nature. While it is important to resolve this point, it is clear that from Israel's founding days Israeli leaders have used acts of terrorism in their foreign policy and have done so because they assumed it was an effective strategy to achieve their purposes. Today, contrary to Israel's public posture against terrorism, major Israeli leaders continue to operate on these familiar assumptions. For example, since 1968 Israeli ground and aerial terrorism, justified by Israeli leaders as a battle for survival against PLO terrorism, has brutalized both property and people in Lebanon. The purposes behind Israel's massive bombardment of Lebanese civilian populations during the 1970s were to turn Lebanese civilians against the PLO forces and the Palestinian population, who had been forced out of Jordan and into Lebanon, and to disrupt the fragile Lebanese political unity existing at the time between Christians and Moslems by setting them against each other. This conclusion seems proper in light of the stepped-up Israeli attacks on Lebanon on December 2, 1975, two days after the United Nations Security Council had pushed to have the PLO included in Middle East peace talks for the first time, and then again following the Shtaura peace accord between Lebanon, Syria, and the PLO in November 1977. Indeed, during this time Israeli leaders shifted their public rationale for Israeli attacks on Lebanese villages and Palestinian refugee camps. Terrorist raids which had been called "reprisals" or "punitive acts" were suddenly termed "preventive."

Typical of the scale and ferocity of its "preventive terrorism," Israel hammered Lebanon with 191 air, land, and sea attacks that destroyed 447 homes and killed 236 civilians during an eight-month period of 1975. The December 2, 1975 Israeli attacks left fifty-seven civilians dead. In 1974, *New Times* reporter Judith Coburn ended her months-long investigation of the Israeli bombing of Lebanon claiming that since 1968 scores of Lebanese villages had been turned into ghost towns by daily ground and air assaults and Israeli commando raids. Coburn says Israeli soldiers routinely blew up houses, killed villagers, took prisoners and engaged in the use of shells, bombs, phosphorus, napalm, and incendiary bombs.[10] Other sources, including United Nations officials, report that by 1975 Israel's "preventive" raids and its "scorched earth" policy in southern Lebanon had killed three thousand five hundred civilians in Lebanon, Syria, and Jordan. Middle East expert Noam Chomsky points out that if the figures are accurate, at the time when PLO terrorism filled the front pages of Western newspapers, "Israel had killed about ten times as many Palestinians and Lebanese in attacks on Lebanon as the total number of Israelis killed in the course of cross-border Palestinian attacks through 1982."[11]

In assessing the first two decades of Middle East terrorism, the conclusion must be drawn that, whether for purposes of provocation or retaliation, Israel has been a major participant in terrorism during the first years of the post-World War II era and beyond. Indeed, since Israel's 1982 invasion of Lebanon, its supporters have had to confront directly the reality of Israeli state terrorism. Israel's purposeful attacks on civilian targets during the 1982 invasion, which killed over eighteen thousand civilians, shocked many of its supporters in the international community.

Israel's current "Iron Fist" policy in southern Lebanon, begun in 1984 and aimed at taming the Shiite population, continues the tradition of Israel's terrorist "reprisal" policy. Under the Iron Fist policy the Israelis have abandoned any effort to befriend the villagers and make no secret that the purpose of their repression is communal punishment and intimidation. According to reports from witnesses and journalists in southern Lebanon, Israeli raids on Shiite villages begin by sealing off target villages at dawn. Troops, backed by armored vehicles, enter the villages shooting at random and often setting police dogs on the women. All the men are rounded up for interrogation. Anyone trying to escape is shot and each house is searched for explosives and bulldozed or blown up if suspicion is aroused. The villages are placed under dawn-to-dusk curfews with curfew breakers shot on the spot. No Shiite is permitted to ride a motorcycle or in a car alone. Sources say the purpose of Israeli reprisal policy against the Shiite community follows the prescription of earlier policy: to terrorize the civilians and turn them against the Shiite resistance. It is a policy of massive terrorism that was successful in turning the Shiite population against the Palestinian guerrillas operating in Lebanon before the

1982 Israel invasion. But witnesses report that, so far, the Iron Fist policy is only increasing Shiite resistance to Israel. If Israeli leaders follow their traditional pattern, we can expect them to respond to Shiite militancy with heightened levels of repression and massive terrorism, especially since the Reagan Administration's bombing of Libya in April 1986 bolstered the ideological climate for Israel's military "reprisal" policy.

The second phase of Middle East terrorism begins with the emergence of the Palestine Liberation Organization as a unified political organization in the mid-1960s. From then to the late 1970s is a decade or so dominated by the confrontation between Palestinian nationalism and Jewish nationalism and the PLO's decision to organize for armed struggle against Israel as a political entity separate from the Arab states. It is a period in Middle East terrorism where the two superpowers, though careful not to confront each other directly, line up on opposite sides, with the United States backing Israel and the Soviet Union supporting the PLO and Arab cause. It began with a few disorganized grenade-throwing raids into Israel by the PLO. However, the scale of terrorism soon increased with the PLO hijacking of three jumbo jets blown up in the Jordanian desert in 1970, the Black September massacre of eleven Israeli athletes at the Munich Olympic Games in 1972, and the Israeli rescue at Entebbe in 1976. In addition, there were Israeli "preventive" aerial terrorism over southern Lebanon during the 1970s and Israel's downing of a Libyan civilian airliner in 1973, which killed 110 people.

The central issue behind the PLO-Israeli terrorism in the second phase is their mutually exclusive claims to the same territory and the denial of nationalist rights to the other side. Israel's position is grounded in its unwillingness to grant any national rights to the indigenous Arab population. Beginning with David Ben-Gurion, this rejectionist stance has been uttered by every major Israeli leader regardless of whether they belong to Israel's Likud or Labor political grouping. In 1936 Ben-Gurion crystalized the Zionist position when he said "there is no conflict between Jewish and Palestinian nationalism becamse the Jewish Nation is not in Palestine and the Palestinians are not a nation."[12] Moshe Dayan expressed similar sentiments when he argued that the Palestinians' cause was "hopeless" and said they should set themselves up in one of the Arab countries. Like Ben-Gurion, Dayan denies any Palestinian attachment or claim to their homes, saying he didn't think "a Palestinian should have difficulties in regarding Jordan, Syria, or Iraq as his homeland."[13] Former Prime Minister Golda Meir echoed this familiar refrain in 1969 with the statement:

It was not as though there was a Palestinian people in Palestine considering itself as a Palestinian people and we came and threw them out and took their country away from them. They did not exist.[14]

This prevailing view among many Israeli leaders, which denies the existence of Palestinian nationalism or a Palestinian claim to a particular territory, is the basis upon which Israel has insisted that the Palestinians are not a legitimate factor in the Israeli-Arab conflict nor have any role to play in any peace settlement of that conflict. On this basis, they have refused to meet or negotiate with any organization, such as the PLO, which claims to represent the interests of the Palestinian national community. From the Israeli point of view, that community west of Jordan simply doesn't exist. And a community that doesn't exist has no legitimate claim to a national territory. Israelis also claim that the Arabs already have twenty-two states, so the Palestinians, who have no claim to self-determination, should select one of those states to live in.

Conversely, Israelis believe the European Jews who established Israel in 1948 do have a valid historical claim to self-determination. It also helps, in their view, that the State of Israel has been determined by the courts to be the "Sovereign State of the Jewish People" and not just of the people living in Israel. As such, the State of Israel stands as a valid national entity willing and able to negotiate a peace settlement with other national entities, i.e., the Arab states.

Similarly, the Arab states have a long history of violent encounters, and they have learned that terroristic policies are often politically successful. The Palestine Liberation Organization was founded at a conference of Arab states in Cairo, Egypt on June 2, 1964. The brainchild of President Gamal Abdel Nasser of Egypt, the PLO was set up as an umbrella organization to unify and coordinate the activities of the multitude of Palestinian resistance groups, among which *Al Fatah*, the Palestine Liberation Front, and the Popular Front for the Liberation of Palestine remain in existence today. Official PLO ideology is expressed primarily in the 1964 Palestinian National Covenant, which delineates the Palestinian territorial claim, the methods of liberation, and the PLO positions on Palestinian and Jewish nationalism. Each point is spelled out in specific articles of the Covenant. The Palestinian territorial claim and right to national self-determination are laid down in Articles 1, 2, 3 and 4.

> Article 1. Palestine is the homeland of the Palestinian Arab people and an integral part of the great Arab homeland, and the people of Palestine are a part of the Arab state.

> Article 2. Palestine, with boundaries that existed at the time of the British mandate, is an integral regional unit.

> Article 3. The Palestinian Arab people possess the legal right to their homeland, and when the liberation of their homeland is completed, they will exercise self-determination solely according to their own will and choice.

> Article 4. The Palestinian personality is an innate, persistent characteristic that does not disappear, and it is transferred from fathers to sons. The Zionist occupation and the dispersal of the Palestinian Arab people as a result of the disasters that befell them do not deprive them of their Palestinian personality and affiliation and do not nullify them.

The PLO's expressed methodologies for the liberation of Palestine from Zionist occupation are armed struggle and "fedayeen" action as spelled out in Articles 9 and 10.

> Article 9. Armed struggle is the only way to liberate Palestine and is therefore a strategy, not a tactic.

> Article 10. Fedayeen action forms the nucleus of the popular Palestinian war of liberation.

In designating armed struggle and "fedayeen" action, which means "one who sacrifices or goes on a suicidal mission," as the basis for its struggle, the PLO connected its mission to the eleventh-century Ismailitic sect of *Hasan ibn-al-Sabbah* and its terrorist doctrine of the assassination of one's enemies. In essence, the PLO purposely chose terrorism as a part of its liberation methodology under the assumption that it was the most effective and thus rational way to achieve Palestinian national goals.

The PLO's rejection of Jewish nationalism and the Zionist presence in Palestine is stated in the Covenant as follows:

> Article 20. The Balfour Declaration, the mandate document, and what has been based on them are considered null and void. The claim of a historical or spiritual tie betwen the Jews and Palestine does not tally with historical realities or with the constituents of statehood in their truest sense. Judaism, in its character as a religion or revelation, is not a nationality with an independent existence. Likewise, the Jews are not one people with an independent personality. They are rather citizens of the states to which they belong.

> Article 15. The liberation of Palestine, from an Arab viewpoint, is a national duty to drive the Zionist imperialist invasion from the great Arab homeland and to purge the Zionist presence from Palestine. Its full responsibilities fall upon the Arab nation, people, and governments, with the Palestinian people at their head.

The Covenant has been modified since 1964, particularly Article 9, which was changed to read that the PLO would struggle by any means, the foremost of which would be armed struggle. Later decisions by the Palestinian National Council further modified the meaning of the Covenant, particularly the 1977 decision authorizing Palestinian participation in a peace conference which included representatives of the State of Israel. But during the second phase of Middle East terrorism, the rejectionist position of the Covenant and the sole reliance on armed struggle dominated the views of the PLO leadership.

It is the confrontation between the mutually exclusive rejectionist positions of the Israelis and the early militant policy of the PLO that served as the dominant framework and rationale for terrorism in the Middle East during the second phase. This stage was preceded by escalating hostilities between Israel and the Arab states in the 1950s and 1960s. Then Israel soundly defeated the Arab armies in the 1967 war. Out of this defeat rose the PLO, under the leadership of Yasser Arafat, as a separate political and military entity. Drawing its political support and guerrilla recruits from the squalor of the Palestinian refugee camps, the PLO set its own agenda, one distinct from and independent of the goals and policies of the Arab states—particularly on the issue of Palestinian nationalism and Arab nationalism, or Pan-Arabism. From its "secure bases," first in Jordan and then in Lebanon, the PLO upgraded and increased its military actions and terrorist operations which Arafat's Al-Fatah and other Syrian-backed and trained terrorist groups had tentatively begun in 1964. Ultimately, PLO terrorism succeeded in placing the issue of Palestinian nationalism in the forefront of regional and international agendas. By 1975 the Arab states and the United Nations had recognized the PLO as the "sole legitimate representative of the Palestinian people."

Reports of PLO terrorism and cruelty have dominated the discussion of Middle East terrorism in the Western media for so long now that we need not detail them in depth here. The important point is that, along with Israel and its "reprisal policy," the PLO engineered the bulk of the terrorism during this period in the name of Palestinian nationalism and in pursuit of the liberation of Palestine from Israel. The scale of this terrorist war between Israel and the Jordan-based PLO escalated in the early years, measured by the number of border "incidents" between Jordan and Israel: they rose from 97 after June 1967 to 916 in 1968, 2,432 in 1969, and more than 1,887 in 1970. They fell to 45 in 1971 after the PLO was pushed out of Jordan in "Black September" 1970. The number of PLO operations in the occupied territories, where it operated from within, also remained high throughout this period.

Several PLO terrorist operations do stand out from the hundreds of others not only because of their horrifying consequences but because of their psychological or political "shock value" on world opinion. Among them are a series of terrorist acts by the George Habash-led Popular Front for the Liberation of Palestine (PFLP). The first PLO hijacking of an airliner in the Middle East took place in July 1968. Three PFLP terrorists commandeered an El Al 707 airliner bound from Rome to Tel Aviv and forced the Israeli crew to land in Algiers. On December 28, 1968 two PFLP terrorists fired on a New York-bound El Al 707 at the Athens International airport, killing one person and wounding another. The two terrorists were arrested but later released in exchange for hostages taken in the hijacking of a Greek airliner to Beirut in July 1970. Another El Al airliner was attacked in February 1969 at the Kloten Airport near Zurich, Switzerland by PFLP gunmen with submachine guns, hand grenades, and incendiary bombs. The co-pilot was killed and the pilot and four others wounded before security guards killed one terrorist and overpowered the others.

The attack in Switzerland was quickly followed by others. PLO terrorists threw a bomb into an El Al office in downtown Athens, killing one child and wounding fourteen others, including three Americans. PLO bombs exploded on board a Swissair jet, forcing it to crash into woods near Zurich and killing all forty-seven people on board. Seven Americans, nine Germans, two Canadians, and fifteen Israelis were among the dead, along with citizens from Senegal, Thailand, Switzerland, Belgium, and England. A February 1970 grenade attack on a bus at the Munich airport killed one Israeli and wounded eleven other passengers. In Asunción, Paraguay, two PLO terrorists murdered the wife of the first secretary at the Israeli embassy on May 4, 1970. On December 17, 1973 the PFLP killed thirty-one people in separate attacks on a Pan Am jet and a Lufthansa airliner in Rome. Collectively, these terrorist operations were successful because of their "shock value" on the international community. They stirred interest about who was behind them and for what reasons.

PLO terrorists also operate inside Israel and the occupied lands. In Jerusalem, the PFLP set off bombs near the oxygen reserve of Hadassah Hospital in February 1970, killing and wounding many people. Five days later a bomb went off at a Jerusalem supermarket, killing two and injuring nine. On May 22, 1970 members of the PFLP, armed with three Russian-made bazooka rockets, opened fire on an Israeli bus loaded with children, killing eight children and a teacher. On May 30, 1972 members of the PFLP and the Japanese Red Army assassinated twenty-five people and wounded seventy-five others in an attack on Lod Air Terminal in Tel Aviv. This attack, along with the monstrous assault on the bus full of Israeli children in 1970, was of particular importance as it brought the PLO worldwide headlines and media coverage. But it also brought universal condemnation and secured for the PLO a reputation for cruelty that continues to this day.

Other terrorist groups under the PLO umbrella were active at this time. The most notorious is Black September, led by Arafat's deputy Salah Khalaf (Abu Ayad) and Ali Hassan Salameh, head of al-Fatah's intelligence unit. Angered by the "Black September" expulsion of the PLO from Jordan in 1970, it aimed its terrorist wrath more at moderate Arab states and the West than it did at Israel. Among its terrorist acts in the West were an attack on a Gulf Oil refinery in Rotterdam in March 1971 and a $1 million fire at an oil storage facility in Trieste in August 1972. Black September launched a letter-bomb campaign aimed at Israeli diplomats throughout western Europe and a series of bombings and hijackings before its shocking massacre of eleven Israeli athletes at the 1972 Munich Olympic Games brought the group worldwide attention, lasting infamy, and its eventual destruction. Before it disappeared, Black September added to its legacy of terrorism by kidnapping two Americans, a Saudi, a Jordanian, and a Belgian at the Saudi Embassy in Khartoum in March 1973 and killing four passengers and wounding fifty-five others in a ground attack in Athens on a TWA airliner on August 5, 1973.

In many ways the massacre at the Munich Olympics serves as a benchmark for the second phase of Middle East terrorism. Arab leaders such as King Hussein of Jordan and, later, Egypt's Anwar Sadat, fearful of growing PLO power, had already moved against the Arafat-led forces, forcing them out of Jordan and into Lebanon. After Munich, Israeli assassinations of PLO leaders and attacks on PLO headquarters and safehouses in the Middle East escalated. In addition, the PLO began to suffer from internal divisions over tactics and ideology, particularly as international pressure began to influence Yasser Arafat and other moderate members of the PLO leadership. Israeli aerial terrorism over Lebanon was also effective in convincing Lebanese civilians that support for the Palestinian cause required too high a price on their part.

While it is difficult to pinpoint exactly, the second stage of Middle East terrorism comes to a close around 1976, when the Israeli raid on Entebbe, Uganda ended a remarkable string of PLO "successes" in terrorist hijackings and when the proliferation of separate organizations within the Palestinian movement, different in ideology and with benefactors ranging from Saudi Arabia to the Soviet Union, finishes off the political unity of the PLO. From this time forward, while the rejectionist confrontation between Israel and the PLO continues to fuel Middle East terrorism and the Arab people condemned to the horrors of the Palestinian refugee camps continue to spew forth nationalist extremists and desperate youthful fanatics ready to die for the cause, other characters and causes come into play and begin to dominate the more contemporary eras of Middle East terrorism.

There is considerable overlap between the second and third phases of Middle East terrorism. The forces that dominate terrorist activity from 1978 to 1983 are Israeli terrorism, intra-communal terrorism in the PLO, and the agents of the Islamic revolution.

The PLO has always been an ensemble of many organizations, some permanent, others lasting anywhere from one day to a few years. As of 1986 there are three important distinctions between the various PLO groups which are presently scattered throughout the world: those who are pro-Arafat, those allied with Syria, and those who operate independently. The many faces of the PLO include the following major organizations:

Al Fatah: Based in Tunis, Yasser Arafat is its leader. This is the largest PLO group, with around eight thousand activists. It presently advocates a dual policy of armed struggle against Israel yet is ready to seek a political settlement to the Palestinian issue. Recently, Al Fatah is reported ready to abandon its peace efforts and begin terrorist actions again because of Jordanian efforts to replace it as the leader of the Palestinian community and Israeli-United States success at isolating it from the Middle East peace process.

Palestine Liberation Front (PLF): Small in numbers (100) and badly split between a pro-Arafat faction, led by Abul Abbas and residing in Tunis, and a pro-Syrian group headquartered in Damascus led by Talaat Yacoub. The Abul Abbas group attempted the hijacking of the Italian liner *Achille Lauro* in October 1985 during which one American was killed. The PLF is dedicated to armed struggle and to terrorism as an effective political tool.

Arab Liberation Front (ALF): A small faction that broke away from Al Fatah and is now backed by Iraq. Headed by Abdul-Rahim Ahmed, who currently sides with Arafat.

Black June (Abu Nidal): An independent group committed to the overthrow of Arafat since 1973. Led by Sabri Al-Banna (Abu Nidal), who is thought to be dead, Black June is credited with the assassination of several moderate PLO leaders in the effort to derail any diplomatic settlement of the Palestinian question. It is currently based in Syria and Lebanon and carries out terrorist operations intended to discredit Arafat and his efforts to negotiate a settlement with Israel.

Democratic Front for the Liberation of Palestine: A small, rigorously Marxist faction headed by Nayif Hawatmeh, a Jordanian Christian. Headquartered in Damascus, it holds onto its independence from Syria but is very pro-Moscow and anti-Jordan. It opposes Arafat's efforts at diplomatic settlement.

Al Intifada: A key dissident faction that broke away from Al Fatah in 1983. Led by Colonel Saed Musa and based in Damascus, its twenty-five hundred members are committed to all-out armed struggle and against any diplomatic settlement of the Palestinian issue.

Popular Front for the Liberation of Palestine (PFLP): Headed by George Habash and based in Damascus, the PFLP is a Marxist-oriented group with more than one thousand members. It is strongly pro-Syrian and leads the PLO rejectionist front in opposing any partial recovery of Palestinian territory.

Popular Front for the Liberation of Palestine—General Command: A splinter group of the PFLP since 1968 and led by Ahmed Jabril. It has around eight hundred activists, all of them combatants, and is considered one of the most militant and least ideologically sophisticated factions. It is extremely pro-Syrian.

Popular Struggle Front: A small splinter group backed by Syria. Under the leadership of Samir Ghusha it broke with Al Fatah in 1983.

In the late 1960s Al Fatah became the dominant organization in the PLO political galaxy and Yasser Arafat its brightest star. But at its height Arafat's leadership did not go unchallenged and his control was never complete. Ironically, as Arafat's star began to rise in the international community in the 1970s, it began to fade within the PLO. As a result, the conflicts between individuals, cliques, and factions that always impacted the PLO began to dominate the Palestinian movement and fostered intra-communal terrorism, i.e., terrorism against other Palestinian organizations and individuals as well as terrorist operations carried out to either enhance one's position or discredit political rivals within the PLO. Typical of the issues and fierceness of the rivalry are the differences between Arafat's Al Fatah and the Abu Nidal of Sabri al-Banna.

The Israeli defeat of Egypt and Syria in 1973 caused a major split within the PLO. On the one side were the moderate factions, led by Arafat, who were willing to accept a Palestinian state limited to the West Bank of the Jordan River and the Gaza Strip, both of which had been occupied by Israel in 1967. The militant or rejectionist factions refused to abandon the original goal of the elimination of Israel and its replacement by a nonsectarian state. Abu Nidal actually broke with Fatah in 1972, accusing Arafat of being soft on Israel and targeting him for assassination. The group also opposed any diplomatic settlement of the Arab-Israeli conflict. Initially called Fatah—"The Revolutionary Command"—and supplied by Iraq, Abu Nidal followed up its threats by assassinating moderate PLO leaders. To date it claims seven moderate Palestinian leaders among its victims. Al Fatah responded by setting up a special counterinsurgency squad and targeted members of Abu Nidal and other Palestinian militants for assassination. The moderate PLO establishment singled out Abu Nidal and sentenced him to death. Backed by the Arab radical states of Libya and Syria since 1980, Abu Nidal has survived and today claims two hundred to five hundred members. Organized into cells, most of the group's members are reported to be in Lebanon, Kuwait, the Gulf States, and a number of European cities. In 1982 Abu Nidal joined the Syria-led anti-Arafat rebellion within the PLO and began a series of terrorist attacks aimed at eliminating pro-Arafat Palestinians and moderate Jordanian officials and at delegitimizing the mainstream PLO. The most spectacular of the Abu Nidal raids were the twin attacks at the Rome and Vienna airports in December 1985. These grisly terrorist attacks on civilian travellers and its other wanton and indiscriminate raids on airplanes, synagogues, sidewalk cafes, schools, and crowded streets since 1984 have caused incalculable damage to the Palestinian cause and the Arab image in world opinion. As demonstrated by the Rome and Vienna airport attacks, Abu Nidal's members are willing to strike a blow at Arafat even if it ends up squandering what international goodwill the Palestinians have left. To them the first requirement of the war against the Zionist enemy is the removal of everyone in the Arab camp who would negotiate with Israel by any means, including violence against innocent civilians.

The Arab militants undertake their terrorist operations knowing that Israel and the Western media have convinced most people in the West that there is no distinction between Palestinian moderates and militants—that they are all terrorists. The wanton terrorism of militants such as Abu Nidal is part of a highly effective strategy to nurture this image by discrediting the PLO moderates regardless of how much they soften their stance toward Israel or try to distance themselves from Palestinian terrorism. Some sources claim that the terrorism of Abu Nidal is also part of a calculated move to bolster Syria's power vis-a-vis Israel in this period before the next Middle East war by forestalling negotiations until the Syrian-led Arab world is strong enough to negotiate from a position of strength. Here again, we have a case where acts of terrorism, which clearly damage the Palestinian case before the court of world opinion, appear to be the work of madmen. Yet when viewed within the framework of the Palestinian intra-communal conflict, they stand as rational and highly effective tactics serving the overall political strategy of the militant Arabs.

We can expect that terrorism will continue until it proves counterproductive to extremist Arab interests. And, at such time when Arafat's strategy of giving political concessions to an intransigent Reagan Administration appears to have exhausted what little patience exists in the squalor of the Palestinian camps, we can also expect groups like Abu Nidal's to be flooded with fanatical recruits, particularly from the camps in Lebanon where they have known only torment and terror, for its suicide missions in the belief that, even if it means certain death, striking out at someone is better than doing nothing.

Despite the unconfirmed death of its leader in 1982, there is substantial proof that Abu Nidal remains at war with Arafat. Members of Abu Nidal are said to be behind the takeover of a Pan American 747 aircraft on the tarmac of the Karashi, Pakistan airport on September 5, 1986, and possibly involved in the September 6 massacre at the Neve Shalom synagogue in Istanbul, Turkey. Both attacks coincided with a meeting in Harare, Ethiopia between non-aligned leaders and Palestinian moderates headed by Arafat. Although two groups, one known as the "Libyan Revolutionary Cells" and a new group, *Jundallah* ("Soldiers of God"), identified as a Lebanese pro-Iranian group, claimed responsibility in the Karashi incident in which twenty hostages were killed, sources say it is more likely the work of Abu Nidal or undisciplined PLO militants acting to discredit Arafat with leaders of the non-aligned movement. The method of operation seemed to match those employed by Abu Nidal, including using false cover names for its operations. Also, the four terrorists were identified as Palestinians.

In addition, a Libyan connection was unlikely, since, contrary to his usual combatant posture, Kaddafi at the time of the Karashi raid was downplaying his role in terrorism in order to forestall another United States bombing raid on his country. It is also unlikely that any Iranian group was behind the attack, since Iran had been backing Arafat loyalists battling pro-Syrian forces in south Beirut and thus had no interest in weakening Arafat's position. The attack on the Istanbul synagogue appeared to be related to the Turkish government's recent decision to upgrade its relations with Israel, a decision that completely stunned Arab militants and delighted Israel and the Reagan Administration.

The revival of the Islam religion spawned new sources of Middle East terrorism during this period. The reasons for this revival, which began in the early 1970s, are complicated. Yet there are four themes which seem to capture its general mood.[15]

First, it has developed out of a sentiment of disenchantment with and outright rejection of the West. As is true in many parts of the Third World, the Western models of political, social, and economic development are viewed more and more as inappropriate or alien transplants. Forced on the Muslim world, these models have no connection to the historical/cultural experience of Muslim societies.

Secondly, there is disillusionment with the political and socio-economic realities of Muslim life. The Western-style political systems and traditions have failed to produce national unity and political legitimacy in the Muslim world. Muslim leaders have tended to be little more than corrupt autocrats propped up by Western governments and multinational corporations. Capitalism has brought only a maldistribution of wealth, unbridled consumerism, and materialism. Marxist socialism is viewed as godless and thus a threat to religion. The process of modernization is rejected as fostering Western values and secularism leading to the breakdown of Muslim society and traditions.

A third theme in the revival of Islam concerns a search for identity and authenticity in Muslim life and a drive to base that process on indigenous cultural values. The revival of Muslim societies rests in a return to Islam, a restoration of Islamic pride, identity, and values in both community and individual life.

Finally, Islam is put forth as an ideology for state and society in which Muslims can only regain their rightful place in world power politics by re-orienting their government and society toward the prescripts of Islamic law. According to Muslim political activists, Islamic history teaches that the early spread of Islam and the creation of an Islamic empire were God's will and a validation of Islam's message.

The ideological framework spurring Islamic activism over the past decade and a half is framed by the following ideas: Islam is a way of life in which religion is integral to politics, law, state, and society; Muslim societies fail when they depart from Islam to follow Western ideologies and values; revival of Islam calls for a revolution based on the Koran and from Mohammed the leader of the first Islam movement; Islamic law, which is the blueprint for Muslim society, must replace Western civil law; and science and technology, while instrumental to the revolution, must be subordinated to Islam in order to protect against the infiltration of Western values.

Contrary to what is commonly asserted in the West, especially during the backlash of the United States-Iranian arms deal, there is much diversity within the Islamic world. Indeed, there are even moderate and radical factions in the radical state of Iran, although the spectrum in Iran's leadership is not as broad as in the larger Muslim community. The principles listed above constitute the moderate position in Islamic politics. Radicals within the Islamic movement, using the moderate framework as their starting point, are guided by the following beliefs: there is a Western Judeo-Christian conspiracy, fueled by neocolonialist ambitions and Zionist power, that pits the West against Islam; it is the will of God, not a choice, that an Islamic system of government be established and thus the duty of all Muslims to obey. Those who fail to comply are no longer Muslims. It is the duty of all true Muslims to wage a holy war (*jihad*) against these non-believers. (Egypt's President Anwar el-Sadat was assassinated in October 1981 by members of Egypt's Jamaat al-Jihad who judged him to be a "non-believer" because he failed to install Islamic law in Egypt.) Finally, radicals believe that Christians and Jews who are not judged "true believers" are "non-believers," or "not people of the book," and thus targets of their holy war. (It is this last principle that explains in part why former United States National Security Advisor Robert McFarlane, as a representative of President Reagan to exchange arms for American hostages, hand-carried a small Bible on his secret mission to Iran in 1986: to enhance his credibility with Iranian radicals he wanted to prove he was a "man of the book.")

The Islamic revolution, particularly its radical ideology, was greatly provoked by Israel's 1967 defeat of the Arab states and Israeli control over the holy city of Jerusalem. This "disaster," as it is known in Muslim circles, was viewed as proof of Arab Muslim impotence and raised questions, particularly among radical elements, about the policies of Arab governments and the appropriateness of the Western model of development. By the 1970s Islam had replaced nationalism and socialism as the major factor in the ideology and politics of Middle East governments and opposition movements. Even though his reinterpretation of Islam has angered and alienated traditional Islamic religious authorities, Kaddafi's Libya stands as the earliest state implementation of Islam and thus an important precedent. After seizing power in 1969, Muammar Kaddafi introduced Islamic law in Libya, though he eventually redefined Islam in his *Green Book*, with the addition of radical socialist ideology. In Egypt, President Anwar el-Sadat, seeking to consolidate his political power after the death of President Gamal Abdel Nasser in 1970, provoked Islamic sentiments and the growth of radical Islamic organizations by using Islamic symbols and Islamic student organizations to neutralize leftist and Nasserist forces. In doing so, he helped legitimize Islam. But he also created an Islamic yardstick by which his and other Arab governments came to be judged as "non-believers" by Islamic radicals and eventually targets of their holy war. Sadat's assassination by members of the radical Jamaat al-Jihad in 1981 still serves as a warning to other "non-believer" leaders in the Arab world. More importantly, it offers clear evidence of the ability and intent of radical Islamic elements to influence events in the Middle East by employing the instrument of terrorism.

The singular event in contemporary Islamic politics was the overthrow of Mohammad Reza Shah Pahlavi, the Shah of Iran, in 1978–79 and the subsequent seizure of the Iranian state by radical Shiite followers of the Ayatollah Khomeini. The Shah's commitment to Western values and modernization and his close ties to the United States, two major adversaries of the Islamic revolution, gave special meaning to his downfall and the general revival of Islam. The coming of age of a radical Shiite Islamic state in an

Islamic religion long dominated by the more moderate Sunni community has also given hope and comfort to disenfranchised Shiites everywhere. But it has also widened the major schism in the Islamic world between Sunnis and Shiites, which in Lebanon and on the border between Iran and Iraq has erupted into fierce and possibly suicidal warfare.

It is the radical Shiite Islamic elements, be they individuals, organizations, or states, and their fanatical dedication to the Islamic holy war who came to be a major source of Middle East terrorism in the third phase and beyond. Shiites (the "party of Ali") view themselves as a disenfranchised community within Islam and blame Sunni-dominated governments for preventing them from assuming their rightful place in Islam. The ideological basis of current Shiite militancy stems in part from the martyrdom of Ali's son Hussein who was killed in 680 A.D. by Sunni Caliph Yazid's army at Karlbala in Iraq. The memory of this "martyrdom," which includes a willingness to sacrifice and die for God, is kept alive by the annual re-enactment of this drama about the struggle of a small righteous party, or army of God, against Satan. Believing that the political realities of Muslim life require "jihad," or armed struggle, radical organizations like Egypt's Jamaat al Jihad and Lebanon's Hezbollah ("Party of God") have dedicated themselves to a policy of violent confrontation. They see their governments as anti-Islamic regimes who through their control over religion or their repression of the authentic Islamic movements stand in the way of the Islamic revolution. As enemies of God, these despotic rulers and their Western allies are legitimate targets for violence and terrorism.

The terrorism of radical Islam is both state- and community-based. The Shiite regime of the Ayatollah Khomeini in postrevolutionary Iran has sponsored terrorist groups and operations in many parts of the world and against many different nationalities. The most famous is the taking of American hostages in 1979, an act which continues to stir so much anger among Americans that even so popular and conservative an American president as Ronald Reagan negotiates with the Iranian government at his political peril. According to *The New York Times News Service*, information gathered by French and Israeli intelligence officials indicates Iran provided the explosives used in the terrorist attacks on the United States Embassy on April 8, 1983 and on the Marine base at Beirut

International Airport in October of 1983.[16] These sources claim that the Iranian government also transferred more than $1 million to the Iranian Embassy in Beirut and used it to buy the explosives. Seventeen Americans died in the embassy attack and two hundred forty-two were killed in the terrorist attack on the Marine compound. In other cases, Iranian embassy personnel all over western Europe have been charged with sponsoring terrorist groups. For example, in 1983 Spanish police arrested a number of Iranians who later confessed they were planning to kill expatriate critics of the Khomeini regime. Also in 1983, French officials expelled several Iranian diplomats after discovering that the Iranian Embassy in Paris served as a center for Iranian terrorists bent on assassinating Iranian dissidents. These Iranian "diplomats" had been trained in camps in Libya and Syria and then sent abroad with diplomatic cover. Beginning in 1983, Iranian assassination squads have been found to operate as far afield as the Philippines and Indonesia. Iranian terrorists have targeted non-Iranian moderates as well. In August 1984 Spanish police arrested four members of the Martyrs of the Iranian Revolution after uncovering a plot to hijack a Saudi airliner. Iranian terrorists hijacked a French airliner and demanded the release of Iranians jailed in France following the attempt to kill former Iranian Prime Minister Shapur Bakhtiari in 1980. Iranian leaders made no effort to cover their involvement in the hijacking, describing it as a "lesson for France" related to French support of Iraq and Iranian dissidents.

Prominent Arab sources claim that two major training terrorist camps opened up in Iran in 1983 to train cadres in "suicide" operations. The largest camp, of about two thousand volunteers, most of whom are selected for training by Iranian diplomats in the Middle East and western Europe, is outside of Qum. Training includes instruction in truck bombing, explosives, and weapons, as well as ideological indoctrination. After graduation, the cadres are assigned to foreign posts or sent on suicidal missions against the Iraqis.

Khomeini's radical regime in Iran has also greatly influenced the emergence of political radicalism in quiescent Shiite communities in Muslim Sunni-dominated states throughout the Middle East, particularly in Saudi Arabia and Pakistan; in Iraq, the Iranians promoted the *al-Hizb al-Da'wah al-Islamiyah* ("Party of the Islamic Cell") which is now located in Teheran and for years has directed its terrorism at Iraqi officials and installations including the Iraqi Embassy in Beirut, Lebanon, in December 1981. This group, which is currently active in Iran, Iraq, Syria, Kuwait, and other Persian Gulf nations, is dedicated to overthrowing the governments of these countries and installing an Islamic republic modelled after Khomeini's Iran. In Lebanon, where Shiites are the largest ethnic community, Iranian volunteers have been training with Lebanese Shiites since 1979. In 1982 members of the Iranian Revolutionary Guard began operating in Lebanon and are credited with organizing terrorist splinter groups such as the Islamic Amal, the Hezbollah, and the Islamic Jihad, who in the early 1980s were responsible for major terrorist operations against Western targets. The Hezbollah carried out the deadly attacks on the United States Embassy and Marine compound in 1983. The Islamic Jihad is tied by some sources to the attacks on the United States Marines and the United States Embassy in 1983 as well as the truck bombing of French military headquarters, the December 1983 bombing of a hotel, and French military court command post.[17] It was also allegedly behind the bombing of the United States Embassy in East Beirut in September 1984, the July 1984 attack on the Soviet Embassy in Beirut, and the hijacking of a Kuwaiti airliner in Teheran in December 1984.

As noted, the Iranian regime helped spur militancy within Lebanon's Shiite community. But terrorism in Lebanon is largely community-based. The mobilization of Lebanese Shiite Muslims was well under way by the mid-1970s, provoked by fifty years of repressive rule by Lebanon's Christian Maronite government which kept the Shiite community in a state of economic and political deprivation. Imam Musa Sadr, an Iranian-born member of the Lebanese Shiite community, formed the "Movement of the Dispossessed," which evolved into "The Battalions of the Resistance" or *Amal*, in the mid-1970s. Under the leadership of Nabih Berri, Amal has emerged as a relatively moderate organization looking for a power-sharing arrangement in Lebanese politics. Though Amal militias have fought against Israel, Lebanese Christian and Sunni forces, and the PLO, Berri remains a force of moderation and played a central role in mediating the release of American hostages during the June 1985 hijacking of the TWA airliner in Beirut. Despite Amal's moderate stance, the general Lebanese Shiite community, particularly its youth, has been radicalized by Iran's revolution, the Israeli invasions of Lebanon in 1978 and 1982, and the subsequent Israeli "Iron Fist" policy in southern Lebanon. While support for Amal's political program remained strong among Shiites in the early 1980s, there was also growing support for the Islamic Jihad and Hezbollah's call for the creation of a separate Lebanese Islamic state and the pursuit of an armed holy war against the "enemies of God" through terrorism, assassination, and suicide attacks.

The radicalization of the Lebanese Shiite community, the Amal attacks on the Sunni-dominated Palestinian refugee camps, and assassination attempts on Sunni leaders such as Paris-exiled Murabitun militia head Ibrahim Qulaylat have in turn spawned radical groups in the Lebanese-based Sunni Muslim community. Most of these neighborhood-based and loosely structured groups have successfully recruited members by capitalizing on the sectarian conflict between the Sunnis and Shiites. The most important of these is the Islamic Military Council, whose leader, Abdul Hafiz Qasim, calls for an independent Sunni identity. Other Sunni militants, such as Sheik Habashi, have fueled sectarian violence within the Lebanese Muslim community by telling Sunni extremists that Islamic law permits the spilling of Shiite blood. Another important Sunni militant is Sheik Said Shaaban, leader of the Tawhid or Islamic Unity Movement. Fanatically anti-Christian, Shaaban calls for an Islamic state and believes that the only alternative to Islam is pagan rule. During his attempt to control Tripoli in 1983 his organization massacred hundreds of leftists and secularists and reportedly dumped their bodies in the sea to rid the earth of their evil influence.

The Armenian Christian community is another source of Middle East community-based terrorism. Today's Armenian militancy is part of the history of struggle for Armenian ethno-cultural survival. This struggle was led by two nineteenth-century nationalist organizations, the Hunchak and Dashnak parties, founded in the 1880s to maintain Armenian identity amidst the surrounding Muslim culture. In 1915 most of the Turkish Armenian community was massacred by the Young Turks. Those who weren't killed were deported to other countries where they gathered into refugee camps. Avenging this massacre is the principal spark igniting contemporary Armenian militancy and terrorism. In 1975 the Armenian Secret Army for the Liberation of Armenia (ASALA) and the Justice Commmandos of the Armenian Genocide began their terrorist operations. They were joined in 1983 by the Armenian Revolutionary Army (ARA). In their early days these organizations were linked to Palestinian organizations and received training in PLO camps in Lebanon until the Israeli invasion in 1982. ASALA split with Arafat's Fatah in the early 1980s and since 1982 has operated out of training camps it has established in Syria and Cyprus. In 1982 it also split internally into ASALA, a military and nationalist wing emphasizing terrorism, and a political wing known as ASALA-Revolutionary Movement. Organized in a self-sufficient cell structure under the General Command of the People of Armenia (VAN), ASALA claims to have cadres in several countries, including the United States, France, West Germany, Switzerland, Italy, Cyprus, Portugal, Greece, Iran, Spain, and Australia. In Lebanon, ASALA has five bases and its headquarters are in Beirut. It receives training from Syria and support from Iran. Greece also gives the ASALA support by way of Cyprus.

In line with their mission to avenge the 1915 massacre, the majority of ASALA terrorist operations are undertaken against Turkish diplomatic officials and Turkish embassies. ASALA terrorists are connected to at least fifty assassinations, including the murders of twenty-nine Turkish diplomats and their families. It is credited with more than one hundred attacks on Turkish targets in over fifteen countries. Among them: in August 1982 ASALA terrorists machine-gunned innocent passengers at the Ankara airport; in June 1983 two people were murdered and twenty-three injured by ASALA cadres in Istanbul; a suitcase bomb at Orly Airport in France was credited to the ASALA in July 1983, as was the attack on two Turkish diplomats in March 1984, and the shooting of a Turkish businessman in May 1984 in Teheran.

The other Armenian group, the Justice Commandos of the Armenian Genocide, said to be based in California, is credited with the assassinations of the Turkish ambassadors in Paris and Vienna in 1975 and then the Turkish ambassador to Yugoslavia in 1983. The newest Armenian terrorist organization, the Armenian Revolutionary Army (ARA) is said to be responsible for the 1983 assassination of a Turkish diplomat in Brussels, and the occupation of the Turkish Embassy in Lisbon. In 1984 ARA terrorists murdered two Turkish officials in Vienna. In March 1985 an ARA raid on the Turkish Embassy in Ottawa cost the life of a security guard.

The Turkish government has countered Armenian violence with terrorist operations of its own. The Armenian communities in Turkey are kept under official surveillance. The government harasses and arrests anyone suspected of aiding the various Armenian terrorist groups. Turkish intelligence counterterrorist operations reportedly include 1983 and 1984 bombings of the Armenian Cultural Center at Alfortville, France, the bombing of the Marseilles Cultural Center in March 1984, and a Paris bombing in November 1984.

The role of Syria in state-sponsored Middle East terrorism is currently the subject of much debate. The question is not whether Syria is involved but for what reasons and to what extent. Many analysts, among them Barry Rubin, a fellow at Johns Hopkins University School of Advanced International Studies, argue that Syrian president Hafez al-Assad employs terrorism and terrorists as a major and very effective tool of his foreign policy. According to Rubin, Syria uses state terrorism more effectively than either Iran or Libya because Assad follows several important rules.[18] First, Syrian terrorism is used for limited, well-defined goals rather than as an instrument to provoke revolution. Following this rule, Syrian-sponsored terrorism has enabled Syria to maximize its influence in Lebanon while weakening American and Israeli leverage, prevent Jordan from making peace with Israel, keep the PLO under Syrian influence, and blackmail wealthy oil-producing Arab states. Secondly, Syria has deployed terrorism in conjunction with military and diplomatic operations. The combination of terrorism, Syrian army occupation, and diplomatic intervention in Lebanon's internal politics has allowed Assad to outmaneuver the United States in many instances and sustain its hegemony over war-torn Lebanon. The third rule Assad invokes is to avoid publicity and to not boast about being involved in terrorism. In addition, he believes terrorism should be sporadic rather than a continuous offensive. Until the trial of Jordanian Nezar Hindawi in October 1986 exposed the level of Syrian-sponsored terrorism, following this rule helped Syria avoid the kind of diplomatic and economic sanctions and military reprisals levelled by the United States and the western Europeans at Libya and its loudmouth leader Kaddafi. Finally, Syria has remained strong enough and close enough to the Soviet Union to forestall military retaliation for its terrorism.

Assad's predecessors openly supported PLO terrorism in the

1960s. As a result of Israel's victory in the 1967 war, Syria's regional power was diminished. When Assad came to power in 1971 it was his goal to re-establish that power but to do so by being more selective and secretive in the use of terrorism. After the Syrian army invaded Lebanon in 1975, Assad effectively controlled events by playing off the various Christian, Druse, or Shiite and Sunni Muslim groups against each other and by either subsidizing or punishing them, depending on Syrian interests at the moment. In this way, Syria sustained its hegemony in Lebanon by engaging in terrorism and assassination to ensure that no party won the civil war. For example, Syria arranged the assassination of Druse leader Kemal Jumblatt in 1966 because he would not abandon his goal of total victory. In 1982 Syria ordered the murder of Lebanon's president, Bashir Gemayel, whose dynamism threatened Syrian power.

It has been known for a long time that Syria is directly supportive of dissident factions of the PLO. The purposes behind Syrian support for Arafat's rivals such as Colonel Abu Musa and George Habash are consistent with the principal Syrian foreign policy goal to become a dominant power in the Middle East by preventing any negotiated solution to the Arab-Israel conflict. At this point a settlement of the conflict would be disastrous to Syria, since it is likely to strengthen Jordan's position on the Palestinian issue, free the PLO from Syrian hegemony, and permit Israel, through Arab recognition, to become a powerful rival state in Middle East politics. Reduced tensions in the region would also demote Syria to a second-rate power while increasing American power and prestige. Through its support of PLO terrorists Syria is able to put pressure on the governments of Lebanon and Jordan without having to get involved in a direct military operation. It also helps ensure that the PLO remains politically divided and thus unable to challenge Syrian leadership in the Palestinian community.

Recent disclosures from American, French, and Israeli intelligence sources confirm that Syrian military experts directed the assembly and emplacement of the bombs by the Shiite Hezbollah that killed the two hundred and forty-two American Marines and seventeen American personnel of the United States Embassy in Beirut in 1983.[19] The disclosure of further information concerning Syria's role in terrorism during the trial and conviction of Nezar

Hindawi for attempting to blow up an El Al airliner at London's Heathrow Airport has convinced British authorities to cut diplomatic ties with Syria. According to Benjamin Netanyahu, Israel's permanent representative to the United Nations, Hindawi's trial proved that Syria masterminds a terror machine that is "implicated in dozens of other terrorist attacks, from West Beirut to West Berlin."[20] Hindawi, a Jordanian-born Palestinian, confessed he was trained in Syria and accompanied to London by a Syrian intelligence agent. Netanyahu claims that the coordinator of the failed London attack on the El Al jet was Colonel Mohammad Kholi, chief of Syrian air force intelligence and a close confidante of Syrian President Assad. One of Kholi's deputies is reported to have personally transported the explosives used in the March 29, 1986 bombing of the German-Arab Friendship League into West Berlin. The Syrian Embassy in East Berlin is alleged to have been the conduit for the explosives. On April 5, 1986 a similar explosive device destroyed La Belle discotheque in West Berlin and killed an American soldier and a Turkish woman.

Syria utilizes three separate terrorist constituencies in pursuing its foreign policy goals. First, as noted above, it is involved with several anti-Arafat Palestinian groups. The most prominent of these are *As Saiqa*, headed by Abu Mesa, the Popular Struggle Front, the Popular Front for the Liberation of Palestine, led by George Habash, and Abu Nidal. These and sundry other PLO groups are headquartered in Damascus. Six of the major dissident factions, led by the PFLP, were organized by Syria under the banner of the Palestine National Salvation Front as an alternative to Arafat's PLO. These groups have carried out terrorist attacks under Syrian sponsorship. For example, from 1983 onward Syria hired its Palestinian surrogates, specifically Abu Nidal, for a successful terrorist campaign to discourage King Hussein from embracing the Reagan Plan or any PLO-led negotiations. In April 1983 PLO moderate Issam Suwas was killed in Portugal by Syrian agents. In October 1983 Syrian-backed terrorists murdered the Jordanian ambassadors to India and Italy and a Jordanian security officer in Athens. In December 1984 Syrian agents killed Fahd Kawasmeh, a former West Bank mayor and PLO executive committee member with close ties to Jordan's King Hussein. In 1985 Syria organized a rocket attack on a Jordanian airliner in Athens, the bombing of a Jordanian diplomat in Ankara, and a Jordanian publisher in Athens. The murders of Palestinian moderate Aziz Shehadeh in Ramallah and Mayor Zahir al-Masri, who was a link between Hussein and Arafat in 1986, are said to be the work of Syrian agents. Also in 1986, members of the Abu Mesa-led As Saiqa, found to be carrying Syrian passports at the time of their capture, successfully exploded a bomb aboard a Trans World Air airliner in flight in February and bombed an El Al airline counter in Madrid in June.

Syrian involvement in terrorism extends beyond the PLO. According to Netanyahu and other Israeli sources, Syria has lent support to and serves as a diplomatic base for most leading anti-Western terrorist groups, including the Italian Red Brigade, the French Direct Action, the Japanese Red Army, the German Red Army Faction, the Basque E.T.A., and Turkish opposition groups such as the Armenian ASALA and the Gray Wolves. Others reportedly represented in Damascus are Kurdish and Tamil organizations, the Patani Liberation of Thailand, and the Polisario of Morocco.[21]

Syria's third terrorist constituents are "freelance" terrorists such as Nezar Hindawi and his brother Ahmed Nawal Mansour Hazi Hindawi, who have little and in most cases no connection to an identifiable terrorist organization. Freelance terrorists are hired for highly sensitive cases where the government desires minimum visibility for its role in terrorism. As Middle East terrorism enters the fourth and current stage, freelance terrorists are playing a larger role and are proving to be increasingly independent from and thus more troubling to their government employers, including Syria.

Along with the continuation of the Arab-Israeli conflict, the third phase of Middle East terrorism was defined by the state-sponsored terrorism of Iran, Syria, and Libya as part of their respective foreign policy strategies. The Islamic revolution gave purpose and direction to state-sponsored terrorism, particularly in the case of Iran. But it also spawned extremism and terrorist groups within the Shiite and Sunni Islamic communities. With the exception of Israel, these terrorist states and groups were guided by a decidedly anti-Western bent. The Reagan Administration has interpreted this anti-Western sentiment as specifically anti-American in focus, even though western European nations have been the major target for Middle East terrorists. To be sure, anti-Americanism does accompany Islamic and Palestinian terrorism, but it is not usually provoked by an instinctive hatred of America. In the case of the PLO it is stirred principally by United States' support of Israel and Israeli acts of terrorism. Anti-Americanism within the Islamic community is a response to the threat American political and cultural hegemony and power is perceived to pose to Muslim identity.

The third phase of Middle East terrorism ends with intra-communal terrorism engulfing both the Palestinian movement and the Islamic Revolution. Syrian and Israeli policies have kept the PLO divided and thus factionalist terror in the Palestinian community alive and well. In the early 1980s the Middle East Islamic community was ruptured on two fronts as Shiites began fighting Sunnis on the Iran-Iraq border and terrorizing each other in Lebanon for control of the Islamic Revolution.

The fourth and current phase of Middle East terrorism begins around 1983 and is dominated by the proliferation of "freelance" terrorist groups and their objectives. Today, a single act of terrorism brings claims, and in many cases contradictory disclaimers, of responsibility from dozens of groups for a variety of causes. For instance, five Beirut-based groups claimed responsibility for the attempted hijacking of an Iraqi Airways Boeing 737 over Saudi Arabia on Christmas Day 1986, during which at least sixty-two people died. Four of the groups claiming responsibility, the Revolutionary Action Organization, the Revolutionary Shiite Organization, the Islamic Revolutionary Movement, and the Islamic Revolutionary Movement (Iraqi Branch), were previously unknown. The fifth group claiming involvement was the well-known Islamic Jihad.

On the other hand, numerous terrorist acts occurring in a short span of time are often credited to completely different sponsors. For example, the suicide attack on the Istanbul synagogue, the series of deadly bombings in Paris, the hijacking of the Pan Am flight in Karashi, the grenade attack at the Wailing Wall in Jerusalem, and the videotape appeals of French and American hostages, all occurring in the early fall of 1986, were credited to different groups with different motivations.

The anarchic nature of violence and terrorism in Lebanon is representative of this new kaleidoscopic age of Middle East terrorism. In Beirut, no less than thirty-three separate organizations have claimed responsibility for terrorist operations carried out or planned in Lebanon over the past four years. Twenty-seven of the thirty-three are not really "groups" in the sense of being an organized coherent body; most have been formed for a specific operation and lack both history and future either to avoid discovery or due to a lack of allegiance. All twenty-seven claimed only one action and were not heard of before or since. The motivation behind these operations ranges from revenge, money, or political beliefs, to simple bravado. The titles these groups claim for themselves reflect the proliferation of "causes." For example, among the groups who claimed responsibility for terrorist acts in Lebanon since 1983 are "The Independent Movement for the Liberation of the Kidnapped," "The National Resistance Army of the Nation's Liberation Faction," "Organization M5," "Group 219FA," "The Front for Confronting Corruption and Debauchery," "The Organization of the Oppressed on Earth," "The Revolutionary Organization of Socialist Muslims," "Black Banners," and "The Green Brigades." There are only a half dozen groups that claimed responsibility for more than one action. The most important of these is "Islamic Jihad," which claimed credit for twenty-seven actions. But it is clear that Islamic Jihad is not a single structured organization, although there may have been a central organization to Islamic Jihad when it began its terrorist operations. Now, other groups adopt the prestigious name of "Islamic Jihad" to take advantage of the notoriety surrounding the original group. These groups have proven difficult to trace and identify because while one "Islamic Jihad" claims credit for an action, another "Islamic Jihad" disclaims responsibility for the same action.

Judging from their titles, targets, and the deals they arrange, at least half of the twenty-seven groups appear to be from the Shiite community. Their attacks also appear to be politically motivated, as they were aimed at the Western powers of France, Britain, and the United States. But often, as in the 1985 kidnapping of a South Korean diplomat by "The Green Brigades" and the demand for a $10 million ransom, some terrorist acts make no political sense or contradict the espoused political goals of the group. There is also evidence that many groups take hostages solely for monetary gain. These shadowy groups sell their victims to the more politically-motivated organizations who in turn take credit for the kidnapping and set the agenda for the hostage release.

The current proliferation of Palestinian terrorist groups is partially a response to Arafat's political isolation and the lack of any success on the peace front. Forced from his bases in Lebanon and Tunis and increasingly isolated from his frontline fighters, Arafat finds his position in the militant Arab world usurped by other leaders such as Hussein Moussawi, a Shiite with Iranian support, George Ibrahim Abdallah, the leader of the Christian Maronite Lebanese Revolutionary Armed Faction, and Abu Nidal. The lack of movement in the peace process has undercut Arafat's moderate strategy and allowed other leaders of the umbrella PLO to exercise their independence. Arafat banned all operations outside Israeli-occupied territory after the fiasco surrounding the pirating of the *Achille Lauro* in October 1985. The subsequent hijacking of the Egyptian airliner in November and the slaughter at the Rome and Vienna airports in December 1985 by Palestinian terrorists demonstrated that Arafat was unable to enforce his ban. Indeed, many Palestinian terrorist operations, such as the recent one at the Karashi airport, are meant solely to embarrass Arafat and discredit his leadership within the Palestinian camps and the Western world. Increasingly the Palestinian refugee-turned-guerrilla is being replaced by the more fanatic foot soldier who is recruited by the renegade Palestinian groups for one-time "suicide" terrorist acts. Two examples are the sixteen-year-old girl Sana Mheidleh, who blew up herself and her car close to an Israeli convoy in southern Lebanon, and Mohammed Sarham, the surviving member of the six young militants who carried out the suicide attacks on the Rome and Vienna airports.

The maze-like world of Middle East terrorism is further complicated by the lack of control exercised by the state terrorist "establishment." By the middle to late 1980s, many of the governments who sponsored or supported terrorist groups in the early years of the decade found they were unable to control the monsters they'd created. Several prominent terrorist groups had abandoned their original sponsor or had adopted several patrons. Abu Nidal, originally supported by Iraq, moved to Syria in 1983 and, until 1990, was thought to be linked to Iraq, but was primarily aided by Libya, Iran and several Eastern European governments. During this period, some terrorist organizations were actually at war with their state sponsors. For example, though the fundamentalist Hezbollah and Syria cooperated in the 1983 bombing of the Marine compound in Beirut, by the mid-1980s their troops often clashed in Lebanon's Bekaa Valley.

In the years preceding the 1990 Persian Gulf Crisis, the proliferation of terrorist groups, states and causes, the factionalism within the Palestinian and Islamic movements, terrorism between Israelis and the Palestinian Intifada and the variety of claims and counterclaims of responsibility which define contemporary Middle East terrorism had created an environment dominated by anarchy and a maze of contradictions. All the major parties involved in the Middle East appeared increasingly willing to use terrorism or traffic with terrorists when it suited their purposes. The Reagan Administration sent thousands of tons of arms to "terrorist" Iran in exchange for the release of American hostages, only to have its efforts rewarded by the kidnapping of three more Americans. Israeli troops created new martyrs for the PLO by killing twelve and fourteen year old rock-throwing Palestinian protesters in the occupied territories. The Shiite population continued its terrorism in southern Lebanon. In Israel, the growing political popularity of the Jewish religio-nationalist fundamentalists to the right of the Likud coalition fueled extremist sentiments within the one hundred thousand-strong Israeli settler community in the occupied areas. French officials paid millions of dollars in ransom to Iran for the release of French hostages in Lebanon as French government and corporate personnel were assassinated by French and Middle East-based terrorists. The streets and neighborhoods of Beirut were ravaged by daily violence as Shiite, Druse and Christian militias battled each other and murdered members of their respective communities. A December, 1986, Israeli "counterterrorist" raid on the Palestinian guerrilla base in the Nahr el-Bared refugee camp claimed twenty-one lives, including that of Mohammed Selim, one of Abu Nidal's top lieutenants. Selim's death provoked promises from Abu Nidal's Revolutionary Council to step up its terrorist efforts against Israel and its allies everywhere. The effort by King Hussein of Jordan to replace Yasser Arafat as leader of the PLO spawned further intracommunal terrorism by Arafat's political rivals culminating in the January 1991 murder of Arafat's two top lieutenants Salah Khalaf and Hayel Abdel-Hamid. Yet, while PLO leaders terrorized each other, support for the PLO and Palestinian extremism rose in the Palestinian refugee camps. As

Adolescents in military training, Iran.

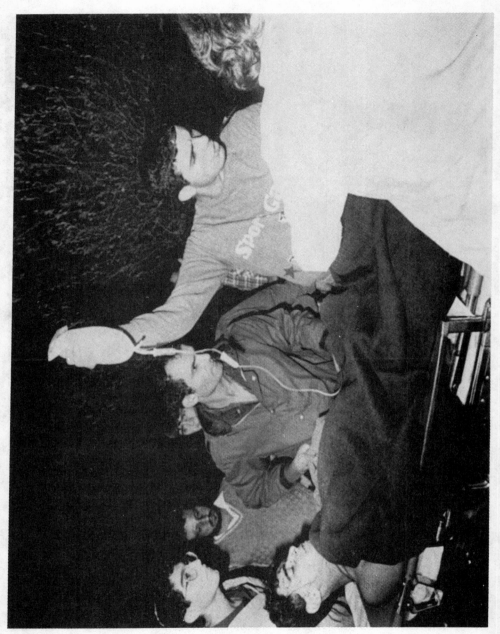

Victims of grenade attack, Wailing Wall, Jerusalem.

Bombed-out synagogue, Istanbul.

Refugee camp massacre, Lebanon.

Arafat-led forces enjoyed a renaissance in the refugee camps of Lebanon in late 1986, and the Syrian-backed Palestine National Salvation Front was battered by desertions to Arafat forces, Syria's President Assad called on his stable of freelance terrorists and Syrian-supported terrorist organizations to forestall any newly developed allegiance to Arafat in the PLO. In the most tragic development, until the 1987 ceasefire, thousands of Iranian and Iraqi teenagers were sent to their deaths on suicidal missions in an Iran-Iraq war fueled by religious and political zealots and massive shipments of arms from a self-serving coalition of states that included the Soviet Union, the United States, Israel and most nations of Eastern and Western Europe.

Throughout the 1980s, the anarchic environment of Middle East terrorism helped destroy any prospect for a comprehensive peace settlement. Even as the thaw in their relations began, the superpowers were limited to supporting their traditional Middle East allies and avoiding any direct confrontation with each other. Despite an increasingly strained relationship, support for Israel remained the cornerstone of United States Middle East policy. Americans were targets of Palestinian and Islamic terrorists, be they community or state sponsored. Meanwhile, Soviet policy continued to side with the Arab cause. In their association with the fragmented Arab world, the Soviets encountered major difficulties and outright failures. For example, despite its anti-Israel posture and its willingness to sell arms to the Arab states, the Soviet Union was unable to allay the suspicious sentiments of conservative Arab states such as Jordan, Kuwait and Saudi Arabia. While the Soviets backed Iraq in its war with Iran, Libya and Syria, their closest allies in the Middle East, supported Khomeini's Iran. The Islamic revolution, which stalled the momentum of Soviet-sponsored socialist movements in the Middle East, was particularly troublesome for the Soviets. Due to their brutal repression of Afghanistan's Muslim population, to increasing numbers of people in the Muslim world the Soviets had become "the terrorist enemy." As the 1980s ended, Soviet citizens and diplomats, like their American counterparts, were viewed by the Muslim world as enemies of Islam and nationalist self-determination and were targeted for kidnapping and murder by an assortment of Middle East terrorist individuals, groups and states.

Our overview of Middle East terrorism centers on two central tenets of the Middle View.

First, our analysis of the four stages of terrorism and the variety of sources from which terrorism springs in and through them confirms the complexity of terrorism. It helps us break down the single-source conspiratorial myth that guides what most of us "know" about terrorism. Our assessment of the ethnic, political and religious diversity in Middle East politics, and the reality of intra-communal and intra-factional terrorism also challenge the notion that terrorism is solely directed against Western capitalist—and specifically American—interests. Indeed, the Arab community, which most Westerners view as the major source of the explosion of terrorism, is victimized by terrorism to a much greater degree than any other constituency in or outside of the Middle East. This is particularly true of Arab women and children in the refugee camps.

Secondly, we have seen that there are a large number of parties in the Middle East, ranging from the states of Israel to Syria to Iran and from right-wing Lebanese Christian groups to left-wing Palestinians, who, believing it to be effective in realizing their goals, adopt terrorism as an integral element in their political strategies. The conclusion that terrorism can be—or is thought to be—an effective political instrument in Middle East politics when added to the increasing vulnerability of modern transportation, communication and energy systems helps provoke the contemporary explosion of terrorism. It also underscores the distressing Middle View prediction that terrorism is likely to be a permanent fixture of the Middle East and politics-at-large for some time to come.

TERRORISM AND THE PERSIAN GULF CRISIS: THE CASE OF IRAQ

Iraq's invasion of Kuwait on August 2, 1990, set in motion a new crisis in Middle East politics, the full dynamics of which are still unfolding. Later, when Iraqi President Saddam Hussein refused to obey the American-sponsored United Nations' ultimatum to withdraw from Kuwait by January 15, 1991, President George Bush, backed by the coalition forces, launched military air attacks against Iraqi troops occupying Kuwait and the nation of Iraq. Forty-three days later, after a six day allied ground offensive routed Iraqi troops from Kuwait, the war ended with the peoples and treasures of Iraq and Kuwait severely damaged. Despite the short duration and decisive outcome of the war, there is little evidence that the political intransigence or belligerent sentiments that define much of Middle East politics have in anyway been diminished. Indeed, the decisive defeat of Iraq and its allies insures that the politics of the past, in which terrorism by all parties plays a central role, will continue into the uncertain future of the region.

Like the previous major crises that have wracked the Middle East since the end of World War II, the war highlights the complexity and permanence of contemporary terrorism. From the very first days of the crisis, multiple parties sought to use terrorism and the threat of terrorism to their advantage. For the coalition forces allied against Iraq, Saddam Hussein's invasion of Kuwait was a local or regional event with international implications, principally because of his alleged nuclear capacity and announced intention to use terrorism to extend the scope of the war beyond the Middle East to all those allied against him in the Gulf War. Because of this, Saddam Hussein rocketed to the top of the Western world's list of most dangerous terrorists. For their parts, Saddam Hussein and his allies in the Arab world insisted that they utilize terrorism as an instrument of war in response to the terror that rained from the skies over Iraqi citizens and the terrorism Middle East Arabs had suffered at the hands of Israel and its Western allies over past decades. From their vantage point, the Israeli leadership is now joined by President George Bush and Soviet President Mikail Gorbachev at the head of the cast of characters responsible for contemporary global terrorism.

It is not surprising that two polarized visions dominate the current discussion of Middle East terrorism. Nor is there any mystery as to why, in the oilrich Persian Gulf, the terrorism of one's enemies was invoked to mobilize support for each side's respective war effort. As we have seen, debates over contemporary terrorism tend to be extremely polarized. As well, the negative connotations attached to terrorism have in the past been invoked for partisan political gain.

However, in the present Middle East context, there are important differences from the past. Now, Americans and Soviets are lined up on the same side of the terrorist issue, a circumstance that requires some adjustment by respective Western and Soviet citizens who, depending on their nationality, were taught to view Moscow or Washington, D.C. as the central headquarters of international terrorism. Secondly, Saddam Hussein publicly repeated his intention to use terrorism as an instrument of war policy, an unusual posture for someone seeking to mold favorable world opinion.

Hidden close to the surface of partisan and polarized politics is a tangled web of political complexity and intrigue that more accurately reflects the realities of Middle East terrorism and highlights the assumptions of the Middle View.

Like his predecessors, George Bush has sought to justify American foreign policy on a moral basis. In his 1991 State of the Union address, Bush called the war with Iraq a battle between good and evil, thus a "just war." Saddam Hussein gave the president's argument ample evidence when he announced that terrorism would be used to bring the war to the populous of nations waging war on Iraq. On February 6, 1991, Saddam Hussein expanded his terrorist rhetoric with a threat to kill President Bush even after he leaves the presidency.

Once Saddam Hussein had warned that terrorism would be a weapon of war, the central concerns became: When would Iraqi-backed terrorism start, where would it hit and what countermeasures were required? The answer to when the terrorism would start came quickly with Saddam Hussein's immediate refusal to allow "foreign guests" to leave Iraq and Kuwait. As a consequence, another American president faced yet another Middle East hostage crisis, this one affecting thousands of people. Fortunately, early in December, the hostage crisis ended without incident when Saddam Hussein allowed all his "guests" to leave.

When the American-led United Nations coalition attacked Iraq on January 16, 1991, Saddam Hussein responded to the attack on Iraq with his own moralistic stance by urging all Muslims to wage a holy war against the enemy. Then, he launched SCUD "terror" missiles at Israeli and Saudi Arabian cities. The start of war also brought isolated incidents of what Western terrorism analysts labeled Iraq-inspired "freelance" terrorism. Predictably, they were aimed at Western, in particularly American, targets in many parts of the world.

In late January, terrorism related to the Persian Gulf war began in earnest. In Turkey, terrorism hit several locations including two incidents in Adana: a car explosion next to the American Consulate and the murder of American Bobbie Mozelle, an American customs officer, outside the NATO airbase. Dev Sol (Revolutionary Left), a Turkish group analysts say has no links to Iraq, took credit for the terrorism, claiming Mozelle was a CIA agent and the bombing campaign was in response to the Turkish government's decision to permit American air strikes against Iraq from bases in Turkey. Athens, Greece, also suffered numerous bombings. Two bombs exploded in late January, one across the street from the American Express office. A week later, explosions rocked two Western banks. In the first two weeks of war there were eight attacks against the United States' allies in Lebanon. Rocket-propelled grenades were fired at the Italian Embassy and a bank party owned by French investors. A dynamite explosion damaged the Egyptian Embassy in Beirut. The next week, Lebanese officials arrested four senior Palestinian guerrillas, including Walid Khalid, a senior aide to Abu Nidal. Five attacks on Western diplomatic and business interests rocked Jordan over the same period.

Outside the Middle East, explosions next to the Paris office of the French newspaper *Liberation* and close to an American library in Manilla provoked a worldwide terrorism alert. By mid-February, over one hundred terrorist attacks, said to be linked to the Gulf War, hit nations far from the Middle East, including Thailand, Germany, Pakistan, Ecuador, Australia and Peru. Between mid-January and the end of the war in late February, one hundred and twenty terrorist attacks had hit American targets—compared with seventeen over the same time period in 1990.

During the first ten days of war, there was no evidence of Iraqi-directed terrorism. Then, on January 26th, Saddam Hussein allegedly ordered the taps on huge Kuwait oil storage tanks opened. Millions of barrels of oil poured into the Persian Gulf, causing what some analysts called the most disastrous case of environmental or eco-terrorism. By early February, Saudi authorities reported they had captured and executed Iraqi terrorists attempting to infiltrate Saudi Arabia to wage a campaign of sabotage and assassination. During the next few days, sporadic attacks hit American troops in Saudi Arabia. Still, some Western terrorist analysts, such as Frank Benchley and Paul Wilkerson, insisted that the hard-core of Saddam Hussein's professional terrorists were being held back waiting for the coalition nations to drop their guard.[22]

The predominantly "spontaneous" or "freelance" nature of the terrorist attacks made the issue of how to counter Iraqi-inspired terrorism the most troubling and complex question to answer. Predictably, most governments of the coalition beefed up security forces at key installations such as airports, government and corporate buildings and military installations. Showcase sporting events, such as the Super Bowl football game, were played under unprecedented security arrangements. Despite all these measures, many top security analysts warned that, because of the anarchic nature of contemporary terrorism, even the expanded security precautions were probably futile. Yet, they argued that a longstanding infrastructure of radical groups in the Middle East region and the European cities of Brussels, Athens, Istanbul, Rome and Vienna made them the most likely and vulnerable targets.

In the United States, security authorities warned Americans to expect terrorist attacks from Arab terrorist organizations based in the United States, including the Iranian-backed Hezbollah and Abu Nidal. According to security consultant Mike Ackerman, New York, Southern California, Chicago, Washington, D.C. and Detroit were the most likely targets. Curiously, public statements meant to calm public fears about Iraqi terrorism from top FBI officials contradicted these warnings. For example, FBI Director William Sessions claimed the risk of domestic terrorism was relatively low and urged Americans to "go about their business as usual." At the same time, his agents raised to new heights the level of security at airports, arms depots, postal operations, hotels and government buildings. They also stepped up their monitoring of radical groups and homeless people, questioned Arab-Americans and began a search for three thousand Iraqis whose visas the FBI said had expired.[23]

In early January, many Western governments began to invoke more controversial anti-terrorist measures. Claiming they possessed proof that Iraqi embassies had become centers of terrorist organizing and Iraqi diplomatic pouches were used to transport weapons of terror throughout the world, they began to expel Iraqi diplomats and any Iraqi citizen "suspected of terrorism." For example, British authorities gave five Iraqi diplomats and a security guard only twenty-four hours to leave the country. Sixty-seven Iraqis, mostly student members of the National Union of Iraqi Students and Youth, said to be used by Iraqi intelligence for spying, murder and intimidation, were also expelled for "reasons of national security."[24] In Germany, authorities tracked down fifty Iraqis for questioning about terrorism. In many countries the commercial world followed the government lead. European schools with heavy American student populations closed when the war started, only to reopen under tight security. Most American corporations with European facilities banned all but "essential" air travel. By early February, 1991, air traffic from the United States to Europe was down forty percent. Early in 1991, Pan Am began refusing to board Iraqis on its aircraft. A month later, under pressure from the New York City Human Rights Commission, Pan Am partially retracted the policy, refusing service only to Iraqis without permanent United States residency.

In the United States, the FBI began detailed questioning, ostensibly about terrorism, of Arab-Americans. This tactic proved extremely controversial as it raised fears that Arab-Americans would be treated like Japanese-Americans were handled during World War II (eventually rounded up and sent off to internment camps). Indeed, shortly after Iraqi forces entered Kuwait, the FBI mounted a "spider web" defense, a strategy involving watching locations in the United States where terrorists were thought to gather. The purpose of "spider web," the FBI said, was to immobilize Iraqi agents and operatives.[25] The strategy involved electronic and physical monitoring, the use of informants and other undisclosed "secret" means of spying on every Iraqi living in the United States. Except for loud protests from the Arab-American community, these and other "anti-terrorist" actions were covertly undertaken. The American public remained compliant in the face of major service disruptions, possible civil liberty violations and warnings from security officials that such measures were unnecessary or, if necessary, probably inadequate against terrorist threats.

Curiously, one important question about Iraqi terrorism goes largely unanswered: Did Saddam Hussein have the capability to carry out his threat of global terrorism? To some American sources and Soviet analysts, Iraq's seizure of Kuwait had indeed produced evidence of a new international terrorist network, this time under the direction and control of Saddam Hussein. Three weeks into the Gulf crisis, Bruce Hoffman, a RAND Corporation security analyst, argued that Saddam Hussein had been collecting terrorist groups for some time, wooing, among others, the infamous Palestinian terrorists Abu Nidal, Abul Abbas and Ahmad Jahril to his command post in Baghdad. Hoffman claimed that, under Saddam Hussein's direction, the ultimate "fifth column," an international terrorist army, stood ready to strike targets throughout the Middle East and Europe.[26] Bush Administration sources fueled support of Hoffman's theory by confirming that in April or May, 1990, Abu Nidal had been allowed to reopen a Baghdad office and that Iraq had given assistance to a foiled May 30, 1990, terrorist attack on an Israeli beach. Pentagon officials suggested Saddam Hussein had control over Baathist cells that had been dormant for years, but which could now be easily activated.[27] According to some media sources, the infamous "Carlos" was also in Saddam Hussein's terrorist stable.

By the January outbreak of war, some American legislators and State Department officials came forward to strongly support Hoffman's conspiracy theory. Senator Orrin Hatch of Utah, a member of the Senate Intelligence Committee, claimed, "Terrorists are being set up by Saddam Hussein all over Europe and the Middle East and even here. I think we are going to see a lot of terrorist acts."[28] State Department spokesperson Margaret Tutwiler alleged an Iraqi-led conspiracy when she said, "We have clear evidence that Iraq is supporting terrorists planning to mount attacks against coalition countries."[29] Other administration sources estimated that around one hundred Iraqi terrorist agents had been sent, in December 1990, to Europe, Asia and Africa to serve as a "deadly core" of the international terrorist network. FBI official William M. Baker revealed that, in addition to fifty supporters of Abu Nidal, members of the Palestinian Liberation Front and the Democratic Front for the Liberation of Palestine were under FBI surveillance in the United States. According to Baker, up to the present, the Iraqi terrorists had committed their terrorism against Iraqi dissidents and opponents of the Iraqi government. Now, on orders from Saddam Hussein, they were ready to terrorize the American public.

The suggestion that Saddam Hussein had direct control over an international terrorist network is new and radically different from analysis of his capabilities provided by Western analysts in the past, thus open to debate. Still, as American officials know well, evidence of Iraqi terrorist capabilities is consistent with past intelligence concerning Iraq's long and bloody sponsorship of terrorism. Iraqi sabotage of Saudi refineries in 1977 had prompted the Carter Administration to place Iraq on the official list of "terrorist" nations in 1979, where it remained until being removed by the Reagan Administration in 1982.

Saddam Hussein came to power in 1979 and, immediately, through execution, development of a personality cult and the use of terror, set out to eliminate any and all opposition to his rule. According to *Saddam Hussein and the Crisis in the Gulf*, at Hussein's first party meeting on inauguration, one thousand people attended. He read the names of those in the room he considered to be traitors and, in the next few days, approximately five hundred people were executed—some personally by Hussein. This was followed by the institution of broad-based police organizations, many of which spy on each other and civilians and routinely use terrorism as a method of control. Terrorism reportedly instituted by Saddam has been perpetrated against the Iraqi exile community throughout the world.

Former CIA terrorism specialist Vincent Cannistrono claims that, during the Reagan presidency and first two years of the Bush Administration, American officials knew Iraq was involved in international terrorism, but turned a blind eye to the evidence. Even after the end of the Iran-Iraq war, when they had proof Saddam Hussein was re-establishing his terrorist links and positioning himself to use terrorism against his neighbors, American officials left Iraq off the official terrorist-state list because the United States was attempting to cultivate favor with Hussein's regime.[30] Cannistrono charges that, in 1982, an American-Iraqi deal was struck whereby Reagan officials dropped Iraq from their terrorist list and began selling foodstuffs to Saddam Hussein's regime in exchange for an Iraqi "promise" to cut any connection with international terrorism: a promise never kept.[31] Noel Koch, head of the Pentagon counterterrorist program during the Reagan years, agrees, saying the United States should not have taken Iraq off the list of terrorist states. In an independent investigation by *The Village Voice,* Koch claims he objected to the decision, but was overruled by higher officials in the administration.[32] *The Village Voice* investigators charge that, during these years of continued Iraqi terror, the United States government and American commercial interests, along with Western European nations, in violation of American law, sold tons of sophisticated arms, weapons manufacturing technology, uniforms and commercial goods and pressured the United States Import-Export Bank to make multi-million dollar loans and credit guarantees to Saddam Hussein to help his war effort against Iran.

Over the 1980s, the Reagan—and later the Bush—Administration did not place Iraq back on the state terrorist list, even when Abu Nidal returned to Iraq in November 1982. Though he was expelled again in 1983, American officials knew that Iraqi support for Abu Nidal's terrorism, including masterminding the Achille Lauro ship hijacking in 1985, remained strong. As late as 1989, State Department publications state Iraq provided safehaven to several Palestinian groups, including the Arab Liberation Front and Abu Abbas's Palestine Liberation Front—groups now cited by Bruce Hoffman and many American officials as central components of an Iraqi-controlled international terrorist network.[33] Over this time, the annual investigation of human rights abuses by the United States Department of State paralleled evidence gathered by private organizations such as Amnesty International about Iraqi terrorism at home and abroad. On the editorial page of *The New York Times,* Amnesty International Chairman James David Barber charged that three hundred Iraqi children had been kidnapped and tortured for political reasons.[34] In a major report on Iraq published in February, 1989, Amnesty claims that the children of Iraq were routinely subjected to torture methods such as extractions of fingernails, beatings, whippings, sexual abuse and electrical shock treatment.[35] Neither the Reagan nor the Bush Administrations acted on either report, nor on State Department charges about Iraqi human rights abuse. In 1989, the United Nations Human Rights Commission passed a resolution asking Iraq to account for its use of chemical weapons against its Kurdish population (up to 100,000 were displaced or gassed, their homes bulldozed and whole towns razed). The Bush Administration did not join its major European allies in sponsoring the resolution, and actively worked against its passage. Finally, in April, 1990, the murder in California of an Assyrian and Kurd by Andri Khosaba, an Iraqi-American, illustrates that the American "hands-off" approach to Iraqi terrorism continued late into this period. Evidence that Khosaba was paid $50,000 for the murder by an Iraqi agent in New York provoked the quiet expulsion of an unnamed Iraqi United Nations diplomat for "abuse of his privileges of residence in the United States." Neither the murder nor the expulsion provoked any official mention of Iraqi terrorism or a possible worldwide Iraqi terrorist network.

Apparently, the conflicting evidence surrounding Saddam Hussein's terrorist capabilities, particularly the alleged Baghdad-based international terrorist network and American acquiescence to Iraqi terrorism in the 1980s, raised too many questions about some aspects of Iraqi terrorism in the face of the Reagan Administration's support of Iraq. As the Gulf crisis deepened, the silence continued.

Saddam Hussein threatened terrorism against his enemies and there is little doubt, based on the past, that he would use it if able. Curiously, in almost the same breath, he sought to rally world opinion to his cause. Such strategy would appear to be self-defeating.

Yet few analysts have raised questions about it. Though one may, as many allies do, see Saddam Hussein as "Hitler-like," and conclude that he does not care about the moral connotations or propriety of terrorism, such an image provides only a partial explanation at best. From the Middle View, there are more germane answers to the questions why Saddam Hussein would use terrorism and freely admit to it: answers that help us understand the "mind set" of Hussein on the basis of his and Iraq's past history. It is these answers that can help us grasp the complexities of contemporary terrorism.

In order to find them, one must first suspend judgement and try to understand current events from Hussein's perspective.

For Saddam Hussein, the moral issues surrounding the use of terrorism must be suspect. He sees almost everyone else, in particularly major and minor powers such as the United States, Soviet Union, Syria, Iran, Libya, Israel, Turkey and other NATO members —not to mention the variety of non-state Middle East terrorists listed previously—using or supporting terrorist agents to serve their interests. Thus, if terrorism is "right" for others, why not for Iraq? If terrorism is deemed effective and proper political and para-military strategy for others, then might it not be perceived as effective and expedient for Iraq?

To Saddam Hussein, launching SCUD surface-to-surface "terror" missiles at Saudi and Israeli civilians must have seemed no different politically or morally than what the Iraqi civilian population endured from the bombing of Iraq, and the interrogation of allied military little different from the interrogations visited upon captured Iraqi military or members of the Arab communities in the United States and Western Europe since the start of the Persian Gulf crisis.

Further, while he has rarely traveled abroad, Saddam Hussein knows his adversaries well, in particular the priorities of his American friends-suddenly-turned enemy. What he understands first hand is that, while invoking highly moral public arguments against terrorism, in private many American officials utilize the terrorism issue to serve their purposes. After all, during the 1980s, Iraq and the United States were principal partners and beneficiaries in such manipulation. He is also painfully aware that Iraq fell victim to such manipulation when the Reagan Administration made the arms deal with "terrorist" Iran in 1986. The conclusion Saddam Hussein has no doubt reached is that, by manipulating the terrorism issue, it is possible—as others have shown—to diminish the impact the negative moral implications of his use of terrorism has on world opinion.

Also, Hussein must be aware, as we all should be, that, though Iraq is not a major power, his own ability to sway public opinion is considerable, given widespread and growing anti-Western, anti-American sentiments, particularly within Middle East Arab and Islamic communities and substantial parts of the Third World. This audience has already tuned out those in the West who have condoned the invasion of Grenada and Panama and supported the likes of Cambodia's Pol Pot and Chile's Augusto Pinochet, and who now would moralize to them about the crimes of Saddam Hussein. For Saddam Hussein, it is that segment of opinion which counts most.

Moreover, Saddam Hussein's decision to use terrorism reflects the power disparity between Iraq and the major members of the American-sponsored coalition. In the Middle View, we have argued that terrorism is a tool of both the strong and the weak. In the event of a direct confrontation between major and minor powers, terrorism by the weak creates a more level playing field. It allows the weak to strike at the power base of the major power, especially in cases where the home territory and populous are beyond the scope of its military capability. In the Persian Gulf war, Iraqi-inspired terrorism against Western interests in the Middle East, Europe and, particularly, the United States is the only way for Saddam Hussein to bring the war home to citizens of coalition states outside the Middle East. Terrorist analysts Brian Jenkins and Robert Kupperman make this exact point when they suggest that Saddam Hussein "is going to have to try to reduce the number of United States allies both in the Middle East and in Europe, so he's got to make it painful."[36] Both analysts think European nations are particularly vulnerable to the demoralizing effects of Iraqi terrorism because they have had to do battle against indigenous terrorism for so long and because of their close proximity to Iraq.

It is the need for a terrorist capacity with broad geographical reach that helps explain Saddam Hussein's public pronouncement of his terrorist intentions. The fact is Saddam Hussein must know his pro-terrorism public posture is the most expedient way he can take advantage of the anarchic nature of contemporary terrorism and connect his cause to the variety of groups and individuals who either directly or indirectly sympathize with his efforts, or who, driven by their own agendas, will capitalize on the war climate to strike against their separate or common enemy.

The potential for the utilization of terroristic methods by minor powers such as Hussein of Iraq became instantly clear on February 7, 1991. Members of the Provisional Irish Republic Army, easily compromising tight anti-terrorist security, fired three mortars at British government buildings in London before escaping. The explosions slightly wounded three people and damaged several buildings, including the 10 Downing Street residence of Prime Minister John Major, where the British War Cabinet was in session. IRA spokespersons said the plans for the assassination attempt predated Britain's participation in the war effort, but radio broadcasts from Baghdad claimed the attack was the beginning of a major terrorist campaign. Again, in the bombing of the Victoria and other railway stations on February 18, 1991, both the IRA and Baghdad claimed responsibility.

Regardless of their intent or purpose, the IRA attacks sent tremors throughout the Western security community and highlighted again just how vulnerable even the most heavily defended sites and persons remain to determined terrorists, even in a climate of high alert. It also made clear, given the anarchic nature of current Middle East and global terrorism, why Saddam Hussein's public announcement to use terrorism makes political sense in pursuit of his Middle East war agenda. More important, as painful as it may be, it served to remind us that, as far as Middle East terrorism is concerned, the past is indeed the future. Whether Saddam Hussein controls terrorism or not, as the major hostilities in the Persian Gulf end, we can anticipate a long period in which not only Iraqi sympathizers but other embittered members of both camps will no doubt seek revenge via terrorism and in which terrorists unconnected to the Persian Gulf War will continue to utilize the hostile post-war environment for their own purposes. Indeed, as the ceasefire took hold, the Party of God, a radical Muslim group based in Lebanon and supported by Iran, announced that the "real mother of all battles" had begun and would be directed against the United States.

11

THE MIDDLE VIEW RE-VISITED

We began this book by exploring what we know and don't know about the explosion of terrorism. We argued that, starting in the 1970s and continuing through the mid-1980s, the debate over terrorism was dominated by two opposing political perspectives. In the West, the political framework of the "ideology of terrorism," which views terrorism primarily as a strategy and deed of the political Left, reigned supreme. Through this view, we came to "know" that the hand of the Soviet Union directed the sinister acts of an international terrorist network reeking havoc everywhere, be it in Ulster, India, Lebanon, El Salvador, or Nyack, New York. Western media coverage of "terrorist incidents" and fictional accounts of terrorists and terrorism in film and print reinforced this vision. As a result, we in the West came to picture all terrorists as wild-eyed, gun-toting fanatics imbued with either Marxist rhetoric or Islamic hatred and backed by evil forces of Soviet Communism and Islamic fundamentalism.

On the other hand, proponents of the Soviet view of terrorism "came to know" that the explosion of terrorism was the work of imperialist forces in the international capitalist system. In the Soviet view, the major international terrorists were the agents of capitalist class interests in the United States, Britain, South Africa, Chile, Israel, Pakistan, Indonesia and El Salvador. Also, high on the Soviet's list of terrorists were groups such as the Nicaraguan Contras and individuals such as Angolan rebel leader Joseph Zavimbi or American mercenaries such as Sam Hall, Eugene Hasenfus and Felix Rodriquez, who man the front lines in Imperialism's battle to overthrow leftist governments in Angola, Afghanistan, Nicaragua and Cambodia.

By the mid-1980s, structured by these polarized and opposing visions, the discussion of the explosion of terrorism became a highly charged political debate. As we have seen, both American and Soviet officials understood and used the negative connotations connected to terrorism, and the positive tenor attached to anti-terrorism, to pursue their respective political agendas. Indeed, the rhetorical battle over terrorism and anti-terrorism often reached obscene heights. It became commonplace for government leaders of all political stripes to call their political foes terrorists, in order to delegitimize them in the court of world opinion and to justify their own acts of violence and terrorism. In this vein, Chili's rightwing President Augusto Pinochet sought to rally domestic and international support for his murderous state of emergency by characterizing the broad range of opposition forces, which included labor unions, church groups, student organizations and small business associations, as "terrorists." In East Germany, the Stalinist government took a similar route, attempting to discredit the cause of striking railroad workers by labeling them "terrorists." In June 1986, Peru's army slaughtered four hundred prison inmates—sixty of them after they surrendered. To the Peruvian military, this massacre was justified, since the inmates were all captured "terrorists."

The rhetorical battle over terrorism took center stage at a time when internal political conditions in many parts of the world were deteriorating. The United States and the Soviet Union were deadlocked in their negotiations on arms reduction—while they were building up nuclear arsenals in Europe. Peace prospects were dismal in the Middle East, southern Africa, Ulster and Central America and the possibility of direct superpower confrontation in these regions was very real. The political rhetoric continued in both the "ideology of terrorism" and the Soviet view interjected into these regional and local crises served to further polarize antagonistic political, religious, and cultural communities and harden already intractable positions. And, since terrorism—which produces its own anger and vengefulness—was exploding all over the world, the situation seemed dismal.

If prospects for better superpower relations and the settlement of the many regional and local crises were to be improved, it was, and is, imperative that the terrorism issues be depoliticized and taken out of the hands of political leaders intent on manipulating public fears to serve their interests. This is a very difficult task, given the fact that terrorism and its threats can be very effective political tools. Still, as we have seen in the various instances in this book, there are no easy solutions to the terrorism of our time—or any time. But, if we cannot end terrorism, we can eliminate the vulnerability of the public to the manipulative qualities of the terrorism issue.

Moreover, if, as partners carving out a new world order, the superpowers no longer manipulate the terrorism issue in their respective favors, much can be done.

CONFIRMATION OF THE MIDDLE VIEW: THE LESSONS OF IRAN-CONTRA

The Iran-Contra scandal was the major catalyst for undermining the "ideology of terrorism" anti-terrorist public policy. Through it, we learned how the terrorism issue could be used successfully to manipulate public opinion.

Iran-Contra shook the American and foreign liberal democratic conscience to the core. For most of us, the long list of revelations about secret arms sales to "terrorist" Iran, purposeful violations of law, duplicity and other criminal activities by high government officials, CIA-Contra drug running and a host of other less publicized activities including widespread domestic spying on American citizens erroneously suspected of supporting terrorism, were hard pills to swallow.

From November, 1986, through two years of the Joint Congressional Committee's investigation of the Iran-Contra affair, the multiple and varied revelations about administration activities stripped away the moral and political basis of America's anti-terrorist posture. The core revelations strike at the heart of how we have been taught to view contemporary terrorism. Out of these revelations flow a myriad of lessons that we need to know in order to construct a new perspective on terrorism closer to the realities theorized by the Middle View.

According to the Majority Report of the Iran-Contra committee:

"The United States simultaneously pursued two contradictory foreign policies—a public one and a secret one.

The public policy was not to make any concessions for the release of hostages lest such concessions encourage more hostage-taking. At the same time, the United States was secretly trading weapons to get the hostages back.

The public policy was to ban arms shipments to Iran and to exhort other governments to observe this embargo. At the same time, the United States was secretly selling sophisticated missiles to Iran and promising more.

The public policy was to improve relations with Iraq. At the same time, the United States secretly shared military intelligence on Iraq and Iran, and Lieutenant Colonel Oliver North told the Iranians, in contradiction to United States policy, that the United States would help promote the overthrow of the Iraqi head of state.

The public policy was to urge all governments to punish terrorism and to support, indeed encourage, the refusal of Kuwait to free the Da'wa prisoners who were convicted of terrorist acts. At the same time, senior officials secretly endorsed a Richard V. Secord-Albert Hakim plan to permit Iran to obtain the release of the Da'wa prisoners.

These contradictions in policy inevitably resulted in policy failure:

The United States armed Iran, including its most radical elements, but attained neither a new relationship . . . nor a reduction in the number of American hostages.

The arms sales did not lead to a moderation of Iranian policies.

The United States opened itself to blackmail by adversaries who might reveal the secret arms and who, according to North, threatened to kill the hostages if the sales stopped.

The United States undermined its credibility with friends and allies . . . by its public stance of opposing arms sales to Iran while undertaking such arms sales in secret.

The United States sought illicit funding for the Contras through profits from the secret arms sales, but a substantial portion of those profits ended up in the personal bank accounts of the private individuals executing the sales while the exorbitant amounts charged for the weapons inflamed the Iranians.

Secrecy became an obsession. Congress was never informed of the Iran or the Contra covert action.

In the case of the "secret" Iran arms-for-hostages deal, although the NSC staff did not inform the Secretary of State, the Chairman of the Joint Chiefs of Staff or the leadership . . . of Congress, it was content to let the following persons know:

Iranian arms dealer Manucher Ghorbanifer, who flunked every polygraph test administered by the United States government,

Iranian officials, who daily denounced the United States, but received an inscribed Bible from the President,

Officials of Iran's Revolutionary Guard, who received the United States weapons,

Secord and Hakim, whose personal interests could conflict with the interest of the United States,

Israeli officials, international arms merchants, pilots and air crews, whose interests did not always coincide with ours,

An unknown number of shadowy intermediaries and financiers . . ."[1]

Other disclosures confirmed the Reagan Administration's negotiations with "terrorist" Iran, as well as a wide array of non-state terrorists, including a series of contacts between United States foreign service officers and PLO and Libyan splintergroups, in contradiction to stated United States foreign policy.[2]

The arms for hostages revelations played havoc with the moral and political conscience of the American public and American allies attempting to abide by America's stated anti-terrorist policy. Suddenly, the high moral purpose and rigidly principled political value system—which the public believed was governing United States foreign policy on terrorism—was gone.

From abroad, European allies expressed dismay and anger at the contradiction between the covert options undertaken by the United States to resolve its hostage crisis and Reagan Administration pressure on them to forego such options. For all concerned, the revelations of the Iran-Contra scandal created a credibility gap which impacted both friend and foe of the United States foreign policy.

On the positive side, the Iran-Contra affair, even for those whose vision of terrorism proved bankrupt, forced all of us to confront how we think about the explosion of terrorism and to discard many of our comfortable and uncomplicated notions about the terrorist phenomenon. First, the Iran-Contra scandal destroyed the single source image of terrorism. In deciding on covert action, including an "off the shelf" operation to secure the release of the hostages, the administration admitted that working through official circles in Moscow, the alleged source of international terrorism, would prove unproductive and possibly counterproductive given the obvious hostility between the atheistic Soviet state and Middle East Islamic Fundamentalists.

Conversely, details about the murky world of official and unofficial Middle East politics reinforced the Middle View's proposition that terrorism is a multi-sourced, multi-dimensional and complicated phenomenon not given to quick or easy solution. In its efforts to gain release of the hostages, the administration sought out individuals and groups on multiple levels of the political landscape, including some accused of anti-American terrorist acts. The cast of characters is a mixed collection of friends and foes. Most notable among United States' allies caught in the web of intrigue are Israel, Britain, Portugal, Denmark, Spain, Italy, and the conservative pro-American, anti-Israel royal families in Saudi Arabia, Kuwait and Brunei. Heading the list of foes are the anti-American, anti-Israeli states of Syria, Iraq and Iran—all of whom the Reagan Administration publicly designated "terrorist states" at the same moment it privately solicited their assistance on the hostage issue. Heading the list of official parties and private individuals whom the administration dealt with directly or indirectly are Iranian revolutionary leaders Abulhassan Bani-Sadr, Hsheimi Rafsanjani, Mohammed Beheshti and Ahmed Kangarlu. The Iranian "moderates" included Prime Minister Hussein Musavi, whom United States intelligence officials believed was behind the 1983 Kuwaiti bombings that initiated the Lebanon hostage crisis, and Interior Minister Mohammed Mohtashimi-pur, said to be responsible for setting up Iran's Lebanese terror network. In addition to the private individuals mentioned in the Iran-Contra congressional report, the administration solicited the aid of several shadowy figures from the underworld of private arms trade, including Iranian Cyrus Hashemi, Syrian drug and arms runner Monzer al-Kassar and Israeli Yascov Nimrodi, as well as others of questionable standing.

However, administration efforts to sensitize its approach to people from unfamiliar cultures and different religious traditions contradicted its own often-stated proposition that all terrorists understand and only respond to direct force. For, if force is the language of the terrorist, why offer to negotiate on any level or offer financial and other material incentives, and why were negotiations held?

From the Iran-Contra revelations, we now know the answers to these and other questions. American foreign policy had a public and private face. The secret policy had very different propositions about terrorism than those presented for public consumption and said to guide allied policy. In addition, akin to the judgements of the Middle View, the real operative principle was that the complex realities of terrorism required flexible and multi-level response.

Finally, from Iran-Contra, America's industrial allies now understand that, as they put their signature to the Tokyo Anti-terrorism Declaration—pledging to fight terrorism "relentlessly and without compromise," the American sponsor of that statement was relentlessly compromising the pledge by selling arms to Iran in exchange for American hostages.

A year before Iran-Contra unraveled, there was concrete evidence of an American administration playing politics with public sentiment on international terrorism. It came with the sudden omission of Syria from President Reagan's June 1985 list of terrorist "outlaw states." The list was accompanied by official White House confirmation that the omission was no accident, but meant as a political gesture of gratitude to Syrian President Hafez al-Assad for his role in gaining release of American hostages held in Lebanon. Obviously, in June 1985, political considerations of the moment made it "appropriate" to "excuse" Syria from the terrorist list. A year later, other political considerations required that Syria be placed back on the list and new sanctions invoked against Assad's government.

This pattern of political "flexibility" involving Syria continued past these years, when, beginning in September 1990, "terrorist" Syria, despite a 1987 State Department study documenting three years of Syrian-sponsored terrorism, George Bush sent Secretary of State James Baker to ask President Assad to join the United States-led alliance against Iraqi President Saddam Hussein.[3] In November, two or three Israeli agents who had infiltrated Syrian terrorist groups were reported murdered. Substantial rumors arose that the motive for the deaths was provided by intelligence information on Syrian terrorism given to Syrian leaders by top American officials at the Baker-Assad meeting. The same month, Bush met with Assad in Geneva to solidify the new American-Syrian relationship.

Iran-Contra taught other significant lessons about the realities of contemporary terrorism. First, terrorism works, or to some degree is effective, as a political strategy of the weak. It forces powerful nations onto a more level playing field, one where their advantages in weapons, military preparedness and economic resources often prove ineffective or even useless. At times, as in Iran-Contra, the powerful nation's military and economic resources become desired goods for the terrorist and thus bargaining chips in the negotiating process.

Secondly, acts of terrorism also enhance the standing of those who otherwise have little chance of influencing the arena of super-power-dominated politics. Iran-Contra demonstrated that the United States' search for an effective strategy forced it to elevate hostile weaker governments and individuals to the stature of legitimacy. Reagan officials also had to secretly negotiate deals in which they surrendered items of value (arms) to those they didn't recognize as authentic players, but who, via terrorism, held items of value (hostages). Concurrently, American officials sometimes betrayed trusted legitimate players and undercut their efforts at a coordinated, Western anti-terrorist policy.

American officials were not the only ones embroiled in this complex dilemma. In 1986, French Premier Jacques Chirac made the same choice when, through direct government-to-government negotiations with Iran, he secured the release of two French nationals held hostage in Lebanon in exchange for a cut in French aid to Iraq in the Iran-Iraq War, settlement of an Iranian loan to a European consortium and expulsion of Iranian opposition leaders from France. Later in the 1980s, the West Germans also cut similar deals for their Lebanese hostages.

In sum, unfortunately, Iran-Contra and the revelations of parallel events involving other states confirm that terrorism can pay. Weaker state and non-state terrorist forces compelled the powerful to play their game on terms that didn't necessarily favor or benefit the powerful. It also confirmed that national egotism and divergent national interests dominate each new terrorist event.

The Iran-Contra scandal also demonstrates the inherent dangers of a crisis management context of "authoritarian democracy" and its potential for spawning an even deeper crisis of democracy.

As distressing as the revelations and lessons have been, without the revelations of the Iran-Contra affair, future prognostication based on the past would be significantly different and potentially more dangerous. It is very likely that we Americans would still be poised to support unequivocally any military action tagged as a blow against terrorism, even as in the case of Libya when it involved responding to terrorism with terrorism of our own. We would no doubt have remained attached to the simplistic Cold War thesis of an international terrorist network directed from Moscow. We surely would be less convinced that the Gorbachev agenda of Perestroika and Glasnost was little more than propaganda or signaled an opportunity to end the Cold War. Overall, it is likely most of us would still view world affairs through the "mindset" of a 1950s newsreel depicting in black and white footage the ongoing struggle between the forces of good and evil.

Without the Iran-Contra affair, we would still be wallowing in official duplicity, still vulnerable to political manipulation, still mobilized to support America's unilateral view of terrorism. Further, we may still not have come to grips with the reality of contemporary terrorism as ripe with complexity, political ambiguity and difficult moral decisions. More importantly, we would not have been provoked into a more mature understanding of the terrorism issue, its manipulative qualities and the need for a sober, new terrorism policy.

It is tempting to see Iran-Contra as an aberration whose lessons should be quickly forgotten. But other events before and after the unraveling of the Iran-Contra anti-terrorism policy underscore the limitations of America's past policy and lead us toward the Middle View's understanding of the complexity and political contradictions inherent in contemporary terrorism.

The year before Iran-Contra, the tangled web of Middle East politics exposed the shortcomings of American anti-terrorist policy. On March 8, 1985, a car bomb killed eighty innocent bystanders in Beirut, Lebanon. Subsequent investigation pointed to the conclusion that the bomb blast was the work of a CIA-trained Lebanese counterterrorist unit.

Whatever the initial high-minded motives of the program, the car bombing exposed the fact that there were American covert efforts going on to prevent and punish international terrorism. These efforts were born out of frustration and then held captive to local political rivalries and activated under conflicting evidence. Charging that the CIA knew the attack was being planned, Lebanese army intelligence sources said the bombing was part of a United States' sanctioned policy "to fight terrorism with terrorism." The target of the bomb was not the eighty civilians of Beirut who died, but suspected terrorist Sheik Fadlallah, leader of the Iranian-backed Shiite group Hezbollah. The *Washington Post* claimed evidence of terrorist activities on the part of Fadlallah, who escaped injury in the blast, was nonexistent. The accusations against the Shiite leader had come exclusively from rival Christian military sources. In fact, Fadlallah had repeatedly made public declarations against terrorism, labeling them "un-Islamic" and urging his Shiite followers to forego acts of revenge against Westerners. Further inquiry led to accusations of American, Israeli and Lebanese intelligence involvement and a promise by Reagan officials to shut down the CIA-trained proxy unit responsible for the Beirut bombing. However, they refused to end the operations of any other proxy units.

In this case, the Administration again sought simple solutions to the complex problem of terrorism and attempted to do so by circumventing established foreign policy principles; indeed, advocating using terrorism as an option to fight terrorism.

As Iran-Contra was breaking in mid-November, 1986, it became apparent that other Western industrial nations were also compromising their idealistic, anti-terrorism postures in order to fight actual attacks of terrorism. On November 10, 1986, the foreign ministers of the European Community agreed to a package of sanctions, including a ban on arms sales, against Syria for its alleged involvement in Jordanian Nezar Hindawi's April 1986 attempt to blow up an El Al jet in London. British officials, who had registered the charge of Syrian involvement, hailed the EC sanctions as "the clearest possible message" that Syrian culpability in the El Al affair was "totally unacceptable."

Britain cut off diplomatic relations with Syria, but the actions of other European nations undercut the firm British posture. During the previous week, French Premier Jacques Chirac had questioned the accuracy of reports of Syrian involvement in the El Al incident, telling reporters that West German Chancellor Helmut Kohl and Foreign Minister Hans-Dietrich Genscher had told him Syria had been framed. French Foreign Minister Jean-Bernard Raimond, responding to the announced EC sanctions, argued that the text of the agreement did not "implicate the Syrian government." One day after the EC imposed sanctions against Syria, the Lebanese Revolutionary Justice Organization released two French hostages as part of a French-Iranian deal in which Syrian officials played a key role.

Like the French, other European leaders questioned the utility of the European Community's action against Syria. Greek representatives refused to sign the agreement arguing that the sanctions would hinder Syrian participation in future European Middle East peace efforts. To Greek officials, Syrian involvement in terrorism was not so unique as "all countries have secret services, and most secret services have perpetrated crimes at one time or another."[4]

Were the French and Greeks "out of step" with allied terrorism policy as they have so often been accused? Or were they "in step" with a context in which national priorities rule the day? In this case, the acrimony, fingerpointing and frantic scramble among EC nations to protect narrow national interests—and their consistent efforts to do so since—underscores the normalcy of French-Greek actions. Indeed, in the opinion of most independent analysts, the EC sanctions, described as "weak" rather than "decisive," are further proof that any coordination or adoption of formidable anti-terrorism policy is difficult even among "like-minded" and culturally homogeneous parties. As in Iran-Contra, we see again how the reality of contemporary terrorism conforms to the Middle View.

USS VINCINNES

In early July of 1988, the American warship USS Vincinnes, on patrol in the Persian Gulf, shot down an Iranian civilian airliner. Two hundred and ninety innocent people were sent to their deaths. Several days of conflicting accounts about what had occurred aboard the Vincinnes were heard. The Reagan Administration mobilized public and official opinion behind the view that the Iranian Flight 655 had been mistaken for an Iranian F-14 jet. Thinking he was under attack, Commander Will Rogers took a "tragic," but militarily "justifiable defensive action."

A vast array of political leaders, including Presidential candidates George Bush and Michael Dukakis, and most media sources, echoed the administration's sentiments. Dukakis argued, "Clearly, we have a right to defend ourselves," while Vice-President Bush praised Commander Rogers for "not wanting to put those heroic kids of his—the finest young sailors this Navy has ever had—in harms way."[5] Most agreed with administration officials that due to the airbus's erratic behavior, the Vincinnes was forced into defensive action which resulted in a tragic mistake. Still, the administration announced on July 11, in keeping with "the humanitarian traditions of our nation," the United States intended to compensate the victims' families.

Public opinion polls on the airbus tragedy illustrate how vulnerable most Americans remained in 1988 to anti-terrorist themes. A *Washington Post*-ABC News poll taken on July 7th found 71 percent of Americans surveyed agreeing that the Vincinnes was justified in shooting at the airbus; 80 percent believed the Captain's decision was proper; 74 percent said Iran was more to blame than the United States; and 61 percent were against the United States compensating the victims' families. In a *Los Angeles Times* poll, six out of seven of those polled blamed the Iranian pilot for the accident, even though British aviation officials and American military sources in the Persian Gulf confirmed that Flight 655 was on time and climbing in altitude, rather than diving towards the Vincinnes. In sum, the court of American public opinion was told, the victim was to blame for the tragedy.

Shock and horror were expressed after the Iranian airbus incident by many American friends and anti-Iranian foes alike. Predictably, foes such as Libya registered the strongest protest, agreeing with Iranian sentiments that the incident was "a barbaric massacre." Ironically, in view of later events, a more restrained President Saddam Hussein of Iraq called the incident "a regrettable accident," strong sentiments echoed through most of the anti-Iranian Arab world. Soviet officials, wary of the incident's possible negative impact on superpower relations, choose a two track approach. While some Soviet sources criticized the American action as "deliberate mass murder in cold blood" and "terrorism," others expressed regret at the accident.

Among European allies, the administration's explanation was first met with support, then, as it unraveled, with public doubt and dismay. British Prime Minister Margaret Thatcher, a strong backer of the Reagan hardline on terrorism, expressed her "profound regret" over the loss of Iranian lives. Likewise, a United Nations Security Council resolution stated "profound regrets" and "deep distress." The International Civil Aviation Organization, without mentioning the United States, deplored the use of weapons against civilian aircraft. The statements of both international bodies, though only mildly critical of American action, do not exonerate the United States from culpability. Still, the mild reactions of these western-dominated institutions was a rebuff to Iran for its role as a "terrorist" nation. And the handling of the tragic incident further alienated the feelings of the Iranian population toward the United States.

PAN AM FLIGHT 103

The tragic consequences of terrorism on innocent victims and their families is certain, regardless of those victims' nationalities. Major contributions to a new understanding of terrorism are being made within the circles of lay opinion. One of the most significant has been forged out of the tragedy aboard Pan Am Flight 103.

On December 21, 1988, a Pan Am Boeing 747 jet enroute from London to New York City broke apart and crashed into the village of Lockerbie, Scotland, killing all two hundred fifty nine persons on board and eleven residents of the small town. After several weeks, British investigators determined that a plastic explosive, most likely Semtex or C-4, had been placed in a cassette player and put on board a Boeing 727 at the start of the first leg of the flight in Frankfurt, West Germany. The British investigators concluded the bomb had been designed to go off over the ocean, but strong headwinds had forced a navigational course that kept the plane over land longer than normal. West German authorities immediately objected to the British report, saying that the bomb was more likely placed in the cargo hold of the Boeing 747 at London's Heathrow airport. In its investigation, the United States Federal Aviation Administration (FAA) found that the American government had alerted airports, airlines and embassies in Europe after the United States embassy in Finland was alerted on December 5th that a Pan Am Frankfurt-New York flight would be the target of a bombing attempt over the next two weeks. Finnish authorities, who claimed they were monitoring events in the wake of the threat, insisted there was no connection between the December 5th phone call and the explosion. Subsequent investigations indicated that at least six FAA warning bulletins were issued with information pertinent to the December 21, 1988 bombing of Pan Am 103. American embassy officials in Moscow posted one of the warnings on the embassy bulletin board to alert diplomatic personnel and their families to the threat.

When told of the Finnish warning, numerous individuals, mostly families and friends of the Pan Am 103 victims, demanded to know from President Reagan why they had not been informed of the threat. Not satisfied with his response that a public statement about every bomb threat would virtually close down international air traffic (a position restated by President George Bush in April, 1989), the families and friends of the Pan Am 103 passengers formed a group called Victims of Pan Am Flight 103 and demanded a special investigation of the bombing and general procedures concerning terrorist threats.

The creation of Victims of Pan Am Flight 103 is a manifestation of the Middle View's recipe for producing important breakthroughs in anti-terrorist policy. The formation of the victims group signals a growing public awareness that, despite the assurances of public officials, there are no easy or surefire solutions to terrorism. Even more significant, the victims group's persistent questioning exposes a lack of public confidence in and increased willingness to challenge the decisions of public officials and security professionals on terrorism and personal safety issues.

Since the December, 1988 tragedy, spokepersons for the Pan Am 103 Victims group, in numerous appearances before Congressional panels and on media news programs, have pointedly asked why the public can't be kept abreast of the risks of air travel.[6] They are outraged that the United States government would inform American diplomatic and military personnel of terrorist threats, but not the general traveling public. They judge it immoral that, since October 1987, the State Department has been selling up-to-the-minute information on terrorist threats to a select group of two hundred international corporate subscribers, but will not allow the general public access to the same information. Finally, armed with FAA reports indicating that, over the first six months of 1988, there were two hundred eighteen bomb threats amongst nearly three million flights and only twenty to twenty-four bomb threats were considered serious during all of 1988, they want to know why it is that public information about terrorist threats will bring the aviation system to a halt or compromise intelligence sources any more than a disastrous act of terrorism?[7]

The formation of the victims' group also follows the urgings of the Middle View for laypersons to be actively involved in the debate on terrorism rather than passively leaving policy decisions to the "experts" of the scientific and political communities. The Victims of Pan Am Flight 103 have experienced first hand the failure of the present system of aviation safety, a system that "experts" have been left, by their insistence on the need for secrecy, to develop unobstructed by public inquiry. From the victims perspective, it is time for a new era in the battle against terrorism; one of public participation, consideration of fresh ideas, thoughtful answers to difficult questions and, if need be, new and possibly different policy and institutions.[8]

The transition into a new era of anti-terrorism has not come easily for the families of those killed on Pan Am Flight 103. Under constant pressure to leave anti-terrorist policy to the experts, yet determined that the public have the opportunity to make an informed decision about personal safety, in its first year, the victims group pushed the Bush Administration for a new policy providing public access to information about terrorist threats against the aviation industry. Instead, in July 1989, the FAA—with the full backing of the Bush Administration—codified its refusal-to-warn policy with regulations imposing $1,000 fines on individuals and $10,000 fines on air carriers that give security warning information to the public.

Disappointed, but undaunted, the victims group stubbornly persisted. They continued to provide valuable testimony to various Congressional investigations including a Presidential commission that found serious systematic flaws in aviation security. Ultimately, in October 1990, they successfully lobbied Congress into passing a bill requiring Federal officials be assigned to major airports to oversee security arrangements. More importantly, the bill encourages Federal officials to alert the public of specific terrorist threats to airlines. Though it still allows security experts considerable latitude about when to notify the public of such threats, the bill does guarantee that if some people are notified, everybody will be. At least, in the battle against aviation terrorists, no longer will there be a policy distinction between first and second class American citizens.

This is an important victory for the proponents of the Middle View. Most credit goes to members of Victims of 103 who, by their probing questions and insistence on their democratic right to know, helped shred the curtain of secrecy and expose the unwarranted smugness of the professional security establishment. In doing so, they set an important precedent.

Emerging from these developments is a more sober and sobering understanding of the complex realities of terrorism. It is the view expressed in my original book, *The Explosion of Terrorism,* as The Middle View. Proponents of the new understanding constitute a new and potentially formidable progressive force creeping in the arenas of expert opinion and the public conscience. By forcing open the discussion of terrorism to new ideas, formulas and realities, they increase the potential for better comprehension of and policy towards the explosion of terrorism which confronts us all.

The central development in recent international politics has been the demise of Cold War hostilities and, with it, the changing nature of the superpower relationship. The reasons for the end of Cold War Two are many and beyond the scope of this discussion. What is important is that in the midst of improving Soviet-American relations and the continuation of state-sponsored terrorism in many parts of the world, accusations concerning the other superpower's sponsorship of international terrorism have suddenly and dramatically ended.

However, the United States continues to aid groups and states that are high on the Soviet list of imperialism's terrorists, most notably rebel forces in Angola, Ethiopia, Cambodia and Afghanistan and the "terrorist" governments of El Salvador, Guatemala, Israel and South Africa. Though diminished by 1990, Soviet support endures for most members of the Reagan Administration's list of terrorist "outlaw" states and for the "terrorist" Namibian SWAPO and South Africa's African National Congress. American accounts of the Soviet withdrawal from Afghanistan claim that the Soviet military continues to terrorize the civilian population in absentia with poisoned food and water, anti-personnel land mines and exploding toys.[9]

Despite these apparent contradictions, beginning in early 1989, the superpowers announced they are now united in their efforts to combat "the scourge of terrorism." On the heels of the exchange of views at conferences between longtime intelligence adversaries Ray Cline and William Colby of the CIA and the KGB's Lieutenant General Fjodor Sherbak and Major General Valentin Zvezdenkov, superpower collaboration has been institutionalized in the United States-Soviet Task Force to Prevent Terrorism. The Task Force's deliberations and complete list of recommendations developed at a September 1990 conference remain secret and under study by Bush officials at the White House, State Department, Justice Department and CIA and members of the Central Committee of the Soviet KGB. But previous recommendations give us a clear sense as to the scope and intent of superpower cooperation. They call for direct superpower cooperation to free hostages; expansion of the United States-Soviet nuclear crisis control center to deal with terrorist use of biological, chemical and nuclear weapons; joint cooperation on narco-terrorism; a bilateral group to exchange information on terrorist groups and coordinate policy during terrorist incidents; joint prohibition of the sale or transfer of military explosives and certain classes of weapons to non-government organizations and sales to governments; joint anti-terrorist training exercises; and sharing of anti-terrorist technology.

These joint American-Soviet actions are aimed at terrorists who now threaten to undermine superpower efforts to impose a new world order. At this point, although chaotic, internal problems within the USSR may change the agenda, both superpowers seem intent on constructing an international order in which terrorist acts can't endanger United States-Soviet relations or pit them against each other in regional or local conflicts. They have already agreed to a draft of an International Legal Convention Against Terrorism, proposed an international tribunal to try terrorists and supported creation of a United Nations Standing Committee on International Terrorism. Security experts on both sides have hailed the new cooperative spirit.

But, as the Middle View conveys, terrorism is a complex, multifaceted problem involving both the superpowers and the other nations of the world. In fact, terrorism is the one field on which all play as equals. Therefore, true resolvement of new explosions of terrorism must involve all nations.

Debris from Pam Am 103.

Hostages released in Tehran.

Conclusion

There is little doubt that the legacy of the partisan views of terrorism espoused during Cold War Two remain formidable. Yet, on the immediate horizon, a constant array of events and revelations are forcing the central message of the Middle View onto the global stage and are beginning to prick the public consciousness. In the end, they are certain to confront us with the contradictions of the past and the need, as we face an uncertain future, to construct a new policy on terrorism.

The more superpowers stake out common interests and goals, the more the polarized Cold War visions of terrorism disappear from the Bush-Gorbachev agenda. Today, we see even more clearly how politicized America's anti-terrorism policy before Iran-Contra was. Today, not only are negotiations with those once perceived as the terrorist leaders of the Soviet "evil empire" in full bloom, but, three months after the 1990 State Department terrorist list was announced, President Bush was actively soliciting the support of "terrorist states" Iran, Yemen and Syria and encouraging the cooperation of all other members of the international community, including the "terrorist states" of Cuba, North Korea and Libya in United Nations sanctions and then war against "terrorist" Iraq. For the Bush Administration, the different political realities of the 1990 Persian Gulf crisis have overruled the past political "realities" of international terrorism.

Even before the Iraqi invasion of Kuwait, the Bush Administration was changing its anti-terrorism policy to fit the global climate of the 1990s. Early in its first year, the Bush Administration decided to honor Yasser Arafat's December 1988 promise to end PLO involvement in terrorism and begin a United States-PLO dialogue. Outraged by this decision, many pro-Israeli critics expressed the view that Arafat's PLO is linked with anti-Western, Anti-Israeli terrorism. They strongly feel that Arafat controls the multiple splinter groups of the Palestinian movement. This thesis was first espoused during the Reagan years and was consistent with the Cold War notion of a Soviet-sponsored international terrorist network. But the March 1990 State Department report on the PLO and terrorism indi-

cates that changed political realities require the Bush Administration
to discard old "evidence" that depicted the PLO as a single-headed
monster under Arafat's control. In essence, the State Department
now views the PLO as the highly splintered, politically diverse and
multi-faceted organization the Middle View claims it to be. The
State Department report argues that there was no clear link between
Yasser Arafat and incidents of Palestinian terror during 1989.

Israeli reaction to the report was vehement and centered on the
accusation that the Bush Administration is manipulating the facts
on Palestinian terrorism to suit its larger political agenda for an Is-
raeli-Palestinian peace process by twisting reality in order to defend
the PLO's reputation.[1] For the first time, the Israelis accused an
American president, rather than Arab sources, of playing politics
with the terrorism issue. Administration officials have denied this
charge. Under pressure from Israel and the United States Congress
after an abortive speedboat raid on Israeli beaches on May 30, 1990,
the Bush Administration reluctantly suspended its dialogue with the
PLO in June. President Bush acknowledged the PLO had disassoci-
ated itself from the attack, but claimed it had failed to sufficiently
condemn the raid. On the other hand, he left the door open to
renewed talks if the PLO "took the necessary steps."

However, the Bush Administration's continuing policy on terrorism is not totally predictable nor totally reliable. In the summer
of 1989, Bush officials, while publicly reaffirming American determination not to negotiate with terrorists, used Swiss and Japanese
officials as third parties to negotiate a deal with Iran for release of
American hostages still held in Lebanon.[2] Contrary to its public re-
proach of French political deals in exchange for hostages, the Bush
Administration privately announced its willingness to soften its
stand against Iran, including the release of Iranian financial assets, if
American hostages were released first. During the same August
week, "hardline" Israel followed suit and proposed a trade of its
Shiite prisoners for Israeli soldiers and foreign hostages.

Such public-private contradiction is, of course, troubling. The
contradictions in Bush's expressed posture of "flexibility" underscore the Middle View's message about the complex and multiple
realities of terrorism. The more attentive we, the public, are to this
message, the less vulnerable democratic opinion will become to future political partisans offering victory in the war with terrorism
through quick-fix solutions and promises of moral salvation.

The rise in Libyan-sponsored, anti-American terrorism in the years since the 1986 air raids on Tripoli should have already alerted us to the dangers of the quick-fix solution. In retrospect, Reagan's decision "for swift and effective retribution" actually escalated terrorist violence, as the use of force often does, and left American citizens and the Bush Administration to confront a far more dangerous world. There is little evidence of Libyan agents harming Americans before 1986; however, there is much evidence that they now target American overseas facilities. Since April 1986, State Department analysts have linked Libyan agents with an average of one terrorist attack a month, including the attempt to blow up the American embassy in Lome, Togo; the 1986 hijacking of Pan Am Flight 73 in Karachi, Pakistan; and the 1988 bombings of a USO club in Naples, aboard Pan Am 103, and American library facilities in Colombia, Peru and Costa Rica. In February 1990, President Bush again extended economic sanctions against Libya for its continued support of international and primarily anti-American terrorism.

Encouraged by most military professionals, the build-up of American anti-terrorist capabilities begun by President Carter and completed under Reagan was undertaken with the understanding that success in anti-terrorism operations is directly related to the development of first rate anti-terrorist military and para-military forces. Yet, just at the moment the Delta forces are in place and ready for action, political realities raise serious questions about whether they will ever be used, let alone used successfully. As the 1986 Task Force on Combatting Terrorism, headed by then-vice-president George Bush, warned, identifying the terrorists with certainty is one thing, striking without harming innocent civilians is another. Steven Emerson, a senior editor of *United States News and World Report*, sees even more formidable problems. In his study of America's top-secret, anti-terrorist forces, Emerson found the troops well financed, well trained and equipped with a dazzling array of high tech weapons. Yet, even under an administration eager to use them, he concluded that technical breakdowns, bureaucratic disarray, presidential political interference and professional jealousy and mistrust had stymied these elite forces to the point of inertia.[3]

It is distressing enough to find that, under the best of circumstances, domestic political realities may have immobilized the United States' anti-terrorist forces. Even more disturbing is the discovery that, in dozens of countries in the Middle East, Africa, Asia and Latin America, the United States supports foreign proxy counterterrorism squads imbued with a "license to kill." Reagan and Bush officials seem to have ignored the warning signs of the 1985 Beirut car bombing disaster. In doing so, they guarantee a hazardous future in which American policy and personnel are held hostage to divergent and localized political interests.

The anti-terrorist proxy training program is yet another lesson in how adept political leaders and security officials are in utilizing the terrorism issue to circumvent Congressional legislation and oversight, in this case laws forbidding domestic use of military units, foreign covert actions and the training of foreign police forces. To "accommodate" the restrictions of a 1974 law forbidding United States military training of foreign police forces, the Pentagon armed and trained "anti-terrorist" units who, under alleged close American supervision, can swing into action against "terrorists" anywhere and at any time. To elude restrictions on domestic use of the military, "anti-terrorist" commandoes are routinely "deputized" as United States Marshals. During the 1984 Los Angeles Olympics and the 1986 Statue of Liberty celebrations, thousands of military "anti-terrorist" personnel were "deputized" as agents of federal law enforcement.[4]

Finally, among the hard lessons with which we are daily confronted is the grim reality that many of our allies—and, by implication, Americans as well—are responsible for the continuing explosion of terrorism. We, and they, have not yet ceased to "put the gun on the table, knowing terrorists would pick it up."

Rightwing death squads continue to torture the citizens of Central America, especially in El Salvador. In mid-October, 1989, American medical specialists charged the United States-backed Salvadoran government with conducting a national campaign of killings, torture and harassment against doctors and health-care workers. In November, a uniformed death squad slaughtered six Jesuit priests, their cook and the cook's daughter at Jose Simeon Canas University. By late 1990, the disappearance of evidence and witnesses had stalled the investigation. But there was enough evidence of Salvadoran army complicity and government cover-up in the killings to force the United States Congress to slash aid to El Salvador from $85 million to $42.5 million for 1991–92. The Bush Administration has also been charged with having participated in the cover-up. The United States Senate is considering testimony on the accusation

from a United States Marine officer in 1991. Adding fuel to the
terrorism issue in El Salvador is a United States congressional study
released in May, 1990, revealing that fourteen of El Salvador's fifteen highest ranking military officers have led troops accountable
for torturing prisoners, murdering civilians, causing disappearances,
refusing medical attention to victims of the war and falsifying documents to hide their terrorist activities.

Elsewhere, in Cambodia the United States confounds allies and
foes alike by backing Cambodian rebel forces that include the
Khmer Rouge, architects of Cambodia's "killing fields" in the 1970s.
In Angola, UNITA rebels routinely terrorize the civilian population
with anti-personnel mines supplied by the United States and South
Africa. Angola now has the world's highest per capita of limbless
people and the highest demand for limb prostheses. A study authorized by the Commonwealth Committee of Foreign Ministers on
Southern Africa shows extensive documentation of a ten year South
African strategy of "apartheid terrorism" that had ravaged its neighbors economies, killed hundreds of thousands of people and left
millions homeless.[5] The terrorist carnage in Mozambique is horrifying. From 1987 to 1989, anti-Marxist rebels of the National Resistance of Mozambique (RENAMO) slaughtered 100,000 people, ten
percent of them children, and forced a million farm families to flee
to the cities, where, as refugees, many have starved to death. In the
1990s, RENAMO continues its terror, including wholesale violence
against refugees and international relief agencies, under the watch-
ful eye of South Africa and with no meaningful protest from the
capitols of the "civilized" Western world.

Finally, at home and abroad the monster known as narco-terrorism creeps ever so slowly into our daily lives, promising to be the
most difficult terrorist reality with which to deal. Yet, when first
introduced in 1985, it all seemed so uncomplicated. According to
Reagan officials in the Defense and State Departments, narco-terrorism was a simple case of Soviet-sponsored leftist guerrillas in Central and South America running drug operations to finance their
anti-government terrorist activities. But now, after closer examination of the global drug network—including testimony during the
Iran-Contra investigation of fabricated evidence on leftwing drug-
running, and the disclosures surrounding American support of Panama's alleged drug-king, General Manuel Noriega—we find narco-
terrorism caught in the same political complexities as other aspects

of the new explosion of terrorism. For Americans, these complexities of modern terrorism are brought even closer to home as increasing numbers of foreigners charge American citizens involved in purchasing and using narcotics with directly financing the global narco-terrorism network.

The more we shed the veil of partisan politics and are exposed to the global scope and multiple practitioners of terrorism, the more we see that America, as well as our foes and allies, is inescapably implicated in terrorism's dastardly deeds, either by our active support for those we were told were "freedom fighters" or by our silent acquiescence.

Given the auspicious predictions concerning the permanence of the explosion of terrorism in its various forms, the difficulty in coming to terms with its complex realities, and the likely continuation of its manipulative qualities, our best hope is to be better prepared as we confront time and again the hard lessons of the past two decades. We can be certain that unless there is a public outcry forcing public debate of different ideas and new global perspectives and global agreements on combatting terrorism, we will remain vulnerable to the old manipulative politics of terrorism.

As optimistic as our aspirations for the Middle View are, it remains clear that there are no easy solutions to the explosion of terrorism. Even a shift to the prescripts of the Middle View will not end the repression, killing and maiming immediately, if ever. Yet, expanding what we know about terrorism, the various rationales behind it, and its place in our lives is a necessary and important first step toward reaching a global accord.

Armed with the lessons of the past and further exposure to the distressing realities of terrorism, we now appear closer to taking that step. In doing so, we must commit ourselves and our political leadership to acting on the implications provoked by the Middle View no matter how politically difficult or inconvenient they may be. Only then can we rob terrorists who do the killing and those who would close open democratic society in the name of anti-terrorism of the public support they require. And, at last, begin formulating realistic plans and finding real solutions.

Notes

CHAPTER 1

1. *The New York Times*, April 15, 1986, p. 7.
2. President Reagan's press conference, June 18, 1985.
3. *Newsweek*, June 10, 1985, p. 58.
4. *The Los Angeles Times*, June 22, 1985, p. 1.
5. *The New York Times*, July 18, 1985, p. 4.
6. *Webster's Third New International Dictionary*, s.v. terrorism.
7. United Nations Charter: Item 92.
8. *The New York Times*, July 9, 1985, p. 1.
9. *The New York Times*, July 10, 1985, p. 1.
10. Noam Chomsky and Edward S. Herman, *The Washington Connection and Third World Fascism* (Boston: South End Press, 1979), p. 6.
11. *Random House Dictionary of the English Language*, College Edition, s.v. war.
12. *The New York Times*, Dec. 12, 1984, p. 8.
13. Claire Sterling, *The Terror Network* (New York: Reader's Digest Press, 1981), p. 1.
14. Michael Stohl, *The Politics of Terrorism* (New York: Marcel Dekker, Inc., 1979), p. 2.
15. Anthony Burton, *Urban Terrorism* (London: Leo Cooper, 1975), p. 5.
16. Paul Wilkinson, *Terrorism and the Liberal State* (New York: New York University Press, 1979), p. 13.
17. Walter Laqueur, "The Futility of Terrorism," *Harpers* 252, No. 1510 (March, 1976): 105.

CHAPTER 2

1. Samuel Huntington, "The Democratic Distemper," in Nathan Glazer and Irving Kristol, eds., *The American Commonwealth* (New York: Basic Books, 1976), p. 15.
2. Daniel Bell, *Cultural Contradictions of Capitalism* (New York: Basic Books, 1976), p. 79.
3. Ibid., p. 41.
4. Martin Diamond, "The Declaration and the Constitution: Liberty, Democracy, and the Founders," in Nathan Glazer and Irving Kristol, eds., *The American Commonwealth* (New York: Basic Books, 1976), p. 49.
5. See: Peter Steinfels, *The Neoconservatives: The Men Who are Changing American Politics* (New York: Simon and Schuster, 1979) for a larger discussion of these connections.
6. See *Facts on File*, March 9, 1984 (New York: Facts on File, Inc.), p. 168.
7. Ibid.

8. Ibid.
9. Ibid.
10. Ibid.
11. Ibid.
12. Quoted from a speech given by David Rockefeller to the Los Angeles World Affairs Council that appeared in *The Wall Street Journal*, April 30, 1980.
13. Michael J. Crozier, Samuel P. Huntington, and Joji Watanuki, *The Crisis of Democracy: Report on the Governability of Democracies to the Trilateral Commission* (New York: New York University Press, 1975), p. 157.
14. Ibid., p. 113.
15. Ibid., p. 173.
16. Walter Laqueur, "The Anatomy of Terrorism," in Jennifer Shaw et al., eds., *Ten Years of Terrorism* (London: Crane Russak and Company, Inc., 1979), p. 20.
17. Paul Wilkinson, *Terrorism and the Liberal State* (New York: New York University Press, 1979), p. 72.
18. Christopher Dobson and Ronald Payne, *The Terrorists* (London: Macmillan, 1979), p. 21.
19. Wilkinson, *op. cit.*, p. 78.
20. Olig Zinam, "Theory of Discontent and Frustration," in Marius Livingston, ed., *International Terrorism and the Contemporary World* (Westport, Conn.: Greenwood Press, 1978), p. 260.
21. Dobson and Payne, *op. cit.*, p. 17.
22. Ibid., p. 52.
23. See: Samuel P. Huntington, "Civil Violence and the Process of Development," in *Civil Violence and the International System* (London: International Institute for Strategic Studies, 1971).
24. See: Bell, *op. cit.*
25. Juliet Lodge, ed., *Terrorism, A Challenge to the State* (New York: St. Martin's Press, 1981), p. 6.
26. Charles A. Russell and Bowman H. Miller, "Profile of a Terrorist," in John D. Elliot and Leslie K. Gibson, eds., *Contemporary Terrorism* (Gaithersburg: International Association of Chiefs of Police, 1978).
27. Ibid., p. 82.
28. Ibid.
29. Sterling, *op. cit.*, p. 131.
30. Ibid.
31. Dobson and Payne, *op. cit.*, p. 41.
32. Ibid., p. 40.
33. Russell and Miller, *op. cit.*
34. Ibid., p. 88.
35. Ibid.

CHAPTER 3

1. See: *Facts on File*, January 30, 1981, p. 46.
2. Samuel G. Freedman, "Across the Country, A Sense of Euphoria and Cries for Blood," *The New York Times*, October 14, 1985, p. 1.

3. Ibid., p. 10.
4. Flora Lewis, "The Big Bark," *The New York Times*, July 12, 1985, p. 23.
5. Ibid.
6. *The New York Times*, July 15, 1985, p. 3.
7. Paul Wilkinson, *Terrorism and the Liberal State* (New York: New York University Press, 1979), p. 128.
8. Ibid., p. 132.
9. Juliet Lodge, ed., *Terrorism: A Challenge to the State* (New York: St. Martin's Press, 1981), p. 6.
10. Lord Grey of Naunton, "Political Problems of Terrorism and Society," in Jennifer Shaw et al., eds., *Ten Years of Terrorism* (London: Crane Russak and Company, Inc., 1979), p. 41.
11. Lodge, *op. cit.*
12. Walter Laqueur, "The Anatomy of Terrorism," in Jennifer Shaw et al., eds., *Ten Years of Terrorism* (London: Crane Russak and Company, Inc., 1979), p. 21.
13. Ibid., p. 12.
14. "Hijacking Court Urged by U Thant," *The New York Times*, September 15, 1970, p. 17.
15. Duncan Campbell, "Lifting the Veil on Police Computer," *New Scientist* 81 (January 18): 160.
16. Carol Ackroyd, Karen Margolis, Jonathan Rosehead, and Tim Shallice, *The Technology of Political Control* (New York: Penguin Books, 1977), p. 169.
17. Campbell, *op. cit.*
18. *State Research Bulletin* (Vol. 2), No. 8 (October-November), p. 3.
19. *State Research Bulletin* (Vol. 2), No. 5 (April-May 1978), p. 77.
20. Ibid.
21. The official title is the "Organization of American States Convention to Prevent and Punish Acts of Terrorism Taking the Form of Crimes Against Persons and Related Extortion that are of International Significance."

CHAPTER 4

1. Charles L. Heatherly, ed., *Mandate for Leadership* (Washington, D.C.: The Heritage Foundation, 1981), p. 939.
2. Robert Kupperman and Darrell Trent, "Terrorism," p. 7.
3. Ibid., p. 37.
4. Quote from a White House Statement, *Facts on File*, December 11, 1981, p. 911.
5. "Return of the Weatherman," *Newsweek*, November 2, 1981, p. 30.
6. Senator John East, quoted in John Judis, "When the Visible Saints Come Marching In," in *The Progressive*, January 1982, p. 21.
7. John Ashbrook, *Congressional Record*, October 27, 1981, p. 4975.
8. *The New York Times*, October 25, 1981, p. 1, "Brinks Holdup Opens Inquiry."
9. Ibid.

10. *The New York Times*, February 16, 1982, p. B4, "Behind the Brink's Case: Return of the Radical Left."
11. *Guardian*, November 4, 1981, p. 19, "New Danger to Civil Liberties."
12. *The New York Times*, October 27, 1981, p. A31, "Is There A Cancer?"
13. *The New York Times*, April 27, 1981, p. A19, "FBI Chief Sees No Evidence Soviets Aid Terrorists in U.S."
14. *The New York Times*, December 23, 1981, p. A14, "Latin Exiles Focus on Nicaragua as They Train Urgently in Florida."
15. Ibid., p. A1.
16. *The New York Times*, December 24, 1981, p. A14, "Latins Training in U.S. Raises Questions of Criminal and International Law."
17. Ibid.
18. *The New York Times*, December 9, 1985, p. B9, "Abortion Clinics are Targets Again."
19. *The New York Times*, December 12, 1984, p. 28, "When is a Terrorist Not Necessarily a Terrorist?"
20. *FBI Analysis of Terrorist Incidents in the United States–1983*, prepared by: Terrorist Research and Analytical Center, Terrorism Section, Criminal Investigation Division.

CHAPTER 5

1. *The Los Angeles Times*, March 19, 1981, p. 1, "Haig Sees Communist Plot."
2. Ibid.
3. James Petras, "White Paper on the White Paper," *The Nation*, March 28, 1981, p. 353.
4. Robert Wesson, "Why U.S. Should Help El Salvador," *The San Francisco Chronicle*, March 28, 1981, p. 34.
5. See: Dial Torgerson, "No One Is Safe From Terrorism in El Salvador," *The Los Angeles Times*, April 16, 1981, p. 1, for further discussion of level of terrorism.
6. See: Frank del Olmo, "For El Salvador's Campesinos, Terror Wears a Government Uniform," *The Los Angeles Times*, April 5, 1981, p. 1 for a detailed analysis of peasant attitudes towards the government troops.
7. *The New York Times*, February 27, 1981, p. 1, "Salvadoran Junta Struggles To End Noncombat Killings."
8. T. D. Allman, "Rising to Rebellion," *Harper's*, March, 1981, p. 32.
9. Petras, *op. cit.*, p. 368.
10. Ibid.
11. *The New York Times*, September 5, 1982, p. 5, "Ex-envoy Dubious Over Cuban Arms."
12. John Dinges, "White Paper or Blank Paper," *The Los Angeles Times*, March 27, 1981, p. 7.
13. Jonathan Kwitny, "Tarnished Report? Apparent Errors Cloud US 'White Paper' on Reds in El Salvador," *The Wall Street Journal*, June 8, 1981, p. 1.

14. See: Michael McClintock, *The American Connection* (Bath: The Pittman Press, 1985) for details of the American military and security contribution to El Salvador since 1961.
15. *The Los Angeles Times*, March 29, 1981, p. 3, "El Salvador: Some See Communists Everywhere."
16. Petras, *op. cit.*, p. 368.
17. *Newsweek*, December 21, 1981, p. 17.
18. Ibid., p. 19.
19. *Time*, December 21, 1981, p. 22.
20. *The New York Times*, December 18, 1981, p. B7.
21. *The New York Times*, December 18, 1981, p. B7, "President Reagan Denies Overreaction by U.S. to Report of Libyan Assassin Team."
22. *Newsweek*, December 21, p. 17.
23. *The New York Times*, December 18, 1981, p. B7.
24. Bernard Weinraub, "President Says Nicaragua Is Trying to Build a Libya," *The New York Times*, April 23, 1986, p. A7.
25. Ibid.
26. Ibid.
27. Senator Christopher Dodd, *The Congressional Record*, April 4, 1984, p. S3792.
28. Senator Paul Tsongas, *The Congressional Record*, April 4, 1984, p. S12945.
29. Senator Edward Kennedy, *The Congressional Record*, October 3, 1984, p. S12945.
30. See: Reed Brody, *Contra Terror in Nicaragua* (Boston: South End Press, 1986).
31. *Psychological Operations in Guerrilla Warfare* (New York: Vintage Books, 1985), p. 57.
32. Martha Holmes, "Contra Polygraphs," *The Nation*, March 29, 1986, p. 445.
33. Holly Burkhalter and Alita Paine, "Our Overseas Cops," *The Nation*, September 14, 1985, p. 197.
34. Alexander Cockburn, "Beat The Devil: Remember El Salvador," *The Nation*, June 1, 1985, p. 662.

Chapter 6

1. Dr. Ray S. Cline is quoted in Herbert Krosney's article, "The PLO's Moscow Connection," *The New York Times*, September 24, 1979, p. 72.
2. Samuel T. Francis, *The Soviet Strategy of Terror* (Washington, D.C.: The Heritage Foundation, 1981), p. 5.
3. Ibid., pp. 22–23.
4. Ibid., p. 5.
5. See: "World Military Expenditures and Arms Transfers," United States Arms Control and Disarmament Agency, 1985.
6. See: "Soviet Military Power," United States Department of Defense, 1985.
7. Ray S. Cline and Yonah Alexander, *Terrorism: The Soviet Connection* (London: Crane Russak and Company, Inc., 1984), p. 31.

8. Samuel Francis, *op. cit.*, p. 16.
9. Ibid., p. 42.
10. *Report of the Economic and Social Council*, "Situation of Human Rights in Afghanistan," submitted by the Secretary General to the United Nations General Assembly on November 5, 1985, p. 25.
11. Ibid., p. 25.
12. Ibid., p. 26.
13. Ibid., p. 29.
14. Ibid., p. 29.
15. Ibid., p. 30.
16. Ibid., p. 31.
17. Jean-Francois Revel and Rosanne Klass, "Agony in Afghanistan," condensed version appearing in *Reader's Digest*, March 1986, p. 133.
18. Ibid., p. 134.
19. Ibid., p. 135.
20. Edward Girardet, "Moscow's War of Terror in Afghanistan," *U.S. News and World Report*, October 15, 1984, p. 43.
21. Ibid.
22. This material is taken from Noam Chomsky and Edward S. Herman, *The Washington Connection and Third World Fascism* (Boston: South End Press, 1979) and Edward S. Herman, *The Real Terror Network* (Boston: South End Press, 1982).
23. See: Alfred M. Lilienthal, *The Zionist Connection* (Dodd, Mead, 1978), and Noam Chomsky, *The Fateful Triangle* (Boston, South End Press, 1983) for this discussion.
24. Chomsky, *op. cit.*, pp. 1–2.
25. Herman, *op. cit.*, p. 84.
26. Quoted in Arthur M. Schlesinger, Jr., *The Bitter Heritage* (New York: Houghton Mifflin, 1967), p. 47.
27. Michael J. Uhl, Hearings Before Subcommittee of House Committee on Government Operations, *U.S. Assistance Programs in Vietnam* (July/August 1971), p. 314.
28. See: " 'Pacification' by Calculated Frightfulness: The Testimony of Diane and Michael Jones and the Massacres of South Vietnamese Civilians by South Korean Mercenary Troops," *Pacification Monograph Number 2*; edited with an Introduction by Edward Herman, Philadelphia, 1976.
29. Kai Bird and Max Holland, "Freedom House Journalists," *The Nation*, May 24, 1986, p. 720.

CHAPTER 7

1. See: "Prevention of Terrorism (Temporary Provisions) Act 1976," in *Statute in Force*, c. 8 (London: Her Majesty's Stationary Office, 1979).
2. "Briefing Paper on the Operations of the Prevention of Terrorism (Temporary Provisions) Act 1976," *NCCL Report*, March 1979, pp. 7–8.
3. *State Research Bulletin*, No. 7 (August-September 1978), p. 125.
4. David Lowry, "Draconian Powers; The New British Approach to

Pretrial Detention of Suspected Terrorists," *Columbia Human Rights Law Review* 9 (Spring/Summer 1977).

5. Ibid., pp. 199–200.
6. Ibid., pp. 205–206.
7. Ibid.
8. See: Frank Kitson, *Low Intensity Operations: Subversion, Insurgency and Peacekeeping* (London: Faber, 1971).
9. Lawrence J. McCaffrey, *Ireland From Colony to Nation State* (Englewood Cliffs, N.J.: Prentice-Hall, Inc., 1979), p. 43.
10. Norbert Paul Engel, "European Court Slams Irish Law on Divorce Ban," *Orange Standard* (June, 1970), p. 2.
11. Edmund A. Aunger, "Religion and Occupational Class in Northern Ireland," *Economic and Social Review* 7 (1975–1976), p. 8.
12. See: Duncan Campbell's interviews with Holroyd in *New Statesman*, May 4, 11, 18, 1984 for extensive documentation of British Army terrorism.

CHAPTER 8

1. Hans Jochen Vogel (CDU), *Bundestag*, 12.vi.75, p. 12437 and 16.1.76, p. 14760. Ernst Benda, "Der Rechtsstaat in der Krise," Stuttgart, 1971, p. 143.
2. "Terrorism and Politics in West Germany," a pamphlet distributed by C.A.B.C., 34 Perowne Street, Cambridge, England, p. 40.
3. *Frankfurter Rundschau*, 28.x.74, p. 2.
4. *Bild*, 4.iii.75, p. 2.
5. Margit Mayer, "The German October of 1977," in *New German Critique*, no. 13 (1978), p. 162.
6. Hans Jochen Vogel (SPD), quoted in *Frankfurter Rundschau*, 14.v.75, p. 4.
7. Hans-Magnus Engensberger, "A Determined Effort to Explain to a New York Audience the Secrets of German Democracy," in *New Left Review*, no. 118 (November-December 1979), p. 13.
8. In order of quotations: Vetter (TUC), quoted in *Frankfurter Rundschau*, 10.iii.75, p. 3; Sabais (SPD), quoted in *Darmstadter Echo*, 1.ii.74; Brandt (SPD), quoted in *Frankfurter Allegemeine Zeitung*, 10.iii.75, p. 1 and *Frankfurter Allegemeine Zeitung*, 21.v.75, p. 1; Wohlrabe (CDU), *Bundestag*, 7.vi.72, p. 10979; CDU/SU Bundestag group, quoted in *Frankfurter Rundschau*, 28.ii.75, p. 2; *Frankfurter Allegemeine Zeitung*, 28.v.75, p. 1; *Der Abeitgeber*, nos. 24–26 (1974), p. 1004; Kohl (CDU), *Bundestag*, 13.iii.75, p. 10777.
9. Mayer, *op. cit.*, p. 163.
10. Oskar Negt, "Terrorism and the German State's Absorption of Conflicts," in *New German Critique*, no. 12 (Fall 1977), pp. 24–25. This scenario is also found in various speeches by police and security officials, one copy of which is in the author's possession.
11. Dregger, "Im Brennpunkt," ARD TV program, 5.iii.75, p. 2.

12. Sebastian Cobler, *Law, Order and Politics in West Germany* (London: Penguin, 1978), p. 93.
13. Ibid., pp. 92–93.
14. Penal Code: Section 129, para. 4.
15. Cobler, *op. cit.*, p. 140.
16. CILIP, pamphlet distributed by *Newsletter on Civil Liberties and Police Development*, No. 2 (January/February 1979), p. 15.
17. Wolf-Dieter Narr, "Threats to Constitutional Freedoms in West Germany," in *New German Critique*, No. 8 (Spring 1976), p. 22.
18. Interior Minister Hans-Dietrich Genscher, quoted in *Deutsche Polizei* 12 (1972), p. 357, quoted in Cobler, *op. cit.*, p. 150.
19. Ibid., p. 150.
20. Mayer, *op. cit.*, p. 158.
21. *Frankfurter Rundschau*, September 12, 1977, quoted in Mayer, *op. cit.*, p. 158.
22. See: Wolf-Dieter Narr, "Threats to Constitutional Freedoms in West Germany," in *New German Critique*, No. 8 (Spring 1976), p. 22.
23. Ibid., p. 32.
24. "For Official Use Only: The Secret Plans of the West German Interior Ministry to Destroy the Russell Tribunal on Human Rights," *Spokesman Pamphlet*, No. 60 (January 1978), p. 6.
25. Ibid.
26. "Terrorism and Politics in West Germany," *op. cit.*, p. 45.

CHAPTER 9

1. See a discussion of this report by Andrew Whitley, "Deaths from Terrorism 'Double in 1985'," *Financial Times*, August 14, 1986.
2. Quoted in Stanley Meisler's article, "Years of Dealing with Terrorists Now Exploding in the Face of Paris," in *The Los Angeles Times*, September 21, 1986, Part V, p. 2.
3. Noam Chomsky, *The Fateful Triangle* (Boston: South End Press, 1983), p. 95.
4. Quoted in Livia Rokach, *Israel's Sacred Terrorism* (Belmont, Mass.: Association of Arab-American University Graduates, Inc., 1980), p. 10.
5. Chomsky, *op. cit.*, p. 2.
6. See: Moshe Sharett, *Personal Diary* (Tel Aviv: Yoman Ishi Ma'ariv, 1979).
7. See: Livia Rokach, *op. cit.*, for further elaboration of these points.
8. *Al Hamishmar*, May 10, 1978, Independence Day Supplement.
9. See: Livia Rokach, *op. cit.*, for further discussion of this campaign.
10. *New Times*, March 7, 1975.
11. Chomsky, *op. cit.*, p. 191.
12. Simha Flapan, *Zionism and the Palestinians* (New York: Barnes and Noble, 1979), p. 134.

13. Amnon Kapeliouk, *Israel: la fin de mythes* (Paris: Albin Michael, 1975), p. 32.
14. *London Sunday Times*, June 15, 1969.
15. For further discussion of these points see, among others, John L. Esposito, "Islam in the Politics of the Middle East," in *Current History*, February, 1986.
16. *The New York Times News Service* reported in "Officials Say U.S. Knew of Iran's Link to Fatal Bombings," *Santa Barbara News Press*, December 8, 1986, p. 1.
17. See reports in the *The Washington Post*, October 25, 1983, and in *The New York Times*, October 24, 1983 and December 22, 1983.
18. See: Barry Rubin, "The Untouchable: Why Assad's Terror Goes Unpunished," *New Republic*, June 2, 1986, pp. 16–17.
19. *Santa Barbara News Press*, December 8, 1983, p. 5.
20. Benjamin Netanyahu, "The Syrian Terror Machine," *The New York Times*, November 23, 1986, p. 25.
21. Ibid.
22. "Iraq's Terrorists Waiting for OK, Analysts Believe," *The Sacramento Bee*, February 4, 1991, p. A9.
23. Ronald J. Ostrow and Robin Wright, "FBI Chief Urges 'Business as Usual;' Cites Low Terrorism Risk," *Los Angeles Times*, January 25, 1991, p. A10.
24. "Precautionary Measures," *Middle East International*, January 11, 1991, p. 11.
25. Ronald J. Ostrow and Robin Wright, "U.S. Fears Iraq is Cultivating Terrorist Ties," *Los Angeles Times*, September 2, 1990, p. A1.
26. Bruce Hoffman, "Saddam Hussein's Ultimate Fifth Column—Terrorists," *Los Angeles Times*, August 26, 1990, P. M5.
27. Ostrow and Wright, "Iraq Cultivating Terrorist Ties," *Los Angeles Times*, September 2, 1990.
28. Muriel Dobbin, "FBI Warning of Terrorist Threat to Cities of U.S.," *Sacramento Bee*, January 25, 1991, p. A27.
29. Ibid.
30. "Ex-Official Says U.S. Tolerated Iraqi Terror," *San Francisco Chronicle*, November 21, 1990, p. A15.
31. Interview with Vincent Cannistrano, CBS News, January 7, 1991.
32. Murray Waas, "What We Gave Saddam for Christmas," *Village Voice*, December 18, 1990.
33. United States Department of State, *Patterns of Global Terrorism: 1989*, April, 1990, p. 10–11.
34. James David Barber, "Lobbies Can't Erase Rights Violations," *The New York Times*, June 9, 1986, p. A23.
35. *Iraq: Children, Innocent Victims of Political Repression*, (London, Amnesty International, MDE 14-04-89), February, 1989, p. 15.
36. Peter Grier and George D. Moffett III, "Iraq's Arsenal: Terror, Sabotage, and Propaganda," *Christian Science Monitor*, August 22, 1990, p. 1.

CHAPTER 10

1. *Far Eastern Economic Review*, February 21, 1985, p. 38.
2. See: *Amnesty International Report, 1984* (London: Amnesty International Publications, 1984) for a larger discussion of Sri Lankan government terrorism.
3. Ibid.

CHAPTER 11

1. Report of the Congressional Committees on the Iran-Contra Affair, November 18, 1987.
2. *New Leader,* December 29, 1986, p. 6.
3. "Syrian Support for International Terrorism, 1983–86," *Department of State Bulletin,* February, 1987.
4. Deputy Foreign Minister Theodore Pangalos, quoted in *Facts on File,* November 14, 1986, p. 851.
5. *Facts on File,* 1988, p. 491.
6. For Congressional testimony, see "Airport Security," Hearing Before the Subcommittee on Transportation, Aviation and Materials of the Committee on Science, Space and Technology, United States House of Representatives, One Hundred First Congress, First Session, February 8, 1989 and "Aviation Security," Hearing Before the Subcommittee on Aviation, of the Committee on Commerce, Science, and Transportation, United States Senate, One Hundred First Congress, First Session on Aviation Security, April 13, 1989.
7. According to FAA statistics, since 1983 the level of threats to airlines has been relatively constant at 400 to 500 per year with less than 30 being designated "high level threats" out of six million flights. See the statement of Daniel Cohen, Member of Families of Pan Am 103 before the United States House of Representatives Subcommittee on Government Activities and Transportation, Hearing on the Bombing of Pan Am Flight 103, Rayburn House Office Building, Washington, D.C., September 25, 1989.
8. For specific recommendations authored by the Victims of Pan Am Flight 103 on security matters, see "Written Testimony of the Victims of Pan Am Flight 103," before the United States House of Representatives Foreign Affairs International Operations Subcommittee, September 25, 1989.
9. Rob Schultheis, "The Soviets' Ugly Exit: Do Atrocities in Afghanistan Belie Moscow's PR?" *Washington Post,* January 8, 1989, p. C1.

CONCLUSION

1. Barry Rubin, "How Long Will We Stoop for Arafat?" *The Los Angeles Times,* March 22, 1990, p. B7.

2. Robert Pear, "White House Reaffirms Antiterrorist Policy While Taking Steps to Work Around It," *The New York Times,* August 4, 1989.
3. Steven Emerson, "Stymied Warriors," *The New York Times Magazine,* November 13, 1988.
4. For full details, see Robin Wright and John M. Broder, "U.S. Secretly Aids Anti-Terror Units," *The Los Angeles Times,* July 2, 1989, p. 1.
5. Phyllis Johnson and David Martin. *Apartheid Terrorism: A Report for the Commonwealth Committee of Foreign Ministers on Southern Africa.* Bloomington: Indiana University Press, 1989.